Fine WoodWorking
TECHNIQUES 4

Fine WoodWorking TECHNIQUES 4

Selected by the Editors
of Fine Woodworking magazine

The Taunton Press
Newtown, Connecticut

Typeface: Compugraphic Garamond and Univers
Paper: Mead Offset Enamel 70 lb.

First Printing: June 1982
Second Printing: October 1982

The Taunton Press, Inc.
52 Church Hill Rd.
Box 355
Newtown, Connecticut 06470

A FINE WOODWORKING Book

FINE WOODWORKING® is a trademark of The Taunton Press,
Inc., registered in the U.S. Patent and Trademark Office.

International Standard Book Number 0-918804-13-2
Library of Congress Catalog Card Number 78-58221
Printed in the United States of America

CONTENTS

INTRODUCTION

The *Fine Woodworking Techniques* series brings together all the technical information from past issues of *Fine Woodworking* magazine and preserves it in durable, easy-to-use volumes. *Techniques 4*, the latest in the series, includes the articles from 1980, issues No. 20 through 25. A variety of ideas about wood, tools, the shop, joinery, cabinetmaking, bending, veneering and finishing are presented in 232 pages of text, photographs and illustrations. You'll hear from some well-known professionals: Tage Frid (on working with hardwood plywood), Ian Kirby (on how to cut dovetails), and R. Bruce Hoadley (on the properties of the dowel joint). You'll also hear from skilled amateurs on subjects ranging from setting up shop to finishing marquetry. And in the Methods of Work pages, you'll find tools, jigs and tricks that readers have discovered after years of experimenting—or just by luck.

Each article and Method of Work in *Techniques 4* is reprinted in its entirety from *Fine Woodworking* magazine; changes were made only where corrections or cross-references were needed. The articles are arranged according to subject matter and indexed for easy reference.

Whether you work wood as a hobby or as a profession, we hope you'll find this book a handy and useful tool.

A Barn for Air-Drying Lumber
Pennsylvania Dutch tobacco sheds inspire design

by Sam Talarico

About ten years ago I came across a huge red oak burl left to rot by lumbermen who had no use for this natural rarity. It led to more than a career in woodworking. I now pursue burls, rootwood and highly figured flitches. I have gathered thousands of board feet, involving many hours of searching, felling, hauling and sawing. I came to be known as a source of hard-to-find, special pieces. I stacked these treasures carefully with stickers, waxed the ends and protected them from the weather with roofing tin. This worked until winter winds wreaked havoc. Too many times I found myself gathering the scattered tin to re-cover the stacks. Piling cement blocks on top caused another problem. Every time someone came for wood, I would have to uncover and unstack many piles to find just the piece or pieces to satisfy him. All of my lumber is bookmatched, so it took extra care to go through a stack. Numbering the pieces with marking crayon

as they came off the sawmill helped. But I needed a shelter for air-drying that would provide easy access to the piles I was constantly shuffling through. It had to be spacious, sturdy and as maintenance-free as possible. I wanted an attractive building with a character to suit its purpose, one that would harmonize with the existing buildings on the property. And it had to be economical and easy to build.

Ideas for this barn came not from books or studies of convection and ventilation, but from everyday farmers, mostly of the Mennonite and Amish sects, whose livelihood depends on getting a good price for their money crop, tobacco. Their tobacco sheds, sound and handsome structures found throughout Pennsylvania and New England, are designed to generate and regulate air flow to eliminate fungus and mold, plagues also to the woodman trying to season green lumber. The pitch of the roof, for instance, not only beautifies the barn and

The drying barn under construction, top left. The floor will be poured concrete, leaving a 6-in. gap below the siding for air to flow in. Open-ended gables will vent air out. At left, the completed barn. Four sets of doors give easy access to lumber racks in the front and flitch piles throughout the lower level. Under front gable, above, stairs, deck and double doors provide access to upper level. Hoist beam extends halfway into length of building and is braced by 4x4s running obliquely into door framing. Swallow hole in gable serves no purpose, except 'for nice,' as the Mennonites put it.

Photos: Jim Penta; Illustration: Christopher Clapp

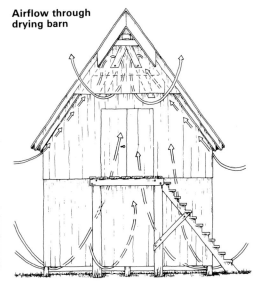

Gaps in flooring of upper level ensure airflow to dry burls and rootwood stored here.

allows headroom upstairs; it also moves air better than a lower roof would. The corrugated aluminum (traditionally tin) conducts the sun's heat, causing the air inside to rise. Fresh air is drawn in through a gap around the bottom of the barn and through spaces under the eaves. Openings under the gable ends serve as exhaust vents, and a 3x5 window in the top of the rear wall provides light upstairs. In a tobacco barn, long narrow doors, rather like louvers all around the building, can be opened and, in conjunction with the open-ended gables, provide maximum draft to inhibit mold and rot. For seasoning lumber, I didn't feel I needed as much draft. The eight wide doors on the side of the barn are mainly for access to the stacks, though in hot, humid weather, I open one or two sets for added ventilation. They also provide adequate light without windows on the lower level; direct sunlight bleaches some woods and its heat can cause surface checks and warp. A stairway on the front of the barn (easier to build than one inside, and it saved storage space), two doors and a hoist beam under the gable provide access to the second floor. The barn is 20 ft. by 40 ft., with the stairs added on to that; it is 23 ft. to the ridge.

I am experienced in the old methods of mortise-and-tenon contruction, held together with oak or locust pins, but these methods are too costly and time-consuming for today's economy. I compromised and used treated-pine pole construction with green oak framing, spiked and lag-bolted together. The lag bolts were old black steel, four 5-gal. buckets of them in various sizes I found for $5 a bucket. Beware of the new zinc-coated ones. I've had many bad experiences with their heads twisting off when you start to bear down on them. It's well worth hunting for the old black lag bolts.

The fifteen main posts, 10 ft. apart, and the two extra posts to frame the stairs and deck are 15-ft. 6x6s resting on concrete footers surfaced exactly the same depth using a transit. Before uprighting them, the posts are notched with saw and slick ("Working with Heavy Timbers," *FWW* #17, July '79) to receive the 2x12 rafter plate at the top and the 2x12 joist plate for the second floor 1 ft. below that. When the 4-in. thick concrete floor was poured, I still had almost 10 ft. of clearance below the second floor. The lower level has no sill, joists or wooden floor.

With the upper floor-joist plates bolted to the posts, braces are nailed flush with the outside of the posts to serve as nailers for the pine siding. At the top of the center posts a 6x8 girder runs the length of the barn. Two-by-eight joists cross the girder from plate to plate, and 1x8 green oak flooring gets nailed on to make the second floor. The gaps that shrinkage produces in this flooring provide good air flow from the lower level of the building through to the top.

The roof is composed of 23 2x6 trusses, laid out on a 15/12 pitch. They're put up on 24-in. centers with poplar lath and 1x6 pine diagonal wind bracing let into the rafters for support. The 6x6 hoist I added serves as part of the ridge pole. It extends 19 ft. into the building, braced into each truss and supported where it overhangs at the front by two 4x4s run diagonally back into 4x4 framing for the upper door. The aluminum roof is nailed on, and then the siding. Rather than paint this, I've chosen to let it weather. I've removed pine siding from barns well over 100 years old, and the boards were sound enough to be used in other constructions.

After the siding is on, hanging the doors is easy. Basically, you frame each 10-ft. opening between the posts with 2x10s notched horizontally into the posts and braced with two diagonals. Cover these with siding, fasten your hinges, cut right down the middle and open the doors. It's best to set your circular saw at an angle inward so the doors can open and close without binding.

For lumber racks I framed out a 10-ft. by 10-ft. area in each front end of the barn to be used for easy access to dimensional lumber and smaller flitches. I lapped horizontal 2x6s into 4x4 uprights and into the 6x6 posts. I stack my large flitches on the floor throughout the rest of the barn on 4x4 blocks. All my shortest pieces, burls and rootwood I store upstairs. To add some extra storage I hung racks from the floor joists and posts in the back center. I've used all the space available and managed to keep things well enough in order to be able quickly to pull a particular flitch upon request.

I'm very happy with this barn; it's served me well, drying large and highly figured pieces with little degrade. It took me and my Mennonite neighbors just seven days to build, except for the concrete and lumber racks, which I did later. It cost me a little under $4,000 when we built it three years ago, and has required no maintenance to speak of since. □

Sam Talarico makes furniture from his prize flitches in Mohnton, Pa.

Alternative Wood-Drying Technologies
Solar energy and dehumidification

Two-thirds of the energy used to manufacture lumber goes into drying it. Burning mill residue supplies only part of the energy used by conventional kilns; most of it is fossil fuel and electrical energy. In the United States, we use more than 10^{13} BTUs of fuel each year to dry lumber. Energy-efficient solar and dehumidifier kilns are important alternatives both to industry and to the individual woodworker.

Drying green wood involves removing both free water and some bound water. Free water is water in the cell cavities, and it evaporates relatively quickly and easily. But at the fiber saturation point (30% for most species) bound water must be extracted from within the cell walls, and shrinkage begins. If a board is dried too quickly, the moisture gradient between the surface and the core becomes too steep. Excessive surface shrinkage precedes internal shrinkage, causing stresses that can result in surface checks, casehardening or internal collapse (honeycomb). Proper drying requires careful pacing and close control of both temperature and humidity throughout the process. (For more on water and wood, drying lumber and conventional kiln operation, see *FWW #4*, Fall '76; *#5*, Winter '76; and *#6*, Spring '77.)

Solar drying—Solar kilns are basically greenhouses that trap the sun's energy and circulate the heated air through stickered stacks of lumber. Most solar kilns consist of a rigid framework with one slanted side facing south for maximum solar exposure. Within the kiln, or mounted on the slanted side, are collectors—either metal plates or some other material painted flat black—to absorb energy. These collectors contact a transfer fluid, usually air. Water-transfer systems have higher heat capacities, but require expensive pipe-embedded plates and more demanding maintenance. Because of the relatively low temperatures required, because it is air that must ultimately be heated to effect the drying, and because of their simplicity and low cost, it is generally agreed that air-transfer systems are more appropriate for solar kilns.

The collectors must be covered with some transparent or translucent material that will allow solar energy to pass through to the collectors while inhibiting the escape of heat. The material should resist deterioration from ultraviolet light, weathering and heat. Glass is an obvious choice—low-iron, tempered glass is best, but more expensive than plain window glass. Glass requires substantial framing and expensive replacement when broken. A number of lighter, less expensive and, in some cases, more transparent materials have been developed specifically for solar-energy applications. They include Teflon and Tedlar solar films (Dupont, Wilmington, Del. 19898), a fiberglass material called Sun-Lite

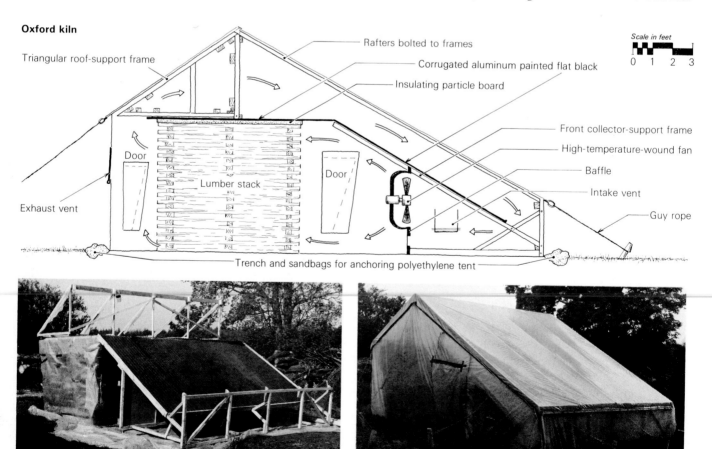

Oxford kiln

Triangular roof-support frame

Rafters bolted to frames

Corrugated aluminum painted flat black

Insulating particle board

Scale in feet
0 1 2 3

Front collector-support frame

High-temperature-wound fan

Door

Door

Baffle

Lumber stack

Intake vent

Exhaust vent

Guy rope

Trench and sandbags for anchoring polyethylene tent

The Oxford kiln with rafters and polyethylene tent yet to be mounted, left, and in operation, right, is light enough to be carried by two or three people from one stack to another. It was designed for use in energy-poor countries.

4

Illustrations: Christopher Clapp

(Kalwall Corp., Box 237, Manchester, N.H. 03105) and ultraviolet-resistant polyethylene and polyester (S.U.N., Box 306, Bascom, Ohio 44809). The polyethylene commonly available from building-supply houses deteriorates in ultraviolet light and cannot be expected to last more than a year.

The other important components of most solar kilns are a fan and vents. Temperature within the kiln can rise above 150°F, so fans with plastic components that may melt should be avoided. Proper air circulation ensures that the lumber will dry evenly and at the safest rate. A timer is generally used to turn the fans on during the day and off at night. It is important that the relative humidity within the kiln be allowed to rise at night, to slow down evaporation from the wood surface. As moisture from the core continues to migrate to the shell, stress is relieved and the moisture gradient is kept moderate. The most critical time is the first week; the kiln should be monitored daily (preferably in the afternoon when the kiln is hottest), lest too rapid drying cause checks. Vents are kept closed at first or opened only a little, to keep moisture exhaust to a minimum and the humidity high. Moisture content should be checked regularly with a commercial moisture meter or by weighing a sample board.

One small, permanent solar kiln has been described in *FWW* #7, Summer '77. A cheaper, simpler, easier-to-construct kiln has been designed by R.A. Plumtree at Oxford University in England. It is portable enough for two or three people to move it from one stack of lumber to another. The design has been particularly effective in developing countries, where drying timber instead of exporting it unprocessed generates badly needed employment and revenue. It consists of two wooden frames, some sheets of corrugated aluminum painted matte black, a couple of fans and a roll of polyethylene that gets draped over the framework.

One of the frames is a triangular truss that sits atop the pile of stickered lumber, the pile having first been covered with an insulating layer of particle board, then with half the sheets of corrugated aluminum. The other frame forms a slanted surface on which the remainder of the aluminum sheets lie. This frame is positioned on the side of the lumber pile where it will receive the most solar exposure. It includes a plywood baffle that houses the fans. The polyethylene tent is draped over the frame and made taut with guy ropes from the top periphery and sand bags around the bottom.

Doors cut into the polyethylene—one between the stack and the baffle, another at the rear of the stack—give access to the lumber for moisture-content readings. The fans draw fresh air through two vents cut on either side of the kiln in

EDITOR'S NOTE: This article was prepared, with help from Roger Schroeder, from material published by the Forest Products Laboratory, Box 5130, Madison, Wis. 53705; the Forest Products Research Society, 2801 Marshall Court, Madison, Wis. 53705; and the Department of Energy, Washington, D.C. 20545. Contact these agencies for more information on wood drying and solar energy. Other publications serving as resources in solar technology include *Harvest the Sun* by Nick Nicholson (Ayer's Cliff Center for Solar Research, Box 344, Ayer's Cliff, Quebec, Canada J0B 1C0; 210 pp., $9.95), *The Solar Age Resource Book*, edited by Martin McPhillips (Everest House, 1133 6th Ave., New York, N.Y. 10036; 242 pp., $9.95), *Solar Age* magazine (Box 4934, Manchester, N.H. 03108; $20 for 12 issues), and *The People's Solar Handbook* (Solar Usage Now, Box 306, Bascom, Ohio 44809; 350 pp., $5.00). Solar kilns and dehumidification systems are undergoing continuing development. If you've had experience building and using them, write and tell us about it. —R.M.

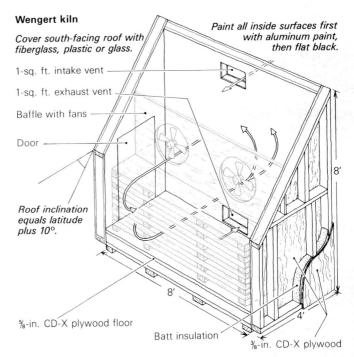

Wengert kiln

Cover south-facing roof with fiberglass, plastic or glass.

Paint all inside surfaces first with aluminum paint, then flat black.

1-sq. ft. intake vent

1-sq. ft. exhaust vent

Baffle with fans

Door

Roof inclination equals latitude plus 10°.

8'

8'

4'

⅜-in. CD-X plywood floor

Batt insulation

⅜-in. CD-X plywood

front of the baffle, and moist air escapes through a vent cut midway on the back side of the kiln. Velcro, a self-sticking material that can be bought in fabric stores, seals the doors and vents.

According to A. Frederick Prins, professor of forest science at Oxford, a kiln that can successfully dry 3,500 bd. ft. of 3-in. oak over the course of an English summer was built for around $1,600 in materials. Prins says the Oxford kiln can be scaled down, at a considerable reduction in cost, using only one fan, less polyethylene and fewer collectors.

Another solar kiln, developed and tested by Dr. Gene Wengert at Virginia Polytechnic Institute in Blacksburg, functions without metal collectors, an expensive component of most kilns. The plan calls for 2x4 stud walls covered inside and out with ⅜-in. exterior-grade (CD-X) plywood insulated with batt between the layers. The south-facing roof is covered with two layers of fiberglass, plastic or glass. Wengert suggests the angle of the roof be 10° steeper than the latitude of the kiln's location, which is between 30° and 50° in the continental U.S. Making it equal to the latitude gives best average exposure, but making it steeper improves winter performance, and summer performance is best moderated anyway. Multispeed, high-temperature-wound fans, mounted in a baffle that sits on a plywood covering atop the lumber stack, can be controlled with timers or thermostats. Instead of metal collectors, Wengert paints the baffle, plywood stack-cover and inside walls first with aluminum paint, then with flat black. The aluminum paint acts as a vapor barrier against the plywood, and the flat black absorbs enough heat to raise the temperature within the kiln, without a charge of lumber, up to 100°F above the outside temperature. A vent at the top of the north wall allows fresh air in and a vent at the bottom exhausts moist air, but the flow of new air is kept to around 5%. As with most kilns, humidity is kept high in the initial days of drying by keeping the vents closed. Doors in the east and west walls provide convenient access to the stack for moisture readings.

Wengert says a kiln of this design, with a capacity of 1,000 bd. ft., can be built for as little as $500. Size is flexible, but there must be at least 1 ft. between the walls and the stack to allow air to circulate, and the proportion of roof area to capacity must remain at about 1 sq. ft. to 10 bd. ft. As with all solar kilns, performance depends on the time of year and the weather conditions, but in good drying weather Wengert has taken green oak down to 6% moisture content in 30 days.

Both the Wengert and the Oxford kilns are open-flow systems that cycle air into and out of the drying chamber. As much as 25% of the heat generated in a solar kiln can be lost in venting. A couple of kilns have been designed as closed systems, employing condensation rather than venting to eliminate moisture. Condensation naturally occurs in solar kilns as a result of daily temperature fluctuations. It reduces degrade by relieving the stresses that build up in lumber as it dries.

Timothy Lumley and Elvin Choong at Louisiana State University have designed and tested a closed-flow solar kiln that incorporates a modification of the traditional flatplate collector, as used in the Oxford kiln. Their collector resembles a large box cut diagonally through two opposite corners, providing four surfaces instead of one for absorption. The diagonal surface is glazed, and vents located in the bottom of the box allow heated air to pass into the drying chamber. The design more than doubles the absorption area of a flatplate collector with the same amount of glazing.

A further advantage of the box-type collector is that because each of its four surfaces is oriented differently, it will pick up solar radiation from different angles during different seasons or times of the day, and energy reflected off any one surface, instead of passing uselessly out through the glass, may be absorbed by another surface. The kiln tested in Louisiana has two box-type collectors, one above the stack and the other in front of it, and has a capacity of 25,000 bd. ft. It was constructed for half the cost of a similarly sized conventional kiln and successfully dried lumber in only twice the conventional-kiln time, and at a fraction of the operating costs. Lumley and Choong believe their design may be commercially competitive with conventional kilns, but that the greatest potential for solar kilns is to replace air-drying before finally kilning down to 6% moisture content. Performance is too dependent on solar conditions to match the control possible in conventional kilns.

Dehumidification—Both conventional and solar kilns dry wood by increasing the temperature of the drying air, which decreases its relative humidity, making it possible for it to take on more moisture as it is circulated through the lumber. The same principle can be inverted: The temperature of the drying air *after* it has circulated through the stack can be *decreased* until it reaches its dew point, when the water vapor evaporated from the wood condenses. Dehumidification is a closed-flow system that employs a heat pump to effect condensation and the drying process. A heat pump transfers thermal energy by compressing a volatile fluid in one section of its circuit (the condenser), then piping it to another section where it is allowed to evaporate. The evaporator section takes on heat from the atmosphere; the condenser gives heat off. In a wood-dehumidification system, both the lumber stack and heat pump are in an insulated chamber. Fans draw air through the stack and past the evaporator section of the heat pump. Here moisture that the air has absorbed from the wood condenses on the cooling coils and is drained away. Now cool and drier, the air passes through the condenser section, where it is reheated with the energy that was extracted from it in the evaporator section. The air is blown back through the stack warm and dry.

The dehumidifier requires only half the energy of a conventional kiln and reaches an operating temperature of around 120°F; each pound of water condensed produces 1,000 BTUs of energy. Still, this is a relatively low-temperature process and as such produces lumber with little degrade. **The system is simpler to operate and maintain than a conventional steam kiln and can require less initial investment. Canadian-based Merkara, Inc. (7290 Torbram Rd., Mississauga, Ont.)** distributes a dehumidification system called Westair that can dry 5,000 bd. ft. of green oak to 6% moisture content in 30 days. At $15,000 the system is about half the price of a comparable conventional kiln. Other manufacturers include Irvington-Moore (Box 40666, Jacksonville, Fla.) and Ebac Ltd. (Greenfield Industrial Estate, Bishop Auckland, Co. Durham, England). The latter sells a dehumidifier with a 1,000-bd.-ft. capacity for $800, excluding the drying chamber. Unfortunately this product is not yet distributed in the U.S.

But the fact that dehumidification uses half as much

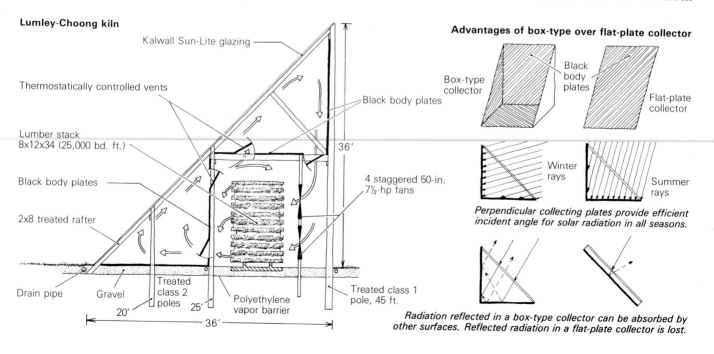

Lumley-Choong kiln

Kalwall Sun-Lite glazing

Thermostatically controlled vents

Black body plates

Lumber stack 8x12x34 (25,000 bd. ft.)

36'

Black body plates

4 staggered 50-in. 7½-hp fans

2x8 treated rafter

Drain pipe Gravel Treated class 2 poles Polyethylene vapor barrier Treated class 1 pole, 45 ft.

20' 25'

36'

Advantages of box-type over flat-plate collector

Box-type collector Black body plates

Black body plates Flat-plate collector

Winter rays Summer rays

Perpendicular collecting plates provide efficient incident angle for solar radiation in all seasons.

Radiation reflected in a box-type collector can be absorbed by other surfaces. Reflected radiation in a flat-plate collector is lost.

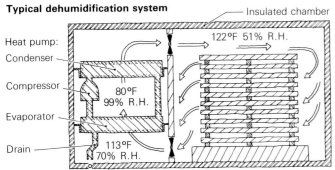

Heat pump:
Condenser

Compressor

Evaporator

Drain

Insulated chamber

122°F 51% R.H.

80°F
99% R.H.

113°F
70% R.H.

As moist air from the stacks is cooled in the evaporator section of the heat pump, water vapor condenses out and is drained away. The cool, dry air (the relative humidity is high only because it is cool) passes through the condenser section where it is heated with the energy absorbed from it in the evaporator section. This lowers the relative humidity, and it is blown back through the stack warm and dry.

energy as conventional kiln-drying must be weighed against the fact that it is electrical energy, which can be three to four times as expensive as fossil fuels. Also, for a heat-pump compressor to begin operating, the ambient temperature must be at least 70°F, necessitating pre-heating outdoor facilities. Most systems must incorporate an electrical coil preheater.

Ultimately, comparing dehumidification with conventional kiln-drying comes to a question of cost effectiveness, and the energy costs at particular installations vary. Where electricity is cheap and for medium-sized lumber-drying businesses (1,000 to 1,000,000 bd. ft./year), dehumidification is worth considering. But on the properties of individual craftsmen and enterprising woodworkers faced with the rising cost of conventionally dried lumber, greenhouse-like structures will be the more common sight. □

Methods of Work

Making little wooden balls
Faced with having to reproduce a number of ½-in. diameter wooden balls (to replace missing ornamentation on an old fireplace), I discovered a virtually painless procedure using a large belt sander. Build a box frame, open on the bottom, and clamp it to the stationary part of the sander so it sits just off the belt. For ½-in. diameter balls, cut ½-in. cubes and toss them in the box frame. Put a cover on the box (Plexiglas is best) and turn on the sander. The sanding belt will throw the cubes around in the frame like dice on a game table, knocking off their corners and edges until they're perfect spheres.

If the cubes don't tumble about but rather line up neatly against the far wall of the frame, glue a wedge there. If this doesn't work, you could vary the number of cubes, presand

Clamp frame
to sander
just above belt

Wedge

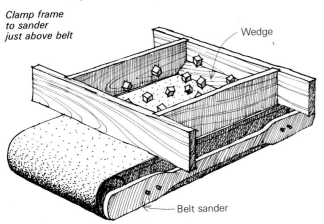

Belt sander

the corners or throw in a few ball bearings to keep the cubes tumbling. Using this method, I produced a dozen or so perfectly shaped balls in an hour's sanding time. Had I shaped the balls by hand it would have taken longer and the result would have been less uniform. Perhaps laziness really is the mother of invention. —*Charles Reed, Washington, D.C.*

Picture-frame clamp
This picture-frame clamp beats anything else I've tried. Make the device from ¾-in. thick, 2-in. wide hardwood strips. I covered the hardwood with smooth Formica for extra strength and for freer action of the parts. You'll need four 16-in. legs, two 4-in. connectors and four 2-in. discs notched to hold the corners of the frame.

To use, determine the positions of the notched discs on the

legs through a dry run. When everything is ready, apply pressure to the frame using a parallel-jaw wooden clamp across the center connectors.
—*John L. Van Scoyoc, Bartlesville, Okla.*

To tighten, clamp across
center connectors

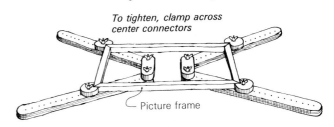

Picture frame

Clamping wide boards
In bookcase construction and other large-carcase work, it is often necessary to join wide boards in an *H*. Without special clamps, it is difficult to achieve the necessary clamping pressure. This simple crowned caul, used with ordinary bar clamps, solves the problem.

To make the caul select a 1-in. thick, 2-in. wide block as

Caul
(crown
exaggerated)

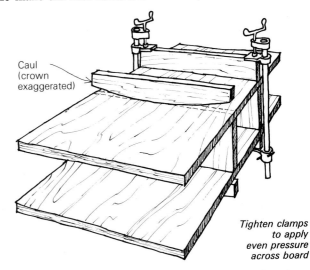

Tighten clamps
to apply
even pressure
across board

long as your lumber is wide. Plane a crown on one edge, leaving the center high and each end about a degree lower. Now lay the caul, crown edge down, across the width of the board to be clamped. As you apply pressure to each end with bar clamps, the end-gaps will close, resulting in even pressure across the joint. —*David Shaffer, Silvercliff, Colo.*

Hardwood Plywood
Modern 'glued-up stuff' saves work, money and wood

by Tage Frid

There is great confusion about how to buy hardwood plywood, about the different grades and qualities, and about its advantages and disadvantages against solid wood. Having a good knowledge of these things makes it easy to decide when to use plywood and when to use solid stock.

The advantage of plywood is that it's more stable and won't change its dimensions, except in thickness. It's easier to make machine joints using veneer-core plywood because the alternating direction of the plies makes for about 50% long-grain to long-grain gluing surfaces. It would be impossible to make much modern furniture without plywood.

The advantage of solid wood is that it can be shaped and carved. Its color is usually darker and its figure more pronounced because it's not cooked and steamed like veneer. The joints in solid-wood constructions can be exposed, making an attractive addition to the design. Solid-wood surfaces are also easier to repair, something to consider when making a piece that will receive lots of wear and possible abuse.

The greatest disadvantages of solid wood are that it doesn't have much strength across its width, and its dimensions never stabilize—it's always moving in width and thickness. The disadvantages of plywood are that it's difficult to repair, its joints usually have to be hidden and its edges have to be faced with either veneer or strips of solid wood.

Many people talk about plywood and veneer as "that modern glued-up stuff." Actually there's nothing modern about it, except the glues used today. Veneering, the basis for plywood construction, was known to the Egyptians 3,500 years ago. The ancient Greeks and Romans used the technique also, but during the Middle Ages the technology was lost, and solid-wood furniture was joined with pegs rather than glue. In the 15th century the Italians rediscovered the technique of veneering and the art spread throughout Europe, reaching its climax of skill and artistry in 18th-century England and France. With the introduction of machinery and the decline in craftsmanship during the 19th century, the art of veneering again suffered. After World War I, the first fumbling experiments were made to use plywood in furniture construction, and since then it has become indispensable.

The flush corners and edges of modern furniture and the development of panel constructions into plain unbroken surfaces would have been impossible without the dimensional stability of plywood. Architecture has been revolutionized by the availability of standard-size sheets of wood that are stronger than ordinary lumber. Exterior-grade plywood made with weather-resistant glue and used for decking and siding has changed our conception of house framing. And with the shortage of wood today, manufacturing veneer for plywood, unlike sawing boards from logs, produces little waste. Almost 100% of the log is made into plywood, except for its center, which is put to other uses.

Plywood means less waste for the craftsman too—there are no knots, checks or other natural defects that must be cut out. Also, more expensive species of woods, such as rosewood and teak, can be purchased in plywood form for about half the cost of an equal amount of solid stock. Generally though, the cost of one square foot of good quality ¾-in. hardwood plywood is about the same as one board foot of solid stock of the same species. Using plywood saves labor as well as material because it's not necessary to glue up large panels from narrow boards or to construct frames to hold the panels. Woodworkers should not rule out using plywood because they think it costs too much.

Plywood veneers are cut in one of four ways, depending on the species of the lumber and the use to which the veneer will be put. Most veneer is rotary cut. This method requires first cooking the log and removing its bark. Then it's placed between centers in a big lathe and revolved into a knife. As the log turns, the knife automatically advances into the stock at a controlled rate, which determines the thickness of the veneer. A cylinder six or seven inches in diameter is left over. Rotary-cut veneer (*FWW* #12, Sept. '78, pp. 83-85) doesn't have the fine figure of sliced veneer, because when rotary cut, the veneer is peeled off the log like a sheet of wrapping paper being pulled from a roll. Because the cuts are always parallel to the annual rings, the grain of the veneer looks unnaturally stretched and doesn't have much character.

For face veneer the finest hardwood logs are used, and the veneer is sliced instead of rotary cut. Whether cut tangentially or quarter-cut, there are several ways to slice veneer. Usually the log is rammed into a fixed knife and automatically advanced between cuts so each slice is the exact same thickness, usually ⅟₂₈ in. The pieces are kept in order as they come from the machine so they can be matched. Sliced veneers are sold in flitches, bundles containing all the stock from one log or from a section of a large log. This makes it possible to panel a whole room with face veneer from the same tree.

Somewhat similar to sliced veneer, but cut instead on a

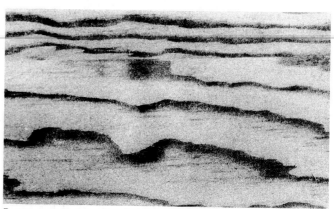

Rotary-cut veneers often lack natural-looking figure because they're cut parallel to the growth rings.

lathe, is half-round veneer. The log is bolted to a stay and mounted to the lathe in eccentric chucks. As the log revolves, it presents only a small arc of its circumference to the knife. Another method of getting veneer is by sawing on a band saw with a thin blade, which makes a narrow kerf. Even so, as much wood is wasted as is saved. Because this way produces so much waste, it is little used.

Though most plywood is made for the building industry, there are several good products available to the craftsman, who can buy them with the face veneer already glued on or with no face veneer at all (so he can veneer it himself). The plywoods commonly used by the craftsman are veneer core, lumber core, particle-board core and fiber-board core. All plywood is built up of an uneven number of plies of various thicknesses, depending on the finished thickness of the sheet itself. But whatever the thickness and the species of lumber used, the grain direction of any ply must be at right angles to that of the adjacent plies. This crossing of the grains gives plywood its great strength and dimensional stability.

The most used and best-known plywood is veneer core. The thinner the veneer used to build up the core, the greater the strength of the plywood. I would never use, for example, three-ply ¼-in. plywood. In most cases such plywood is made of cheap materials, especially the core, so any imperfection in the core telegraphs right through the face veneer. Assuming that the face veneers are ⅟₂₈ in. thick, this makes the core about ⅕ in. thick, and because the grain of the core must cross the grain of the face veneers at right angles, the plywood is weak along its length and easy to break. If ¼-in. plywood is made out of five plies, the center ply and the face veneers run in the same direction, and with the two crossbands, it's stronger and more stable.

The quality of veneer-core plywood varies greatly. Cheaper plywood contains voids and unsound knots in its inner plies. Voids in the crossband, the plies directly below the face plies, make the face veneers weak in those places because there's nothing to back them up, and they can break through. A better veneer-core plywood is a Russian product called Baltic birch. The quality of the wood is good, but the plywood itself tends to twist, and lately I've found that the layers sometimes separate. Most Baltic birch plywood is made to metric dimensions—standard sheets are 150 cm by 150 cm (roughly 5 ft. square) and the thickness also is in millimeters. Another very good veneer core is made in the Philippines and is sold under the general commercial name lauan. It is very stable and the core is good. Its color is close to mahogany.

Lumber-core plywood is made up of two face veneers, two crossbands and a solid-wood core. Because the core is much thicker than the crossbands and its grain runs in the same direction as the face veneers, it has great strength lengthwise. Most lumber-core plywood is made up of edge-joined strips in its center; poplar and basswood are common, though mahogany is better. These strips vary in width, but 3 in. is usually the maximum. The strips are glued together and then dressed to the necessary thickness. Next the crossbands and face veneers are glued on. Lumber-core plywood can twist because the glued-up core acts like one piece of wood.

Imported lauan plywood is also available in lumber core. The difference between the lauan lumber core and the ordinary commercial kind is that the core strips in the lauan are not glued up into one solid sheet. They're held together by the crossband plies with small spaces between the strips. This

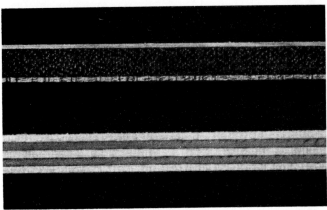

The three-ply material, top, is weaker than the more expensive five-ply material, bottom. Defects in the three-ply core will telegraph through the face veneer.

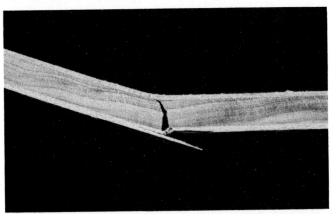

Three-ply ¼-in. plywood breaks easily, especially if it is used in narrow strips.

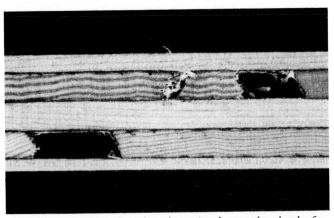

Voids in cheap plywood weaken the entire sheet and make the face veneers vulnerable because there's nothing to back them up.

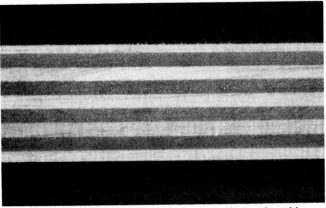

Baltic birch plywood, a Russian import, contains no voids and has exceptional strength and good working properties. Though it sometimes twists and delaminates, it's generally a superior product.

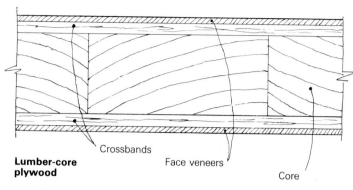

Lumber-core plywood

Crossbands

Face veneers

Core

Two bookmatched veneers. When taken from the flitch, one piece is flipped over, as you would open a book.

An entire panel can be made up of bookmatched veneers by flipping every other piece as it comes from the flitch.

Slipmatched veneers have a different look because there's no mirror-image effect.

allows each core strip to move independently, making the plywood more stable and more suitable for cabinetmaking. This lumber-core plywood is available without face veneers in 4x8 sheets that the craftsman himself can veneer.

When veneering plywood yourself, take the pieces of veneer from either the top of the flitch or the bottom. Don't pull them out of the center or any other place in the bundle because that splits up the flitch and makes it impossible to match the figure later on. There are two ways to match veneer on a panel. One is called bookmatching, because the piece on top is flipped over, as though you were opening the cover of a book. Bookmatching can be done with more than two pieces of veneer, and this is usually how good-quality sheets of plywood are faced. The other way of matching is to use veneers in the order they come from the flitch, only without flipping them. This is called slipmatching.

When working plywood of any type, the cardinal rule is that what you do to one side you must do to the other. Whether you veneer your own plywood blanks or buy them with the face veneers already glued on, make sure that the face ply and the back ply are the same species. If two different face veneers are used, for example, walnut on the front and poplar on the back, the two will expand and contract at different rates. There are plywoods available with plies of the same species on the front and back, though usually the quality of the front veneer is better and allows for fewer defects.

There are other materials that can be veneered or that come already faced with veneer. These are sold under the commercial names of particle board and fiber board and are usually less expensive but not nearly as strong as plywood. The greatest advantage in using these materials is that because they're made out of sawdust or fibers they don't have any grain direction, so the veneer can be applied with its grain going in any direction. The greatest disadvantage of this type of material is that it doesn't have much strength and that it's not easy to join together, because the joints must be reinforced with splines made of some other material. Another disadvantage of particle board is that it will bow if it's used to make doors that slide in a track on the bottom. This is because there's no grain direction to support the weight. To prevent this from happening, either put a wide facing on the edges of the doors or hang them from a frame at the top.

The U.S. Department of Commerce has established voluntary product standards for grading hardwood plywood. This grading system is different from the one used to grade softwood plywood, and the two should not be confused. Premium-grade veneers are given the symbol *A*, while other quality veneers are designated by a number: good grade—1, sound grade—2, utility grade—3, backing grade—4, and a specialty grade—*SP*. Any combination is possible, the first symbol representing the quality of the face veneer and the second the quality of the back veneer. Plywood grade *A-3*, for example, has a premium-quality face veneer and a utility-grade back veneer. The absolute best would be *A-A*. Often the back veneer is a different species from the front veneer, so it's a good idea to ask about this when ordering because the grading system doesn't take this into account. For more information, write the Hardwood Plywood Manufacturers Association, Box 2789, Reston, Va. 22090. □

Tage Frid, professor emeritus at Rhode Island School of Design, is senior editor of Fine Woodworking *magazine.*

Methods of Work

Unwinding lumber

Here's a method for recovering short lengths of twisted lumber too wide for your jointer. First tack a strip (wider than the lumber is thick) to one edge. Lay the work on the saw table and tack an identical strip to the other side so that both strips lie flat on the saw table and are precisely parallel. Now run both sides of the work over a dado head (or flat, three-lipped cutter) to obtain a flat board.

—*Pendleton Tompkins, San Mateo, Calif.*

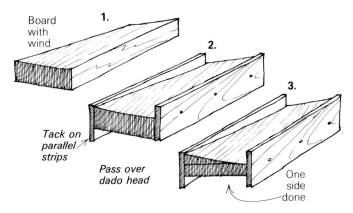

Surfacing wide boards

My jointer is small, but that doesn't stop me from surfacing boards wider than 6 in. Say you've found the perfect piece of cherry for a drawer front, but it's 9 in. wide, cupped or slightly twisted. To rip and reglue the board would spoil the gorgeous grain pattern. What I'd do is rabbet the two edges of one surface, run the new narrow width over the jointer, then flatten the top through the thickness planer. Flip the board over and plane the true board to thickness.

Naturally the nature of the cup, bow or twist and the thickness of the finished piece determine the depth of the rabbet. And, if you must rabbet both edges, you'll likely have to remove the regular fence from the jointer to center the work over the blade. —*Donald Leporini, Newton Centre, Mass.*

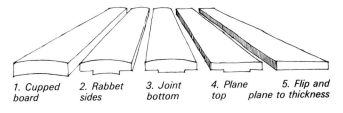

1. Cupped board 2. Rabbet sides 3. Joint bottom 4. Plane top 5. Flip and plane to thickness

Making miniature shingles

To make small wood shingles for miniature buildings, start with a length of straight-grained 2x4. Any softwood will do, but white cedar is best as it is quite flexible. To make pointed shingles, cut ⅜-in. notches across the end of the 2x4 with a band saw, using a regular (not skip-tooth) blade. To make square-end shingles, substitute a series of ½-in. saw kerfs for the notches. Now cut off a ⅞-in. length from the notched (or kerfed) end of the 2x4. Continue notching and cutting off ⅞-in. blocks until you have plenty to complete the job.

To prepare your band saw for slicing gang shingles from the blocks, saw straight into the center of a piece of ¼-in. plywood and stop. Clamp a wood fence on top of the plywood and as close to the blade as the thickness of shingle you want (1/16 in. or so). Use a push-stick to hold the block snugly up against the fence. Slice gangs of shingles from the block until the block is cut down to ¼ in. Glue this remnant to the next block to be sliced.

Alternately, the slicing operation can be done on the table saw using a fine-tooth plywood blade. To keep the thin slices of shingle from falling through the space beside the blade, tape a thin, flat board to the saw table against the rip fence and over the blade. Elevate the blade through the board to provide a gap-free surface.

You should taper by hand the first course of shingles around the eaves of your miniature building. If you don't, the second course won't lie right. To accomplish this, build a hand clamp (useful for other work as well) from two pieces of hardwood and a hinge as shown. Pinch a gang of shingles in

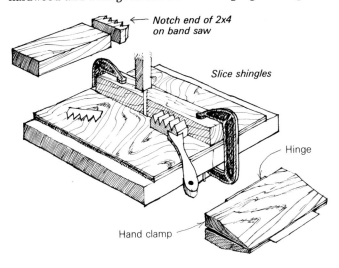

the clamp (points in) and feather the back end of the shingles by pressing lightly on a belt sander.

To install the shingles, match up the ends and glue in place on a line. Hold each row in place with masking tape until the glue sets. —*Floyd L. Lien, Aptos, Calif.*

Wooden mallet

At least one wooden carpenter's mallet belongs in every woodworker's tool chest. The advantages of wood over steel are obvious—less damage to tools, work, thumbs and eyes. For the price of one steel hammer, you can make a dozen mallets, each tailored to a particular job.

The traditional mallet has a solid-wood head mortised through for the wedge-shaped handle. My laminated head design is just as strong and much easier to make. Begin by cutting the handle and two center laminations for the head from the same 1-in. thick board (this saves a lot of fitting later). Copy the handle's wedge angle (no more than ½ in. of taper) onto one of the side laminations. Then glue up the head block, carefully aligning the center laminations with the wedge-angle pencil lines. When the glue has cured, bandsaw the head to shape. Then chamfer all the edges to reduce the chances of splitting and insert the handle.

—*Daniel Arnold, Viroqua, Wis.*

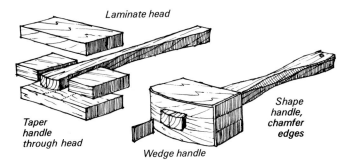

any one thing but versatile enough to be used for everything. Chestnut's rot resistance rivals the heartwood of white oak, and abundant shingles, doorsteps and sills testify to its durability. Easy to work, it found wide service in barns, carriage houses and out-buildings. Chestnut also takes a fine finish, and was popular in the cabinet shop and for items as diverse as barrels and caskets. This tree's fast growth ensured a steady supply of posts and rails as America fenced herself in in the 1880s. When blight-infected trees flooded the market in the 1930s, telephone poles and highway guard rails helped absorb the glut. Boxes, crates, veneer core and railroad ties were also made from chestnut.

Chestnut was available. Usually growing in mixed hardwood forests, it composed from 15% to 50% of the standing timber. Pure stands also occurred. Chestnut trees can put on an inch in diameter in a year during their youth. One 70-year-old specimen was 5 ft. in diameter. With little effort, a farmer could get posts at 15 years, beams at 25, lumber at 50 and feed his hogs on the nut crop every fall in between.

In 1904, trees infected with a fungus, brought into this country on chestnut trees from the Orient, were noticed at the Bronx Zoo in New York City. The chestnut blight, as the fungus came to be known, attacked the bark of the tree, girdling the trunk with cankers. These cankers interrupted the vital flow of water from the roots and killed the tree. The wind-borne blight advanced 25 miles per year. It was first seen in central Connecticut in 1910, and uninfected trees were hard to find by 1915. In Pennsylvania, state foresters cleared large areas of forest, hoping to halt the epidemic's advance. But pockets of infection broke out far in advance of the blight's front and spread, eventually decimating the chestnut throughout its entire natural range. By 1940, loggers were sharpening their saws to drop the last big sticks in the South.

In the wake of the blight was economic disaster. Nuts disappeared as an important source of food for man and animal alike. Dead chestnut hulks inundated the sawmills, depressing lumber prices. In Appalachia, the tanning industry collapsed, adding more hardship to that already impoverished area. Upland soils eroded at an alarming rate with the sudden disappearance of such

a dominant forest member. In place of chestnut, less desirable trees grew. Land that gave timber now gives cordwood.

Chestnut persists today, but only as a shrub. It sprouts from the stumps of the former giants and grows several inches in diameter before the blight grabs it again. How long this cycle will last is anybody's guess, but these remaining small trees offer hope. Dr. Richard Jaynes, of the Connecticut Agricultural Experiment Station in New Haven, is working on a disease to infect the disease. In Europe and a few isolated areas in the U.S., chestnut trees with resistance to the blight have been found. In these trees, a virus infects the fungus. Dr. Jaynes is looking for a method to spread this virus to American chestnut sprouts. Success would be an economic miracle for our eastern timberlands.

Locating and using chestnut

Chestnut wood is often confused with oak, ash, elm and hickory, all ring-porous woods, but there are ways to distinguish it. I don't stress color because it is unreliable. Fresh cut, the wood is blond, but with aging mellows to a wide variety of reddish browns. The surest way to identify it is by looking at the end grain. The pores that form the earlywood rings, best seen with a hand lens, are oval in chestnut and frequently occluded with tyloses—shiny, bubble-like structures. The transition from these rings to the denser latewood rings is more gradual than in other ring-porous woods. An obvious difference between chestnut and oaks is that the oaks have prominent rays, which on the end grain appear as light lines radiating from the center of the tree and on the face grain (tangential view) appear as dark flecks. Rays are less prominent in elm, hickory and ash, but they are visible; they are not visible in chestnut. Chestnut is the lightest and softest of the ring-porous woods (with a specific gravity of 0.43). Lastly, chestnut because of its high tannin content will stain black in contact with iron salts. Boiling shavings in a ferric chloride solution will not distinguish it from oaks, which are also high in tannin, but elm and ash, low in tannin, will discolor only slightly.

Knowing where chestnut was commonly used is valuable when looking for wood to recycle. I pay close attention to sills, joists and other pieces close to ground level where rot resistance is a

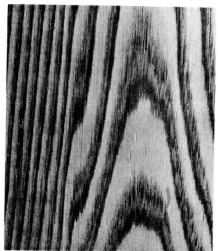

Usable pieces of plainsawn chestnut may be salvaged from framing members of turn-of-the-century buildings.

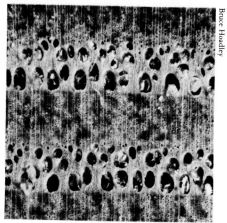

Bruce Hoadley

Large, oval pores in chestnut, visible in 10× cross-sectional view, are often occluded with tyloses. Earlywood/latewood transition is gradual. Rays are fine, barely discernible.

must. Fencing also merits close scrutiny. Buildings from early in this century are my favorite haunts. Two structures on my property are dated 1914, just when blighted trees were abundant. Not surprisingly, they are framed completely in chestnut. In general, white oak is the only other ring-porous wood commonly found as a framing member. In furniture, where finishes obscure the wood, identification can be tricky. Chestnut never hides beneath painted millwork and was usually considered too soft for flooring, although I do know of a few examples.

Heavy boots, gloves, a crowbar and a sharp knife are all the would-be chestnut hunter needs to bring along. Time-encrusted roughsawn lumber doesn't display its grain. If the wood cuts like pine to reveal an open grain, I give it a second look. Where an old house or barn is being torn down, the wood is often free for the asking.

When I've amassed a pile of wood, I

American chestnut
(Castanea dentata)

chestnut—whence the name wormy chestnut. The holes, if not too plentiful, are attractive. These holes are the excavations of the chestnut pole borer, which attacks moist heartwood in standing dead chestnut and oak. The cavities are packed with the borers' excrement, which looks like fine sawdust. It can be packed so tight as to obscure the hole. I use the air pump at a service station to clean the wood. Goggles and a mask must be worn because the dust is extremely irritating. Cleaning the holes with small pins is time-consuming and not very satisfactory.

No two pieces of chestnut are the same. In my haunts I occasionally come across pieces stained black on the outside. Always found in close contact with the soil (iron salts react with the tannin in the wood), these uglies conceal a real treasure. Inside, the wood is mellowed to a soft brown with creamy white streaks running with the grain. It's incomparably beautiful.

When dressing this rough stock, I rip off about ⅝ in. The stain on this surface has the best effect. If I saw too far into the board, I usually get regular-colored chestnut, and if too shallow, black wood. Cutting shallow is preferable though, because the surface can be planed to change the intensity of the stain. In constructing with this wood you must bear in mind that there is only one beautiful face; the other is either black or typical chestnut, and the edge shows the transition.

Salvaging from older structures is not the only way to obtain chestnut. One woodturner I know gets wood from old chestnut hulks he finds on the ground in remote forests. He goes as far as Ohio and South Carolina for logs passed over during the post-blight salvage. Often these choice pieces are inaccessible, perched on a steep hill miles from the nearest road. It is remarkable that after 30 or 40 years some hulks remain unrotted. Sometimes the center of the tree rots out, leaving a hard, useless shell. Crotch areas often remain solid, though, and are usually symmetrical with beautiful figure. Turning must proceed cautiously, as the wood splits easily if the tool catches.   □

Jon Arno lives in Brookfield, Wis.; Victor DeMasi lives in Redding, Conn. Both are amateur woodworkers. DeMasi's article was prepared with the help of research by Roanna Metowski.

sort the pieces according to destination—the saw or the woodstove. I inspect the good pieces for rot and nails and crosscut these out with a bowsaw. Before pulling out individual nails, I mark the area around each with a red crayon in case the nail breaks off. Black spots should be crayoned too. These are iron stains from nails, pieces of which might still lie buried in the wood.

It helps to have a definite project in mind before you start ripping. You can then saw for the right sizes. I work backward, however, and must always see the wood before I can decide on a project for it. Plainsawn chestnut, which has wavy face grain, is more attractive, I think, than quartersawn stock. Most chestnut was plainsawn to begin with, so I cut parallel to existing edges and usually obtain attractive figures. I use a circular saw with a guide, or a bench saw for wider boards. Cheap blades are best; if I hit a big nail, I change the blade. After a few too many

damaged blades I got better at avoiding those nails. When all my stock is ripped I again crosscut to eliminate the few remaining nails that I missed. I don't send any wood that has nails into a planer. When the wood is surfaced and jointed, it is tightly stacked and weighted down to minimize warping.

Working with chestnut is a real pleasure. It rips cleanly with a sharp blade, but on older pieces the end grain always tears during crosscutting. The wood almost leaps together when it is glued. It sands easily, but grits below 100 should be avoided because they scratch the wood and make even more sanding necessary. The finest sanding stages can be frustrating, as a slightly raised grain persists. The problem can be solved by wetting the surface with paint thinner. Tung oil is a suitable finish for chestnut, and brings out the beautiful color on older, salvaged wood.

Small wormholes are common in

Limited space need not mean an inefficient workshop. Open central area of Henry Jones' former shop gives ready access to bench and machinery, leaving ample room for assembly. Platform in alcove at right is piled with 8/4 mahogany, out of the way but easily reached.

Setting Up a Small Shop
Five woodworkers tell how they'd do it

How can you set up a serious woodworking shop on a slender shoestring? Many readers have asked us variations of this question, so we made up our own composite question and put it to five expert craftsmen:

"I am an amateur woodworker, and I wish to start building a proper shop. As my skills improve, I'd like to make at least part of my living from the craft. I can move into a single-car garage (about 10 ft. by 20 ft.) with an overhead door. I have some basic hand tools, but no machines yet. What machines should I buy first, and what should I add as my finances permit? How should I arrange them in the available space? What about lighting, ventilation, storage, finishing?" The answer men are as follows:

—Henry Jones of Vineyard Haven, Mass., an industrial designer turned professional woodworker. His article on how to produce square frames in batches of 100 appeared in the Sept. '79 issue of *Fine Woodworking*.

—Tage Frid, professor emeritus at the Rhode Island School of Design and senior editor of *Fine Woodworking*.

—Franklin Gottshall, of Boyertown, Pa., cabinetmaker and author. Eleven of his fifteen books, including *How to Design and Construct Period Furniture*, are still in print.

—Andy Marlow, consulting editor of *Fine Woodworking*, a professional wood craftsman and author of several books on reproducing antiques. His most recent book, *Classic Furniture Projects*, contains plans and instructions for 13 different pieces of furniture, most of them with inlay.

—Frank Klausz, a cabinetmaker in Bedminster, N.J. His article on cutting mortise-and-tenon joints appeared in the Sept. '79 issue of *Fine Woodworking*.

We invite readers to send us their own floor plans and ideas so we can treat this subject again in a future issue.

Leave room in the middle

by Henry Jones

When I opened a commercial cabinet shop about six years ago, I had to decide whether to rent suitable space or attempt to work in my detached single-car garage. The convenience of having a shop only a few steps from my front door was incentive enough to favor the garage, but economic considerations decided the issue, and I set about transforming the tiny 10-ft. by 26-ft. building into a production shop.

To cram my entire operation into 260 sq. ft. meant that I would have to use every available square inch. My first step was to prepare a diagram that included every machine, fixture and cabinet and the clearance paths required for the use of each machine and for my bench as well. I had to make many changes once I actually started setting up, but the original plan helped me decide that the limited space could be made to work. From the plan I knew that if I managed the space properly, I wouldn't have to move my machines around much to make room for other operations and that I would still have storage for lumber, fixtures, supplies, patterns and miscellaneous tools. In the midst of all this I had to have room to set up and assemble work in progress, without having to shift furniture parts and tools all over the shop every time I needed to use a given machine.

Deciding from the outset to limit stock length to 12 ft. or less on all but rare occasions, I was able to compute the amount of space needed to operate each machine. A 12-in. planer requires an unobstructed path 26 ft. by 24 in. by 6 in. A radial arm saw or a shaper needs about the same. A 4-in. to 6-in. jointer needs a space about 16 ft. long and 8 in. wide. And my 8-ft. workbench has to have at least 10 ft. on either side of the vise. Having satisfied myself that I could fit all these into the existing space, I was confident that somehow I could squeeze in my band saw and my Shopsmith.

With only minor modifications and several simple, inexpensive additions to the basic structure, I managed to produce a meager but acceptable income in this shop for five years. But last year I tore away about half of the garage and built it anew, doubling the floor space and tripling the volume. However, the methods I worked out to cope with limited space and which I'll describe here were successful in enabling me to run a cabinet shop on a small budget until it was financially feasible for me to enlarge the space.

To make the old shop workable, but without disturbing the existing roof or major structural members, I added a narrow shed and a bay clear of the ground—a kind of elevated alcove—to provide areas for storing and working large plywood sheets. I also cut ports through the two walls at opposite ends of the planer so the machine could be operated across the short end of the shop. The ports were then fitted with lift-out covers that latch in place. Because the arrangement precluded the use of a table saw, obliging me to use my radial arm saw for ripping (which I find entirely satisfactory), I cut another port in the wall that stands about 10 ft. from the saw. This lets me rip boards as long as 14 ft. and provides almost unlimited crosscut capacity.

I located my shaper to the left of the radial arm saw's 6-ft. table, and the band saw to the right of it. To keep the work

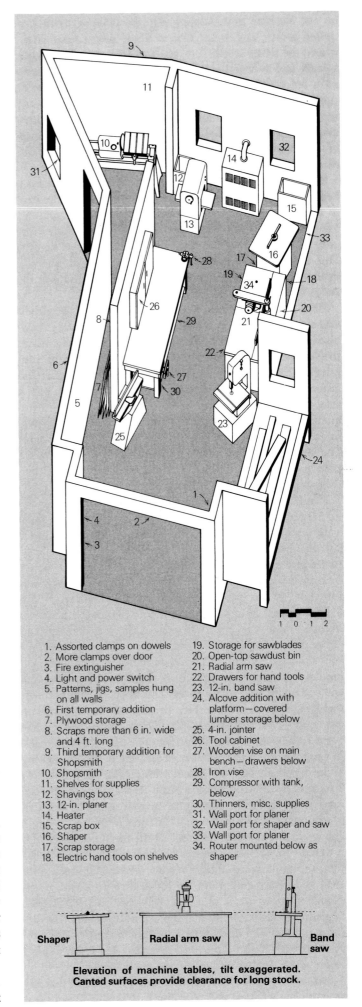

1. Assorted clamps on dowels
2. More clamps over door
3. Fire extinguisher
4. Light and power switch
5. Patterns, jigs, samples hung on all walls
6. First temporary addition
7. Plywood storage
8. Scraps more than 6 in. wide and 4 ft. long
9. Third temporary addition for Shopsmith
10. Shopsmith
11. Shelves for supplies
12. Shavings box
13. 12-in. planer
14. Heater
15. Scrap box
16. Shaper
17. Scrap storage
18. Electric hand tools on shelves
19. Storage for sawblades
20. Open-top sawdust bin
21. Radial arm saw
22. Drawers for hand tools
23. 12-in. band saw
24. Alcove addition with platform—covered lumber storage below
25. 4-in. jointer
26. Tool cabinet
27. Wooden vise on main bench—drawers below
28. Iron vise
29. Compressor with tank, below
30. Thinners, misc. supplies
31. Wall port for planer
32. Wall port for shaper and saw
33. Wall port for planer
34. Router mounted below as shaper

Shaper   **Radial arm saw**   **Band saw**

**Elevation of machine tables, tilt exaggerated.
Canted surfaces provide clearance for long stock.**

Illustrations: Robert Croston

High ceiling, wood floor, good light

by Franklin H. Gottshall

A good shop should have a high ceiling. A minimum height of 7 ft. will do, but 8 ft. or 9 ft. is much better. My shop, a part of which is shown in the photograph, has a 9-ft. ceiling. I do not like a cement floor in a shop, and unfortunately most garage and basement shops have one. A wooden floor is much easier on the feet and the work, and if either a garage or a basement is to be made into a workshop I strongly advise superimposing a wooden floor over the cement, though this will mean lowering the ceiling. Walls and ceiling should be adequately insulated to keep the shop warm and dry.

Proper lighting is extremely important, and is often inadequate both in home workshops and in buildings used for commercial purposes. You need natural daylight as well as enough artificial lighting. Walls and ceiling should be white to make full use of all the light you can bring into the shop. Good eyesight is precious.

The drawing shows what I think is an ideal natural lighting situation, with the workbench situated to get lighting from the north. This eliminates a lot of glare and shadows you might get having to work facing in another direction. You need enough overhead lighting at your machines and workbench to eliminate shadows and eyestrain, and in my shop it is possible to move some lights as necessary.

As to equipment and machinery, first priority should be given to a good workbench, equipped with a good vise or two. I recommend a bench with a flat, hardwood top, 2 in. or more thick, and a substantial base. It should not be fastened to the floor, because you may need to move it.

Machinery should be the best quality obtainable. I recommend buying single-purpose machines and avoiding multi-purpose machines that combine saw, jointer, lathe, and what-have-you. They are inefficient because too much time must be spent on the adjustments and changes needed to carry out sequential operations. All of my machines have sturdy cast-iron bases, and each has its own electric motor.

If I were to purchase machinery for a shop, one item at a time, I'd buy a good table saw first. You should be able to tilt either the saw or the saw table, and it should be equipped with a 10-in. combination crosscut and ripping blade and with a dado head. A radial arm saw could be substituted here but would require more room. My table saw has a ¾-HP motor, which meets all my cutting requirements.

Next, I would buy a 6-in. jointer, equipped with a ⅓-HP or ½-HP motor. A 14-in. or 16-in. band saw should be your third machine, and for this a ⅓-HP motor is adequate. A floor-type drill press (⅓ HP will do) should be next, and it would pay you to equip it for hollow-chisel mortising.

Fifth, get a woodturning lathe with one or more faceplates, as well as a good set of woodturning chisels. If possible buy a lathe equipped with an index head and a bed long enough so you can turn spindles 38 in. or more. A ⅓-HP motor will be adequate for this machine. A 12-in. surface planer is a good machine if you can afford one, but it might crowd you for space in a small shop. You need floor space for assembling large projects and for safety—don't sacrifice it for equipment you can get along without.

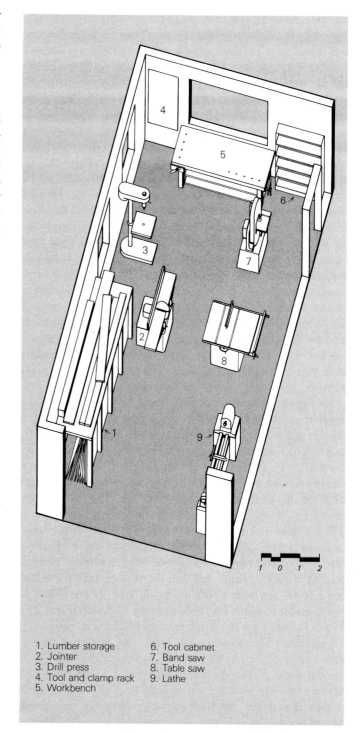

1. Lumber storage
2. Jointer
3. Drill press
4. Tool and clamp rack
5. Workbench
6. Tool cabinet
7. Band saw
8. Table saw
9. Lathe

Gottshall in his own shop, somewhat larger than 200 sq. ft.

Get a big band saw and a jigsaw too

by Andy Marlow

For a home shop I would start with a 10-in. table saw. This is one machine that requires space in all four directions for work maneuverability, so it must be placed with the fence running parallel to the length of the building and equidistant from all four walls. Though the power cable should come up through the floor (this is not too difficult to arrange if the floor is wood), it may not be worth the trouble of chipping away cement to bury the conduit. So to keep from tripping over the conduit, simply border it with chamfered strips of wood on each side. Your jointer, for convenience of operation, should be placed next to your table saw and can be powered by the same cable.

The placement of other machines and equipment is optional and deserves careful consideration. I would place the lathe along a wall somewhere near the workbench because extra space at the ends of this machine is unnecessary, and operational space out into the general shop area can be held to a minimum. A band saw is an indispensable tool, so don't buy a small toy. I believe that a 16-in. throat is the minimum, not only because of its width capacity but also because on smaller size saws the blade will wander, distorting the shape on the bottom of the cut, especially if the stock is thick. The column of the band saw may be placed quite close to a wall, though there should be plenty of room on the other three sides to move your body and negotiate the workpiece.

Two more machines I consider necessary are a drill press and jigsaw. As you continue to use your shop equipment, you will begin to realize how many different operations can be done on a drill press. In addition to light shaper work, you can do dowel boring and mortising. True perpendicular boring is, in many cases, quite important. A jigsaw is indispensable for fine scroll work on thin stock, and no other machine can saw a complete inside cutout. If you look at the shop sketch, it will become apparent that space is running out. Fortunately a jigsaw can be mounted on a table with casters so that you can move it about the shop. Two more machines for later consideration are a bench shaper and a homemade 6-in. belt sander needed for larger work.

The idea is to get as much daylight as possible on the bench, so you might want to place it close to the entry door. You could get by with a bench top as small as 48 in. by 20 in. At least 95% of your work will be performed at the right end of the bench (if you're right-handed), where two 7-in. woodworking vises should be mounted. The vise on the end should have a dog, and on the bench, in line with this dog, should be a series of 7/8-in. diameter holes to receive a bench stop. You can make a suitable bench stop by starting with a block 1 1/4 in. square by 2 5/8 in. long. Put it in your lathe and turn a 7/8-in. by 2-in. dowel on the end of it. This stop can be inserted in any one of the holes in the bench to hold workpieces of various lengths.

The kind of lighting you use is optional, but your fixtures must be placed so that no shadows will be cast on your work. Only one other suggestion—don't use a fluorescent light over your lathe. Rapidly revolving objects appear to writhe and squirm under this kind of light.

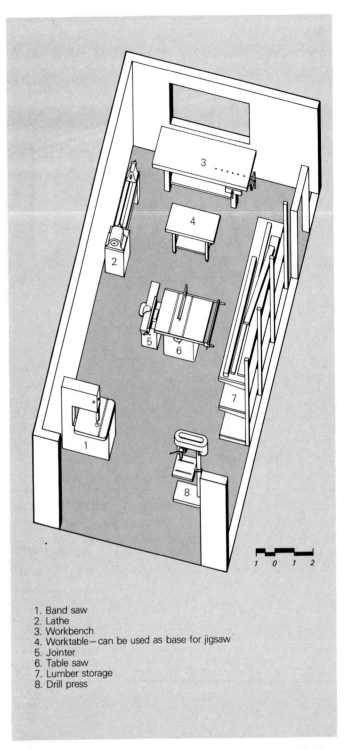

1. Band saw
2. Lathe
3. Workbench
4. Worktable—can be used as base for jigsaw
5. Jointer
6. Table saw
7. Lumber storage
8. Drill press

Though his shop is not much larger than a typical single-car garage, Marlow works quite comfortably and efficiently here reproducing period furniture. His work includes multiple productions and one-of-a-kind pieces.

2. A Plexiglas template (Plexiglas allows defects to be seen and avoided) is used to mark band-saw cuts on the 8/4 drawer blanks. The cuts produce what will be the center carcase lamination, the drawer (the saw kerf will be glued back together and clamped with motorcycle inner tubes) and a central waste piece, which is used to make another design, the shell box. Drawer and carcase members are numbered and later rejoined to maintain continuity of figure.

1. Because the designs are already known, it is most efficient to mill the stock to blanks as soon as the lumber shipment has been checked for moisture content and drying stresses. The blanks can then be stacked in space-saving, fire-safe piles and left to reach equilibrium moisture content with the shop atmosphere. Here a 3-roll, 8-speed automatic feeder by Forest City, which can also be used on the jointer and shaper, helps to rip egg-box blanks safely, quickly and cleanly. The saw is a dual-arbor 16-in. Yates American with 5 HP per arbor. There's a 32-tooth carbide, glue-joint-ripping blade on one arbor and a 60-tooth crosscut blade on the other.

3. The insides of the drawers are shaped to identical size with a shaper jig before rabbeting the lower edge for press-fitted drawer bottom. Handles screw down to clamp drawer blank in place. Heavy ⅜-in. steel base (laminated with Masonite to slide easily on shaper table) dampens vibration as precision-ground cutout is guided around fixed shaper collar. An adjustable angle-iron indexer for positioning the drawer blank also acts as a scatter shield. The segmented carbide cutter is quieter than standard cutters.

allow it to harden for 12 to 36 hours. Then it is buffed at high speed with non-impregnated soft nylon (also made by Norton) leaving a lustrous but not glossy finish.

Over the years we have kept careful records of what new technology has worked for us or why it didn't and what might be changed to improve it. Abrasive manufacturers in particular are interested in this kind of feedback, and specialized sales representatives can be very helpful in suggesting and sometimes engineering products that suit your needs. The important thing is to do your homework first, acquire the basic knowledge of the product, and go back to the manufacturer with specific experiences and requirements.

Design and construction—Because our shop makes a commitment to each design, long-term refinement is possible. It is a continuous, slow, and carefully thought-out process, making the most of available resources in balance with the realities of being in business. Once again, superficially conflicting concerns, like quality and efficiency, turn out to be compatibly interrelated. For instance, we make our freeform

cutting boards in only six basic shapes that over the years have proven the most practical and the most aesthetically pleasing. These shapes have also been developed to make maximum use of stock: The free-form templates are paired to fill various standard rectangular blanks.

Commitment to a limited number of designs also makes possible the long-term refinement of construction techniques. Quality equipment, custom bits and special one-piece cutters (which are safer and faster to set up) can be purchased and amortized over an extended period of anticipated return. Specialized jigs, fixtures, clamps and tools can be devised not only to expedite the construction process, but also to improve working tolerances and quality and to increase safety. Waste and cutoffs can be used to maximum advantage by designing new items out of predictable leftovers.

The egg box, whose production is illustrated above, is one of our first production designs, and it still has strong appeal after 10 years. I was impressed with the simple beauty of Art Carpenter's bandsawn boxes and the shapes Wendell Castle gets out of laminated wood. Starting with a few prototypes,

4. Parts are selected according to figure, and 4/4 top and bottom are glued to 8/4 carcase center. Using aliphatic resin glue for joint elasticity, the gluing surfaces are sized (precoated for maximum fiber penetration) and stacked in specially made egg-box clamp. Pressure applied evenly through threaded rods achieves optimum 0.002-in. glueline.

5. Because there are fewer and easier machine setups, the rest of the production run is divided into smaller groups so more attention can be given each box. Drawers are fitted to their carcases and, after bandsawing the outline and rounding it over on the shaper, the top and bottom surfaces are crowned on the stroke sander. A padded, graphite-covered hand platen is used first, then a graphite-coated glove.

6. At the pneumatic sander, far left, the surface is smoothed, first with 50-grit at 12 lb. to 15 lb. of pressure, then with 120-grit at 6 lb. to 8 lb., and then with 240-grit at 4 lb. to 6 lb. The shape of the box, carefully chosen abrasive products and their backing, and the use of a tire pressure gauge make possible the radical increments in grit. Adjustable dust-collection intake and point-source lighting add to the comfort and accuracy of this operation. Left, sharp edges are sanded by hand before final sanding (to 500-grit) on Vonnegut flap sander.

the initial run was seven boxes of black willow. Since then the egg box has been made in eastern walnut, claro walnut, cherry, Tennessee cedar, butternut, African naga, California oak, elm, shedua and most recently Hawaiian koa. The design has undergone refinements that typify the interrelationship of design and construction improvements. The first drawers, for instance, were hogged out of solid wood. Not only was this time-consuming and wasteful, but the resulting drawer tended to warp and stick closed. We tried bandsawing out the whole center of the drawer and inserting a plywood bottom, which was faster, but the hardwood drawer sides would contract around the unyielding plywood bottom, cup and still stick closed. Shaving down the back of the drawer to clear the inside of the carcase only made the drawer too loose, on being pulled out, to remain in its track. The solution we have developed is to use 1/4-in. thick sugar pine for the bottom. It is press-fitted and glued into a rabbet in the bottom of the hardwood drawer sides, and because it is solid wood and more yielding than the hardwood, it expands and contracts compatibly with the sides.

The waste from the insides of the drawers accumulated until we could hardly move through parts of the shop. Finally we conceived of the shell box (photo, p. 28), made by resawing this waste, hollowing out the halves and hinging them back together. The corners of the rectangular blank from which the egg box is bandsawn were more pieces of waste until we designed a segmented toy snake, and now we use those too.

I can't honestly say that I'm proud of every single box we've made over the last ten years. But, having put the necessary time and effort into the egg box, we have been able to refine the design and technique to where only a small percentage is unusable. The screening for quality begins with the rough wood. For a variety of reasons, units or parts of units will fall out of production along the way. The final product is also inspected, and only about 50% of the finished output can be considered gallery quality. Those of unusual quality we prefer to sell directly and that way are assured that the customers know and appreciate what they are buying. □

Dean Santner Woodworking is located in Emeryville, Calif. Santner is available as a design and production consultant.

Mobile-Home Wood Shop

by Anthony Wheeler

Few can afford to build a shop, but a house trailer affords a good solution to the one or two-man business or to the serious hobbyist. Since the house trailer is somewhat mobile, it allows for changes in residence or even for the building of a new shop while already having a completely functional one. The cost can be as low as $5/sq. ft., with internal alterations kept to a minimum; a fixed-foundation building of equal size would run $10 to $12/sq. ft. Most trailers are designed with windows on one side, good for solar heating. The basic shape of a trailer accommodates long stock, and even plywood can be maneuvered in trailers 12 ft. or 14 ft. wide. The longest trailers are 950 sq. ft. (14 ft. by 70 ft.), with low ceilings; thus the size and variety of the equipment that can be used is limited.

I live on rented property out in the country, where a 1974 Shultz 14-ft. by 70-ft. house trailer has become an extremely functional shop for about $7/sq. ft. It had been damaged in a fire. In hunting it out, I saw other trailers ranging from a 1965 10-ft. by 50-ft. for $600 to a 1976 14-ft. by 70-ft. with expanded living room for $7,600. My fire-damaged trailer cost $5,000 (this may have been high), plus $2,000 to lay a new plywood floor, replace interior walls with drywall, replace over half the windows, rewire for power-tool equipment and fluorescent lighting, repair the ceiling and put in bench areas.

An extra-heavy block base was constructed to spread the trailer's weight over soft earth. The location required blocking one end up about 5 ft., and once skirted, this space has provided a good storage space for lumber. All of these details can increase the cost of setting up this type of shop.

The long narrow shape of the trailer is well suited to a cabinet shop. My shop is laid out so that work moves in one direction, from the front door as rough stock to the finishing room in the rear. The first and largest room (13 ft. by 30 ft.) is devoted to wood storage and power-tool work. A narrow storage area here will hold approximately 15 to 20 sheets of plywood and 100 bd. ft. of lumber. The power tools include a 10-in. table saw, a 12-in. band saw, a jointer, a panel saw and a Shopsmith. The table saw and Shopsmith are on casters so they can be moved when working on odd-size stock. The panel saw's proximity to the lumber storage area saves work. The Shopsmith has been an adequate tool thus far. For this room I made a large router table that can be stored vertically when not in use.

The second room (13 ft. by 20 ft.) is the bench room and is separated from the first room by a large sliding door, which reduces dust flow. This room contains a woodworking bench and an auxiliary bench and is where final assembly and gluing are done, and all carving. The adjacent area includes an office, converted from the bathroom, a gas furnace and a woodburning stove. The last room is used for wood finishing, stained-glass work and storage. I plan to install a large bank of sunlamps to improve finish results. Once a piece is finished it makes a single trip back through the shop and out to the customer. There is really no place to store completed work. □

Tony Wheeler, 30, of Nevada, Iowa, is a self-taught professional woodworker.

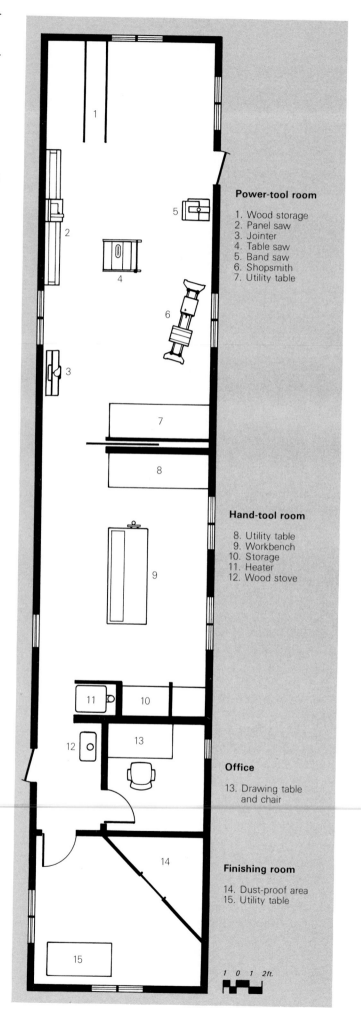

Power-tool room

1. Wood storage
2. Panel saw
3. Jointer
4. Table saw
5. Band saw
6. Shopsmith
7. Utility table

Hand-tool room

8. Utility table
9. Workbench
10. Storage
11. Heater
12. Wood stove

Office

13. Drawing table and chair

Finishing room

14. Dust-proof area
15. Utility table

Converting to 3-Phase Power

More surges per cycle can save you money

by Mac Campbell

Recently I had the basement of my house wired to supply the power that's required to drive both the single-phase and 3-phase machines I need to run a one-man, custom woodworking shop. From a two-pole, 60-amp fuse box, I get enough power to drive portable hand tools as well as my standing shop machinery. I have a 10-in. table saw (2 HP, single phase), a central dust-collection system (3 HP, single phase), a 14-in. jointer (2 HP, 3 phase), a 24-in. thickness planer (7½ HP and ¾ HP, 3 phase), a stationary belt sander (1½ HP, 3 phase) and a 30-in. band saw (5 HP, 3 phase). I use a phase converter to provide the power I need to drive the 3-phase machines. This converter takes the 220-volt, single-phase, alternating current that's supplied to my house and changes it to 3-phase electricity, as is normally found in commercial and industrial zones.

Before saying more about the advantages of 3-phase power and about making a phase converter, a warning is necessary. Electricity must be treated with respect, deliberation and caution. Improper planning, poor layout or failure to observe those safety standards set forth in the National Electrical Code (NEC) or the Canadian Electric Code (CEC) can result in blown fuses, burned-out motors, shop fires, personal injury or death. So if in the process of setting up your shop and installing your electrical system you have doubts or run into problems you can't readily solve, call in a licensed electrician. You may have no choice in the matter because in many cities and towns only licensed electricians are authorized to do the kind of electrical work I describe here.

In addition to observing standard safety practices when wiring your shop, you'll need to put each machine on its own separate circuit, which will protect the individual motor from overload with either a fuse or circuit breaker. Each machine will also require its own power switch that's rated to match the voltage and current draw of the motor. And for maximum safety, especially on concrete floors, each motor circuit should be equipped with a ground-fault interrupter. This device senses current leaks and breaks the circuit before the leakage gets powerful enough to cause a harmful electrical shock.

Next to safety, the efficient use of energy should be your chief concern, and here's where 3-phase electricity is important. Consisting of three separate sources of single-phase alternating current, 3-phase electricity is generated so that the voltage peaks of each phase follow one another at regular intervals, dividing the duration of one cycle of single-phase current (⅟₆₀ second) into even sixths. So instead of two voltage peaks every ⅟₆₀ second, you get six, each ⅟₃₆₀ second apart. Electric motors get their driving force from surges of electromagnetic energy, a power surge occurring with each voltage peak (one positive, one negative). At 60 cycles per second, an 1,800-RPM motor running on single-phase current will receive about four power surges per revolution. But an 1,800-RPM, 3-phase motor will get three times as many power surges per revolution, and will produce smoother, more efficient rotary power and higher starting torque. Single-phase electric motors are to 3-phase motors as two-cylinder gasoline engines are to six-cylinder engines. Aside from getting more energy efficiency, the woodworker who's supplied with 3-phase power has ready access to the used machinery market and can equip his entire shop, if he wishes, with superior industrial-duty machines, most of which have 3-phase motors. Such machines sometimes can be purchased for what it would cost to buy new consumer-grade tools with single-phase motors.

Three-phase wiring requires three insulated conductors plus a ground wire, rather than the two conductors plus a ground needed for single-phase wiring; the practical advantages of 3-phase are numerous. Three-phase motors contain fewer internal parts. They do not, for example, require a separate starter winding and centrifugal switch or a starting

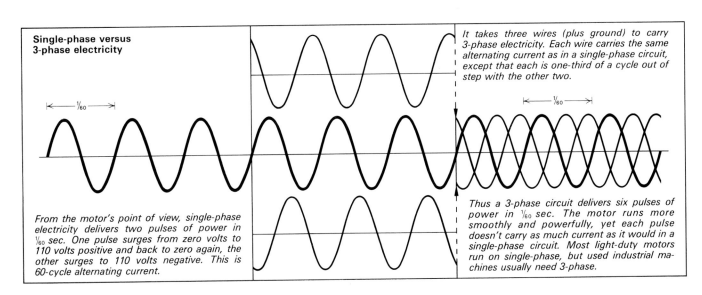

Single-phase versus 3-phase electricity

←— ⅟₆₀ —→

←— ⅟₆₀ —→

From the motor's point of view, single-phase electricity delivers two pulses of power in ⅟₆₀ sec. One pulse surges from zero volts to 110 volts positive and back to zero again, the other surges to 110 volts negative. This is 60-cycle alternating current.

It takes three wires (plus ground) to carry 3-phase electricity. Each wire carries the same alternating current as in a single-phase circuit, except that each is one-third of a cycle out of step with the other two.

Thus a 3-phase circuit delivers six pulses of power in ⅟₆₀ sec. The motor runs more smoothly and powerfully, yet each pulse doesn't carry as much current as it would in a single-phase circuit. Most light-duty motors run on single-phase, but used industrial machines usually need 3-phase.

Comments on "Converting to 3-phase power"

Mac Campbell's article on 3-phase conversion (pp. 33-34) contains some misconceptions which, while they won't prevent his converter from operating properly, should be corrected.... First is an apparent confusion between power, voltage and current.... The instantaneous 3-phase power is constant rather than sinusoidal like single-phase power. This is why 3-phase motors run smoother—there are *no* power surges. Second, the reason that single-phase power is sufficient to keep the conversion motor running is because its total load (electrical plus mechanical) is less than two-thirds of the motor's power rating....

—Tony Armendariz, La Honda, Calif.

...3-phase power is more economical for the industrial user as it comes from the power company but Campbell's system introduces inefficiencies that will make his overall system use more, not less, energy.

The smartest thing one can do with a 3-phase motor and only single-phase power is sell the 3-phase motor and use the money to buy a single-phase motor. Or, in a real bind, a 3-phase motor can be run single-phase up to about two-thirds of its rated capacity if started by some external means.... The solid-state converters available are expensive and have poor efficiency and usually poor starting torque. A motor-generating set—single-phase motor driving 3-phase generator—would give the best power and performance, but is also expensive and has efficiency losses. You just can't get something for nothing. *—Mike Graetz, Lakeland, Minn.*

...There are numerous types of single-phase motors; there are also a lot of types of 3-phase motors. These motors differ in many ways such as full-load efficiency, speed regulation etc., and 3-phase motors don't necessarily have higher starting torque. For example a single-phase repulsion-induction motor would start a much heavier load than a normal 3-phase motor. Furthermore, starting torque is quite pointless in woodworking machinery; I know of no examples where the machine must start under working load.... Rather than allow the converter to run with no mechanical load, Campbell might really be able to save some power by using it to drive some permanent load like the fan of his central dust-collection system.... He could get rid of the motor that drives his fan, eliminating one motor—and its losses, which now must be supplied by the converter....

—E.W. Jones, Wilkes-Barre, Pa.

...To illustrate the efficiency advantages of 3-phase motors over single-phase motors, the article used a chart of motor currents. The electrical to mechanical power conversion efficiency of a motor is a function of current, voltage and power factor, and it is not valid to compare currents alone and expect a meaningful result. For example, an average 1-HP, 110-volt single-phase motor draws as much as 16 amps at full load, versus 3.8 amps for a 1-HP, 230-volt 3-phase motor. In terms of power consumption however, the single-phase motor will use about 1,040 watts versus 960 watts for the 3-phase motor. Thus the single-phase motor draws about 400% more current but only 8% more power. If the motors were on a small saw, run at full load for one hour per day, and electricity cost 5ᶜ per kilowatt hour, the single-phase motor would use about a dime more energy per month than the 3-phase motor. Even the dime would disappear if the user had to convert single-phase to 3-phase because of the energy consumed by the converting equipment.... *—T.J. Cotter, Mauldin, S.C.*

...When using a 3-phase motor as a converter as described, a second motor is not needed to start it. Simply place a motor-starting capacitor (readily available for about $10 from electrical suppliers and sources such as W.W. Grainger, Woburn, Mass.) in series with a push button as shown in the diagram below. After turning the power on, pushing the button will cause one winding of the converter to act as a starting winding. A 3-phase motor can also be used directly on 220-volt single-phase in this manner, with an output of roughly two-thirds its rated output. Capacitor size ranges from about 150 μfd for a 1-HP motor to 650 μfd for a 5-HP motor.

—Bruce Fortier, Essex, Mass.

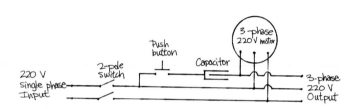

EDITOR'S NOTE: We received a dozen letters discussing the conversion to 3-phase power, several of them from electrical engineers who took the time to explain the intricacies in exhaustive detail. The excerpts printed above are the points on which the engineers agree. To validate their advice, we asked our New England correspondent, Richard Starr, to explore the question with Eric LaWhite of South Royalton, Vt. LaWhite is a mechanical-engineering consultant who has well-equipped metal and woodworking shops and for 20 years has run about half of his machines on 3-phase current supplied by a small idler motor. Starr's report:

"LaWhite's idler, a 3-HP, 3-phase motor, sits inconspicuously in a corner of his woodworking shop. To get it running he spins its shaft with the rubber sole of his shoe (up to about half its rated 1,200 RPM), then switches on its 220-volt single-phase power supply. The biggest 3-phase motor in the shop, which drives a pedestal belt sander with 5 HP, caused the idler to buzz slightly as it generated the third leg of the sander's starting current. His 3-phase powered equipment includes the sander, a table saw, a wood lathe, several machinist's lathes, a surface grinder and a dust collector. LaWhite can run all these tools simultaneously, without overloading the idler.

"LaWhite explained that the function of an idler is to generate the third leg of 3-phase current. Any motor in the circuit can do it. If your idler seems to overload while starting or running a large motor, you can augment its capacity by running a second or third motor in the circuit—for example, run your idler and disc sander to start your table saw. In fact, as long as any two motors are running, they are both operating on 3-phase current. But take care using this method; there is risk in running power tools unattended. The advantage is that you don't need to waste current operating an oversized idler. LaWhite suggests using a conversion motor whose horsepower rating equals the average shop motor. The diagram at right shows the circuitry LaWhite recommends, with Fortier's capacitor starter included. Note that each leg of the 220-volt input requires its own circuit breaker, that the starter circuit for the idler motor should be enclosed in a metal box (capacitors can explode if something goes wrong), and that each additional motor should have its own starter switch with heaters for overload protection.

"Considering the conversion losses and the nuisance of setting up a second wiring system, why bother with 3-phase power? A major advantage to machinists, says LaWhite, is the instant reversability of 3-phase motors. Single-phase equipment can be run backwards by reversing the wires in the starting circuit but the motor must first be stopped. When you switch a 3-phase motor into reverse at full speed, it is like hitting a brake. This is very handy on lathes and milling machines, and could be useful on woodworking tools. Reversing drum switches are available at electrical supply houses for about $15.

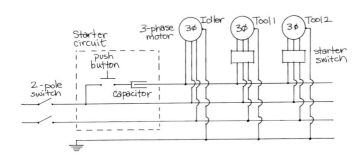

"New 3-phase motors sell for 10% to 30% less than the price of comparable single-phase motors, require less maintenance because they are simpler, and can be had in much larger sizes. They are slightly more efficient than single-phase motors.

"But for the small shop, the main advantage is in the purchase of used 3-phase equipment, and the advantage is twofold. First, the motors and the tools they power are built to industrial standards and are far more durable than 'home-craftsman' models. Second, since these tools are not in demand they can be had for bargain prices. LaWhite prowls the classified ads, used-tool shops and auctions.

"Consider these points when shopping for used 3-phase motors:
—Recent motors are usually more efficient than old ones; they have better magnetic properties. Ball bearings usually indicate a newer motor. Ball-bearing motors will run freely when spun by hand; they have grease fittings or permanent lubrication, while sleeve bearings have oil cups. When shopping for an idler, get a modern motor.
—For use as an idler, choose a lower RPM motor. It is easier to start, will run quieter and have fewer internal losses. There's no need to match speeds among motors and idlers. But whatever starting method you use, be sure that your motor is running at rated speed once started. Always start in the same direction; a reversed idler will run the other motors backward.
—You will seldom (if ever) find a 3-phase motor with a ground lead, so don't reject a motor if one is not present. Three-phase equipment is usually wired to metal conduit or *BX* cable, which provides grounding. If you wire with plastic-sheathed cable, be sure to ground the frame of each motor.
—Check the motor with an ohmmeter. Three-phase motors have either three or nine leads, and there's usually a wiring diagram on the housing or inside the cover of the wiring box. None of the leads should show a connection with the frame of the motor. A motor with a current leak is dangerous.
—Run the motor. It should sound right without excessive hum or grumble.

"Commercially built converters come in two types—static and rotary. The static variety generally consists of a box of capacitors tuned to a particular motor, which supply the starting current and then drop out of the circuit. It's designed for running a single motor under constant load. A rotary converter, which consists of a matched motor-generator set with capacitor start, is much more suitable for woodworking machinery. It works the same way as scavenged equipment, except it's designed for the job rather than cobbled together. One model, rated to handle a total of 9 HP and to start 3 HP under load, lists for $428. Suppliers of both static and rotary converters are Ronk Electrical Industries, 106 E. State St., Nokomis, Ill. 62075; Arco Electric Corp., P.O. Box 278, Shelbyville, Ind. 46176; and Cedarberg Industries, 5408 Chicago Ave. S., Minneapolis, Minn. 55413.

"In most conversion setups, two legs of current are supplied directly from the power lines at full-line voltage. LaWhite found that his idler was supplying only 160 volts on the third leg. Motors run on unbalanced 3-phase start slower and lose efficiency. Most 3-phase motors can be wired to run on either 220-volt or 440-volt. By wiring the output leg of his idler to 440-volt, LaWhite found that it would supply close to line voltage. But he warns that this reduces its current-carrying capacity, increasing the likelihood of overloading.

"Finally, LaWhite advises craftsmen to keep in mind that electricity is deadly, and wiring of this sort should not be attempted by inexperienced persons. In many jurisdictions, local codes make it illegal to wire without a licensed electrician. In any case, it pays to have a competent electrician check your system before you use it."

Methods of Work

Heating the shop

Heating a woodworking shop can be a problem—sawdust and paint vapors present a fire hazard. Local heating firms suggested several approaches including a separate "heating room," a gas wall heater, infrared heating and electric baseboard heating. All these approaches were either too expensive, a fire hazard or both. Finally, I chose electric hot-water baseboard heat for my just completed 14-ft. by 22-ft. woodworking shed. I was a little worried about the operating cost, but surprisingly, costs have been only slightly higher than gas heat. The unit keeps the water at an even temperature and doesn't cycle on and off like other heating systems. Hot water baseboard units weigh less than 30 lb. and can be purchased as portable or permanently mounted models. They don't stir up the air—an ideal situation for a dusty shop or paint room. Because the units operate at a continuous low heat, they're not a fire hazard.

I chose the largest model the supplier had—a 220-volt portable unit that sells for about $150. It measures 4 in. by 9 in. by 107 in. long and produces 6,800 BTU. The supplier: Intertherm Inc., 3800 Park Ave., St. Louis, Mo. 63110.

—*R. Voorhees, Ft. Wayne, Ind.*

Light stands

For temporary lighting in my new shop, I built a couple of light stands from 2x4s with 1x4 legs. Two or three inexpensive clamp-lights completed the fixtures. The poles are easy to move around and don't take a lot of room. They're versatile and inexpensive. Although I've added overhead lighting now in my shop, I haven't been able to do without my light stands.

—*A. Miller, Lakewood, Colo.*

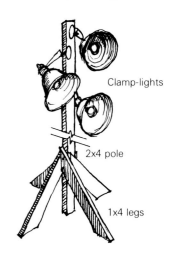

Clamp-lights

2x4 pole

1x4 legs

Electric-cord suspension

It is much easier to use portable electric tools if the cord can be suspended from above so it doesn't drag across your workbench. This cord suspension arm is designed to move easily to different heights or to different locations in the shop. The arm pivots on electrical conduit pipe, which is cheap and light but strong enough. The conduit slips into 1-in. screw-eyes spaced so that when the arm is raised, the lower pipe will disengage for removal.

—*Pendleton Tompkins, San Mateo, Calif.*

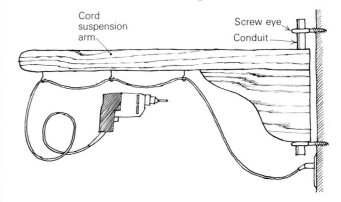

Cord suspension arm

Screw eye

Conduit

A Joiner's Tool Case
Wooden box holds all the essentials

by Tony Taylor

A few years ago I worked alongside a joiner who impressed on me the advantages of carrying your tools in a wooden case. His own case was a masterpiece of inventiveness and caught the eye of every visitor to our work site. The number of items he kept in this case amazed me. In addition to a full range of hand tools, he could produce on request just about anything the rest of us didn't carry—spare knife blades, chalk and line, scissors, tweezers, knife, fork and spoon, and, in case he worked overtime, toothbrush and paste, razor and aftershave and a corkscrew. Not everyone may feel the need to be so readily equipped for the contingencies of the working day, but those who regularly work away from the shop are familiar with the need to carry an organized tool kit.

My finished tool case weighs 16 lb. unloaded and up to 55 lb. when full, so don't count on walking to work if you make one of similar size. Strength of construction is vital; your tool case may have to withstand rough handling. So unless you can guarantee its safety, I would advise against making anything too fancy. A simple, well-made case will give years of service and will protect your tools. Because each tool has its own place, it's easy to find, and you'll notice if any are missing at the end of the day. Furthermore, an attractive, well-made case will always get the attention of prospective clients and employers, and it will serve as a good example of your work.

Whether you plan to build a fine showpiece or a simple plywood box, careful planning is essential. List on paper all the tools you want to carry and sort them into categories according to size and usefulness. The saws can fit into the lid, where they lie flat and are easy to reach; a square can fit in here as well. Small tools fit easily into removable drawers or trays. Divide the drawers into separate compartments for chisels, files, brace bits and screwdrivers. Allow extra drawer space for mortise gauges, marking tools, measuring tape, drill bits and punches. My spirit level hangs on blocks glued to the back panel underneath the lowest drawer. This leaves the larger, heavier tools—oilstone, planes, hand drill, brace, pump screwdriver, coping saw and hammer—to lie in the bottom of the case.

The carcase is made of ⅝-in. thick pine boards dovetailed together. Front and back panels are of ¼-in. plywood. The depth of the lid must be determined before you lay out the

A sturdy tool case puts everything in its place for on-site work, with three drawers for small hand tools, saws inside the lid, and a storage compartment below for large, heavy tools. Top right, a tenon saw starts the cuts in the two upper corners and makes the beveled cut through the face of the front panel to form the lid. Note that the kerf neatly divides a dovetail pin. Once the corners and the panel have been cut, a portable jigsaw finishes the cuts along the sides and top. The lid will fall away as shown, lower right.

Photos: Tony Taylor

Wooden tool case

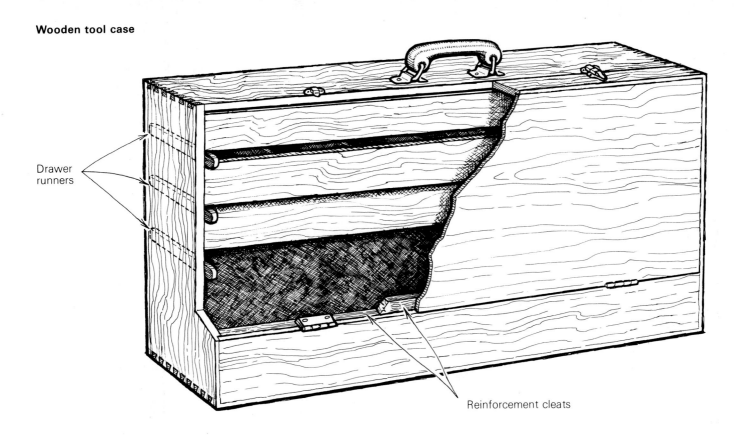

Drawer runners

Reinforcement cleats

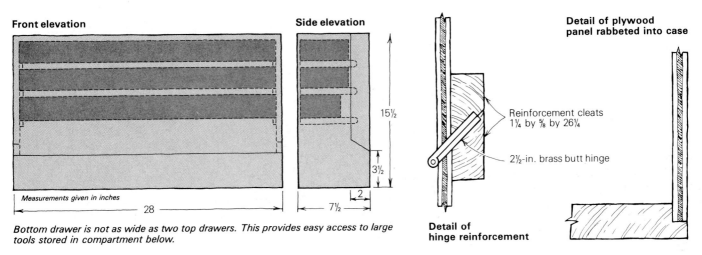

Front elevation

Side elevation

15½

3½

2

Measurements given in inches — 28 —

— 7½ —

Bottom drawer is not as wide as two top drawers. This provides easy access to large tools stored in compartment below.

Detail of plywood panel rabbeted into case

Reinforcement cleats 1¼ by ⅝ by 26¼

2½-in. brass butt hinge

Detail of hinge reinforcement

dovetails so the sawcut that will separate the lid from the case will pass through the middle of one of the pins. It's best to glue the plywood panels into rabbets cut in the carcase rather than to fit them into grooves. The latter way may seem stronger, but will rob space from the inside of the case. Remember to allow for the rabbet when laying out the dovetails.

With the carcase glued up and the panels glued in place, the box is now completely enclosed. So the next step is to saw off the lid. Mark the depth of the lid with a gauge, and then make the first cut along the front plywood panel using a tenon saw. Cut from the outside edges of the panel towards the center, gradually lowering the angle of the saw as the cut proceeds. Complete the cut down the beveled line on the carcase sides. Next, saw in from the top corners so the kerfs will pass through a dovetail pin and will end at the beveled line on the carcase side and at the center of the top of the case. At this point the lid will fall free. Some cleaning up of the sawn edges will be necessary, but it should be kept to a minimum or else the gap between case and lid will be too wide.

Before fitting the hinges, the sawn edges of the front plywood panel must be reinforced and made thicker by gluing in

two pieces about ⅝ in. thick and 1¼ in. wide. Install the hinges at this stage and then remove the lid from the case, to work on each part separately. To fit the saws into the lid, cut contoured blocks to fit inside the saw handles. These should be 1/16 in. thicker than the saw handles. When they are glued into position, screw on the latches. It may be necessary to provide holders or rests for the blades of the saws to hold them in position.

Using butt joints throughout, I made the drawers from ¼-in. plywood with ⅛-in. plywood bottoms. You may prefer using solid wood with delicate dovetails. To permit easy access to the bottom compartment of the case, I made the lowest drawer 1 in. narrower than the upper two. The drawers slide on hardwood runners screwed to the sides of the carcase. The runners extend beyond the drawer fronts to allow the drawer to be pulled out farther than would otherwise be possible. When fitting the insides of the drawers for partitions, cut more dadoes than required; this will let you arrange things differently should the need arise in the future. □

Tony Taylor, 25, is a cabinetmaker and writer in London.

41

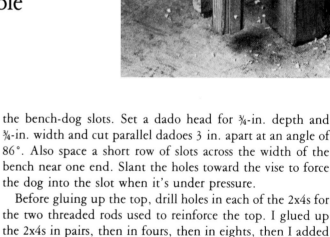

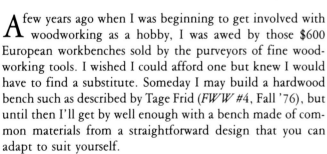
Three leg vises and three rows of dog holes give Schuldt's bench large holding capability. Side view of leg vise, right, shows threaded rod, pivot foot and steel strap stiffener.

A Softwood Workbench
Leg vises keep it versatile and affordable

by Ted Schuldt

A few years ago when I was beginning to get involved with woodworking as a hobby, I was awed by those $600 European workbenches sold by the purveyors of fine woodworking tools. I wished I could afford one but knew I would have to find a substitute. Someday I may build a hardwood bench such as described by Tage Frid (*FWW* #4, Fall '76), but until then I'll get by well enough with a bench made of common materials from a straightforward design that you can adapt to suit yourself.

Before determining the dimensions of your bench, evaluate your needs and the size of your shop. I chose a length of 60 in. because of space restrictions and a width of 27 in. to provide enough workspace to assemble casepieces. After determining the required dimensions, begin by making the bench top.

All the wood used in this bench is fir, readily available at any lumberyard. The bench top is made of 2x4s set on edge. Take extra care in selecting the pieces for the top. They should be straight, and the edges that will be the top should be as free of knots as possible. Most dimensioned lumber has rounded edges, so rip off enough of the edge to get the corners square to provide for a smooth, flat surface when the boards are glued up. Select the two best 2x4s in which to cut

the bench-dog slots. Set a dado head for ¾-in. depth and ¾-in. width and cut parallel dadoes 3 in. apart at an angle of 86°. Also space a short row of slots across the width of the bench near one end. Slant the holes toward the vise to force the dog into the slot when it's under pressure.

Before gluing up the top, drill holes in each of the 2x4s for the two threaded rods used to reinforce the top. I glued up the 2x4s in pairs, then in fours, then in eights, then I added one more to make two halves each of nine pieces.

Then I took the two halves to a high-school woodshop and ran them through a thickness planer. You could plane these by hand, but I took the more expeditious way to the end result. With the two halves completed, run two ½-in. Redi-Bolt threaded rods through the predrilled holes to join the two halves of the top and to reinforce the glue joint. Mortise out enough of the outside pieces to countersink the washers and nuts of the rods. As the top dries from the 17% moisture content of kiln-dried dimension lumber, the nuts will have to be tightened. Depending on the length of your bench, you may want to install a third or fourth rod.

Next work on the legs. In positioning the legs, the center of the legs must line up with the center of the bench dog slots. Chop through mortises in the 4x4 legs for the stretcher tenons

Photos: Ted Schuldt; Illustration: Ric Lopez

and the vise positioners. I cut these by drilling holes at opposite corners of the mortise and cutting out the waste with a saber saw to within 1/32 in. of the line and cleaning up with a chisel. Now, drill a 13/16-in. hole for the vise screw in three of the legs and mortise out just enough to countersink a 3/4-in. nut at both ends of the hole. Also drill for a 1/2-in. draw pin for each mortise in the leg. Cut tenons on the stretchers, fit, drill holes for the draw pins 1/8 in. off center to pull the tenons into the joint and then glue up the leg assembly and pin the tenons with 1/2-in. birch dowels.

To fasten the top to the legs, drill a 3/8-in. hole down through the top into the end rails in four places. Drill a 1-in. hole to intersect the above hole and set into it a cylindrical "washer"—a short piece of pipe or electrical conduit. This will keep the captured nut from indenting the wood. Countersink the bolt in the top enough to cover the head with a wood plug. Now come the leg vises. I made mine out of 2x4s stiffened by two 1/8-in. by 3/4-in. steel straps screwed into grooves on their edges. If I had it to do over again, I would make the vises out of 4x4s. Make the vise positioner (pivot foot), and fit it onto the end of the vise so it will pivot on a 1/2-in. dowel pin. The vise screw is 3/4-in./10 Redi-Bolt threaded rod. It comes in 36-in. lengths, so each vise screw is 12 in. long. Screw the rod into the two nuts mortised into the leg and use it to line up the hole in the vise for the screw, then bore it to a 1-in. diameter. The nut nearest the vise must be restrained from coming out as the vise is tightened. This is done with a retainer made of steel straps filed to allow the rod to pass through. The retainers are screwed to the leg. The nut on the other side can be secured with a piece of 1/8-in. hardboard because it's under no stress.

With the vise screw and vise in place, drill 1/2-in. holes in the pivot foot so that the leg is perpendicular to the bench top at jaw spacings for common thicknesses of lumber (3/4 in., 1 1/2 in., 2 1/2 in., 3 1/2 in.) or whatever spacings suit your needs. Placing the holes too close together, however, will weaken the pivot foot, which takes considerable stress as it keeps the vise jaws as parallel as possible. I glued sandpaper to the jaws of one vise but it did not significantly improve its holding power. The bench dog slots can now be drilled and chiseled out in the end grain of the leg vise if you use a 4x4; but if you use a 2x4, make the slot using a dado cut into the end of the 2x4 and glue a 2x4 block to the back of the leg to house the slot. Again, incline the slots at 86° toward the bench top to ensure proper clamping dynamics.

A handle can be made for the threaded rod by screwing a 1/2-in. T-pipe fitting onto it. Secure this by drilling a hole through the T and the vise screw and pin them together with a nail or hardened steel pin. The pitch of #10 threads makes for slow going, but I can get the holding power I need using my hands on the T without using a long handle for leverage. I pinned the threaded rod just on the inside of the vise jaw so that the jaw opens when the rod is loosened.

I made bench dogs in two sets of four out of some scrap oak flooring. One set sticks 1/2 in. above the bench top, and the other sticks up 1 in. for larger pieces. I drive the bench dogs in with a rubber hammer and out by using a short rod and hammer from underneath the bench. If you don't like the idea of driving the dogs in and out, you may want to dimension them to an easy fit and equip each with a bullet catch to hold them in place (FWW #15, March '79, p. 20). The tool tray is held on by two lag bolts, and a support for long pieces

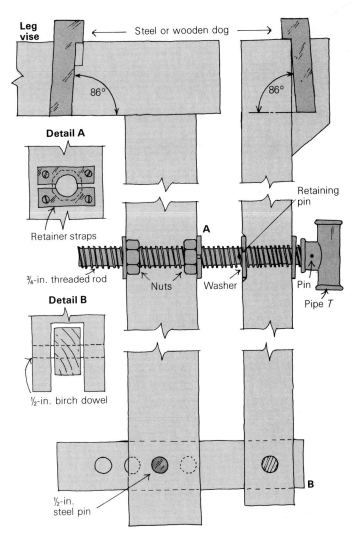

Detail A

Retainer straps

3/4-in. threaded rod

Leg vise

Steel or wooden dog

86°

86°

Retaining pin

A

Nuts

Washer

Pin

Pipe T

Detail B

1/2-in. birch dowel

1/2-in. steel pin

B

Bill of materials		
Quantity	Length	Item
1	12 ft.	4x4 fir
13	10 ft.	2x4 fir
2	4 ft.	1/2-in. birch dowels
1	3 ft.	3/4-in. threaded rod w/ nuts and washers
2	3 ft.	1/2-in. threaded rod w/ nuts and washers
4	4 in.	3/8-in. hex bolts w/ nuts and washers
3		1/2-in. T-pipe fittings
1	5 in.	1-in. pipe or conduit (sawn into four 1-in. lengths
2	2 in.	1/4-in. lag bolts and washers
2	3 ft.	1/8-in. by 3/4-in. steel strap
1		qt. yellow glue

of lumber is made using 3/4-in. dowel in a 2x4 screwed to the legs of the bench.

This bench has given good service for two years now. I have not had the courage to bear down on any of the vises just to see how much it takes to break one. But none has ever failed to hold a workpiece firmly. Fir might not be the best material for a bench top, but it's inexpensive and can be resurfaced easily with a hand plane and scraper. The bench is very heavy, and this gives it good stability when all my weight is put into planing a piece. It is versatile too, but best of all it would cost less than $100 to build today. □

Ted Schuldt, a minister and amateur woodworker, lives in Toledo, Wash.

A Shoulder Vise and Clamping Dogs
Attachments make a table a workbench

by R. J. Silvestrini

Tage Frid's workbench (*FWW* #4, Fall '76) offers two features I had long sought—a shoulder vise with its jaw unobstructed by the usual screw and guide bars (it can grip irregular objects, as well) and a tail vise with a traveling dog. Since my workbench has a radial arm saw mounted on one end of it and I don't have room for another bench in my shop, I chose to adapt these two features to the bench I already had.

After studying Frid's plans, I decided that the shoulder vise could be made separately and then attached. But the tail vise was a different story. I wanted its traveling dog so I could hold long workpieces on my bench, but I really didn't need the vise jaws, and besides, my radial arm saw was sitting right where these would go. I resolved this dilemma by doing away with the vise part of the system and rigging a traveling dog in a sliding, screw-driven housing. This mechanism, together with a row of dog holes, could be mounted on the edge of my bench top in one long unit. I decided to make all of these components—the shoulder vise and the bench-top clamping system—so they could be removed later on, should I want to mount them on a new bench.

For the shoulder vise, I followed Frid's design, making necessary changes where I had to. I used an acme-threaded bench

EDITOR'S NOTE: Plans for Tage Frid's workbench are available for $6 from the Taunton Press, Box 355, Newtown, Conn. 06470. For more on workbench design see Donald McKinley's article in *FWW* #16, May '79, pp. 72-75.

screw (from Woodcraft Supply Corp., 313 Montvale Ave., Woburn, Mass. 01888) for the vise jaw. To hold the cantilevered arm in place and keep it from being pushed outward as the vise is tightened, I used a ½-in. threaded rod, which is passed through the arm and spacer block and secured by a captured nut let into the top of the bench.

I departed from Frid's design when making the row of dog holes and the moving housing that opposes them. Instead of cutting the slots in a solid strip as Frid does, I cut a lot of parallelogram-shaped spacer blocks (angled 4° off the perpendicular so the dog would be canted appropriately) and sandwiched them between two strips 3 in. wide and as long as the bench. Each block is 4¹/₁₆ in. wide, and to make the holes, I spaced the blocks ¹⁵/₁₆ in. apart. The little slots in the front of each hole (Frid chisels these in by hand) which accommodate the head of the dog, I easily cut by elevating the blade on my radial arm saw and using a 3-in. high fence.

I designed the sliding dog housing after having looked at a drawing of a similar one made by David Powell of Leeds Design Workshops in Easthampton, Mass. While his uses a lot more hardware, I made mine with a minimum of metal parts by connecting two spacer blocks with a pair of wooden bars. These bars serve also to guide the housing as it travels, riding in grooves cut into the two strips that form the back and face sides of the dog unit. These grooves should be long enough to allow the slide to travel about 7½ in., approximately 1½ times

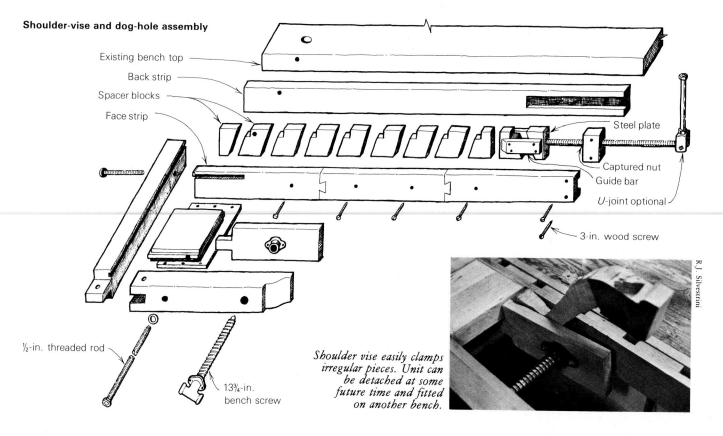

Shoulder-vise and dog-hole assembly

Existing bench top

Back strip

Spacer blocks

Face strip

Steel plate

Captured nut

Guide bar

U-joint optional

3-in. wood screw

½-in. threaded rod

13¾-in. bench screw

Shoulder vise easily clamps irregular pieces. Unit can be detached at some future time and fitted on another bench.

R.J. Silvestrini

44

the distance between dog holes. The threaded rod is attached to the slide by means of a metal plate, which is drilled in its center to receive a ⅛-in. bolt. The threaded end of this bolt is epoxied into a hole drilled in the end of the ½-in. threaded rod. Before attaching the plate to the slide with wood screws, the slide must be counterbored to accommodate the head of the ⅛-in. bolt.

The last piece of the slide assembly to make is the block that holds a ½-in. captured nut in which the threaded rod turns to advance or retract the slide. Once all the pieces are cut, the spacer blocks are glued to the back strip. Then the face strip is attached. I made a separate face strip to be attached only with screws to cover the part of the unit that's involved in the slide mechanism. This gives me access to the guts of the thing if it needs tuning or repair. When the system is complete, it's affixed to the edge of the bench top with 3-in. wood screws that are countersunk into the face strip. □

R. J. Silvestrini, 56, is president of an industrial equipment distribution company in Huntington, W. Va.

Wooden Vise

by G. Barry Ellis

The jaws, the screw, the guide rods and the handle of early vises were all made of wood. Modern vises like the one I will describe here have a metal screw, nut and rods, which you can buy from catalog supply houses or find used in a second-hand store. The jaws must be strong and durable. Many species of wood will work, but I think green ash, maple, beech (the traditional choice) and pecan are best. The size and shape of the jaws will depend on your requirements. Most European vises have relatively shallow throats and thick jaws, a combination that produces great clamping pressure and is suitable for use with bench-top clamping systems. If, however, you need large holding capacity in a vise with only moderate clamping pressure, then a wooden-jaw vise modeled after North American steel vises will do the job.

The jaws need to be a matching pair. On my vise they are 12 in. long, 6 in. wide and a full 2 in. thick. For proper alignment, the two jaws should be clamped together when drilling the holes for the screw and the guide rods. I use ½-in. black pipe for the guide rods and standard pipe nuts for attaching the rods to the front jaw. This requires threading the pipe 2 in. along its length on the front end and about ¾ in. at the back where it screws into the drag bar, a horizontal piece of wood or metal that holds the trailing ends of the guide rods and screw in alignment. The length of the guide rods is determined by the length of the screw you use and by how they are attached to the front jaw and to the drag bar. If you make

Wood-jaw vise with steel bench dog, above, can be made with standard hardware items. The front jaw is attached to the guide rods by two pairs of pipe nuts. Rear view of vise, right, shows how guide rods are affixed to drag bar by means of pipe flanges. Braces dadoed into rear jaw provide added strength and stability.

Dick Glenn

your drag bar out of wood, you can fit it with threaded flanges and screw the guide rods into them as shown above. Keep in mind that the two guide rods should be slightly higher than the screw to prevent a workpiece from resting on an oily screw. And when you attach the rods to the front jaw by means of two pairs of nuts, you must recess the two nuts on the inside of the jaw so the vise will close completely.

The rear jaw of the vise can be secured to the edge of your bench with lag bolts or with machine-thread bolts screwed into barrel nuts let into the bench top from underneath. In either case, you must counterbore the rear jaw for the bolt heads. For extra strength you can dado the backside of the rear jaw to receive a pair of braces that fasten to the underside of the bench. The addition of a bench dog is easy once the vise is affixed to your bench. Just bore a hole directly above the screw (or several of them if you want to use more than one dog at a time) into the top of the front jaw. For the dog I use a steel pin with a head on it and file a flat on one side of the head where it will contact the workpiece. Another hole bored in the side of the jaw holds the dog when it's not in use. □

G. Barry Ellis, of Calgary, Alta., is a workshop specialist who writes for Canadian newspapers.

Post-and-Spar Lumber Rack

by Richard Starr

The storage rack I designed for the junior-high-school woodshop where I teach consists of four units like the one in the photo below, set on 4-ft. centers. Each unit has three oak spars, through-mortised and pegged into 6x6 fir uprights. The 40-in. spars are tapered to add capacity to the next lower storage area and neatness to their appearance. The mortises were chopped very tight, and each spar was driven in with a sledge hammer. There is a ½-in. shoulder at the top and bottom of each tenon.

The uprights of the rack are mounted against a concrete-block wall, but not sup-

Post-and-spar lumber rack has large capacity and great inherent strength. Wedge-shaped strips added to top edges of spars cant the load backwards, reducing the likelihood of lumber falling off the rack accidentally.

ported by it. Their main strength comes from tying them into the rafters of the building using the little cleats shown in the drawing. The cleats are cut from 2-in. oak, open-end mortised into the upright and pinned with a 1-in. dowel. Carriage bolts hold the cleats to the rafters. Before being erected, the bottom end of each 6x6 was nailed to a 2x6 block, then the 2x6 was nailed to the concrete floor. This locates and stabilizes the bottom end.

The advantage of a cantilevered woodrack is that you can approach it from three sides. It is easy moving wood around to find the one piece you need and quick to load up with new material when it arrives. The capacity of this thing is enormous. If you load it with 16-ft. boards to a depth of about 26 in. per shelf (compensating for the taper in the spars), you get about 5,550 bd. ft. Of course it's less if you sticker your wood, but more if you allow for overhang over the ends of the thing, which are 16 ft. apart. We've never fully loaded the top shelf, but with the bottom two spars loaded solid with pine, there is no sign of flexing in the uprights or in the spars. I'm sure the rack could be loaded to the brim with unstickered hardwood, if the building itself could take it. If the rack were to hang in a frame building, I'd think over the scantlings of the entire structure. □

Richard Starr lives in Thetford Center, Vt.

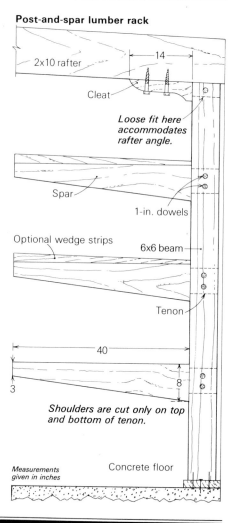

Post-and-spar lumber rack

2x10 rafter — 14

Cleat

Loose fit here accommodates rafter angle.

Spar

1-in. dowels

Optional wedge strips

6x6 beam

Tenon

40

3 — 8

Shoulders are cut only on top and bottom of tenon.

Measurements given in inches — Concrete floor

Double-Top Workbench
Design increases workspace and clamping capability

by Ramon Sanna

With its tail vise and shoulder vise, the Scandinavian-style cabinetmaker's bench (*FWW #4*, Fall '76) offers a number of ways to hold a workpiece, and its design is well suited to most shop operations. But for those of us who like to have a lot of room on our benches—room for project parts and for tools—a larger work surface is desirable. Without sacrificing any of the clamping features of the Scandinavian bench, I designed mine with two tops, four rows of dog holes, a center tool well and three vises. This gives me a work surface that's a full 28 in. wide, in addition to an out-of-the-way place to keep all the hand tools I'm using at a given time.

Each top is glued up from five pieces of 8/4 maple, three boards for the work surface and two for the aprons. Edge-joined with ¾-in. thick splines, each top surface measures 11 in. wide, just right for being surfaced to 1¾ in. thick on my Parks 12-in. planer. The aprons are also splined to the underedges of the tops, which gives them a finished thickness of

4¼ in. The center aprons are rabbeted on their bottom outer edges to receive the tool tray, which separates the tops and provides a 6-in. wide well between them (see drawing). Finally, each end of the bench is fitted with a facing board 28 in. by 4¼ in. These facing boards are joined to the bench tops with ¾-in. thick splines and are best attached by bolts and barrel nuts, one pair for each apron, two pairs for each top. The counterbores for the bolt heads can be plugged. When the tandem top is finished, it's mounted onto a single base frame.

Instead of using the conventional rectangular bench dogs, I bored two rows of ⁵⁄₁₆-in. diameter holes in each top and counterbored the undersides of each hole ²⁵⁄₆₄ in. to accept a ⁵⁄₁₆-18 short-prong *T*-nut. These are available from the Sharon Bolt and Screw Co., 60 Pleasant St., Ashland, Mass. 01721 (#TN-355Q). Using horizontal counterbored bench stops made of pine (see photos), I can securely hold workpieces of almost any size and shape by bolting the bench stops into any

Right, Sanna's workbench with three vises, tool well and storage shelf beneath is spacious and sturdy. The bench and tail-vise jaws have a total of 56 dog holes, each containing a T-nut. Tail vise, below left, clamps board to bench top. Stops are bolted into place rather than just slipped into holes. Both tail vises, below right, can hold a single long piece, or with stops on both vises, they can become part of a four-point clamping system.

Section through bench top

Facing boards are bolted onto each end of bench top and held firmly by barrel nuts let into underside of top. All other parts are splined together, except for tool tray, which is glued into rabbets.

Tool tray

4¼"

— 11" — — 6" — — 11" —

½-in. diameter bore

To secure the T-nuts, you should drill a couple of small holes in their flanges and brad them to the underside of the top.

⁵⁄₁₆-in. T-nut

of the 56 *T*-nuts in the two tops. These serve also as hold-downs for jigs and other fixtures.

The two tail vises, also bored and equipped with *T*-nuts, can be used as part of the bench-stop system or as woodworking vises. Because they are both on the same end of the bench, I can use them together to clamp a long board edge up, something the Scandinavian bench won't do at all. Rather than making a shoulder vise of the kind Tage Frid recommends, I got an ordinary woodworker's vise with a steel dog and mounted it on the front of the bench (opposite the end with the tail vises). I can use the dog in conjunction with the bench

stops or use the vise to hold long cumbersome pieces like doors.

Since my tool well is in the middle of the bench, I can work on both sides of my bench and always be within easy reach of my tools. Though it takes more time to bolt the stops into place than it does to slip a dog into its slot, I find this disadvantage to be offset by the increased versatility and firm clamping capability of the bench-top system. The more I use my bench, the more I am convinced that it's the most important tool in my shop. □

Ramon Sanna, 34, of Madison, Wis., is an amateur woodworker.

Bigfoot Tool Rack

by Ted Wick

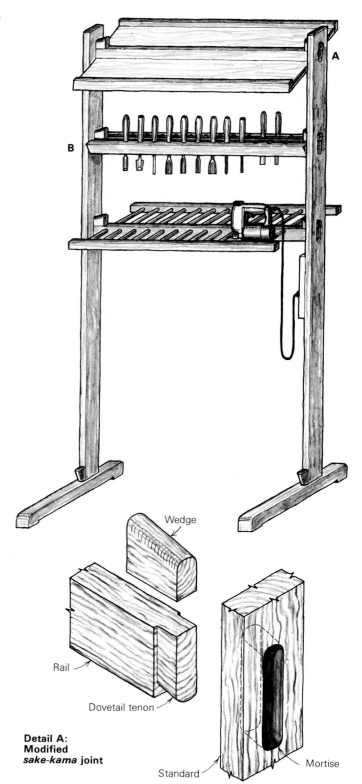

A simple way to get your hand tools within easy reach of your workbench is to design and build a free-standing tool rack. I didn't have enough space in my shop for a wall-hung tool cabinet, which lacks the convenience of portability, so I made "Bigfoot," a tool rack with long feet for stability and an upper structure that can be adapted to changing needs as time goes by. To attach the crossmembers to the uprights, I adapted a Japanese joint called *sake-kama*, a modified through-dovetail joint held tight with a wedge, as shown in detail *A*. I used this assembly so I would be able to knock the rack apart easily and alter its brackets to accommodate changes and additions to my hand-tool collection. I used no glue or fasteners on Bigfoot so these future alterations would be easy to make. You can increase the capacity of the rack simply by using longer crossmembers or by adding more shelves and racks.

For the bottom rack, I made something that resembles a round-rung ladder lying flat. Between its rungs it holds mallets, squares and other tools with large heads and narrow shafts, and its design lets dust and shavings fall right through to the floor. I also keep all of my electric hand tools on this lower shelf, where they can remain plugged into the six-outlet fixture I've attached to the right-hand standard below shelf level. I like being able to use these tools right when I need them, without having to plug them in and then unplug them when the operation is finished. Their cords drop neatly behind the bench when they're not in use.

The middle rack, for my chisels and gouges, is a compound piece that works much better than a strip of wood with holes bored into it. My basic design is shown in detail *B*. I began with a board 1½ in. square and bored ¾-in. diameter holes on 3-in. centers all the way down its length. Then, setting my sawblade at an angle of about 75°, I ripped this board in two. These two halves, their slots staggered, were then joined with ⅜-in. dowels to a 1-in. by 2½-in. center strip so that there was a ⅜-in. gap remaining between the center strip and the two strips with the half-round slots in them. The gap, in conjunction with the angle, serves to accommodate the tapered sockets and handles of the chisels, holding them always perpendicular to the rack and keeping them from flopping around in their holes and damaging their edges by scraping against each other.

The top crossmember is a shelf for planes, spokeshaves and the like. The edges of the shelf are lipped, with the crossmember down the center. The back shelf is located high on the crossmember, while the front-shelf is located at a low position on its front. The shelf is angled slightly towards the front; this elevates the tools on the rear half of the shelf and makes getting at them easier. □

Ted Wick, 43, an amateur woodworker, is campus chaplain at Pacific Union College, Angwin, Calif.

**Detail A:
Modified
sake-kama joint**

Top of mortise is angled to accommodate wedge; bottom of mortise is angled in the same direction to house dovetail on tenon.

Detail B

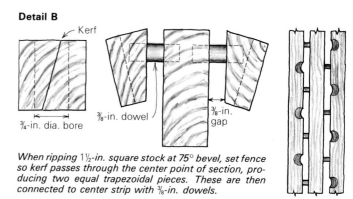

When ripping 1½-in. square stock at 75° bevel, set fence so kerf passes through the center point of section, producing two equal trapezoidal pieces. These are then connected to center strip with ⅜-in. dowels.

Methods of Work

Bench-top hold-down

An old steel roofing square makes an excellent workbench hold-down and glass-cutting aid. Drill mating ⅜-in. holes in the ends of the long side of the square and in the bench top. Insert 1-ft. lengths of ⅜-in. threaded rod through the holes with washers and wing nuts above and below. For butting glass, make two short sections of non-threaded ⅜-in. rod

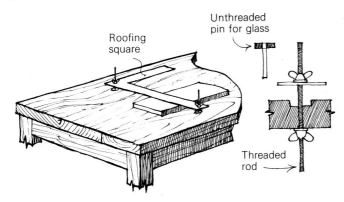

Roofing square

Unthreaded pin for glass

Threaded rod

capped with dowel heads to use in place of the threaded rod. The non-threaded pins are easier to install and remove. Use the shorter side of the square as a backstop or measuring aid. If it's in the way, just flip the square over.

—Malcolm McKeag, Peace Dale, R.I.

Bench dogs: round versus square

While building a European-style workbench, I experimented with both square and round bench dogs. I concluded that round dogs (wooden or steel) are superior in several important ways. First, it is much easier to put a round hole into a bench top (or anything else). Second, the round dogs are easily made in a variety of shapes that will rotate in the hole to conform to the shape of the work. Square steel dogs cannot rotate, more easily mar the work, and can drop through the hole in the bench top.

Round dogs can be turned on the lathe or built up from ¾-in. doweling by gluing hardwood shapes to the tops of the

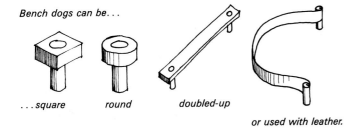

Bench dogs can be...

...square   round   doubled-up

or used with leather.

dowels. A wide variety of shapes, padded or in combinations, can be used as the work requires.

If I had a bench with square dogs, I would convert it to use round dogs by filling the square holes with wood of the same density as the top and redrilling new round holes.

—William E. Betzner, St. Petersburg, Fla.

Gain two clamps

In exchange for a little ingenuity you can gain two large-capacity, versatile clamps: your drill press and lathe. Just clamp the work between quill and drill-press table or between headstock and tailstock (remove centers).

—Michael Bavlsik, Paterson, N.J.

Preventing tear-out

The problem of excessive tear-out at the bottom of drill-press holes can be solved with a simple metal collar. I discovered the collar solution during a 30-unit production run of a small piece of furniture. Each unit required a drilling operation of eighteen holes in warped 1x12 pine. Without question, the tear-out problems I experienced were because the warped stock was inadequately supported on the drill table.

I'm aware that the classic prevention for tear-out is to support the stock to be drilled with a scrap back-up board. This I wished to avoid because of the hazard, nuisance and expense. I used my small metal lathe to turn a substitute for the back-up board—a steel collar with a ⅛₂-in. protruding lip to compress and support the wood in the area of the hole. When the wood is adequately supported and compressed in advance of the rotating bit, the result is a clean hole.

The profile of the collar is shown in the sketch. Except for matching the collar's bore to the drill bit used, the dimensions are arbitrary. Turn the bottom of the collar flat (perhaps even a shade concave) to prevent the collar from rocking.

To install the collar on the drill press, put double-sided tape on the bottom of the collar and slip it over the drill bit. With the bit lowered into the table, carefully slide the collar down and press it onto the table. Counterboring the hole in the table will prevent shavings from jamming the collar hole.

—Carl Hogberg, North Chatham, Mass.

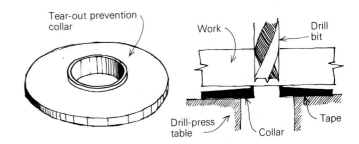

Tear-out prevention collar

Work

Drill bit

Drill-press table   Collar   Tape

Reversing belt-driven tools

It's easy to reverse disc sanders and other belt-driven tools if the motor is mounted perpendicular to the shaft it drives, so there's a quarter-turn in the belt, as shown. To reverse, loosen the belt, flip 180° (on either pulley) and tighten. The twist in the belt seems to dampen vibrations —an added advantage.

—Roger Lynne, Bloomington, Minn.

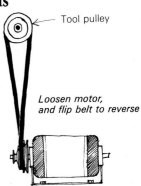

Tool pulley

Loosen motor, and flip belt to reverse

Sanding block for beaded edges

On a recent mantle clock project I needed to sand the beaded edges without rounding the crisp corners or flawing the uniform curvature of the bead. Hand sanding with a folded sheet of sandpaper would just not do. I made a reverse-image sanding block by routing a cove into a small piece of wood. Then I cut strips of sandpaper and glued them to the cove with 3M's feathering disc adhesive. This adhesive, used by auto body men to attach discs to disc sanders, was excellent for my purpose. Since it remains tacky, I could attach new strips of sandpaper as the old strips wore out without reapplying the adhesive. It also works well for attaching wooden protective pads to the jaws of C-clamps and bar clamps.

—John Searles, Xenia, Ohio

Sawhorses

Basic design adapts to several workshop tasks

by Sam Allen

"You can judge a man by his sawhorse" was a remark made often by a carpenter I once knew. When he was foreman on a job site, he would have job applicants build a pair of sawhorses. The one who built the best pair got the job. A craftsman who takes pride in his work wants his tools to reflect that pride. But what usually happens with sawhorses is that a temporary pair gets thrown together for use on a particular job, then becomes a permanent fixture in your shop. Why not take time now to build a sturdy, good-looking pair of sawhorses that you can be proud to own?

Construction—To build a basic pair of sawhorses you'll need one 8-ft. 2x6, three 8-ft. 1x6s plus a few 1x6 scraps for braces. Fir or pine is the usual choice because of its strength and light weight. All operations in sawhorse construction can be performed with hand tools, but power tools make the job faster and easier.

Start by cutting two 42-in. long pieces of 2x6 for the saddles. Some people prefer to use a saddle 48 in. long, but the 42-in. length is handier for working on doors and still gives plenty of support to a 4x8 sheet of plywood. Next cut eight legs 28 in. long from the 1x6 stock. Once the sawhorses are assembled, the legs will be trimmed to give an overall height of 24 in. Taper the legs on one edge starting full width at a point 8 in. from the top and tapering down to 3½ in. at the bottom. This makes the horse lighter and more stable.

When the legs are done, cut the gains (notches) in the saddle to receive them. This is probably the most critical part of making sawhorses. The gains are cut on a compound angle, and much of the strength of the sawhorse depends on a good fit. Use a steel square to mark the angles. Make the first mark 3½ in. from the end of the saddle. Place the square on the edge of the 2x6 so the 3-in. mark on one leg and the 12-in. mark on the other line up with the face corner of the 2x6, and

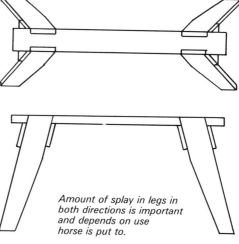

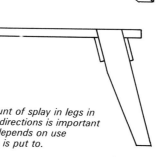

General-purpose horse

Painter's horse

Amount of splay in legs in both directions is important and depends on use horse is put to.

With legs of pine and saddle of fir, sawhorse is both sturdy and attractive.

Left, legs are sawn flush with saddle after they're secured in place and braces are attached. You can add a central slit, above, for ripping boards of any length using a handsaw.

Photos and Illustrations by the author

scribe a 4:1 (75°) slope. Line up a 1x6 leg with this slope and use its opposite edge to make a second mark. This gives you the lengthwise slope of the leg. Now determine the spread of the legs across the width. There are two dimensions in common use. For a sawhorse used in house framing, the spread should be 14 in., as this allows it to be carried between studs that are on 16-in. centers. A 20-in. spread is better for finish work and shop use because of the added stability.

Mark the gains for this angle on top of the 2x6 by scribing a line ¾ in. in from the edge between the two marks previously made. On the bottom make a line that will vary according to the spread you choose. For the 14-in. spread, it should be ½ in. in from the edge; and for the 20-in. spread, ⅜ in.

Using a handsaw, cut along the marks on the edge of the 2x6. Stop cutting when the teeth touch the lines on the top and bottom of the 2x6. Now make parallel sawcuts about ½ in. apart between the first two cuts, stopping at the top and bottom lines also. Use a chisel to clean out the gain. Cut the leg braces from the leftover pieces of 1x6. Hold a piece in position and mark the angles of the legs on it, making sure the legs are spread to the correct degree and the angles are equal. Use this as a pattern to cut the rest of the braces. Bevel the top of each brace so it will fit flush under the saddle. After the braces have been fastened with glue and nails, trim the legs flush with the top of the saddle using a handsaw.

With the horse standing on a flat surface, measure the distance from the top of the saddle to the ground. Set a scriber for the difference between this measurement and 24 in. Scribe around each leg to get a cutting line that will allow the legs to sit flat. Chamfer and sand all the corners and edges to avoid possible slivers and cuts, then finish with oil.

Lowboy—A short sawhorse (usually about 12 in. high) called a lowboy is often used in cabinet shops for elevating furniture and cabinets to a convenient working height. It's especially useful when fitting drawers and cabinet doors. Sometimes a 2x8 is used for the saddle to give a larger area of support to the cabinet.

Ripping horse—If you do a lot of ripping with a handsaw, you'll appreciate this horse. A 1-in. wide slot is cut in the center of a standard sawhorse saddle. Stop the slot at the point where the legs attach so the joint won't be weakened. To use this sawhorse, place the board to be ripped on the horse with the cutting line over the slot and the end of the board about 8 in. from the slot end. Put the sawblade through the slot and start ripping. When the blade reaches the end of the slot, move the board forward and begin ripping again.

Painter's sawhorse—When you're painting something supported on sawhorses, invariably some of the paint will drip down the edge of the work and land on the saddle of the sawhorse. Then it seeps between the saddle and the work and leaves a mark on the back of the object. If the object being painted has two sides that show, a door for example, this is not good. A narrow point of contact between the work and the sawhorse will help solve this problem.

Make the painter's sawhorse out of 1x6s. The saddle is a 1x6 turned on edge. On top of the saddle nail a ¾-in. by ¾-in. strip, which can be changed whenever it gets coated with a lot of paint drips. To reduce further the point of contact with the work, the top strip can be beveled so that only a

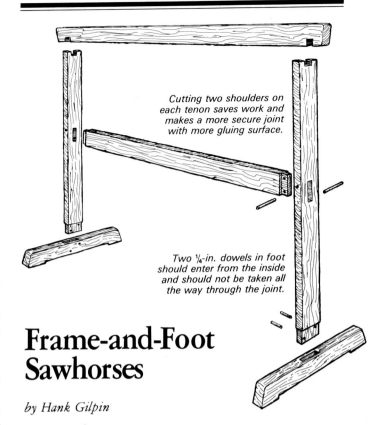

Cutting two shoulders on each tenon saves work and makes a more secure joint with more gluing surface.

Two ¼-in. dowels in foot should enter from the inside and should not be taken all the way through the joint.

Frame-and-Foot Sawhorses

by Hank Gilpin

For supporting cabinets and carcases while you're working on them, for laying out cuts in long boards and for various other jobs around the shop, here's a sawhorse (basically a frame on two feet) that is light and strong, yet stores easily without taking up a lot of space. I made mine out of red oak (only because I had a large quantity on hand), but you can make them out of almost any wood you choose. All the pieces are ¹⁵⁄₁₆ in. thick and 2½ in. wide, except for the foot, which is 1³⁄₁₆ in. wide. The uprights are through-tenoned into the feet and secured with glue and a couple of ¼-in. pegs. To receive the stretcher, I chopped through-mortises in the uprights. The tenons, all of which I cut long to use the same saw setting, were trimmed to length after assembly. They are pinned also with ¼-in. dowels, though wedges would do as well. Both of the uprights and the saddle member are notched to make a secure double-lap joint, which can be pinned or not.

These horses can be made quickly and in quantity with a minimum of materials and fuss. I have a couple dozen of them. They travel well, taking up much less space than conventional four-leg horses, and they nestle together neatly when not in use. □

Hank Gilpin, 34, makes cabinets and furniture in Lincoln, R.I.

small point is left on top. However, this may be undesirable if the underside of the work has been freshly painted, because the point will cut into the paint.

Because of the narrow saddle, you can't cut gains for the legs. Cut the ends of the legs to the appropriate angle so they can be butted against the sides of the saddle. Notch the leg braces so they will extend part way up the saddle.

Padded saddle—If your sawhorses are to be used with finished pieces, you can avoid scratches by padding the saddle. A strip of carpet is one of the best pads. Glue it down or fold it over the edges and tack it to the underside. □

Sam Allen, 28, builds furniture in Provo, Utah.

The Router Rail

Using a router to surface large panels

by Giles Gilson

How often have you needed to plane a large surface such as a tabletop? The usual choices are to use a very expensive 2-ft. to 3-ft. planer or to use hand-controlled tools such as a plane or belt sander. Having faced this problem, I looked for a router accessory that would hold a router at a set elevation while allowing it to travel over a large area. I couldn't find such a device for sale anywhere, so I built an inexpensive one.

The router rail is fairly easy to build, and there are several designs possible. The principle is simple: A carriage just large enough to hold the router runs on rollers in two rails that form the long sides of a narrow frame, thus providing lateral motion. The frame itself has rollers at its narrow ends, and these ride in two rails that form the sides of a larger frame, thus providing longitudinal movement. Bars attached to end plates support the stock to be planed, and elevation wheels raise and lower the larger frame and the stock-support bars independently of one another. The dimensions of my system are 72 in. by 48 in. by 12 in., excluding the sawhorses.

The materials can be obtained from a well-stocked hardware store or by scrounging in the scrap barrels of a metal distributor. The carriage is made from a piece of aluminum plate and has two rollers on each side. The rollers on my system are from a conveyor belt that happened to be living in a friend's junk-shop. A wiper, made from felt cut to the shape of the inside of the track, should be mounted next to each roller so that the track is kept clean ahead of the rollers. The rails can be made of garage-door track. Stiffeners (angle iron or plywood gussets) may be necessary on rails over 5 ft. long if the system feels bouncy. The ends of the large rail frame and the stock-support bars can be made of aluminum or wood. The stock-support bars should hold the work without flexing; the stock is clamped to these bars. The pieces are fastened together with corner brackets, bolts, and hex nuts or wing nuts, as shown in the drawing.

Eight elevation wheels allow for independent adjustment of the rail system and the stock-support bars. I use a 4-ft. level to level the rails first, then the stock. The elevation wheels can easily be turned from a piece of wood or composite board with a nut captured in the center, and the jackscrews on which the wheels run are threaded rod. To capture the nut I first counterbore a hole in the wheel blank the diameter of the distance across the nut's flats. Then I bore a clearance hole through the wheel for the threaded rod and use a bolt with a washer to draw the nut into the counterbore. The nut will cut its way into the wood and remain there when the bolt is removed.

The end plates and stock-support brackets are made of wood: 2x6s for the end plate, and birch plywood for the stock-support brackets. These brackets have cutouts in the

A router becomes a planer, using garage-door track and conveyor-belt rollers to control its movement on two axes. Small work can be surfaced if it is mounted on boards spanning the stock-support bars.

Four wing nuts disassemble the whole system for storage.

Photos: Giles Gilson and Rick Siciliano; drawing: Robert Croston

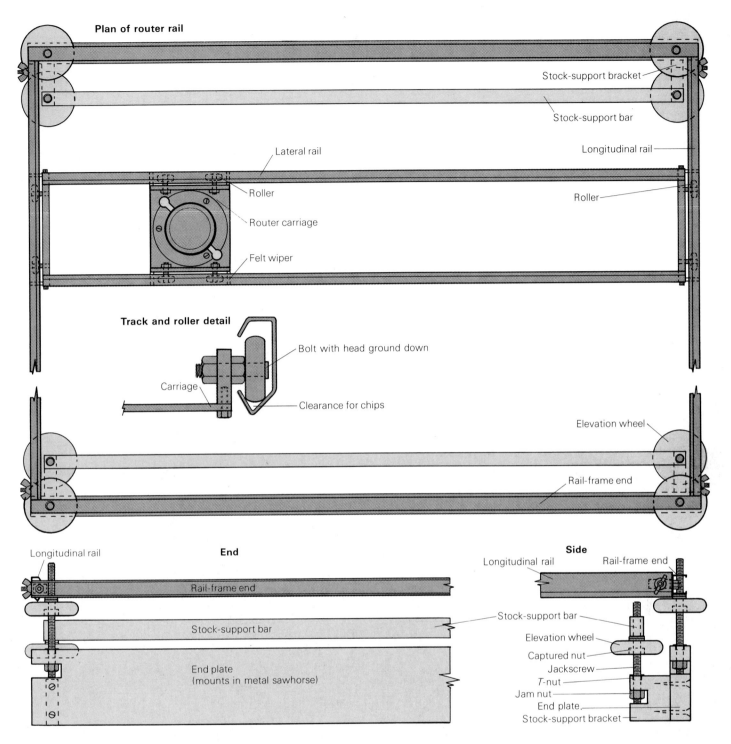

Plan of router rail

Stock-support bracket

Stock-support bar

Lateral rail

Longitudinal rail

Roller

Roller

Router carriage

Felt wiper

Track and roller detail

Bolt with head ground down

Carriage

Clearance for chips

Elevation wheel

Rail-frame end

End

Longitudinal rail

Rail-frame end

Stock-support bar

End plate
(mounts in metal sawhorse)

Side

Longitudinal rail

Rail-frame end

Stock-support bar

Elevation wheel

Captured nut

Jackscrew

T-nut

Jam nut

End plate

Stock-support bracket

ends and a clearance hole drilled from the top through to the cutout. Fit a *T*-nut in the top of the clearance hole, screw the jackscrew in and secure it with a jam nut at the bottom in the cutout. The stock-support brackets can be fastened to the end plates by long wood screws and glue, or by through-mortising the end plate and cutting a tenon on the bracket long enough to be wedged crossways. The end plates mount in metal folding sawhorse legs that clamp to it when opened.

Bolts with wing nuts hold the larger rail frame together. Removing these breaks down the system into the endplate assemblies, including the stock-support bars and elevation screws, the two longitudinal rails, and the lateral rail assembly, including the carriage. The disassembled parts can be hung on a wall for storage.

The router rail is particularly well suited for planing end-grain panels, like butcher block. Although the largest bit I

feel safe with in a router is a 1¼-in. carbide-tipped straight-faced bit, still I can surface a 6-ft. by 3-ft. tabletop in less than a half hour, including setup time, and that's significantly faster than I can do it by hand. Someday I'll build a heavy-duty version rigid enough to support a 2-HP motor that will take a 3-in. diameter cutterhead.

The router rail has possibilities for other routing operations besides planing. Stops can be placed on the long rails to allow the router to move only crossways. The carriage can be clamped, allowing only lengthwise movement, or stops can be placed to allow only a certain length of cut, for making stopped dadoes and slots. A sharp individual can get pretty inventive with one of these gadgets—so get to work.   □

Giles Gilson, of Schenectady, N.Y., is a woodworker and sculptor who makes many of his own machines.

Methods of Work

Laminated bowls

The method I use to make six-sided bowls creates boldly repeating patterns and reduces layout and blank-assembly time. I start by laminating a wedge-shaped beam with 60° sides, sandwiching veneer of various thicknesses between four ¾-in. hardwood boards. The widest part of the wedge (which I make of a highly figured wood) will be the outermost part of the bowl, and 5 in. here will produce a 10-in. diameter bowl. The length of the wedge will determine the bowl's height.

I set the jointer fence at 30° and joint off two sides of a scrap 2x4, leaving a chunk of wood angled 60° on each edge. Then I cut off six thin wafers, arrange them in a circle and check for proper fit. If there are gaps, I adjust the angle of the jointer fence and try again. When the angle is correct, I joint both sides of the laminated beam deep enough to clean out depressions and glue. Then I cut the beam into six equal sections and dry-fit.

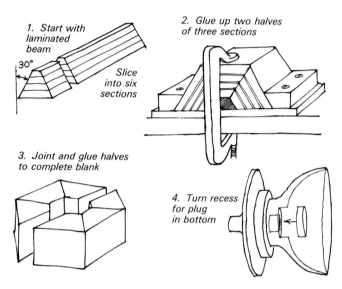

1. Start with laminated beam

30°

Slice into six sections

2. Glue up two halves of three sections

3. Joint and glue halves to complete blank

4. Turn recess for plug in bottom

Now glue up two bowl-blank halves of three sides each. Use a clamping jig. Next, dry-fit the two halves and, if they don't fit perfectly, run the faces of the two sections over the jointer. Glue the two halves together to complete the blank. When you turn the blank, simply make a recess for a round plug to fill the hole in what will be the bottom of the bowl.

—Roy Ashe, Luther, Mich.

Turning ringed objects

An effective mandrel for turning napkin rings and other annular objects can be made as follows. Choose a suitable hardwood (such as hard maple) and mount the wood to the faceplate with the grain oriented perpendicular to the axis. Turn down the end of the mandrel to give a slip fit with the workpiece, leaving a larger-diameter locating shoulder on the base as shown in the sketch. Next, drill and tap the end of the

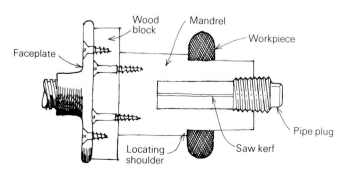

Faceplate

Wood block

Mandrel

Workpiece

Locating shoulder

Saw kerf

Pipe plug

mandrel for a tapered pipe plug of suitable size. First select the recommended tap drill size for the pipe thread and drill into the end of the mandrel ¾ in. or so deeper than the locating shoulder. Then tap the hole so that a pipe plug will thread in halfway. The resulting threads, though rough in appearance, are quite strong if the grain is oriented as suggested. To complete the mandrel, cut two crossed saw kerfs to the same depth as the hole.

To use, slide on the workpiece and screw the pipe plug in the hole. The plug will expand the mandrel, gripping the workpiece firmly. —*Edward F. Groh, Naperville, Ill. and Charles E. Cohn, Clarendon Hills, Ill.*

Turning lamp bases

Here are a couple of tricks to turn tall lamp bases. I don't have a large drill press; I drill the electric cord hole on the lathe with a homemade extended bit and a wooden guide block. To make the long bit, weld the turned-down shank of a ⅜-in. bit in a ¼-in. hole drilled in the end of a 24-in. length of ⅜-in. drill rod. Clean up the weld with a file and sandpaper. Make the guide block as shown in the sketch, screw the block to the stock over the center and carefully drill the cord hole. Back out the bit frequently to remove the chips. The guide block helps keep the hole tight on line through the center of the stock.

To prepare the stock for turning, glue a short length of ⅜-in. dowel in the top end of the cord hole. Screw a faceplate to the other end of the stock, centering the faceplate over the hole. Now mount the stock in the lathe, centering the tailstock's cup center on the dowel insert. When the lamp base is done, remove the faceplate and drill out the dowel insert.

—*Bob Kurz, Hartsville, S.C.*

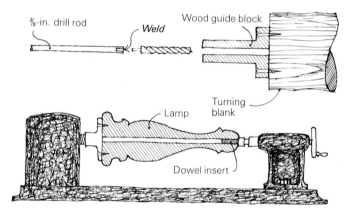

⅜-in. drill rod   Weld   Wood guide block

Turning blank

Lamp

Dowel insert

Duplicate turning gauge

This handy device is invaluable in turning duplicates. Used in multiples, it gives the correct position of control cuts and

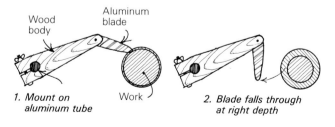

Wood body   Aluminum blade

1. Mount on aluminum tube

Work

2. Blade falls through at right depth

measures the depth as well. Several of the gauges—the number depends on the complexity of the work—are mounted on a metal tube or dowel fastened behind and level with the work. Select ½-in. hardwood for the gauge body and 1/16-in.

aluminum for the blade. Drill one end of the body to fit the metal tube and slot the other end to fit the blade. The blade should fit loose in the slot and pivot easily on the pin. Set the position of the gauges by sliding along the tube. Then vary the angle of the body to set the depth. In use the blade will ride on the work (in the parting-tool cut) and fall through when the right depth is reached.

—*Bayard Cole, Marietta, Ga.*

Assembling staved cylinders

Here's a method based on the principle of canvas-backed tambours that simplifies the assembly of staved cylinders. Lay the staves side by side on a flat surface and carefully align the ends. Apply rows of tape (I use 2-in. wide plastic tape) to the outside surface. Turn the assembly over, apply glue to the stave edges and roll up the cylinder. Apply a strap clamp to complete the job. —*Pope Lawrence, Santa Fe, N. Mex.*

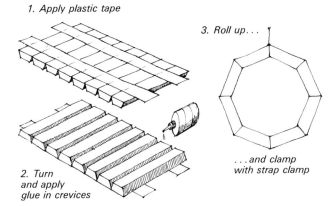

1. Apply plastic tape

2. Turn and apply glue in crevices

3. Roll up...

...and clamp with strap clamp

Sanding block for lathe work

For years my woodworking students invariably burned their fingers sanding bowls and other lathe work. Then I hit upon the solution—sanding blocks cut from sheets of ½-in. thick rubbing felt. The felt sanding block shapes itself to shallow curves and can be deliberately shaped to match any contour of a compound curve.

Rubbing felt is available in 1-ft. squares from H. Behlen & Bros. (Box 698, Amsterdam, N.Y. 12110) and other suppliers. A similar material, used for typewriter cushions, is available from office-machine suppliers. Cut the pad with a razor knife and rule. One block lasts indefinitely.

—*Russell Anderson, Torrington, Conn.*

Sanding mop

To sand hard-to-get-at spots, make a sanding mop from a nut-and-bolt arbor and a handful of small pieces of sandpaper. Overlap the sandpaper like shingles around the arbor and chuck it in a drill. The irregular edge eliminates the hard sanding line produced by rubber-backed discs.

—*Allan Adams, San Francisco, Calif.*

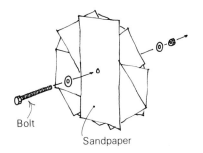

Bolt

Sandpaper

Another lathe chuck

This easy-to-make lathe chuck simplifies turning small bowls and other faceplate work. Mount a solid-wood block to a plywood base and turn a short cylinder with a flared lip as shown in the sketch. For flexibility, cut a saw kerf nearly through the cylinder. Then cut a mortise through the saw kerf and fit two wedges to the mortise. A dowel or bolt through the cylinder's base will add strength.

To use the chuck, bandsaw the blank to shape and mount

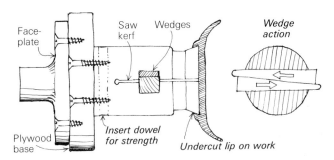

Face-plate

Saw kerf

Wedges

Wedge action

Plywood base

Insert dowel for strength

Undercut lip on work

it on a screw center, screwing into what will be the waste from the concave part of the bowl. Shape the outside of the bowl, then carefully undercut a dovetail recess in the base to fit the lip on the chuck. Remove the stock from the screw center and the screw center from the lathe, attach the chuck, then slip the work over the chuck's lip, carefully orienting the grain to take the pressure. Drive home the two wedges to spread the lips and lock the work in place. For safety's sake, wrap a band of masking tape around the wedges to prevent their flying out.

—*W. W. Kelly, Clinton, Tenn.*

Deep-throat clamp

If you need a deep-throat clamp and none is available, substitute a conventional C-clamp and two blocks of wood arranged as in the sketch below. Though direct pressure is less than with expensive specialty clamps, the system works fine for gluing inlays, guitar bridges and other simple joints.

—*Bob Osbahr, Tucson, Ariz.*

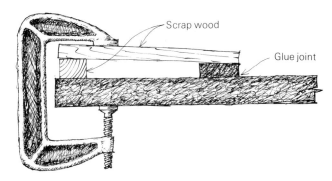

Scrap wood

Glue joint

Triangular scraper

This graunching tool (that's what we called it in the old days back in New England) is used for deburring metal, enlarging holes, scraping paint or glue from hard-to-reach places and many other jobs where a sharp, hard tool is necessary. Break off an old triangular file, hollow-grind it to the shape shown and mount in a handle.—*H. Norman Capen, Granada Hills, Calif.*

Cross section

Shop Math
With a little help from Pythagoras

by C. Edward Moore

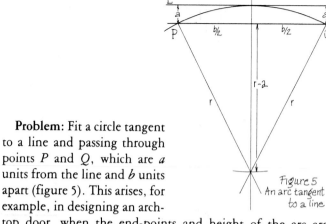

Figure 5
An arc tangent
to a line

You can use shop geometry without knowing why it works, but you will be able to solve more real-world problems if you understand the basic principles. Our point of departure is the right-angled triangle and the theorem of Pythagoras. The terms "right," "square," and "90°" all mean the same thing.

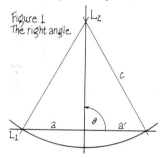

Figure 1
The right angle

The symbol θ, the Greek letter *theta*, designates any angle. In figure 1, we swing an arc of radius c whose center is on line L_2 so that it cuts through line L_1 in two places. This results in two triangles. By definition, whenever the two triangles are symmetrical $(a = a')$, the lines L_1 and L_2 form a right angle.

You use this understanding in reverse to construct a right angle, anywhere you want one (figure 2). First draw the baseline L_1 and mark the point x where you want the corner (vertex) of the right angle. Set a compass to any convenient radius (a), put the point on x, and mark points a and a' equidistantly on either side of x. Now enlarge the compass setting, again by any convenient amount (c) and scribe intersecting arcs above L_1, from centers a and a'. Connect the point thus found with x.

The theorem of Pythagoras tells us that if θ is a right angle, then $a^2 + b^2 = c^2$ and conversely if $a^2 + b^2 = c^2$, then θ is a right angle. The best-known example of this is the 3-4-5 right triangle (figure 3), where $3^2 + 4^2 = 5^2$. Carpenters have used the 3-4-5 triangle, or the 6-8-10 triangle, to square frames for centuries. With a knotted or marked rope and stakes, it is the way to lay out the corners of a building.

The circle is a set of points that all lie the same distance from a fixed point, the center. We create this relationship simply by setting a compass or trammel. On a grid of squares, with horizontal coordinate x and vertical coordinate y, we have the equation $x^2 + y^2 = r^2$, because of Pythagoras. All the values of x and y that produce the same value for r lie on the same circle (figure 4).

Problem: Fit a circle tangent to a line and passing through points P and Q, which are a units from the line and b units apart (figure 5). This arises, for example, in designing an arch-top door, when the end-points and height of the arc are known, and it is necessary to find the center.

Solution: Any tangent to a circle is by definition perpendicular to a radius. Thus the center of the circle will lie on a line drawn at right angles through the midpoint of the line PQ. Pythagoras shows that

$$r^2 = \left(\frac{b}{2}\right)^2 + (r-a)^2 = \frac{b^2}{4} + r^2 - 2ar + a^2,$$

so

$$2ar = \frac{b^2}{4} + a^2 \text{ and } r = \frac{b^2}{8a} + \frac{a}{2}.$$

This equation may be more useful in the form:

$$r = \frac{b^2 + 4a^2}{8a}$$

It can be transformed to find the third parameter of a circular arc when any two are known, that is, the width b can be found if you know the radius r and the height a, or the height a can be found if you know the radius r and the width b:

$$b = 2\sqrt{a(2r-a)} \qquad a = r - \sqrt{r^2 - (\tfrac{1}{2}b)^2}$$

These relationships apply where a is less than half of b, the same as saying that line PQ is in the top half of the circle in figure 5. When the line moves below the circle's diameter, the last equation becomes

$$a = r + \sqrt{r^2 - (\tfrac{1}{2}b)^2}$$

When working equations like these on an electronic calculator, you must either become adept at moving results into

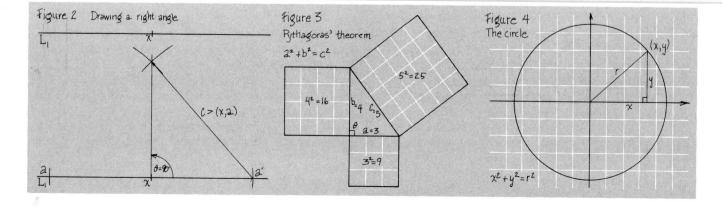

Figure 2   Drawing a right angle

Figure 3
Pythagoras' theorem
$2^2 + b^2 = c^2$
$5^2 = 25$
$4^2 = 16$
$3^2 = 9$

Figure 4
The circle
(x,y)
$x^2 + y^2 = r^2$

and out of the calculator memory, or else keep running notes with pencil and paper. In general, you start inside parentheses and work outward. For example, to solve for a, the height of an arc, when the radius r and width b are known, you would first find ½ of b, square it, and store the answer. Square r and subtract the previously stored result, then find the square root of this answer. Finally, subtract from r.

A useful property of the circle is the fact that if a triangle PQR is drawn with its long side on a diameter and its vertex touching the edge of the circle, that vertex will be a right angle. We can verify this by drawing the circle with its center at O on rectangular coordinates, and applying Pythagoras' theorem (figure 6), after showing that $(PQ)^2 - (PR)^2 = (QR)^2$. We know that wherever on a circle P is, the location of P can be described by coordinates x and y, and $x^2 + y^2 = r^2$. Since length $QR = 2r$, then $(QR)^2 = (2r)^2 = 4r^2$. We also know that $(PQ)^2 = (r - x)^2 + y^2$, and that $(PR)^2 = (r + x)^2 + y^2$. Thus $(PQ)^2 + (PR)^2 = (r - x)^2 + y^2 + (r + x)^2 + y^2$. If you do the algebra you'll find that $(PQ)^2 + (PR)^2 = 4r^2$, and we already found that to be the square of length QR. Thus the triangle PQR is right-angled $(\theta = 90°)$: a diameter and any point P elsewhere on the circle always determine a right angle. Conversely, the legs of a right angle whose vertex is on the circle always cross the circle at the ends of a diameter.

Problem: Find the center of a circle or disc.

Solution: Place the right angle of a square or drafting triangle on the circle, and mark where the sides of the square cross the circle. Rotate the square about a quarter of a turn and again mark where it crosses the circle. Draw the two diameters you have thus located. They intersect at the center of the circle (figure 7).

This relationship can be used to verify whether a trough or semicircular cutout is in fact semicircular—just put the vertex of a framing square into it (figure 8). If the vertex and sides of the square all touch, the cutout is exactly half a circle. The relationship is also another way of constructing a right angle—draw a circle passing through the point where you want the right angle to be, draw in a diameter, and connect the ends of the diameter to the point.

Several recent *Fine Woodworking* articles have referred to proportional division by parallel lines. It is the way shaper-knife profiles are derived, and a way to divide boards for dovetailing. Suppose lines L_1, L_2 and L_3 are parallel and lines M_1 and M_2 intersect them as shown (figure 9). The resulting line segments are proportional, that is,

$$\frac{a_1}{a_2} = \frac{b_1}{b_2}, \ \frac{a_1}{b_1} = \frac{a_2}{b_2}, \text{ and } \frac{a_1}{a_1 + b_1} = \frac{a_2}{a_2 + b_2}.$$

Problem: You have a line divided into two unequal parts. You want to divide another line of different length into the same proportions, that is, locate Q_2 below.

| P_1 | P_2 | P_3 | Q_1 | Q_2? | Q_3 |

Solution: Draw an auxiliary line through Q_1 at any convenient angle and beginning at Q_1, mark on it lengths P_1P_2 and P_2P_3. Then place a straightedge and drafting triangle so that an edge of the triangle connects P_3 with Q_3. Hold the straightedge in place and slide the triangle along it to P_2. A line drawn here will be parallel to P_3Q_3, and thus locates Q_2 (figure 10).

If you wanted to divide a line into five equal parts, you would use the same strategy: draw the auxiliary line, and

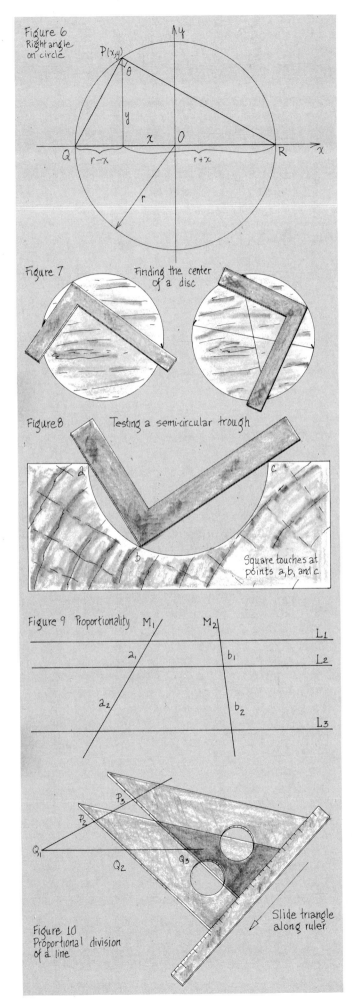

Figure 6
Right angle on circle

Figure 7
Finding the center of a disc

Figure 8
Testing a semi-circular trough
Square touches at points a, b, and c.

Figure 9 Proportionality

Figure 10
Proportional division of a line
Slide triangle along ruler

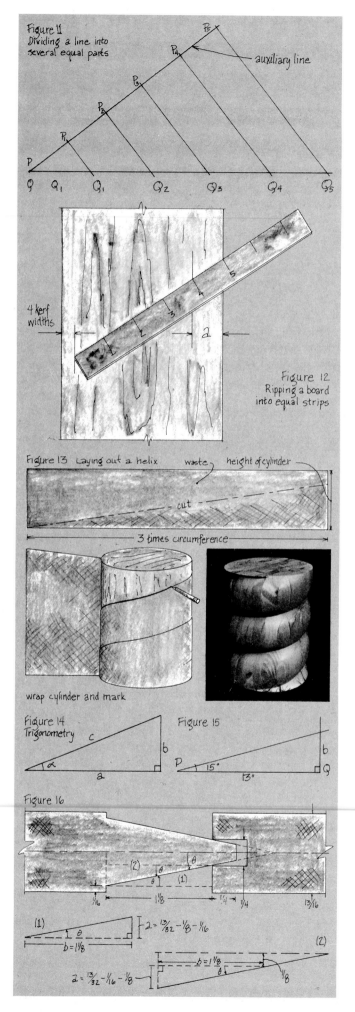

Figure 11
Dividing a line into several equal parts

auxiliary line

4 kerf widths

Figure 12
Ripping a board into equal strips

Figure 13 Laying out a helix

waste   height of cylinder

cut

3 times circumference

wrap cylinder and mark

Figure 14
Trigonometry

Figure 15

Figure 16

$a = \frac{13}{32} - \frac{1}{8} - \frac{1}{16}$

$a = \frac{13}{32} - \frac{1}{16} - \frac{1}{8}$

measure five equal, but convenient, intervals along it. Then use the square-and-ruler method to drop parallels from these points on the auxiliary line to the line you want to divide (figure 11).

   Practical applications: You want to rip a board into *n* equal strips, for example, five strips. First make a test cut into scrap and measure the width of the kerf. Then mark off four kerf widths from one edge of the board. Start a ruler at this point and incline it until it crosses the other edge at some multiple of five. Mark at the fourth multiple, and measure squarely from there to the edge (*a* in figure 12). The width *a* is the distance from the rip fence to the inside of the sawblade.

A related problem is marking off threads on a cylinder, as for a twist carving. My version is the laminated pine table, shown in figure 13 without its round ½-in. glass top, carved from a cylinder 17 or 18 in. high and 14 or 15 in. in diameter. I wanted the thread to go around three times, so I wrapped a string around the cylinder three times, and cut it off there. Next I cut a piece of brown paper the same length as the string, and marked off the height of the cylinder on one edge. Then I cut along the line from the corner to this point, making a long triangle, which I wrapped around the cylinder, its bottom edge aligned with the bottom edge of the wood, and marked along the long side of the triangle as I went.

Here is a brief introduction to trigonometry, the study of relations between the sides and angles of triangles. Trigonometry is sometimes seen as a fearful creature, but with an electronic calculator and a note of the basic relationships, you can tame it for shop use.

Suppose you start with some angle α (the Greek letter *alpha*) and complete the triangle as shown (figure 14) so that side *c* is opposite a right angle. The side of the triangle opposite a right angle is called the hypotenuse. Now, no matter how large or small the triangle is drawn, the ratios *a/c*, *b/c* and *b/a* are fixed numbers. They are completely determined by the angle α. These ratios are given names: sine, cosine and tangent. We write

$$\sin\alpha = \frac{b}{c} = \frac{\text{opposite side}}{\text{hypotenuse}}$$

$$\cos\alpha = \frac{a}{c} = \frac{\text{adjacent side}}{\text{hypotenuse}}$$

$$\tan\alpha = \frac{b}{a} = \frac{\text{opposite side}}{\text{adjacent side}} = \frac{\sin\alpha}{\cos\alpha}.$$

Pythagoras shows that $(\sin\alpha)^2 + (\cos\alpha)^2 = b^2/c^2 + a^2/c^2 = 1$, since $a^2 + b^2 = c^2$.

   Problem: Suppose it is necessary to mark off an angle of 15° from the vertex *P*, where the length *PQ* is 13 in. That is, find length *b* in figure 15. We know that tan15° = *b*/13. From the calculator or from tables, we learn that tan15° = .2679. So, $b = 13 \times .2679 = 3.48$.

   Practical application: What is the correct table-saw angle for cutting the taper on raised panels in a door?

   First solution: Draw the cross section full-size or larger, and measure with a protractor.

   Second solution: From the drawing, extract the relevant right-angled triangle and establish the length of two sides by subtracting known dimensions. Figure 16 shows two ways to do this, giving opposite side *b* of $\frac{7}{32}$ in. and adjacent side *a* of 1⅛ in. tanθ = $\frac{7}{32}$/1⅛ = .09144. You can use trig tables to identify θ or punch tan⁻¹(.01944) into the calculator and get 11°. On some calculators this operation is marked "arctan." □

Oblique Miters in Stock of Variable Thickness

by Jim Cavosie

In my job at a harpsichord shop, I had the task of mitering ¾-in. veneered plywood at oblique angles, so that both the inside and outside surfaces lined up flush. This caused me a lot of headaches because ¾-in. plywood comes from the factory plus or minus ¹⁄₃₂ in. The standard procedure was either to measure the thicknesses, make a drawing and measure the resulting angles with a protractor, or to rely on trial and error and experience. I found a faster and more accurate way using trigonometry and a pocket calculator. The derivation was difficult, so I'll just give the resulting equation.

To find the exact miter angles, you first need to find the length x of the line on which the two thicknesses can join flush. Measure the thickness of the two boards (a and b) and find the total angle of the miter joint (angle A plus angle B). Then find x by solving the following equation:

$$x^2 = \frac{a^2 + b^2 + 2ab\,\cos(A + B)}{\sin^2(A + B)}.$$

Once length x is known, finding the two miter angles is easy. Since $\sin A = a/x$ and $\sin B = b/x$,

$$\text{angle } A = \sin^{-1}\left(\frac{a}{x}\right)$$

$$\text{angle } B = \sin^{-1}\left(\frac{b}{x}\right).$$

If $(A + B)$ approaches 180° and a is much greater than b, it is possible for angle A to be greater than 90°. If this is the case,

$$\text{angle } A = 180° - \sin^{-1}\left(\frac{a}{x}\right).$$

When many miter joints have to be cut at any given total angle, it makes sense to calculate a table of values for angles A and B over a range of values for a and b.

Jim Cavosie lives in Carrboro, N.C.

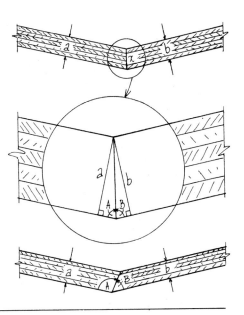

Boring Angled Holes

by Jacob N. Frederiksen

Here is a way to set up the drill press for boring angled holes, as in the seat of a Windsor chair. Most instructions call for tilting a bit brace back at some angle A, and to the side at another angle B. When using a drill press, it's easier to rotate the work through an angle of $R°$ in the horizontal plane, then, by means of an auxiliary table, to tilt the work to an angle T. The tilting table consists of two squares of plywood hinged along one edge and fixed to the drill-press table. The tilt is achieved by fitting blocks of wood under the back edge of the top piece of plywood.

The basic equations are:

$$\tan R = \frac{\tan A}{\tan B}$$

$$\tan^2 T = \tan^2 A + \tan^2 B.$$

When the angles are given in terms of R and T, they can be converted back to angles A and B using the equations:

$$\tan A = \tan T \sin R$$

$$\tan B = \tan T \cos R.$$

Here is an example. I have been building a Windsor chair using Michael Dunbar's plans, purchased through Woodcraft Supply (313 Montvale Ave., Woburn, Mass. 01888). The rear legs of this chair tilt 13° outward (angle A) and 14° to the rear (angle B). The front legs tilt 15° outward and 9° to the front. These angles are measured from a line

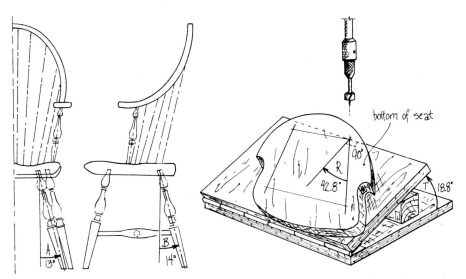

bottom of seat

perpendicular to the bottom of the seat. For the rear legs, the work should be rotated on the table through an angle R:

$$\tan R = \frac{\tan 13°}{\tan 14°} = \frac{.230868}{.249328}$$
$$= .925962$$

so angle $R = 42.8°$.

The table should then be tilted at an angle T:

$$\tan^2 T = \tan^2 13° + \tan^2 14°$$
$$= (.230868)^2 + (.249328)^2$$
$$= .115464,$$

so $\tan T = .339799$, and angle $T = 18.8°$. For the front legs, where A is 15° and B is 9°, angle R is 59.4° and T is 17.3°.

Having done the calculations, I drew reference lines back-to-front on the bottom of the chair seat, through the points to be drilled, as shown in the drawing above. Then I added a second line through the hole centers, at angle R from the fore-to-aft reference line. I rotated the work so that this new pencil line was perpendicular to the back of the table, then tilted the table to angle T. The height of the spacer block to produce angle T can be found by trigonometry, or by trial with a protractor. The important thing is to rotate the work before it is tilted, else you will introduce error, and it is good practice to convert angles R and T back to angles A and B, to guard against mathematical mistakes. □

Jake Frederiksen, 53, of Chevy Chase, Md., builds reproduction furniture for his family.

Drawing the Ellipse
Several ingenious methods

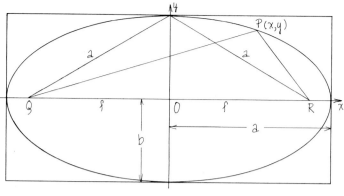

Everybody likes an ellipse. We use them for picture and mirror frames, tabletops, inlays and carved decoration. Everybody also seems to have trouble drawing an ellipse of the size and proportions he wants. First, a definition. An ellipse is a closed curve traced out by maintaining a constant sum of distances from two fixed points in a plane.

If points Q and R are $2f$ units apart and P is a point that is allowed to move so that length PQ + length $PR = 2a$ (a constant), then P will traverse an ellipse that fits into a box measuring $2a$ by $2b$, where $b = \sqrt{a^2 - f^2}$. If we place the center of this box on coordinate axes, then each point P on the ellipse with coordinates (x, y) satisfies the equation:

$$\frac{x^2}{a^2} + \frac{y^2}{b^2} = 1.$$

The major axis of the ellipse has length $2a$ and the minor axis has length $2b$. Points Q and R are called foci or focal points of the ellipse. The size and shape of the ellipse are wholly determined by our choice of a and b (half the length of the major and minor axes). These dimensions define the rectangle into which the ellipse will fit, and only one ellipse will fit any particular rectangle. If a is much greater than b, the ellipse will be long and thin. As a approaches b, the ellipse becomes more nearly circular, until $a = b$, whereupon the foci P and Q coincide at the center of a circle of radius a.

The usual shop problem is to draw an ellipse inside a rectangular box whose dimensions are given. There are a number of ways to do it.

The best-known solution (method *A* below), but not necessarily the easiest or best, is to draw the major and minor axes inside the rectangle, locate the two foci, drive two nails or push-pins there, and loop a string, monofilament line or braided fishline of length $2a$ around the pins. A pencil is pushed against the string and pulled around, keeping the string taut.

You can make the string come out to length $2a$ by driving a third pin at b on the vertical axis. Tie the string tightly

around the three pins, then remove the third one. It doesn't matter whether you make loops at both ends of the string, or tie it into a loop around all three pins.

The distance f of each focal point from the center of the ellipse can be calculated from the formula $f = \sqrt{a^2 - b^2}$ or found geometrically. Set a compass to length a, put its point at b on the vertical axis, and scribe arcs to intersect the horizontal axis. These intersections are points Q and R, the foci of the ellipse.

With method A it is difficult to make the looped string exactly the right length. A way to do it is shown in method B. Push-pins go at the foci, as before, but the third pin goes outside

the ellipse and below the first two. Tie a loop in one end of a long string and drop it over the third pin. Run the string over the focal pins and around them twice, bringing its end over to the center of the ellipse. Then put your finger on the strings between the two pins. Pick up the last pass of string with the pencil, put just enough tension on it to keep from breaking the pencil point, and move the pencil up to the top center of the rectangle *(b)*. Keep the string taut, and sweep the pencil to the right to draw a quarter of the ellipse. Repeat the exercise three more times, moving the third pin above the center line after completing the top portion of the ellipse.

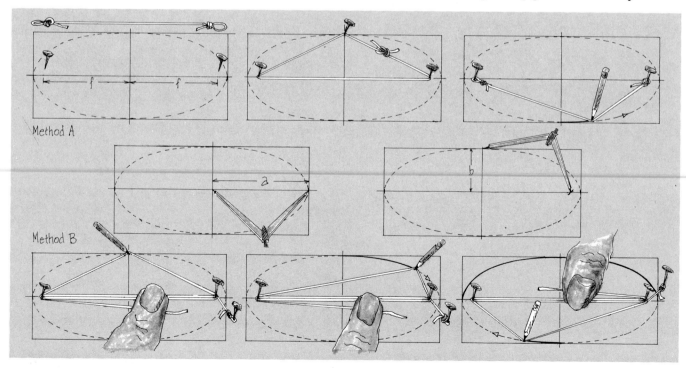

Method A

Method B

The trouble with the looped string methods is that it is quite difficult to maintain string tension and still keep the pencil at exactly the right tilt. The simplest and most accurate way to draw an ellipse is the so-called paper-strip method, which avoids focal points and string altogether.

Begin with coordinate axes and mark off length *a* to the left and right, and point *b* above and below, to define the rectangle in which the ellipse will fit, as shown in the drawing at right. On the edge of a separate strip of paper, tick a point and label it *O*. From point *O*, tick off length *a* and label it *A*. In the same direction from *O*, tick length *b* and mark it *B*.

Now, whenever this edge is placed so that *A* falls on the vertical axis and *B* falls on the horizontal axis, *O* has found a point on the ellipse. Slide the strip along the axes, mark as many points as you find reasonable or necessary, and connect them to obtain the ellipse.

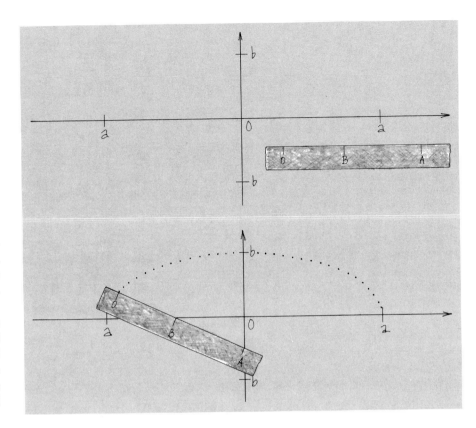

A simple device can be made for drawing ellipses by substituting for the strip of paper a trammel beam carrying two points and a pencil. You draw the axes as before, and set the trammel so that point *O* is the pencil, with lengths *a* and *b* held by the trammel points, as shown in the drawing below. If you can keep the points on the axes, the pencil will draw the ellipse. The Dominy family of woodworkers and watchmakers, who worked on Long Island from about 1760 to 1830, used an ingenious home-made trammel that ran in tracks, making it possible to draw ellipses blindfolded (photo). The track is simply two strips of wood, crossed at right angles and grooved to take the trammel points, which are not sharp but turned like a short dowel. The points slide along the beam and are fixed by wedges; thumbscrews would do as well. The Dominys probably tacked the track to the work and used an iron point to scribe the ellipse. A linkage like this might be arranged to guide a router directly into the stock, but we don't know anybody who has tried it.

One final note: to make two ellipses with parallel sides, as for a picture or mirror frame, two complete ellipses must be drawn because they will have different foci. The governing parameter for each is the box inside which it will fit, and the width of the resulting frame is the difference between the dimensions of the two boxes. □

This account was compiled from information sent by Ed Moore (definitions), Rufus Winsor and Fred Johnson (string methods), C.W. Beringhaus (paper method) and Steele Hinton (trammel method). Moore, a woodworker and associate professor of math at the U.S. Naval Academy, will field shop math problems in our Q/A column, Box 355, Newtown, Conn. 06470.

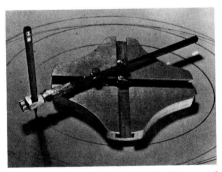

Ellipse trammel by Trevor Robinson of Amherst, Mass., has steel sliding blocks. The distance from pencil to farther pivot is half the major axis, and from pencil to nearer pivot is half the minor axis. Right, the Dominy trammel: birch beam is 39 in. long, sliding blocks are maple with satinwood wedges. Crossed tracks shown are a modern replacement. Photo from With Hammer in Hand *by Charles F. Hummel, courtesy the Henry Francis du Pont Winterthur Museum.*

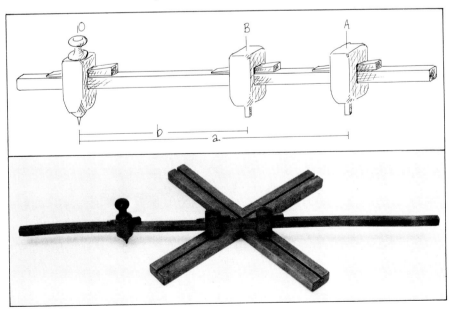

Japanese Planes
The preparation and use of *kanna*

by Ted Chase

Photos: Ted Chase

Woodworkers, both amateur and professional, have been hearing lately about Japanese tools. Ads mention "superior edge qualities," pulling instead of pushing, and assorted other exotic advantages. Interested people who have purchased a Japanese tool may have brought it to the shop, used it for a while and gone back to work with their original tools. Others have found that the tools they bought "didn't work" at all. As with all fine tools, knowing how to care for and prepare them is essential for premium performance.

A brief history — Probably the most striking thing about traditional Japanese woodworking is that much of it is done in a sitting position. The earliest of Japanese tools, the *chona*, or adze, was used long before the introduction of the ripsaw (late 14th century) to rough-surface lumber that had been split with wedge and/or chisel. The adze handle was wood and the blade socket was of primitive and thin metal. A person's full, standing force behind this tool would break the socket—thus the seated position. Nor was this unusual to the lifestyle. Japanese homes have long been designed for multiple-purpose living with minimal furniture; sitting on the floor has been the typical posture for work and for eating. Woodworking was similar. Because few woodworkers had large, permanent shops, a great number of master carpenters, carvers and apprentices would be gathered for a commission by an emperor, feudal lord or military leader. These artisans would set up shop at the construction site, so putting the work on the ground eliminated the need for a workbench. Since less power was applied to the work, it required no mechanical clamps or vises. Because the adze was used across the grain rather than along the length of the piece, the stroke was shorter and a worker could keep one hand free to hold or position the piece. Both feet were available as clamps and weights. Even today, Japanese craftsmen prefer to work sitting down. And where workbenches are used, they're much lower than Western benches, and without vises. The worker planes against a bench stop. Because the bench is low, he can place a foot or leg up on it to hold down the work.

It wasn't until the late 1300s that Japanese blacksmithing and iron manufacturing improved significantly. Along with the refinement of military weapons and ceremonial swords came the introduction of the ripsaw. Lumber cut with these saws could be surfaced more smoothly with a new tool introduced from China via Korea. Its blade, stronger than the *chona*, was set in a block of wood that was moved over the length of the piece to yield a smooth, flat surface. These planes, as used in China and Korea, were designed to be pushed, not pulled. The early imports had a dowel or piece of

Ted Chase, who now makes furniture in Concord, Calif., spent a year in Japan studying with master craftsman Kennosuke Hayakawa.

wood used as a handle, extending through either side. However, these handles soon disappeared, and the craftsman pulled the plane over the work from a seated position.

There have been numerous explanations for the reluctance of the Japanese to adopt the push stroke. Earlier tools and the lifestyle had established deep precedents. Pull-type crosscut saws were used as early as 800 A.D. Given the state of the blacksmith's art at this time, thin blades did not have the stiffness to be pushed through the wood. Perhaps the pull stroke in carpentry goes back to the earliest farming methods, characterized by pulling the hoe rather than plowing through the soil. Consider too that the most common and cherished building materials were straight-grained cedar and cypress; saws and other tools do cut these better on the pull stroke.

Japanese planes have changed little over the centuries. Unlike Western planes, which began in wood and matured to metal (and now are back to wood), the block of solid wood, usually oak, is still the basic modern Japanese plane. The only major refinement came in the late 1800s with the introduction of the subblade, or chipbreaker, positioned a fraction back from the tip of the primary blade.

A *kanna* is simpler than the standard metal block plane. It has no handle, no adjusting mechanism, no screws and levers—just a solid block of wood with two blades wedged in behind a pin that runs the width of the body. The design has been the same for 400 years. Its components are the *kanna no ha*, the plane iron, and the *dai*, the body.

The *ura* face — Most Japanese cutting blades, whether used in planes, chisels, gouges or spokeshaves, are different from Western blades. The standard Western blade is a solid piece of high-carbon steel. The steel of a Japanese blade is a laminated composition of high-carbon and low-carbon steel. The angled or beveled side, *omote*, is never double-beveled. And the other side, *ura* (the flat side of the Western tool), has a hollow ground. The laminated composition and hollow-ground shape offer a number of advantages. The actual cutting edge is the high-carbon steel and the rest of the blade is softer, more pliable steel, which can absorb shock when planing a board with knots or irregular grain patterns; the blade has less tendency to skip or chatter as the plane hits an irregular point. Another advantage is that the hollow-ground section of the *ura* side does not require regular attention. Because there is less surface area, it offers less resistance as it is guided over a board or grinding stone, so keeping this side flat and sharp is easy.

The first procedure in the preparation and care of any Japanese tool with this kind of blade is to obtain a completely flat surface on the *ura* side. Instead of a grinding stone, a *kanaban*, or "iron board," is used in conjunction with a series of grinding powders beginning with *kongosha*, a coarse material from sandstone. The other two powders are residual

64

grinding material that comes from the medium and fine grinding stones. A pinch of *kongosha* is dropped on the iron board with a bit of water and the flat surface of the blade is ground back and forth, yielding a streaked surface. When the streaks are uniform over the face, wash the board and continue with a pinch of the second grinding powder, residue from the medium stone, and a bit of water. This yields a finer, but still streaked, surface. When the streaks are uniform, wash the board again and continue with a pinch of the third grinding powder, from the finishing stone, and some more water. The final step is to put only a drop of water on the board and work the blade face over the board until it is completely dry. Continue to work the blade on the dry surface until there is a completely unstreaked mirror finish on the *ura* face. This is the "basic face" because it is prepared first, after which it remains relatively untended.

The *omote* face — The next step is to sharpen the beveled side of the blade, the *omote* face, on the medium stone. The *omote* face is a bit more difficult to prepare than the basic face, because only the angled part of the blade is held against the stone so it is easy for the blade to twist or roll. The medium stone is also used with water, not oil, and kept clean when not in use by being submerged in water, usually standing on one end. When sharpening, add enough water to provide an easy, but not resistance-free, movement across the stone. As you sharpen, water and stone material will ac-

cumulate at both ends of the stone. Save this as the second powder for the iron-board treatment of the *ura* face. As you sharpen the bevel, a burr will develop on the cutting edge, felt from the *ura* side. When it spans the entire cutting edge, change stones and work with the finishing stone. Grind only the *omote* face on the medium stone, never the *ura* side.

Begin on the finishing stone by working the *omote* face in the same manner as on the medium stone.* Then turn the blade over and work the *ura* face over the stone as done on the iron board to begin to remove the burr. Return to the *omote* face and work, then back to the *ura*. The ratio of working the *omote* to working the *ura* is about 10 strokes to 2. Continue until the burr is gone from the *ura* and a mirror surface appears on the *omote*.

Obviously you should keep your iron board and stones completely flat. Sharpening thin blades that do not cover the entire surface of the board or stones can change their shapes. To keep them flat, sharpen on different areas of the board or stone, covering its full length. Check the surface regularly and, as needed, rub together two wet stone faces, of different

---

*The medium stone is usually synthetic. The finishing stone comes in both synthetic and natural stones. I use the King deluxe 1000 (available from Woodline/The Japan Woodworker, 1004 Central Ave., Alameda, Calif. 94501, for $9). I have both synthetic ($15 to $25) and natural ($50 to $5,000) finishing stones and find the synthetic adequate for the average worker. However, as one's techniques become more refined, the natural stone is, subtly, much better.

Omote, *or beveled side of a* kanna *blade, left, reveals laminated composition: high-carbon steel at the edge; softer, shock-absorbing low-carbon steel for the rest of this side, including the back of the bevel, which appears lightest in this photo. The* ura, *or basic face, right, is hollow-ground.*

Japanese *kanna*

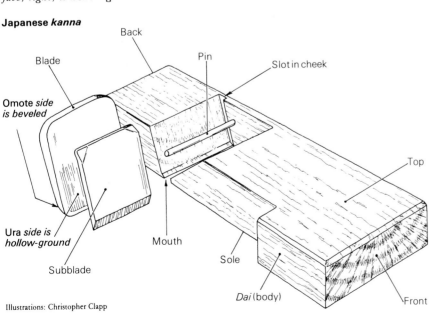

Illustrations: Christopher Clapp

A kanaban, *or iron board, sharpens the* ura. *A series of grinding powders pictured at top— kongosha, right (a sandstone grit), and second and third grinding-stone residues, center and left— are mixed with water on the* kanaban *and the blade ground back and forth over it to bring up a mirror finish. Bottom, because of the low-carbon steel in the blade laminate, the hollow ground on the* ura *can be pushed out by tapping the bevel on the* omote *with the pointed edge of a hammer while the blade rests on the corner of a hard metal surface. This is done when, after repeated sharpenings, the edge has been ground back into the* ura *hollow.*

or of the same grit. This can also be done with two iron boards, with water in between.

Refinishing the *ura* — It would appear that when the *omote* has been sharpened and resharpened down to the hollow itself, the cutting surface has run out. When the front edge can no longer be worked or sharpened, the hollow-ground surface of the *ura* must be pushed out, providing more surface area for the basic face. Because of its low-carbon-steel composition, you can tap the *omote* face with the pointed edge of a hammer to push the *ura* face out.

Hold the *ura* face tightly against an anvil or the edge of a heavy metal work surface. With the blade at a 45° angle to the edge of the anvil and using the pointed edge of a hammer, gently tap the *omote* face along a line across the whole face. The line, actually a series of indentations, must be made two-thirds of the way down from the tip of the blade. Steady, firm taps are necessary, spaced right next to each other in an even line. Later, with proficiency, it will be possible to tap the line halfway down from the tip. This takes less time but more skill. An improperly placed tap can seriously damage the blade. Use gentle, yet firm and evenly placed, taps. Too much force can crack the blade.

This completed, return the blade to the iron board and, using the second powder, begin to rework the basic face. If the front edge does not yet yield enough high-carbon steel, return to the anvil and begin again. This process cannot be hurried, and you may have to repeat it a number of times.

A good blade made of high-quality metal can last a lifetime if it is treated with care and respect. Many old Japanese craftsmen are proud of their *chibi*, or shortened blades, reshaped and sharpened through many years of work.

Usually, the first 15 mm of a new blade does not produce the finest-quality edge and cut, not because the steel is different from the rest of the blade, but rather because through a process of sharpening, finishing, shaping and refinishing, the blade is tamed, custom-fitted to the craftsman. And in some ways, the blade tames the worker as well: The particular composition of each blade is different, so through use and care, a worker will come to understand what is expected of him. Over a period of many years a craftsman will be able to determine which planes to use for rough work and which for finish work, which for soft woods and which for hard.

Using a finely tuned blade becomes an experience in feeling, or "tasting" with one's hands. The taste is different for each person, depending on the style of work, and comes only with experience. But, by watching a good craftsman at work, one can see the plane cutting smoothly over any angle of grain. Then, if the blade tastes like it is not cutting (not passing smoothly over the wood), a sensitive and patient worker will stop, return to the medium stone and resharpen the blade. This takes place many times during the course of a day whenever the blade is not cutting the way it should feel.

The *dai* — I have been told of legendary master carpenters who could sharpen their plane blades so keenly and prepare the *dai* (the plane body) so finely that if they placed the *kanna* on one end of a board and tilted the board, the plane would cut by itself as it slid down the board. Carpenters' mythology, perhaps, but it sets a standard of excellence that these craftsmen are constantly trying to achieve.

Preparation of the *dai* is essential to proper tool care and functioning. Because all Japanese planes are made of solid wood and affected by changes in temperature and humidity, *dai* preparation becomes an ongoing technique for the life of the plane. Improper *dai* preparation probably causes the most problems for those Western woodworkers who buy a Japanese plane and find it useless from the start or after the first change in the weather.

Usually the blade of a new *kanna* does not fit down completely into the mouth and extend out enough to cut. This is sometimes because the seasoning process continues after the *kanna* is manufactured. The first procedure is to correct the groove in the *dai* for the blade to fit snugly, yet deeply enough to cut. In *kanna* with both a blade and a subblade, to allow adequate room to work on the groove, remove the pin that holds the subblade against the main blade. Place the *dai* on its left edge and grasp the pin tightly with pliers. Tap the pliers firmly with a hammer. When the pin protrudes from the hole in the side of the *dai*, pull it out with the pliers.

Now using a short-bristle brush, paint ink on three sides of the main blade. Do not ink the *ura* face or the cutting bevel itself. Chinese calligraphy ink is best. Before the ink dries, place the *omote* face against the angled groove of the *dai* and push in by hand. Gently tap the top end of the blade down further, using a metal hammer with a convex face or a wooden mallet. The tapping should become increasingly firm until the blade fits in the groove. Listen, and when the sound is "solid" (a higher-pitched tap), the blade is snug. To remove the blade, tap the end of the *dai* (behind the blade) firmly with the hammer until the sound indicates the blade is loose. Tap the upper corner-edge of the end of the *dai* on either side of the midpoint, first one side then the other, back and forth. Be sure to tap the corner edge squarely so as not to chip the *dai*. By placing the thumb of the hand holding the *dai* against the blade, you can exert pressure outward with the taps of the hammer, which will also prevent the blade from shooting out of the *dai*, and onto the floor or your foot.

With the blade removed, you can chisel away the ink impressions left on the tight parts of the groove and refit the blade to sit deeper in the *dai*. Chiseling should remove only a thin amount of wood, almost like a powder, and the process of inking and refitting the blades is repeated many times. Chisel only on the wide face that touches the beveled side of the blade and along the sides where the blade fits into the groove; do not chisel the top of these side grooves.

When refitting the blade, don't force it any deeper than it can go with gentle to moderate tapping. Again, listen to the taps. When you begin to sight the blade along the sole of the *dai* just protruding from the mouth, the process is complete. It will take time, especially when the plane is new. After that it won't be necessary to refit unless the temperature or humidity changes significantly or the seasoning process is still extremely active. Then minor inking can be done.

The process sounds complicated and time-consuming, but it is necessary and, with practice, easy. It might happen that too much of the groove has been chiseled. In this case, glue a piece of paper on the wide part of the groove that supports the *omote* side of the blade.

The sole — Sometimes planes are used on their sides, planing, for example, on a shooting board. The Japanese *kanna* is tipped on its right side for this. The sole and right side of the plane therefore must be square. Planing the side might be

Paint the lower face and the two edges of the blade with ink, left, and while the ink is still wet, tap the blade in to register the high points in the groove. When the blade is tapped out, ink remains on the areas to be pared down, above.

necessary. Be careful when chiseling the groove to fit the blade. After many years you may weaken the right side with excessive chiseling, so favor it.

The next step in preparing the *kanna* for use is to make the sole completely flat. The best method for doing this uses a special plane called a *dainaoshi*, whose single blade, set at 90° in the *dai*, scrapes fine, powder-like shavings from the sole of the *kanna*. It is possible to use a wide chisel in the same way. (In fact it is necessary to correct the sole of the *dainaoshi* itself in this way.)

By holding a straightedge across the sole of the *dai* in front of a light and tilting it slightly, you can watch for light to shine through underneath and illuminate the high and low spots across the surface of the sole. Hold the straightedge in many different positions: along the width, length and diagonal. Move it slowly and mark the high spots with a pencil.

Now take the *dainaoshi* (or a chisel) and begin removing the pencil marks, and with them a thin shaving of the sole. Be sure to plane evenly so as not to create extremely low or twisting spots. It is sometimes wise to plane across the *dai* from one side and then turn the *dai* around so planing can go across from the opposite side. This will ensure even planing. Always plane across the *dai*, not lengthwise. You can, however, turn the *dainaoshi* at different angles to the sole of the other *kanna* to smooth the planing action. After removing the pencil marks, again check for flatness with the straightedge and mark new pencil lines for the next shaving. Repeat until you've rendered the *dai* completely flat.

Some books, both English and Japanese, suggest using coarse abrasive paper to sand down the sole of the *dai* to flatness. However, this method is not advisable. The grit from the paper can lodge itself in the sole of the *kanna* and can mar the surface of the lumber being finished. It can also transfer grit into the lumber and then chip the blade as the *kanna* makes its next pass. Further, any other method of treating the sole after sandpaper has been used risks damaging the tool used for the second refinishing.

Depending upon the climatic conditions of the shop and the seasoning qualities of the *dai*, secondary *dai* refinishing with the *dainaoshi* will be necessary at various times. Again, the feel of the cut is the best way to tell whether you should check the sole for changes in flatness. For the *dainaoshi* and finger planes, a flat sole will suffice for smooth cutting. However, large-body *kanna* require further treatment to

create a "wave" pattern on the sole that facilitates accurate and smooth cutting. Locate four points on the sole of the plane: Point A is the front of the *dai*. Point B is the part of the sole just in front of the mouth, or opening for the blade. Point C is that part of the sole just behind the mouth. And point D refers to the opposite end or back.

With the *dainaoshi*, plane the sole between points A and B, taking care to keep those two points the same height. The area between should be approximately $\frac{1}{64}$ in. lower. Now, working back from point C, plane C just a fraction lower than B and continue to plane the sole out toward the back to about $\frac{1}{32}$ in. lower than A and B. By eliminating the surface area between points A and B you reduce the surface of the *kanna* in contact with the wood. Further, the area between points C and D is a fraction lower than point B or the blade would be lifted off the wood and would not cut, or would cut erratically. The figures given are basic rules of thumb for relative

Not to scale

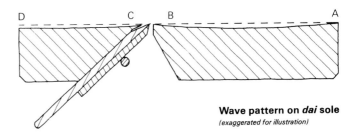

Wave pattern on *dai* sole
(exaggerated for illustration)

Dainaoshi *(planes whose blades are set at 90° to produce a scraping cut for truing plane soles) are used always across, never along, the length of the sole. Larger plane soles are planed not flat but in a wave pattern to reduce friction.*

highs and lows for all points. The best-prepared *kanna* would use fractions of these fractions, and the quality of the cut would be unmatched.

When preparing the sole with *dainaoshi* or chisel be sure to back the blade out of the mouth area, but keep the blade just snug enough in the groove to warrant removal with a hammer, not a hand. This will exert force on the sole behind the mouth so the highs and lows one measures during correction will be the same as when the blade is in the cutting position. Otherwise, the blade might force the area behind the mouth higher than point *B*.

Even after many, many years of seasoning, a *dai* may still need correcting. Again it becomes an experience in feeling to determine when the *dai* is not cutting or moving across the wood efficiently. By examining the sole for shiny spots, you can sometimes detect the high spots without a straightedge. However, this is a preliminary step and should be followed up with the techniques presented here to correct and prepare the *dai* for further use.

Once you've prepared the sole of the *kanna* with a *dainaoshi*, a few minor adjustments must be made for the final finish. A newly purchased plane has a bevel running the length of the *dai* on either side of the sole. After fitting the blade in the *dai*, you'll find these bevels do not reach the mouth. To eliminate unnecessary contact between sole and work surface, increase the size of the two bevels right up to the mouth area. Then chisel a cut at either side of the mouth, angled back toward the end of the *dai* and out onto the beveled sides. This angled cut acts as an escapement for fine shavings that would otherwise become clogged in the mouth. Finally, on the upper edge of the mouth, or the edge closest to the back of the *dai*, chisel a thin 45° bevel across the entire edge. This bevel can reflect light and silhouette the blade as one sights it down the length of the *dai*, facilitating easy and proper gauging of the blade depth.

These procedures may sound complicated. One might ask, "Why not the marvels of modern metal planes?" However, if you are interested in using a Japanese plane and you can complete these steps, you'll be rewarded with an unparalleled

cutting tool that will become easier to operate and to maintain as you work with it. Consider the greater sensitivity of a wooden *kanna* over a metal plane; the pull stroke keeps the work between *kanna* and body. In a short time you'll develop a different sense of control over your work. Another advantage of Japanese planes is that because they are made of solid wood with no moving parts, they can be modified and adapted to fit an infinite variety of shapes and surfaces.

Choosing your *kanna* — The usual manner of making and buying *kanna* in Japan is for a craftsman to purchase one from a master *kanna* maker or from a shop that sells *kanna* made by others. Then he either uses it as is or changes it to suit his needs. The process of making a *kanna* can involve both hand and machine work to a greater or lesser degree, depending on the tool's quality and cost.

I was introduced to a man who makes *kanna* in the Nagoya area of Japan. He and his son run a small tool and hardware shop. They would first cut and square pieces of wood to approximate size using a table saw and a jointer. This wood is then stored anywhere from 2 to 25 years. Much concern and respect are shown for the seasoning process. Better-quality *kanna* are seasoned longest and made by hand. The groove is cut either entirely by hand or with a mortising machine and then finished by hand. The *kanna* master usually buys a variety of blades from different sources, again at varying quality and cost. He builds the *dai* to fit its chosen blade. An expensive *kanna* will have a *dai* seasoned 25 years, and will be made completely by hand, including the blade. It will cost about $250.

Japanese *kanna* can be purchased in a variety of standard sizes. The standard ones are mostly flat-soled. However, it is possible to find tool shops that also sell *kanna* with shaped soles for specialized planing. Finger planes are usually bought in the standard shape and the *dai* recut to fit the job at hand.

Here are some hints on what to look for in a *kanna*. Check the end grain of the *dai*; it should be running horizontally, not vertically as in Western planes. The rays will run vertically and should be well-defined. Check to see that the mouth of the *dai* is not too large and that the escapement angle for the shavings is sharp. There should be no gaps along the groove where the blade fits into the *dai*. To check for this, hold the *kanna* up to a light source and check for light in the groove between blade and *dai*. Test whether the blade fits tightly in the groove. If the *dai* has two blades, it will have a pin to wedge the blades together. Check the positioning of the pin. If the *dai* has been expanding and contracting in the shop, the pin may be pushed through or near the opening of the hole. A tight-fitting blade and evidence of pin movement indicate a better plane; the *dai* has been around for a while, so it is older and therefore more seasoned. Another important thing to check is that the *ura* side of the blade(s) is well shaped and has a well-defined concave face.

The processes involved in preparing and maintaining Japanese *kanna* are rigorous at first. The attention to detail on such seemingly simple tools is, without a doubt, not for everyone. However, for a craftsman who is willing to put mental, as well as physical, effort into preparing and caring for these planes, the rewards can be profound. The craftsman becomes so intimate with his *kanna* that it is, indeed, an extension of his hands, putting him in touch with the process of making, as well as with the end result. □

Kanna *newly purchased, left, and after complete preparation of the sole, right. The large bevels that run the length of the sole decrease the surface area, the notches at the sides of the mouth are for fine-shavings clearance and the chamfer along the back edge of the mouth is for reflecting light to sight proper blade depth.*

Making a Modern Wooden Plane

Nuts and bolts adjuster controls depth

by Karl Dittmer

Photos: Ray Jones

When I yearned for a quality wooden try plane, I took one look at the price and decided to build one using rock maple. Modern glues are trustworthy, so I elected to build it in four layers, using two ¾-in. pieces for the inner layers and ½-in. pieces for the outer. This made it a simple matter to cut the throat area, usually a chore.

The result was quite successful, except that the old-fashioned wedge system proved a bit coarse, particularly when trying to back off the blade for that final light cut. After some thought, I came up with an acceptable depth adjustment that engages the head of the screw attaching the plane iron to the chipbreaker. I have eliminated free play through careful fitting and now have a precise, uncomplicated adjustment mechanism that is almost as smooth and accurate as the one on a Primus plane I acquired during an extravagant moment. Lateral adjustments are made by forcing the top of the plane iron to one side. Come sharpening time, the homegrown mechanism shines because the iron comes out without any of that Primus-type hassle.

The modernized try plane worked so well, I bought more irons and turned out a few more planes. All are a pleasure to use and construction is simple, thanks to being able to work on the throat area before each is assembled. I make my throats small, then after the sole is finished, file them to fit. Don't despair if you get the throat too big. A thin shim epoxied under the plane iron near the throat opening will cure it.

Most of my planes have the iron at 45°; smoothing planes should be at around 50°. Dimensions were determined by the width of the plane iron and what I felt would be appropriate for my style. If you are not certain just how long to make your plane, make it oversize, then cut it off later. □

Karl Dittmer builds furniture in El Reno, Okla. For more on making planes, see Fine Woodworking, *Winter '75.*

Jack plane, right, with depth adjuster and glued-up body is easy to build; most of the throat area can be sawn before assembly. For stability, grain in adjoining pieces of wood is alternated. The adjustment screw, threaded through a brass block mortised into the plane body, is bound to a sliding carriage that fits the plane-iron screw. After the center laminates are sawn, left, they are positioned on the side pieces using steel pins. The sides are cut with a saw and chisel to taper in toward the mouth. Here Dittmer cuts a mortise to accept the depth-adjustment mechanism.

Depth adjuster

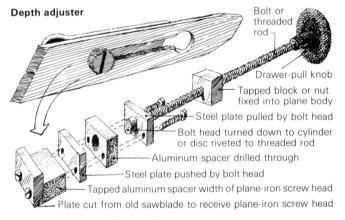

- Bolt or threaded rod
- Drawer-pull knob
- Tapped block or nut fixed into plane body
- Steel plate pulled by bolt head
- Bolt head turned down to cylinder or disc riveted to threaded rod
- Aluminum spacer drilled through
- Steel plate pushed by bolt head
- Tapped aluminum spacer width of plane-iron screw head
- Plate cut from old sawblade to receive plane-iron screw head

Gentleman's plane, disassembled above, is even easier to make than the all-wood-bodied planes. It uses the same adjusting mechanism, but has steel side straps and a pin to hold the wedge and plane iron in. With the toe removed (which reveals its mouth-adjustment capability) and an alternate, shorter set of side straps, it could be used as a bullnose plane.

Some of Dittmer's handmade planes.

Methods of Work

Tool holders

This tool holder is simple to build from scrap lumber and Masonite. The hole spacing can be varied for different tools. A mounting hole on each end allows the rack to be hung from the wall, the workbench or even a door.

—*Jay Wallace, Gilbert, Ariz.*

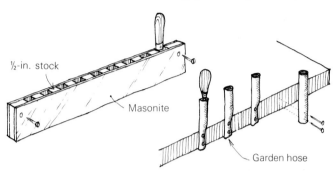

Six-inch lengths of garden hose fastened to the wall or bench with two nails at the bottom make excellent tool holders for screwdrivers, awls, etc. Tools are easy to remove, and the soft, flexible hose won't damage sharp edges.

—*Carl R. Vitale, Cranston, R.I.*

Recycling tool handles

One way I beat inflation is by making my own tool handles from old mop, broom and shovel handles, usually made of ash, hickory or beech, that the average homeowner pitches in the garbage.

Here's how I make octagonal handles for new carving-tool blades (which I buy unhandled). First, clamp a beech mop-stick in the vise, leaving about 6 or 8 in. protruding diagonally at the top. Mark the handle length and taper the sides from this line to the ferrule end with a drawknife. Take shallow cuts at first, turning the stick frequently for uniformity.

For the ferrule, use the metal end of a spent 20-ga. shotgun shell. If you're not a hunter, look for empty shells at a skeet shooting area. To separate the ferrule from the shell, drill through the center bottom (where the shotgun hammer hits the shell) with a ¼-in. bit. This releases the hull and inner packing, which can then be pulled out with pliers. The hole that's left is usually the right size to receive the carving tool's tang. To mount the ferrule, mark its length on the handle,

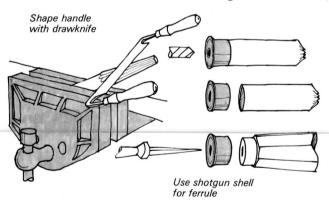

Shape handle with drawknife

Use shotgun shell for ferrule

and with a second-cut wood file, remove enough wood to seat the ferrule snugly.

Beech works well for carving-tool handles, but other woods are more suited to striking-tool handles. Old shovel handles (usually hickory) are best for replacement hammer handles; I work them down also with a drawknife. Broken ash baseball bats (check the local high school's practice field) are excellent

for hammer, hatchet and lathe-tool handles. I finish all these handles with a couple of coats of tung or linseed oil.

—*Rob Russell, Joliet, Ill.*

Socket reamers

Here are two spur-of-the-moment, large-diameter reamers that work well for tapering candlestick sockets and the like. Since a candlestick reamer won't be used often, practically any scrap of steel will do for the cutter on the "deluxe" version. Install the sharpened cutter in a saw kerf with a screw. Use two screws or pin the blade through the dowel body if the cutter shifts in use.

You don't need a lathe for the sandpaper version—it can be whittled and filed sufficiently round by hand. Install one end of a sandpaper strip in a slot in the head. Then wrap the strip around the reamer; there's no need to fasten the other end of the strip. —*Van Caldwell, Cincinnati, Ohio*

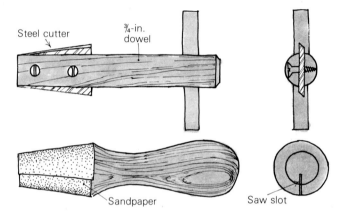

Adjustable tool rest

Here is an adjustable bench-grinder tool rest that's accurate, easy to use and cheap to build. Cut a 1½-in. thick pine hinge-block at the angles shown and mount it to the base with screws from underneath. Cut down two Stanley 10-in. lid supports to make the table-adjusting hardware. Drill out the center rivets and replace with screws into the 1x1 hardwood block. Pin the ⅜-in. threaded rod in a mortise in the pine hinge-block. Now mount the plywood or Formica-covered, composition-board table as close to the grinding wheel as possible. Recess the hinge into the bottom of the table if necessary. —*Mike Perrin, Knoxville, Tenn.*

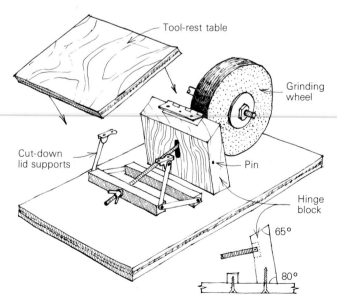

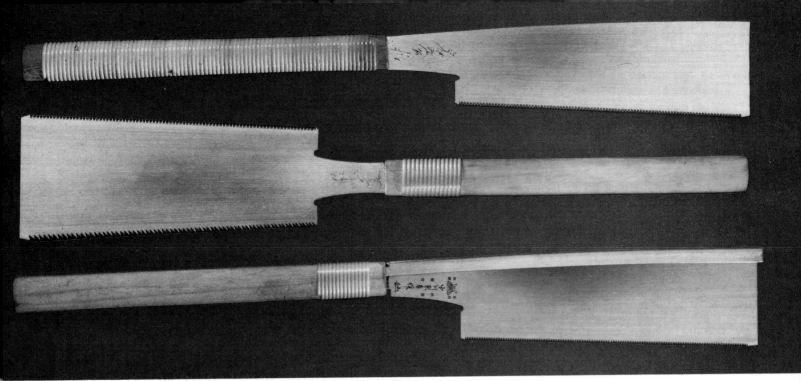

Top to bottom: a kataba, ryoba *and* dozuki, *each approximately 22 in. long.*

Japanese Saws
Thin, flexible blades cut on the pull stroke

by Robert Ghelerter

The *kataba, ryoba* and *dozuki* are the three primary hand-saws for the Japanese woodworker. The *kataba* and *ryoba* roughly correspond to the cabinet saw or carpenter's saw, and the *dozuki* is equivalent to the backsaw or dovetail saw. They differ from their Western counterparts in that all the teeth face back toward the user—they cut on the pull stroke rather than on the push. This allows the blades to be very thin and light. My *ryoba* weighs less than 6 oz. All in all, I find them less tiring to use and more accurate than Western saws.

In Japanese the words *"kataba," "ryoba"* and *"dozuki"* are often followed by the word *"nokogiri,"* which means "saw." *Kataba-nokogiri* is a saw with teeth on one side; *ryoba-nokogiri,* a saw with teeth on both sides (one edge for ripping and the other for crosscutting); and *dozuki-nokogiri,* a saw with guard adjoined.

The first saws came to Japan from China via Korea between the 14th and 15th centuries. The Japanese were never on friendly terms with the Chinese, and everything from China came via Korea. There is some evidence of saws before this time, but they weren't widely used. The first saws introduced were large, for felling and resawing trees. The other saws evolved from them.

The *ryoba* is relatively new, created about 100 years ago. Before this combination saw, woodworkers needed two *kataba*, a rip and a crosscut. Both *ryoba* and *kataba* are for rough cutting and can be used with one or two hands. The saws are versatile and can bend to get into difficult places. When cutting flush to a surface, I prefer the *kataba* because its back can be rested on the wood without scratching the sur-

face. The blades of both *ryoba* and *kataba* are thinner in the center than at the edges to reduce friction in the kerf.

The *dozuki* is used for accurate work, and when cutting angles a guide block can be used. To trim a board to length, draw lines on four sides of the board with a square and a sharp pencil; a thin pencil line will be easier to see, especially on light wood, than a marking-gauge line. Begin the cut at the far corner of one side, gradually leveling the saw until the kerf is about ¼ in. deep. Then turn the board and do the next side. When all four sides have been started, the cut can easily be completed, the kerfs guiding the saw.

The *ryoba* and *kataba* can be used this way too, and the same method cuts shoulders on tenons. For crosscut work I find these saws superior to electric saws in that they leave no tear-out. They are especially handy for cutting 4x8 sheets of ¼-in. paneling. They can be every bit as accurate as a machine and often faster. Although *dozuki* are usually filed for cross-cutting, their teeth can also be shaped for ripping.

There are a few different styles of *kataba, ryoba* and *dozuki* to choose from. The *ryoba* and *kataba* usually come with the teeth in a straight line, but sometimes carpenters prefer a saw with a convex cutting edge (*anabiki*) to begin cuts in the middle of a board or panel. On *dozuki*, the teeth are always in a straight line but the amount of arch in the stiff back varies,

EDITOR'S NOTE: A 210-mm *ryoba* saw costs $46.50 at Woodline/ The Japan Woodworker, 1004 Central Ave., Alameda, Calif. 94501; and $11.75 at Tashiro Hardware, 109 Prefontaine Pl., Seattle, Wash. 98104. Many mail-order catalog houses also sell these saws: Garrett-Wade, $17.50; Woodcraft Supply, $17.40; and Leichtung, $10.95.

Dozuki with guide block cuts the beveled shoulder for a beveled mortise-and-tenon joint.

Board is cut to length by sawing in from each of the four sides in turn.

Ryoba crosscut edge trims tabletop.

changing the angle of the handle to the saw body. There is also a small version of *ryoba* known as *azibiki*. Its blade is usually no longer than 100mm (4 in.), is thick and will not flex much. The cutting edges are convex. I have seen these saws used only by carvers for roughing out, though I understand they are also used in joinery.

When choosing a saw, first consider usage. Carpentry and cabinetmaking saws differ in size, flexibility, hardness and thickness. Standard blade sizes are as follows:

	Cabinetmaking	Carpentry
Kataba and *ryoba* length	210mm to 240mm (8¼ in. to 9½ in.)	270mm to 420mm (10⅝ in. to 16½ in.)
Dozuki length	210mm to 240mm (8¼ in. to 9½ in.)	240mm to 315mm (9½ in. to 12⅜ in.)
Dozuki depth of cut	40mm to 55mm (1⅝ in. to 2 in.)	60mm to 95mm (2⅜ in. to 3¾ in.)

Carpenter's saws are bigger, thicker, harder and have fewer teeth per inch than cabinetmaker's saws. *Dozuki* usually have from 25 to 30 teeth per inch. *Kataba* and *ryoba* crosscut blades range from 15 to 20 teeth per inch, and ripsaws have from 6 to 8 teeth per inch. *Kataba* and *ryoba* teeth are slightly smaller near the handle, for starting the cut.

There are three grades of Japanese tools based on the quality of the steel: "Yellow" is the lowest, "white" the middle, and "blue" the highest quality. It is difficult in this country to distinguish these grades except by price. Saws of the yellow rank (their blades have a yellowish tinge) are cheap ($2 to $13) and not used by serious craftsmen. Most middle and high-grade tools are made from white steel and can cost from $20 to several hundred dollars. A few extremely expensive tools are made from blue or sword steel. Those that are hand-made are easy to differentiate from machine-made saws; the surface is rough and they can cost several thousand dollars.

For general cabinetry, a good saw to start with would be a 220mm *ryoba*. For fine joinery you should also have a *dozuki*—240mm is standard. Beginners should stay away from the thinnest (paper-thin) *dozuki*, which, although more accurate, are harder to control and can easily break. A good saw maximizes hardness and flexibility; it will bend considerably (the *ryoba* and *kataba* into a half circle) and still return to its original shape. Yet because it is thin, it will break before it deforms. Cheap saws are thicker, softer, less flexible, and less likely to break.

Good saws generally come with the handles unattached. The handles are usually wrapped with bamboo cane, for strength. Some are wrapped only at the end where the saw fits in, others the entire length. Handles come with a hole for the tang, but the holes are usually too small and should be enlarged with a keyhole saw. Cut only a little at a time, trying the saw tang for fit. Push the tang into the handle and strike the handle end with a hammer. Never strike the saw itself.

In Japan most woodworkers send their saws to a shop for sharpening by hand. Saws can be sent back to the factory to be sharpened by machine, but hand-sharpening, which leaves the teeth rough from the file, is considered superior. It is not difficult and with a little practice can be done rapidly. If this is your first time sharpening a saw, before beginning, cut a kerf in a piece of wood so that the newly sharpened saw can be compared to how it was before.

If the blade is warped or kinked, sometimes a result of friction-caused heat expanding the metal at the cutting edge, hammer it out with the same hammer that will be used to set the teeth. The saw is placed on a piece of iron, concave side of the warp down, and struck lightly to stretch the metal evenly. Never heat the blade; you can easily ruin its temper.

Sometimes the blade of the *dozuki* slips a little from the backing. It is held only by pressure and is not actually bonded. A loose blade can become badly kinked, but is easily remedied by tapping the saw's back on a piece of wood. After straightening, hold the blade in one hand, resting on a firm surface, and joint the teeth. The Japanese use a special tool, but a flat metal file serves the same purpose. Two or three strokes ensure that all the teeth are the same height. Now the saw is ready to sharpen.

Sharpening must be done with a special feather file (a thin diamond in cross section), which should be available where the saw is purchased. It is best used only once and comes unhandled, so it's a good idea to make a simple, reusable

Photos: Robert Ghelerter

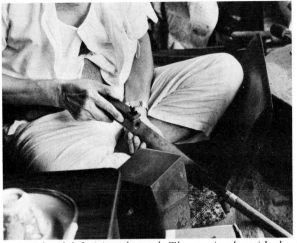

A special tool, left, joints the teeth. The saw vise alongside the sharpener's knee is used with a diamond-profile feather file, as at right, to sharpen the lead side of a rip tooth.

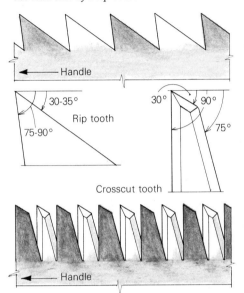

After filing, gentle tapping sets the teeth.

handle. The Japanese prefer a thin branch from a cherry tree, but a piece of dowel stock with a drilled hole to receive the tang will work as well. To hold the saw, the Japanese use a flat, wide vise whose two jaws, hinged in the middle, are driven together with a wedge at the bottom. The jaws are shaped so they grasp the saw only near the teeth. Two shaped boards held together with screws and wing nuts will suffice.

Rip teeth and crosscut teeth have different shapes and are filed differently, except that filing is always done on the push stroke and on teeth that point away from you. For the rip teeth, hold the file 90° to the saw body and file the lead side of every other tooth (the side closest to the handle), then turn the holder around and file the lead side of the remaining teeth. Push simultaneously sideways and down, to cut a little into the body of the blade. One or two strokes are adequate. Next file the trailing side, also 90° to the saw body, once again doing every other tooth, then turn the holder around to file the remaining teeth. File until a new point is formed.

Japanese crosscut teeth are quite unlike any Western saw teeth, in that each is sharpened with a bevel not only on the leading and trailing edges but also at the apex of each tooth. The leading and trailing edges of adjacent teeth are filed on the same stroke, then the top facet is filed. Start with the handle of the saw on the right. Hold the file at a 60° angle to the saw body, pointing toward the handle. One stroke, pushing down and toward the left, should cut the leading

edge of the tooth set away from you, while the other side of the file rubs lightly on the trailing edge of the tooth to the right, set toward you. Next file the top of each tooth set away from you, trying to duplicate the existing angle, which is about 60° to the saw body, but slanted away from the handle. Again, one stroke is adequate. Then turn the holder and with the handle and file pointed to the left, and applying more pressure on the stroke to the right (on the leading edge of a tooth set away from you), file the other teeth.

Because the blade is so thin and sharpening can bend the teeth, they are set after filing. A hammer with a face no wider than a single tooth is used. Hold the edge of the saw on the rounded edge of a piece of flat iron so the tooth to be struck almost touches the iron. Bring the hammer down lightly, or allow it to fall of its own weight. The small crosscut teeth require considerable skill. Look down both sides of the saw to make sure the teeth are in line. *Dozuki* teeth need little set, although the amount can vary with personal preference. If in use the saw is difficult to guide, the teeth may need a little more set. After setting, deburr the saw by running a piece of metal along both sides of the teeth. Occasionally, rub a little oil into the blade to keep it from rusting. □

Robert Ghelerter, 26, has recently returned from a year and a half studying woodworking in Japan. He now builds furniture in Berkeley, Calif.

Sharpening Saws
Principles, procedures and gadgets

by Jules A. Paquin

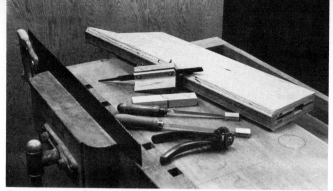
Crosscut saw with reconditioning apparatus.

A handsaw is a tool with a blade of tempered steel in which teeth have been cut. Different kinds of saws are made to perform different functions. The number of teeth to the inch and their shape vary according to the work the saw has to accomplish. The two basic woodworking saws are the crosscut saw, designed to cut across the grain of the wood, and the ripsaw, designed to cut with the grain. The crosscut-saw tooth cuts like a knife. The ripsaw tooth cuts like a chisel.

The teeth of a saw become blunt from regular use, particularly from sawing hardwood. New saws have been shaped, set and sharpened by precision machines at the factory, but many saws can be improved, and old saws reconditioned, by following the step-by-step instruction offered in this article. It is not always necessary to go through the complete sequence, but wherever you start, you should follow through the rest of the order.

For regular maintenance it is a good idea to file the teeth lightly as soon as they have lost their sharpness. One or two filings of this kind will not affect the set of the teeth. Generally it will take three or four filings before resetting is needed. At this stage you can check the shape of the teeth. If the previous filings were done with care and attention, and the saw has not been misused, only setting and filing will be needed. If the teeth have been damaged or made uneven by excessive filing, it will be necessary to go through the five restoring operations: jointing, shaping, setting, filing and honing.

The only equipment you need is a saw set, an 8-in. smooth mill file and a fine-cut triangular file, slightly tapered and with 60° angles to match the angles between the teeth of most handsaws. The saw sharpening vise and various filing guides shown here you can easily make yourself.

Jointing — This operation consists of filing the points of the teeth with the mill file to make them even or in line along the saw. The jointing guide (figure 1) will keep the file flat on the tips of the teeth and square with the blade. Run the file gently along the top of the teeth, holding the guide flat on the side of the blade. This cuts a flat on the tip of the teeth, which varies in width according to how far out of line each tooth was. Jointing must touch all the teeth but cut none down more than is necessary to bring them in line. If the teeth are very uneven and a considerable amount of jointing is necessary, you should alternate jointing with the next operation, shaping, otherwise the shape of the teeth may be lost.

Shaping — This operation restores the teeth to their regular form. Place the saw in the sharpening vise (figure 2), the teeth close to the top so the thin metal will not vibrate when filed, and clamp the saw vise in the bench vise. Inserting the tip of a triangular file firmly on a tilting guide (figure 3), file straight across the saw, at right angles to the blade. Note that there are two tilting guides, one for ripsaws and one for crosscuts. Shape first the teeth that have been leveled most. The jointed flats or brights on the tips of the teeth will be taken off in two stages: The triangular file will wear half the flat on one tooth and half the flat on the next tooth. Take care that the top of the tilting guide remain horizontal while filing and that the stroke of the file be perpendicular to the blade. Don't file the gullet too deeply. To make the teeth equal and regular, often you will need to press more against the front of one tooth than against the back of the next tooth, or vice-versa. After shaping, all the gullets should be of equal depth, the front and back of the teeth at the proper angle and all the teeth the same size. Check by looking at the saw from the side. All the teeth will have been shaped from the same side of the saw and there will be no bevel toward the front or back of the teeth. Before setting, rub both sides of the saw with an oilstone to remove the burr left by the file, and brush away any oilstone residue left in the gullets.

Setting — The goal of setting is to make the kerf that the saw will cut wide enough so the blade will not bind. This is accomplished by bending outward the upper part of each tooth. To work properly, a saw should have no more set than is necessary. Only one-third of the height of the tooth should be bent, producing a saw kerf that is a little less than one and a half times the thickness of the blade, thus the set on each

Fig. 1: Jointing guide

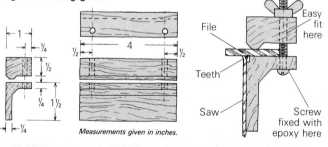

Measurements given in inches.

To joint the teeth, place the saw in the bench vise and a smooth mill file in the jointing guide. Hold the guide flat against the side of the blade and run the file gently over the top of the teeth. The saw vise pictured on the bench is used in subsequent steps.

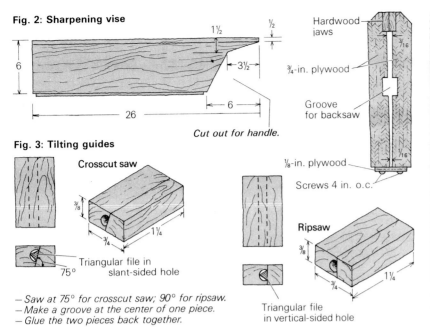

Fig. 2: Sharpening vise

1½
½
6
3½
6
26

Cut out for handle.

Hardwood jaws

¾-in. plywood

Groove for backsaw

3/16

⅛-in. plywood

1/16

Screws 4 in. o.c.

Fig. 3: Tilting guides

Crosscut saw

3/8
¾
1¼

Triangular file in slant-sided hole
75°

Ripsaw

3/8
¾
1¼

Triangular file in vertical-sided hole

— Saw at 75° for crosscut saw; 90° for ripsaw.
— Make a groove at the center of one piece.
— Glue the two pieces back together.

Shaping is done with the saw in the saw vise and a tilting guide on the tip of a smooth-cut triangular file. The stroke should be level and at 90° to the sawblade.

Fig. 4: Saw set

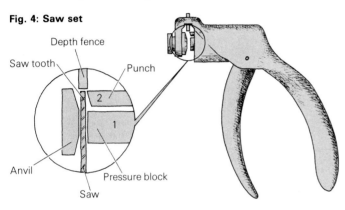

Depth fence

Saw tooth

Punch

2

1

Anvil

Pressure block

Saw

side should be one-quarter the thickness of the blade. Trying to bend the teeth too much may break them off or cause a crack at the bottom of the gullets. Work in hardwood requires less set than work in softwood.

Setting is done with a special tool called a saw set, which operates with handles like those of a pliers. The principle is to press the tooth with a beveled punch against a little anvil. There are several styles of saw sets on the market. The most practical one (figure 4) does two operations simultaneously: A block presses and holds the sawblade on the anvil, and a beveled punch pushes the tooth onto the inclined part of the anvil. The saw-set anvil is usually an adjustable wheel with numbers around it. These numbers correspond approximately to the number of teeth to an inch of the saw. Bring the number to the appropriate index mark, and the anvil is in po-

sition to set all teeth to the same proper inclination. Set first the teeth that point away from you on one side, then turn the saw around and set the other teeth. Never reverse the set of a tooth. When you are finished check to see that you have not missed a tooth. The set must be the same from end to end of the blade, otherwise the saw will not cut straight, but snakey.

Filing — Filing sharpens the saw and is the most important operation in reconditioning. Depending on the point size of your saw, select a slim triangular file: for 11 to 18 points per inch, a 5-in. file; for 7 to 10 points, a 6-in. file, and for 4 to 6 points, a 7-in. file.

Except for differences in tilting and bearing angles, filing crosscut saws is the same as filing ripsaws. Mount the saw in the saw vise, the bottom of the tooth gullets ⅛ in. above the vise jaws and the handle of the saw to your right.

For a crosscut saw, place the bearing guide (figure 5, next page) on the top of the teeth, and the crosscut tilting guide (figure 3) on the tip of the file. The bearing guide may be placed to the right or to the left of the tooth being filed, but as close as possible to it without getting in the way. It is a device with which to line up the file by eye and is moved along the saw as needed. Start at the toe of the saw and place the file in the gullet to the left of the first tooth set toward you. The file should be parallel to the bearing guide, and the tilting guide should be horizontal. Push the file straight forward, holding it firmly at both ends. Exert slight pressure on the forward movement, but lift the file on the backward movement. The

Reconditioning a saw			
Process	**Aim**	**Necessary**	**Recommended**
1. Jointing	To make the teeth the same height.	If the teeth have been seriously damaged by careless handling of the saw.	After several filings to make the teeth the same height.
2. Shaping	To restore the shape of the teeth.	If the jointing has left a large flat top at the tip of some teeth.	If the flat on the teeth is not nearly the same.
3. Setting	To widen the kerf by bending alternate teeth in opposite direction.	If you have done processes 1 and 2.	After four or five filings not preceded by processes 1 or 2.
4. Filing	To sharpen the teeth.	Processes 1, 2 and 3 are always followed by filing.	When teeth become dull.
5. Honing	To remove the burr that appears on the sides of the teeth.		Highly recommended for delicate saw work.

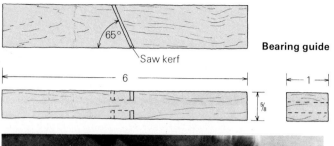

Bearing guide

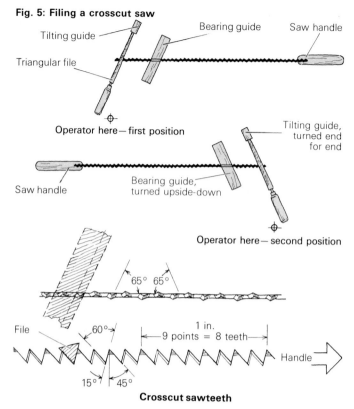

Fig. 5: Filing a crosscut saw

Crosscut-saw filing is aided by a bearing guide on the saw and a tilting guide on the file. Maintain consistent pressure for an equal number of strokes in each gullet, with a tooth set toward you always closest to the saw handle.

stroke should be always horizontal. This operation will wear both the front of the tooth set toward you and the back of the preceding tooth set away from you. Count the file strokes and note the pressure you exert because you will have to repeat the same number of strokes and the same pressure all the way along. After the first gullet go to the third gullet, skipping the second; then go to the fifth, skipping the fourth; and so on every second gullet up to the handle.

Turn the saw around so the handle is at your left. Turn the bearing guide upside-down and the tilting guide around, end for end. Work the other side of the saw in the same manner, starting at the toe and in the gullet to the right of the first tooth set toward you. After filing a few teeth on this side, check them. The filing should have brought the teeth to a fine point with a bevel to the front and to the back of each tooth. Do not remove any more metal than is necessary to make the bevels meet at the top of the tooth. Continue filing along the length of the saw.

A crosscut saw is filed well if you can slide a needle between the tips of the teeth without it falling.

For a ripsaw (figure 6), place the ripsaw tilting guide (figure 3) on your triangular file and file perpendicular to the face of the saw; rip teeth have no bevel. A well-trained eye and hand can easily keep the stroke perpendicular without the aid of a bearing guide. File the first gullet, the third, the

fifth, etc. Turn the saw and file the other gullets so the filing will be uniform on each side; otherwise the saw will cut on a slant. For ripsaw teeth, the alternation of the direction of the stroke and its evenness are the only differences between filing and the earlier operation of shaping.

Honing — Filing leaves a burr or wire edge at the sides of the teeth. A burr won't make any difference in rough work, but for fine work it is best to get rid of it. To do this, put your saw flat on your bench and run a fine oilstone gently against the teeth on both sides. Honing will also correct small irregularities in setting.

The angles I use are good. I have adopted them with satisfaction. But there are other workable angles and they should not be ignored. For a crosscut saw some prefer a bearing angle of 55°, and others 60°. Some prefer the handle end of the file about 10° below the horizon. For a ripsaw some prefer a tilting angle of 8° instead of 0°. You can adopt the standards that best fit your needs, but when you have made your choice, be consistent. Remember, though, you will have to alter the guides shown in the figures accordingly.

Those who haven't tried it think that maintaining a handsaw requires a lot of time, but this is not the case. Here is the time it took me to recondition completely a 24-in. crosscut saw, with 12 teeth per inch. The work, which was performed without haste, took only 47 minutes. Jointing and shaping required 17 minutes; setting, 8 minutes; and filing and honing, 22 minutes. If the same saw were to require only filing to renew the cutting edge, it would take no more than 12 to 15 minutes.

Take good care of your handsaws. When not in use, keep them in a tool rack that will protect them from damage. Wipe the blade frequently with a lightly oiled cloth. □

Jules Paquin, 63, is a wood patternmaker and an amateur woodworker. He lives in Laval, Quebec.

Fig. 6: Ripsaw teeth

File

60°   90°

1 in.
9 points = 8 teeth

Handle

A Set of Carving Gouges
Grind the profiles you need

by Fred J. Johnson

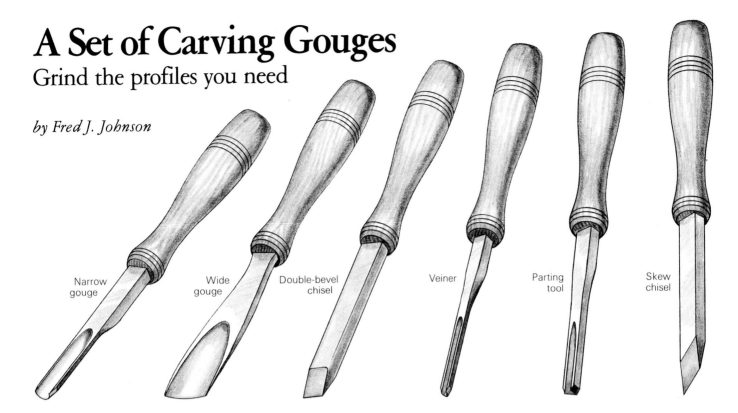

Narrow gouge   Wide gouge   Double-bevel chisel   Veiner   Parting tool   Skew chisel

About six years ago I reached that stage in my furniture making where I wanted to stop whittling and start carving. I had read and reread A. W. Marlow's *Fine Furniture for the Amateur Cabinetmaker,* and wanted to do what Marlow described. The only thing I lacked was a set of carving tools, which I couldn't afford, so I decided to make my own. Here is how I went about it.

Before starting to grind, I had to decide what tools to make. The 1974 Woodcraft catalog listed 116 different tools in their "professional" category; there are 148 now. This was confusing. So I reread Marlow again, looked at all of the pictures and sat down to design the set of tools I would need.

My gouges would have to outline scrolls and spirals with fair, sweet curves. This would require their edges to be arcs of circles. With a compass and a circle template, I laid out a series of increasingly smaller arcs spaced at regular intervals (drawing, bottom right). I had previously learned that any arc of greater diameter than 12 in. could be cut with a series of short, straight lines. I ended up with 21 diameters and decided to make 24 gouges, the extra three being narrow duplicates of the 2-in., 1-in., and ½-in. curves for removing backgrounds. These diameters refer to the cross section of the gouge at its edge, not to its width. The wide, flat gouges are often called "sweeps," the small, tight ones, "veiners." The rest of the set would consist of two *V*-shaped parting tools (one 60° and one 90°), five sizes of single-bevel chisel (¾ in., ½ in., ⅜ in., ¼ in. and ⅛ in.), two double-bevel chisels (½ in. and ⅜ in.), and a ⅜-in. skew chisel, 34 tools in all. I already had two shallow bent gouges that I had used in gunstocking. I bought enough steel for three extra blanks, so if the need for a particular shape arose, I could grind it. So far, I've found the set to be entirely adequate.

A friend who knows about metals recommended oil-hardening tool steel. It will crack and deform less with quenching and is easier to harden than some of the other choices. The only oil-hardening tool steel that we could locate in small quantities was the precision-ground stock that is sold in metalworking tool supply houses for making tools and dies. It comes in a wide variety of rectangular cross sections, in a dead soft state. I already had a ⅛-in. by 1-in. by 6-in. length of this material, so I made a gouge with a 6-in. diameter cutting edge to try out the process. It came out just fine.

I decided to go ahead. I bought a Sears grinder on sale with an extra 6-in. by ½-in. carborundum wheel and a wheel-dressing stick. The steel sold locally came in 18-in. and 36-in. bars, and since two cuts would make three blanks out of the 18-in. length, that's the size I bought—eleven bars of it. The current price would be about $10 per bar, maybe $3.50 per tool.

Shaping the steel — The procedure consists of these steps: saw the bars apart; shape the steel and grind the steel; finish-grind, file and stamp; harden and temper; clean up and maybe polish the steel; make and attach the handles; and sharpen. It's time-consuming only because there are so many tools in a set.

You need a template for each gouge. For the large sizes above 1⅜ in. in diameter, cut templates from cardboard. Save both the inside and the outside of the arc. The concave part is for checking the curvature of the wheel, and the convex part is for checking the tools. For the smaller arcs, use a draftsman's circle template like Pickett No. 1200, about

The cross sections in a set of gouges are a series of 21 circular arcs.

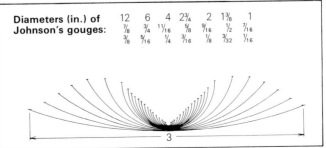

Diameters (in.) of Johnson's gouges:	12	6	4	2¾	2	1⅜	1
	⅞	¾	11⁄16	⅝	9⁄16	½	7⁄16
	⅜	5⁄16	¼	3⁄16	⅛	3⁄32	1⁄16

$1.50. Cut it apart on the center marks so that you have semi-circles. Dress a ¾-in. wide, 60-grit wheel to the required curvature for the largest diameter and after grinding, progressively re-dress the wheel to the next smallest size. Dressing a grinding wheel is like scraping on the lathe. Rest the dressing stick on the tool support and press it gently against the wheel. Keep the stick moving and check only after turning the grinder off. Resist the urge to touch the template to a spinning wheel. If the wheel seems to run forever after you turn it off, slow it down with the dressing stick. When you get to the ½-in. tools, switch to the ½-in. grinding wheel—not as much material to remove.

1: Steps in shaping a gouge

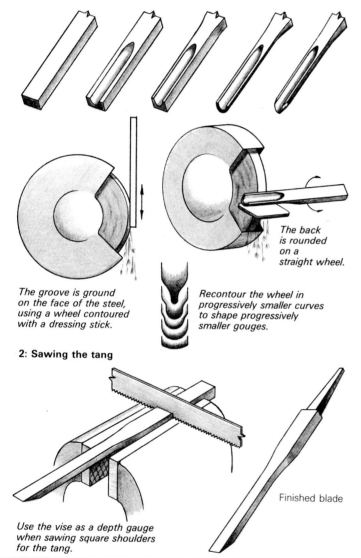

The groove is ground on the face of the steel, using a wheel contoured with a dressing stick.

The back is rounded on a straight wheel.

Recontour the wheel in progressively smaller curves to shape progressively smaller gouges.

2: Sawing the tang

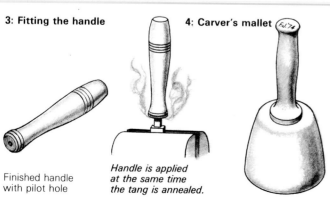

Use the vise as a depth gauge when sawing square shoulders for the tang.

Finished blade

3: Fitting the handle

Finished handle with pilot hole

4: Carver's mallet

Handle is applied at the same time the tang is annealed.

Grind the hollow of each gouge by holding the steel vertical, tang end up (figure 1). Start at the bottom and grind a shallow groove. Then lower the steel to extend the groove toward the tang. Slide the steel up and down on the wheel, keep it moving, and don't use a lot of pressure. Keep the groove centered on the steel and parallel to its sides. Narrow, deep grooves are far easier to grind than wide shallow ones.

Now you need to decide how long to make the groove. Most commercial tools are forged. It is just as easy to stamp a long groove as a short one; thus the groove usually runs almost to the tang. You can grind your tools this way, but I made the grooves of mine only about 1½ in. long for three reasons. First, it saved grinding and wheel-dressing time. Second, I will never sharpen that much steel away in my lifetime. Third, and most important, a tool is more comfortable to hold and easier to control with the left hand if its shaft is rectangular with nicely rounded corners.

After the blank is ground to the proper width and depth, check its curvature with the circle template held against the bottom end of the groove. Keep in mind the way gouges are sharpened. Most have a large bevel on the outside, a few have all of the bevel on the inside, and some are in between. The outside bevel is convex, not straight and not hollow ground. Then there is a smaller bevel on the inside, put there during sharpening. This is no accident—the double bevel makes the tool easier to control, and its edge more durable. The way each gouge is to be sharpened will determine the diameter of the groove that you grind. A fully sharpened tool with a profile of 3/16-in. diameter may start with a groove of 9/32 in.

After you grind each groove, shape the grinding wheel to the next smaller size. Contouring the wheel is easy, but messy—wear a mask to keep from breathing the dust, and vacuum it up promptly. When finished with the gouges, reshape the wheel to the angles chosen for your parting tools.

After you have put the groove in the face of each gouge, veiner and parting tool, clean them up with files. This is especially important for the parting tools if a sharp angle rather than a radius is wanted at the bottom of the groove.

Next, round off the back of each gouge to match the curve of the front. This is done by first hogging off the corners and then by rolling the blank in your hands while moving the steel back and forth across a straight wheel. Hold the gouge horizontal, 90° to the wheel, and keep it moving with a light touch. Check it often, then file everything smooth and grind each gouge to an almost finished edge. Make the straight chisels by grinding and filing their sides to the required width and thickness. Then grind the desired bevels and clean up with files. But don't make the cutting edges sharp enough to cut yourself with until the very last step.

Now the tools are ready for forming tangs. A 1½-in. tang that is 3/16 in. by ¼ in. at the base and tapers to about 1/16 in. by ⅛ in. at the tip will do. Lay out on all four sides of the steel, clamp it in the protected jaws of a vise and hacksaw to the required depth on all four sides (figure 2). This will make a square shoulder for the handle to abut. Grind the tang to the approximate dimensions on a coarse wheel and finish with a coarse file. Keep in mind when handling and clamping tool blanks that they are soft and easily scratched.

Put as much finish on the tools as your sense of fitness demands. At least, round the edges and smooth the surfaces. Rust forms more readily on a rough surface than on a smooth or polished one. I marked each of my gouges with the diam-

Johnson's tool case holds 40 carving tools. Right, piecrust table carved with them.

eter of the cutting edge, using a set of number stamps and stamping near the handle.

Hardening and tempering — Each bar of oil-hardening tool steel comes in an envelope with hardening and tempering instructions printed on it. Heat-treating specialists (look under Heat Treating—Metals in the Yellow Pages) will harden and temper this many tools for about $20, their minimum. Tell them what kind of steel you have and the hardness you want. But there is no magic to heat-treating, just temperature control, and you can do it yourself.

First heat the metal to 1,450°F to 1,500°F, then quench in hot oil (120°F to 140°F). Motor oil will do, but be ready to put a lid on the oil if it catches fire; proper quenching oil has a higher flash point. Don't let the tools get hotter than 1,500°F and don't leave them at that temperature. You can buy temperature-indicating pellets (about $3.50 for 20) or crayons (about $3.50 each) from the supplier who sold you the steel. Quench by plunging the tool straight down into the oil, then move it around, keeping it under the surface. Plunging vertically minimizes distortion. Your heat source might be a forge, an acetylene torch, a kiln or a heat-treating oven. Unless you have experience with a torch, don't heat the tools directly. Put them in a small firebrick oven or on a steel plate and heat everything, being careful not to get above 1,500°F.

Clean the oil off the tools and wire-brush them. Then temper according to the instructions that came with the steel. Most carving tools are tempered in the range of 56 to 60 on the Rockwell C-scale. I followed directions to obtain 57 Rockwell for my tools. The harder they are, the better the edge. If they are too hard, though, the edge breaks off. If they are too soft, they won't stay sharp. The instructions specify a tempering time of one hour at 400°F to get about 60 Rockwell, at 500°F for 58 Rockwell, and 550°F for 56 Rockwell. This can be done in your kitchen oven, but unless you know that its thermostat is correct, use temperature-indicating pellets or crayons. Now you can smooth, buff and polish to your heart's content.

Handles — I turned handles out of scrap oak (railroad dunnage) that was thoroughly dried. I made them 5 in. long when finished. You can make them any shape you like, and out of any wood that is strong and appeals to you. They are your tools and your hands, so experiment to find what feels good. Make some prototypes and try them out.

To mount the handles, drill a pilot hole in the wood and clamp one of the blades in a metalworking vise with all of the tang pointing up (figure 3). Heat the tang with a propane torch until it is red hot. Press the handle firmly down on the tang. Stop short of the shoulder by 1/16 in., remove the handle and let it cool. You may have to heat the tang more than once to get the handle on. When the tool is cool, clamp it firmly in the vise and drive the handle down against the shoulders. Heating the tang serves two purposes. It anneals the tang so that it is not brittle and subject to snapping off, and it fire-hardens the handle hole. To get a handle off requires quite a tug. If you ever have a handle loosen, put some plaster of Paris into the hole. That will mount the blade firmly again. I varnished one handle and found that I preferred the feel of the raw wood. Since your tools will have a reasonably well-formed edge on them, ground before they were hardened, they will be easy to sharpen.

There are really two more things to do before you can consider your toolmaking project complete. One is to make a carver's mallet (figure 4) and the other is to make a case to hold the carving tools (photo, above left). I made a case for forty tools that consists of four trays of ten compartments each, plus a cover. They are all hinged together on the back and latched on the front with small brass hooks. The sides of the trays have rabbets for 1/8-in. hardboard bottoms and slots for hardboard dividers. A handle screwed to the top finishes the case.

I discovered why carvers use round mallets the first time I tried to use a square-faced one. You don't have to look at them when you strike. A square head glances off if the angle is not just right. I turned light and heavy mallets out of oak and they seem to hold up well. The head of the mallet should curve a little from the top to the handle for the same reason that it is round. I enjoy and treasure my tools very much. They suit my carving needs and they give me a feeling of pride and satisfaction because I made them. □

Fred Johnson works as a package designer and makes furniture for his home in Long Beach, Calif.

The Drawknife
Learning to use this simple tool

by Drew Langsner

Although many woodworkers own a drawknife, I am continually surprised to learn how seldom these tools are used. Drawknives are among the most versatile handtools available to woodworkers. They are fast and easy to use for roughing out stock and for some kinds of finish work. Traditionally drawknives were needed by a wide range of skilled woodworkers. I first used one during a summer of intensive training with a Swiss cooper. Other craftsmen who once depended on drawknives include furniture makers, carpenters, turners and wheelwrights. Drawknives are perfect for dressing shingles, making tool handles, debarking poles and pointing fence posts and pickets. They're also excellent for quickly making odd-size dowels, pegs and wedges, especially from straight-grained, riven stock. There's no better tool for adding a decorative chamfer to furniture parts and even house parts.

A drawknife is a viable alternative (or addition) to machine tools for various kinds of work, especially for individual pieces or small production situations. Chairmaker John D. Alexander, Jr., for example, used to work with sawn lumber which he turned on a lathe. His book, *Make a Chair from a Tree: An Introduction to Working Green Wood* (The Taunton Press, 1978) gives good reasons for his becoming a drawknife convert. Ring-porous hardwoods can be split out quickly and shaved with a drawknife to graceful dimensions while maintaining the strong, continuous grain structure. There is also

the pleasure of working in a shop with quiet tools that run on human energy. And the waste from a drawknife is shavings, not sawdust that can cause various respiratory problems.

Old drawknives were often homemade or produced in small runs at local blacksmith shops. A good source of steel for forging a drawknife (see "Basic Blacksmithing," *FWW* #9, Winter '77) is a worn-out file or rasp. Grind off the file teeth along the drawknife cutting edge before doing any forge work.

Early tool catalogs list a wide variety of drawknives for general and specialized uses. The basic drawknife has a straight blade, 6 in. to 10 in. long, with a handle at either end, usually at right angles and in the same plane as the blade. Most often only one side of the blade is beveled, though some old drawknives have symmetrically shaped blades, beveled like a knife or an ax. Slightly dished drawknives (with a bevel on the concave face) are used for dressing flat surfaces, such as the slats of a ladderback chair. Radically curved drawknives, called inshaves, can be beveled on either side. For hollowing (as for barrel staves) or quickly reducing the thickness of a board, a bevel on the convex surface is best. A bevel on the concave face is used for finer work.

There are also variations in the angle between the handles and the blade. Coopers and wheelwrights sometimes used a drawknife with one of the handles extending straight from

Various drawknives satisfy different needs. Above, from top to bottom, straight blade is for general-purpose work. The second can be used to slice wood with the blade at an angle or, with its straight handle out, to chamfer the inside of a bucket rim. The third has a slightly curved blade with the bevel on the concave face—best for light cuts and finishing work on flat surfaces. At top right, a similar drawknife, but with round, French-style handles, takes a fine shaving. The fourth drawknife has a radically curved blade with the bevel on the convex face. This tool makes fast work of hollowing out barrel staves, removing large shavings (photo, right). Also known as an inshave, it is the drawknife equivalent of the scrub plane.

Photos: Tad Stamm

the blade, so the tool was shaped like an *L*. It could be pulled with the blade at an angle for a slicing action without the handles bumping into the bench or workpiece. Drawknives with both handles extending straight from the blade are used for work where angled handles are in the way, for example when shaving the exterior of a bowl, secured rim down on a workbench. Like spokeshaves, straight-handled drawknives are pulled or pushed, whichever is more convenient. It's harder to control a straight-handled drawknife; standard handles provide leverage for controlling the cutting angle.

I sometimes use drawknives while standing at a workbench. However, the best workmate of the drawknife, used long before screw vises were invented, is the shaving horse, an ingenious foot-operated hold-down that grips the work fast and sure. Over the centuries various shaving horses were developed. In one style, called a dumbhead, a central arm pivots in slots mortised through the bench. Jaws on either side of the head hold the work against a ledge 8 in. to 10 in. above the bench seat. The treadle can be a cross peg or a board mortised to the tenoned bottom of the swinging arm. An English shaving horse, sometimes called a bodger's bench, uses two lighter arms pivoted at the sides of the bench and connected by a top crossbar that holds the work, and a bottom crossbar that is the treadle (see "Holding the Work," *FWW* #12, Sept. '78). Like Roy Underhill (*FWW* #14, Jan. '79, p. 4) I prefer the single-arm, dumbhead horse pictured at top right.

If you've used a drawknife and been disappointed with its performance, it's probably because it was poorly shaped or dull. Many new drawknives are ground at an angle that makes them practically impossible to use. Like other edge tools, drawknives must be sharpened with care and precision. Sharpening should begin with a check of the blade bevel angle, usually 30° to 35°. Very thin drawknives, such as the Marples, work well with a 25° bevel.

The wide blade and bent handles of a drawknife require adaptations of standard sharpening procedures. Herr Kohler, the Swiss cooper I worked with, uses a small sandstone wheel whenever rough dressing is necessary. For honing, he props one handle against the work-ledge support on the shaving horse while holding the other handle in his left hand about chest height. In his right hand Kohler first lubricates with spit a small natural stone, then rubs it in circles up and down the blade. When a slight wire edge develops, he flips the knife over and whets the flat side, using the same circular motion until the wire edge disappears.

This method is slow and results in a hollow area gradually developing in the handstone. Wille Sundqvist, a Swedish woodworking instructor, teaches a method that works faster and maintains a flat whetstone. Sundqvist mounts his stone in a shallow cavity chiseled into the side of a wood block. The block is secured in a vise or with dogs and wedges on a workbench. The block's thickness keeps the drawknife handles above the bench surface when the blade is bevel down on the stone. Sundqvist begins with a coarse or medium-grit synthetic stone, depending on the condition of the edge. He holds the right end of the blade, bevel down across the far end of the stone and pulls the drawknife diagonally towards his chest and to the right, so that the left end of the blade is whetted by the end of each pass. He repeats this motion until a wire edge develops across the entire bevel. The wire edge on the flat side, Sundqvist says, should be removed using the next harder-grade stone. Usually a new wire edge forms on

Drawknife and shaving horse offer an ideal combination of direct shaping and quick, sure gripping of green stock.

Two methods of sharpening drawknives. A Swiss cooper teaches supporting the drawknife on the shaving horse, center, and rubbing a handstone first over the bevel, then over the flat face, moving it up and down the length in small circles. A Swedish woodworking instructor teaches mounting the stone in a block of wood held in a vise, above. The drawknife is drawn diagonally over the stone, toward you and toward your right, so the entire length of the blade is whetted in each stroke.

Pieces that do not fit under the shaving-horse head can be held between the end of the shaving horse, in a notch or rabbet, and a roughsawn breast bib. Note that cuts do not start on the end grain; the waste at the far end of the stick will be removed after the stick is turned end for end.

the bevel side. He turns the knife and lightly whets across the bevel. The final wire edge on the flat side should be gently removed with a soft Arkansas stone. The bevel can be dressed very lightly once again with this last stone. Throughout the procedure he's sure to maintain a flat bevel at the proper angle. Whetting a microbevel is faster but necessitates frequent regrinding or coarse-dressing. Sundqvist also emphasizes keeping the flat side perfectly flat.

Drawknives are relatively easy and safe tools to use. It's almost impossible to pull the blade into your belly, though I have seen torn pants and cut legs. Skill is a matter of practice; tuning up with this freehand tool takes time. I generally work with the bevel down. The bevel acts as a slide and fulcrum for directing the angle and depth of cut. Some woodworkers use the drawknife bevel up. Drawknives with a slight bevel on the "flat" side will work in either position. The particular job and tool used should dictate the method. Practice different cuts, from shallow plane-like shavings to rougher work, shaving to ½ in. Then try curves, concave dips and other shapes. Drawknife technique is a combination of strength with the careful control necessary for doing accurate work. With practice it's possible to shape elaborate curves, using a narrow blade and pulling slowly, but with maximum muscular exertion and control—like an isometric exercise.

Drawknives work best with straight-grained woods, especially softwoods and ring-porous hardwoods. It's possible to shave dense woods like beech or dogwood, but convoluted figure requires working back and forth from each direction. This is where quick setups with a shaving horse really pay off. Wild grain may work better with an adjustable spokeshave.

A fast technique for roughing straight-grained wood to approximate size is to start a very deep shaving, then raise the handles to split off the waste wood. To drawknife very thin strips, such as basket splits and bucket hoops, place the work on a 1x2 extension stick held under the shaving-horse head. It's even possible to dress across the end grain of softwoods. Dampen the end grain a few minutes before starting. Use a keen drawknife. Work bevel up, from a low area to a high point. Pull the knife diagonally across the grain with a side-

ways slicing action, cutting only halfway across the section.

Here's a typical procedure for shaving a 1½-in. diameter chair leg from a split piece of wood roughly 2 in. square. If possible use straight and clear-grained green oak. Grip the stick on the shaving horse with the growth rings oriented vertically; radial surfaces are easier to cut than tangential ones. The first cuts will take the stick down to 1½ in. square. Start by tilting the drawknife slightly down on the right and take a shaving off the upper right corner of the stick, so the vertical side of the stick becomes 1½ in. high. Next tilt the drawknife slightly down on the left and do the same. These two cuts will leave a slight apex on the top surface. With the drawknife level, shave this off. Now rotate the stick 90°, and tilting the drawknife first left, then right, take the two shavings that will bring the other two sides of the stick down to 1½ in. Hold the drawknife level and remove the apex on the top surface. The stick is now 1½ in. square for the half of its length close to you. Turn the stick end for end and repeat the procedure to make the whole stick 1½ in. square.

The next step is to shave the square into an octagon. Tilt the drawknife 45° to the right, then 45° to the left, to shave the corners off the square. Try to make the three planes this produces equal in width. Rotate the stick 180° and chamfer the other two corners of the square. When all eight planes are the same size, you should have a regular octagon 1½ in. across. Turn the stick end for end and repeat the procedures to make the whole stick octagonal.

Now to produce a perfectly round chair leg, it's simply a matter of taking thin shavings off the corners of the octagon, rotating it between strokes and checking it occasionally with a go/no-go gauge. It can be finished up with a spokeshave. Alternately shaving and repositioning the stick proves the value of the shaving horse; the hands can concentrate on the work while the feet quickly hold and release it. The dumbhead horse is particularly advantageous because the work can be slipped out the side to turn end for end, instead of drawing out its whole length from under the head, as is necessary with the English-style horse.

Slipping can be a problem with very green wood and hard-to-hold shapes. Check the shaving-horse head for height and jaw-angle adjustment. If slipping continues, place a small block with coarse sandpaper glued to both faces between the work and jaw of the shaving horse. Woodland craftsmen who continually shaved slick wood sometimes inserted a strip of serrated metal into the upper jaw. I've used a small rasp.

Sometimes it's necessary to drawknife a piece of wood that won't fit into the shaving-horse jaws. Or you may want to shape a flare or curve going into the grain at the end of the wood. A method developed before screw vises uses chest pressure to hold the piece against a rabbet or in a notch cut in the end of the shaving-horse work ledge. A breast bib (a small plank hung by a string around one's neck) distributes pressure and protects against accidents. Breast bibs are made from roughsawn wood; a planed surface will slip against the work.

For drawknifing large work use a conventional wood vise or a peg and wedge-holding system. A machinist's vise with wooden jaw-inserts is excellent for drawknifing irregular shapes or small work. The narrow jaws located above the workbench allow drawknifing at a variety of angles. □

Drew Langsner is director/instructor at Country Workshops, a school for traditional woodworking in Marshall, N.C.

Methods of Work

Sharpening jointer knives

Here is a jointer-knife sharpening jig that saves money, eliminates frustrating at-the-sharpening-shop delays and gives the woodworker a bit more independence. The jig, used with a drill press and cup stone, consists of a ¾-in. plywood or particle-board base and a sliding knife-holder. The holder, slotted to accept the jointer knife at the right sharpening angle, slides in an accurately sized channel in the base. Several thumbscrews, tightened in threaded holes, threaded inserts or T-nuts, lock the knife in the holder slot during grinding. (To tap wood, drill pilot holes, use a tapered tap and back the tap out often; maple and other hardwoods tap about like hard brass and hold as well.)

To use the fixture, chuck a medium-grit 1½-in. cup stone (contact Norton Co., 1 New Bond St., Worcester, Mass. 01606 for distributors) in the drill press. True the stone if necessary (I use an old masonry blade). Then clamp the base in position on the drill-press table so the knife and stone are aligned as shown in the sketch. Lower the quill until the stone barely touches the knife, lock the quill and grind the knife by sliding the holder under the stone. Lower the quill a bit and grind again. Repeat this operation until all knicks have disappeared. When the final depth is reached on the first knife, set the drill-press stop to preserve the setting for sharpening the second and third knives.

To avoid warping the knife by heating unevenly, take light cuts, move the holder smoothly and use plenty of thumb-

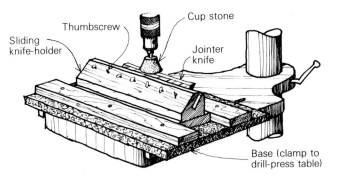

Thumbscrew / Cup stone / Sliding knife-holder / Jointer knife / Base (clamp to drill-press table)

screws to lock the knife in the holder. Long knives are especially prone to warping, so mist them or let them cool between passes. —*James E. Gier, Mesa, Ariz.*

Cleaning file teeth

A blind sharpening-shop operator showed me this simple file-cleaning tool—it works better than a file brush. Hammer flat the pointed end of a 16d or 20d nail and grind the front edge straight. Remove the head of the nail and fit into a drilled dowel handle. Now push the straight edge of the tool along the grooves of file teeth. Soon tiny teeth will form in the edge of the tool which push metal, grease and rust out of the file. Turn the tool on edge to remove stubborn particles in one or two file grooves. —*John Foote, Clarksville, Tenn.*

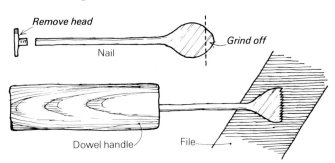

Remove head / Nail / Grind off / Dowel handle / File

Lineshaft sharpening

This inexpensive sharpening setup puts a keen edge on tools in seconds without the usual heat build-up problems of powered abrasive wheels. To construct the setup, laminate four 7-in. wheel blanks from plywood or particle board. Epoxy the blanks to shaft collars, which are set-screwed to the ½-in. lineshaft. The shaft turns in pillow blocks mounted on an oak frame. If a lathe is not available, the wheel blanks can be trued right on the lineshaft with a chisel and a temporary tool rest.

Cement emery-cloth strips (80 grit and 320 grit) to two of the wheels, lining the wheels first with burlap-backed cork (from a linoleum dealer). Cement leather to the other two

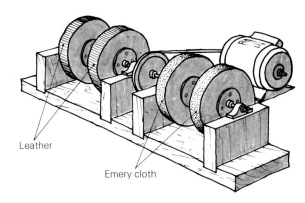

Leather / Emery cloth

wheels. Mount the leather flesh side out to one wheel and hair side out to the other. Charge the "flesh" wheel with emery, the "hair" wheel with rouge. Using rubber cement for all mountings will make replacement easier later on.

An old ¼-HP appliance motor will provide sufficient power. Size the motor and lineshaft pulleys so the wheels turn at 500 to 600 RPM up and away from the operator.

Dull tools may need treatment on all four wheels. But most tools can be sharpened on only the finer two or three wheels. —*Robert L. Koch, Tarlsio, Mo.*

Sharpening fixture

I have always had problems grinding points on tools with tapered shanks. With this simple fixture, it's easy.

To construct the fixture, drill a hole a little larger than the shank of the tool through a hardwood block. Then drill a 1-in. hole from the top, partway through. Glue a scrap of rubber inner tube to the bottom of the block to keep it from slipping about.

To use, insert a finger in the top hole to apply slight pressure against the tool shank. Rotate the tool against the grinder or belt sander with the other hand. —*Jay Wallace, Ashland, Ore.*

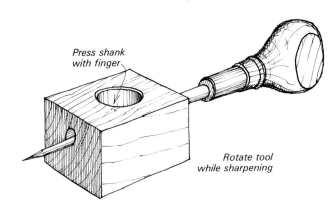

Press shank with finger / Rotate tool while sharpening

Hewing
Axwork shapes log directly

by Drew Langsner

There are three basic types of axwork: chopping, where the axman works diagonally to the grain, as in felling trees and bucking logs; splitting, where the wood is cut with the grain, as for firewood; and hewing, the most sophisticated of the three, in which the woodworker combines techniques of chopping and splitting. Hewing used to be common practice, and still has a place in the modern woodworker's repertoire. Craftsmen who traditionally hewed wood include post-and-beam carpenters, turners, furniture makers, coopers, boatbuilders, carvers of woodenware, wheelwrights and makers of tool handles and agricultural implements. Wood sculptors have also used hewing techniques to advantage. Hewing is perhaps the fastest and certainly the most direct way of bringing a log to approximate size, shape and flatness.

Axes — There are two basic types of hewing axes. Symmetrically beveled axes are shaped and sharpened on both sides of the blade. These may be similar to woodpile axes, except that the blade is usually slimmer and more perfectly maintained. Many have specially shaped handles, and there is a wide variety of ax-head patterns—the result of local traditions, different needs, and available materials. Symmetrically beveled axes permit a scooping action, good for concave cuts. They are also excellent for convex cuts, rough and complex shaping, and fine carpentry.

Broad axes (named after the massive axes used to hew timbers for buildings, railroad ties and bridges) have a bevel on only one side of the head. The other side is flat from the eye straight down to the cutting edge. These axes work like superbroad chisels, and generally are used to create smooth or moderately convex planes. The flat side allows the ax to work at a close angle, skimming the surface in a straight line.

Symmetrically beveled axes and broad axes are also available as hand hatchets—handle length, not head weight, is the determining factor here. Hatchets have shorter handles, and while they are generally lighter (1½ lb. to 2 lb.), some hewing hatchets weigh upward of 5 lb. Axes weigh from 2 lb. to 12 lb.

The evolution of axes probably reached a peak in the Middle Ages, when a wide variety of special types were made for various trades. Though industrialization resulted in the large production of a limited variety, it is still possible to find some special styles of axes in junk and antique shops.

Almost any hatchet or ax can be reshaped or sharpened for use in woodworking, but common hardware-store hatchets tend to be too thick in cross section. The short bevel necessitates chopping at a wide, unwieldy angle, and the thick head has more of a wedging effect, which means the wood is more likely to slip out of control. You can more easily slice into

Drew Langsner is director/instructor at Country Workshop, a school for traditional woodworking in Marshall, N.C.

wood at a close angle with greater precision using a hatchet of thin cross section.

Woodworkers' hatchets and axes also tend to have a longer cutting length than common camp axes. Many craftsmen prefer a shape that flares back from the eye to allow gripping close to the cutting edge, which makes the cut easier to control. An ax or hatchet with a straight cutting edge can be used on thin stock like a chair post. However, a curved edge facilitates severing the grain and is therefore easier to use for hewing wider pieces, shaping the exterior of a large bowl, for instance, or hewing a beam.

The handle of a woodsman's chopping or splitting ax is generally made as thin as possible for a slight whiplike effect and to help absorb shock. Woodlot ax handles require a smooth finish so that the user's forehand can slide freely with each swing. In hewing, the craftsman generally uses a much shorter stroke, keeping both hands in one position—a comfortable grip therefore results from a thicker handle and a rippled or whittled surface.

Handle length and shape are matters of taste. The handle on a heavy broad hatchet may be shorter than a foot, while the handle on a Japanese broad ax may exceed 4 ft. I prefer a handle that gives good leverage, but which is not awkward—about 28 in. long. The axis from eye to handle foot should be straight except in broad axes, where a single or double bend ensures the knuckles will clear the work during each swing.

Ax handles should be split from clear, straight-grained hickory, ash, birch, maple or oak. Green handles are shaped about 10% oversize, then seasoned for at least one month before fitting. Handles made from preseasoned rough blanks can be fitted to the ax eye early on, which allows testing for feel and alignment as shaping progresses.

Broad-ax handles can be bent green immediately after fashioning or after fitting to an ax head. I boil the fitted handle for a half hour, then bend it in a jig (photo facing page, bottom right) and let it set for two to four weeks. After it has cured, I touch up the handle with a knife or rasp, sand it a little, and finish with linseed oil.

Hatchet hewing — Hatchets can be used on stable massive timbers, such as in post-and-beam construction and boatbuilding, but they are generally used for much finer work that must be held in place by hand. For this kind of work, you'll need a support to prop the stock against. A waist-high hardwood stump set in the ground or on the shop floor is ideal. You can also make a small chopping block from a slice of a log and place it directly over a leg on top of your workbench, handy in shops with limited space or where hewing is only an occasional undertaking. A shallow depression on one side of the chopping surface, made with a hatchet or chain saw, keeps the wood from slipping, especially when you're hewing at an angle. The edge of the stump or slab can also be used for support. Keep the striking surface clean—dirt and grit will dull a hatchet fast.

Hatchet weight and shape and your strength and speed will determine the effectiveness of your hewing strokes. Fine hewing is easier if you hold the hatchet at an angle, thereby slicing into the wood. For delicate work I sometimes wrap thumb and index finger around the hatchet head. In hatchet work both hands are busy, as you must also pay attention to the non-hewing hand that holds the work. All axes and hatchets are easier to control in vertical strokes, so it is constantly necessary to invent ways of holding the wood.

In most cases, begin hewing a few inches above the end set against the stump. Progress upward with succeeding strokes. You can start at the upper end and work down, but there will be more risk of the wood splitting or going out of control. Hew notches and concave shapes with conventional hatchets and axes, beveled on both sides. Place the wood on the stump, end grain down, and hew toward the center of the desired shape. Work from both sides to make a *V* or *C* shape with small, easy strokes to avoid splitting. Making a sawcut down the center of a concave shape to full depth also helps prevent splitting.

Hewing a spoon blank.

Any hatchet is effective for hewing close to the grain angle. But you can chop a steep angle only with a sharp hatchet and the work well supported (hold the work over the edge of the stump), taking small shavings with each stroke.

Hewing a beam — Most areas grow at least one timber species that is suitable for log work. Some typical hewing woods include the pines, fir, spruce, redwood, tulip poplar and oak, but you can also hew other woods such as black locust or maple. Within a species, certain trees will be more suitable than others. Knots add to the work involved, and the butt section of a tree is often much tougher than wood a few feet farther up the trunk. Most projects call for relatively straight trees. In North America, logs are generally worked green, but most European craftsmen prefer to hew seasoned logs, which are less likely to check, split or warp.

Before beginning, it's important to be aware of the problems in dealing with a material as heavy as logs, which weigh green between 40 lb. and 70 lb. per cubic foot. It's often difficult to get a log moving, but when gravity takes over, the log becomes hard to stop. Always be careful when lifting or moving logs. Learn to use leg muscles, which strain less easily than the back. Make use of levers, fulcrums, block and tackle, and rollers. Large and small peaveys and cant hooks are almost indispensable. I like to lift and haul logs with a partner on the other side of a timber carrier (photo top left, p. 87). It consists of a pair of grab hooks that hang from a swivel in the center of a 4-ft. or 5-ft. pole. Each person lifts an end of the pole; the front end of the log is in the grab hooks between them, the far end is supported by a pair of wheels in a wooden truss.

Most log hewing is done with broad axes, but though they're wonderful tools, you don't need one to try hewing. In fact, some beginners find a 7-lb. to 10-lb. broad ax intimidating, awkward and backbreaking.

The broad ax that I use has a 9-lb. head with a 13-in. cutting edge. An important feature of this ax, often not understood, is that the inside face of the head is not flat. The side curves along a horizontal line, forming an arc about 3/16 in. deep. This causes the ax to cut with a slight scooping effect. Vertically, the inner face is perfectly flat from the cutting edge to the poll. Broad-ax handles vary in length from 15 in. to 30 in. For most hewing techniques, the handle must take a radical bend immediately behind the head where the lead hand is positioned. This provides the necessary clearance between the hewer's fingers and the log.

The method of hewing I use was developed by Peter Gott, an accomplished craftsman who has refined his hewing technique and style during 18 years of log-building. Many axmen hew by eye, snapping one or two chalk lines down a log, and then hewing. This can be tricky because logs taper, bend and bulge, making it difficult to eyeball a flat plane. Gott's technique, which practically guarantees good results, uses a series of accurate pencil and chalk guidelines that are all perpendicular or parallel to one another, and can be used for hewing one, two, three or four surfaces. Flat planes facilitate notch work, mortise-and-tenon joints and other detailed refinements. You can also adapt Gott's technique to carving and sculptural projects.

Begin hewing by barking the log. Some trees (such as tulip poplar) peel in large slabs, others require more work. Slash a narrow strip with an ax, then try to peel by inserting a barking

At left, hatchets (top to bottom): A symmetrically beveled Kent hatchet, characterized by a diamond-shaped flange around the eye, a well-defined poll and symmetrically flared shoulders; a German broad hatchet; a Japanese daiko ono, whose light head (less than 1 lb.) and extremely back-flared blade (you can hold the hatchet directly above the blade) make it maneuverable enough for making furniture and chopping bowl exteriors; and a reproduction of a 12th-century Viking hatchet, probably an all-purpose tool used for woodworking, butchering and self defense. Axes and hatchets are of two basic shapes. The broad ax (center photo, left) is flat on one side and ideal for smoothing plane surfaces. The symmetrically beveled ax (center right) cuts with a scooping action and is best for roughing out and for concave cuts.

Handle-bending jig (for broad axes) is made from 1-in. thick board, two C-clamps, a wooden wedge and a piece of twine. Heat the handle in boiling water, clamp the head to the board and bend the handle up, by hand, to an angle slightly more than is needed (to allow for springback). Slip the wedge between plank and handle, and tighten the twine with a winding stick to pull the handle into a reverse curve. Shape the handle to align your two hands and the ax head in a straight line.

Hewing a beam

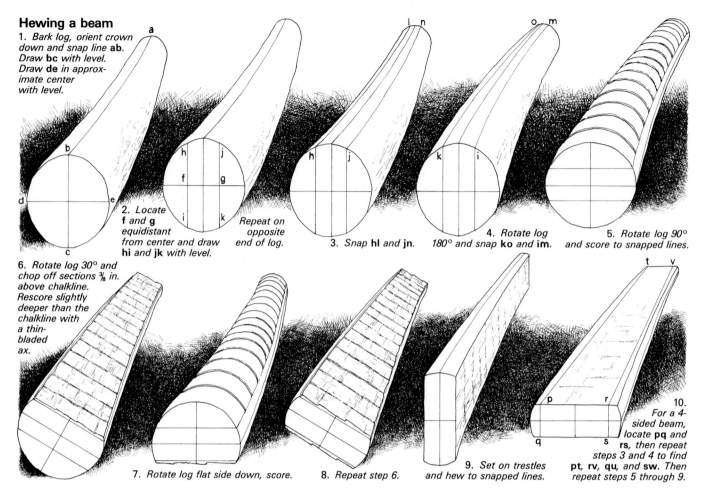

1. Bark log, orient crown down and snap line **ab**. Draw **bc** with level. Draw **de** in approximate center with level.

2. Locate **f** and **g** equidistant from center and draw **hi** and **jk** with level.

Repeat on opposite end of log.

3. Snap **hl** and **jn**.

4. Rotate log 180° and snap **ko** and **im**.

5. Rotate log 90° and score to snapped lines.

6. Rotate log 30° and chop off sections ⅜ in. above chalkline. Rescore slightly deeper than the chalkline with a thin-bladed ax.

7. Rotate log flat side down, score.

8. Repeat step 6.

9. Set on trestles and hew to snapped lines.

10. For a 4-sided beam, locate **pq** and **rs**, then repeat steps 3 and 4 to find **pt**, **rv**, **qu**, and **sw**. Then repeat steps 5 through 9.

spud or garden spade at the cambium. You can also ax off bark or use an extra-large barking drawknife.

Move the clean log onto a pair of cribs (3-ft. to 4-ft. cross logs with center notches to prevent rolling). Sight the log from each end to determine dominant swag or crown, and, with a short peavey or cant hook, rotate the log so that it is crown down. Put an awl through the loop of a chalkline and stick the point into the approximate center of one end of the log. Reel out the line and stick a second awl into the other center, pulling the string taut. A chalk line snapped on a rounded surface can easily result in a curve—avoid this by locating the angle for snapping the line with a vertically held carpenter's level. This is particularly important when working on nonlevel ground, as it's difficult to judge plumb by eye.

Draw a vertical line down the end of the log, using the level as a straightedge. Then draw a perpendicular line somewhere near the middle. Locate the edge(s) to be hewn by drawing vertical lines across the perpendicular line. (On a log to be hewn on two sides, these lines are equidistant on either side from the original vertical line.) Use your level.

When your lines are drawn, knife a small *V*-notch where they meet the side of the log. Repeat this procedure at the other end of the log. Snap new chalklines along the length of the log to locate the hewing lines, using the *V*-notches to hold the chalkline in place. Rotate the log 180° (crown up) and snap parallel hewing lines along the crown.

Rotate the log 90° so the side to be hewed faces up. Remove bulk waste by first scoring to the hewing line every 8 in. to 24 in. on center, using a symmetrically beveled ax, a handsaw or a chain saw. Then rotate the log 30° and remove the end chunk, placing the ax edge ⅜ in. to the waste side of the

chalkline and striking the poll with a mallet. Continue down the log, splitting wood off and leaving the same ⅜-in. margin above the chalkline so the broad ax, which will be used to finish the surface, will have something to bite into. After you have removed most of the waste, chop another series of vertical scoring marks slightly deeper than the chalk hewing lines with a sharp, thin-bladed ax. These cuts should be about 4 in. apart; their pattern will show slightly after hewing is finished. Deep scoring prevents fiber from tearing inward, especially around knots, and is also more attractive than rough saw kerfs. Then flip the log and repeat the entire process on the obverse face.

Set the log on a pair of trestles about 30 in. high—diameter of log, size of craftsman and personal preference dictate different trestle heights. Place the log on edge, and temporarily hold it steady with makeshift wedges placed underneath. Use the level and a vertical guideline on one end of the log to adjust for plumb. A variance of a few degrees makes hewing considerably more difficult.

One traditional way to hold a log steady on edge is with hewing dogs—iron staples with one end driven into the log and the other into the trestle or crib log. Some large logs can be wedged upright, or you can wrap a chain with a light load binder (a lever and cam device used to tighten the chain) around the log and trestle. You can also improvise excellent bracing using 1x1s cut to various lengths and secured to the log and the trestles with box nails. With this system it's possible to make any number of lightweight staples in dimensions as needed. They're virtually free and have the advantage of being mainly wood—there is little chance of dulling an edge tool. I generally begin with two staples on either side of

Photos: Tad Stamm; Illustration: Christopher Clapp

Two-person timber carrier and trolley, left, bring log to where it can be scored with a symmetrically beveled ax, hand saw or chain saw, center. Then log is rotated 30° and waste wood chopped with a symmetrically beveled ax to within ⅜ in. of the chalkline, right.

Broad ax, left and below, leaves a smooth surface in plane.

With both sides roughed out and rescored with a thin-bladed ax, log is steadied on trestles with 1x1 staples. Finish hewing can then begin.

the far end of the log, and one nailed on the opposite side from where I begin hewing. On a long wobbly log I'll set a fourth staple after I've hewn past the first trestle.

The hand grasps used in hewing are different from those used for chopping wood. The best hewing grasp consists of holding one's accustomed hand immediately behind the ax head (thumb extended forward and fingers tucked close to the handle), with the unaccustomed hand somewhere near the handle end. Rather than lean over the log, I prefer to bend both legs, keeping my right leg well forward (something like an advance position in fencing, but not as extreme). I like to stand close to the log, so that my vision is straight ahead along the hewing line. I take short and deliberate strokes.

Carefully hew down the right-hand vertical guideline on the log end, with the length of the log in front of you. Start with short, careful strokes. Hold the ax slightly askew (outward) so that you chop a shallow bevel, trying to split the upper line, but stop after about 2½ ft. Go back and hew straight down, concentrating on the area between the log and the inner side of your ax blade.

I hew about half to two-thirds through from the upper line, then move on. It's easy otherwise to break off wood along the bottom edge, or to go off plumb. Another advantage of not hewing straight through is that I'm continually hewing into waste wood, so the ax doesn't fly free, throwing me off balance or out of rhythm.

Hewing is a skill that combines muscular exertion with subtle accuracy. It's important to find a steady rhythm. Hewing through knots takes extra muscle—extra scoring across and around them minimizes excessive tearing. Sliding your

forward hand toward the middle of the ax handle results in more power. Try to remove thin shavings.

When I get to the far trestle I remove the staple and renail it at the first trestle, if one isn't already in place. I carefully hew down the vertical end, stopping often to glance down the line. (It's not visible from the hewing posture.)

In hewing two surfaces of the log, switch staples and work down the other side. Turn the log over, restaple and finish hewing. For hewing a three or four-sided beam, continue the same procedures. Chalklines for each side of the log can be taken from the original horizontal pencil line made when the log was round. Scoring the third and fourth sides is awkward, because it's necessary to see both hewn edges while sawing. If you're using a chain saw, I recommend stationing a friend on the opposite side who can signal just as the cutters approach the chalkline.

Once you develop a feel, it becomes possible to hew fairly large slabs and to move along at a steady pace. In cool weather I hew one side of a 15-ft. log 15 in. in diameter in about half an hour. Seasoned experts are considerably faster. However, the total time needed to hew two sides of the same log, from initial barking and layout to final hewing, adds up to several hours. The job should be virtually perfect, requiring no touchups with an adze or slick. □

AUTHOR'S NOTE: Woodcraft Supply Corp., 311 Montvale Ave., Woburn, Mass. 01888, sells a fairly nice Kent hatchet imported from England. Modified Kent broad hatchets are currently made by Blue Grass and True Temper, available in hardware stores. Some fine broad hatchets are being imported from Germany and Austria by Woodcraft, The Garrett Wade Co., 302 Fifth Ave., New York, N.Y. 10001, and Frog Tool Co., 541 N. Franklin St., Chicago, Ill. 60610.

Turnings Without Screw Holes
Make sectored-jaw faceplate chucks to hold the work

by E. Carroll Creitz

Traditional methods of mounting workpieces for faceplate turning leave something to be desired. Screw mounting leaves holes that must be plugged. Jam-fitting the workpiece to a recess in the faceplate requires critical fitting. Glue-and-cardboard mounting works well but the cleanup is time-consuming and irritating: The glue and paper fibers quickly ruin a sanding belt, which is costly these days. Washing off a water-soluble glue is a chore, and it raises the grain, which requires additional sanding before the finish can be applied. It seemed there had to be a better way.

The machinist's pot chuck (figure 2) appeared a likely candidate for adaptation to the wood lathe. The three jaws are sectors of a circle, and since pot chucks are usually furnished as blanks, the machinist can cut as many concentric gripping rings, of whatever diameter, as are required. Actuation is by a draw bolt in typical collet fashion: The chuck is pulled back into a tapered section, causing radial compression of the jaws. Pot chucks are not generally available for wood lathes, and they can't be made by most amateurs. But sectored jaws and the convenience of draw-bolt actuation are features worth having.

There are several ways to transmit longitudinal motion through 90°, the most practical of which is the bent lever. The evolution of a bent lever into a sectored faceplate is shown in figure 1. The chance of success in using a curved pivot point (figure 1c or 1d) seemed doubtful. So I temporarily shelved this design in favor of a bent lever whose movement would be provided by pressing a slotted disc into a dish-shaped cavity (figure 1e). The flexibility this would require could be provided by a

thin, good-quality plywood, to which could be attached a jaw ring. The chuck I thus constructed is presented in figure 3. No dimensions are shown because they are a matter of convenience rather than necessity. Note, though, that the support plate must be thick enough that the screws attaching it to the faceplate will not interfere with recessing its face. Make the outside diameter of the jaw ring about ½ in. to ¾ in. larger than the diameter of the workpiece to be gripped. The thicker the stock from which the ring is cut, that is, the larger the distance between the base and top of the jaw, the larger the travel and the less the force on the workpiece.

I started with 8/4 stock to form jaws to hold a 4¾-in. diameter workpiece. This combination permitted a jaw travel of ³⁄₁₆ in. I made the jaw ring about 1 in. wide to allow for a good solid glue joint (I used epoxy) between it and the ⅛-in. plywood, which forms the flexible member of the chuck. I centered this jaw assembly (ring and plywood disc) by first turning a flat-bottomed recess in the support plate, about ⅛ in. deep, and of a diameter slightly larger than the jaw assembly. Then, using a ¼-in. drill in the tailstock chuck, I drilled all the way through the support plate at its exact center. I unscrewed the faceplate from the headstock with the support plate still attached, inserted the jaw assembly into the recess, plywood side next to the support plate, and drilled a ¼-in. hole through the center of the plywood using the support plate as a guide. I next inserted a ¼-in. machine bolt, with washers, through both support plate and jaw assembly and tightened it to hold the jaw assembly in place.

The faceplate with its various attached parts was then returned to the lathe and the jaws turned. In the machinist's pot chuck, several concentric gripping surfaces can be used because they all move together and all exert the same force on the workpiece. Multiple gripping rings on a bent-lever chuck are not recommended because of the inverse relationship between motion and force. Accordingly, I turned only a single ring on this chuck. It is necesary to undercut the gripping ring a few degrees to form a circular dovetail of the required diameter. I then removed the jaw assembly from the support plate and remounted it in the recess with the plywood side out, so I could use the headstock index to mark for sawing the radial slots. I removed the jaw assembly and sawed the radial slots, leaving a 1⅜-in. dia. circle of solid plywood 1⅜ in. in diameter around the center hole. I deepened the recess in the support plate about ³⁄₁₆ in. at the center hole, tapering to the outside edge of the recess.

A pressure plate is needed to press the plywood disc into this dished recess, so I cut a piece of ¼-in. Baltic birch plywood to fit inside the jaw ring and turned its inside face to about the same taper as the support-plate recess. I squared the hole in its center to accept the head of a ¼-in. x 20 carriage bolt, slipped the carriage bolt through and connected it to a draw bolt (¼ in. x 20 threaded rod) using a ½-in. piece of aluminum rod, drilled and tapped. A thick nut would do. The draw bolt passes through the hollow shaft of the headstock to the outboard side, where I attached a handwheel: a brass cone and a Lucite disc. The handwheel draws the pressure plate against the jaw assembly and tightens the jaws. Because the saw kerfs limit the radial motion of the jaws, I enlarged them with a handsaw.

I turned about 25 bowls and plates using this chuck, first screwing the blank to an ordinary faceplate and turning a foot to about the diameter of

Fig. 1: Evolution of chuck designs

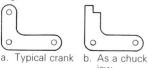

a. Typical crank b. As a chuck jaw c. Expanded to a sector d. Bead pivot e. Sector of a flexible disc

Drawings: Robert Croston

Shop-built faceplate chucks hold the work without marring it and without large waste blocks attached. On the ways are dished-action chuck, left, and bead-pivot chuck, right. Expanding dished-action chuck, mounted on the lathe, is for bracelets.

Fig. 2: Machinist's pot chuck

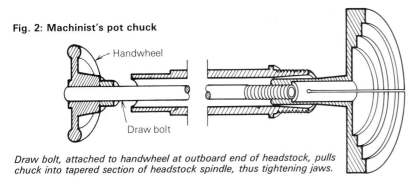

Draw bolt, attached to handwheel at outboard end of headstock, pulls chuck into tapered section of headstock spindle, thus tightening jaws.

Fig. 3: Dished-action chuck

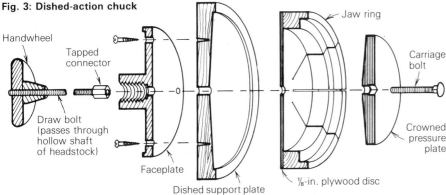

Pressure plate forces plywood disc to conform to dished surface of support plate, thus tightening jaws.

Fig. 4: Bead-pivot chuck

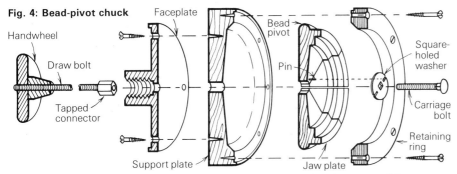

The eight separate sectors of the jaw plate pivot on a bead captured in the groove of the support-plate/retainer-ring assembly.

Fig. 5: Expanding, dished-action chuck

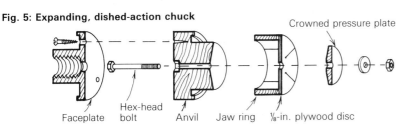

the jaws. The method was so successful that I made additional chucks for 3-in. and 6-in. workpieces. The holding power seems equal or superior to that of a screw center.

The success of the dished-action chucks prompted a return to the pivot-point type of bent-lever chuck, specifically the bead pivot (figure 1d). Thus I made the chuck shown in figure 4. Instead of the jaw ring being applied to a flexible disc and then segmented, I turned the jaw plate from one piece of hardwood, cutting a bead at the base that would pivot in a groove cut into the support plate and retainer ring. I left the bottom of the jaw-plate thick because sawing it into sectors would result in two sectors short-grained at their narrowest ends. I tried a one-piece support plate but found that a separate retainer ring alleviates tedious fitting of the jaw sectors. You can turn the jaw plate to an exact diameter, adding one saw-kerf width for the reduced diameter caused by sawing into sectors. Then the support plate can be turned, its recess dished, and the groove for the bead cut, all with the retainer ring attached. Unscrew the retainer ring and insert the jaw plate, sawn into sectors. The carriage bolt, with a square-holed washer, keeps the sectors from falling down. Pin the washer to two of the sectors to prevent it and the carriage bolt from turning.

Partly because of curiosity about how much punishment ⅛-in. ramin plywood would take, I made the expanding chuck in figure 5. I built it on a 3-in. faceplate, using a piece of 1⅞-in. thick pine as the anvil against which the pressure plate deforms the plywood and expands the jaws. I left a shoulder on the anvil to help align the workpiece. Since the end of this chuck is left exposed, a nut and washer replace the handwheel and draw bolt of my other chucks. The machine bolt to which these attach is countersunk into a hexagonal hole in the anvil to prevent its turning when the nut is tightened. I made two of these chucks in diameters of 2½ in. and 2⅝ in. and with them have turned more than 70 bracelets. The surface of the jaws of the larger of them is getting slick and will soon need pieces of sandpaper glued onto its surfaces. □

Carroll Creitz, a retired research chemist, lives in Kensington, Md.

An Improved Screw Chuck
Good engineering refines a common design

by Richard Starr

The screw chuck is a convenient way to mount work on the lathe for faceplate turning. It requires little preparation of stock, wastes little wood and the work is easy on, easy off. An avid amateur turner, Jerry Glaser of Playa del Rey, Calif. focused his engineer's eye on the screw chuck and came up with a superior device. A perfect replica of Glaser's chuck would require machinist's tools and skills, but some of its features might be used to improve existing chucks.

First, Glaser emphasizes that a faceplate chuck should screw to the spindle of the lathe rather than be secured in the tapered socket. Morse-tapered chucks are fine for work between centers but are not built to resist much radial thrust; a taper-fitted screw chuck not secured by a draw bolt is likely to wear the taper and the spindle socket, eventually resulting in a loose fit.

Next, Glaser examined the contact between the work and the faceplate. Stock is seldom faced off perfectly flat. Work with a hollowed face will sit securely against a flat faceplate, but slightly convex or uneven ends will wobble and soon become loose when held by a single, central screw. Glaser dished out his faceplate, leaving a narrow rim at its edge; this shape is more forgiving of inaccurate facing off of stock. It also gives a tighter fit since all the compression between stock and faceplate is concentrated at a maximum radial distance from the screw.

Glaser's major innovation is a specially designed screw that is cylindrical in shape with a thread whose section is almost knife-thin. A screw's holding power is directly proportional to its diameter. A tapered screw's grip is concentrated where it is thickest, getting progressively weaker toward its tip. But a cylindrical screw maintains its full diameter, and full holding power, along its entire length. For screws of the same nominal diameter, cylindrical screws hold better. Where shallow penetration is desired for delicate work, the tip of a tapered screw is almost useless.

The tapered screw might be preferable in soft woods where work can be threaded right on the screw without predrilling; some production turners, for example, fit stock on a running lathe. But in harder woods a pilot hole is necessary to avoid splitting the stock. Many turners grind a drill bit to a taper matching that of the screw in their chucks, but Glaser has to drill only a cylindrical hole the minor diameter of his screw. The very thin threads cause minimum damage to the fibers when entering the wood and have little tendency to split the work. They grip better than screws with thicker threads because they take up less room, and there is a larger volume of undamaged wood retained within the diameter of the screw. This is especially important when holding in end grain, as screw chucks usually do.

The screw holds so well that it is sometimes difficult to remove work from the chuck. Glaser recommends waxing the threads before mounting the stock. To keep the chuck from turning he inserts an allen key in the setscrew, propping the key against the tool rest. He then unscrews the stubborn work with a strap wrench improvised from some rope and a stick.

Soft metal won't do for a screw with tall, thin threads. Glaser has his cut in a steel called 17-4 P.H., which comes heat treated to 32-35 Rockwell C (the limit of machinability is about 45 RC). He suggests that it could be cut in drill rod that has been hardened and tempered to a medium straw color. It would be risky to try hardening or casehardening this delicate thread after cutting, for fear of burning its edges. A machinist can cut these threads using the same technique used for cutting acme threads. A square-ended cutter is ground with sides shaped to half the included angle of the screw, but narrower than the space between threads. While feeding the cutter at right angles to the work, a helix is cut to full depth, then subsequent cuts are made setting the tool over to the right until the crest of the thread is sharp.

The front end of the thread should have a ¼-in. lead of a diameter tapering to the core of the screw. The end of the thread is tapered with a file while turning in the lathe so the thread seems to rise in height from the core of the screw. This leading edge is sharpened with a jeweler's file. The thread is polished by brushing some lapping compound on it and screwing a block of wood on and off a few dozen times.

The shaft of the screw has a flat ground onto it as a bearing surface for the setscrew that keeps the shaft from rotating in the chuck. The tension of the screw is taken by a pin through the shaft bearing against the inner surface of the faceplate (see drawing). The screw's protrusion is controlled by adding or removing washers between the pin and the chuck. It is an absolutely secure system capable of small increments of adjustment.

One advantage of the chuck, according to its designer, is the almost perfect recentering of rechucked work it affords. This has allowed him to mount specialized wooden chucks or spuds on the lathe, confident that they will always run true. He also uses a pot chuck that is simply a block of wood with a conical socket turned into its end. The outer surface of the block is turned round and kept from splitting by wrapping it with nylon cord glued with epoxy, a quick and easy ferrule. Work is crudely whittled to fit the taper and jammed into the socket for turning.

For Glaser, the joy of using this screw chuck is its easy versatility. He has used it for turning tiny, very thin objects as well as for big jobs, like an olivewood vase 14 in. long and 8 in. in diameter, turned green. Examples of Glaser's work appear on the facing page. □

Richard Starr, of Thetford Center, Vt., is Fine Woodworking's *New England correspondent. Glaser's screw chuck will soon be commercially available from Turnmaster Corp., 11665 Coley River Circle, Fountain Valley, Calif. 92708.*

Fig. 1: Improved screw chuck

Add or remove washers to adjust screw protrusion

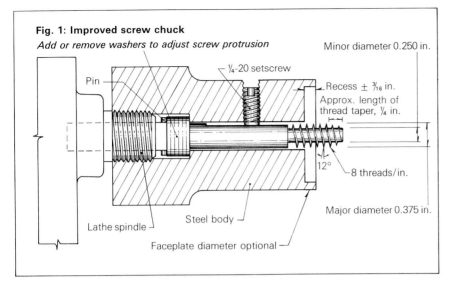

Minor diameter 0.250 in.

¼-20 setscrew

Pin

Recess ± ³/₁₆ in.

Approx. length of thread taper, ¼ in.

12°

8 threads/in.

Lathe spindle

Steel body

Faceplate diameter optional

Major diameter 0.375 in.

Sharp, wide threads of Glaser's adjustable-depth screw chuck secure work with minimal penetration of stock. Optional screw pockets supplement holding power for turning large blanks.

With wooden pot chuck, left, screw chuck can turn the tiniest of goblets. Alone it grips larger stock for vibration-free turning along the full length of mallet, right. Mushroom boxes with putumuju tops, below, evidence more of the versatility and precision possible.

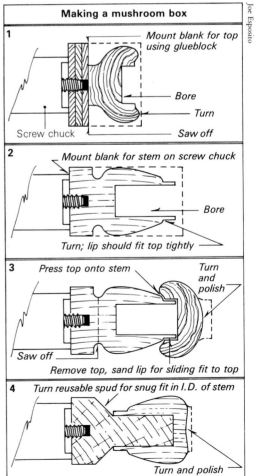

Making a mushroom box

1 Mount blank for top using glueblock

Bore

Turn

Saw off

Screw chuck

2 Mount blank for stem on screw chuck

Bore

Turn; lip should fit top tightly

3 Press top onto stem

Turn and polish

Saw off

Remove top, sand lip for sliding fit to top

4 Turn reusable spud for snug fit in I.D. of stem

Turn and polish

Joe Esposito

The Dial Indicator

by R. Bruce Hoadley

An indispensable tool in our shop is a dial indicator with a magnetic base. Although this tool is usually associated with metalworking, we routinely use it for a host of jobs, from aligning equipment and setting up cutterheads to precise measuring of wood samples and deflection in joints.

The dial indicator works by coupling a plunger-type spindle through internal gearing to a sweep hand. When the instrument is held firmly in position, any slight in-and-out movement of the spindle results in greatly magnified movement of the hand around the dial. The spindle is lightly spring-loaded so its tip will follow variations in the surface it contacts, and it can be fitted with a variety of contact points for special situations. Our instrument has a full inch of spindle travel, and its dial is graduated in units of 0.001 in. Indicators are made with greater accuracy, but the trade-off is a smaller measuring range.

The indicator comes with a universal-jointed arm that holds it in virtually any position relative to its magnetic base, which can be demagnetized by the push of a button. When the button is "off," the base retains only a whisper of magnetism, just enough so it will rest snugly against a steel surface. Once in position, the magnet is turned "on," whereupon it locks with about 50 lb. of force.

When the base is locked to a drill-press table and the indicator positioned perpendicular to the quill, the trueness of quill rotation can be measured. Similarly, measuring against the shank of a drill will reveal whether the chuck is centered. Out-of-round, out-of-center and bent shafts and mandrels of all kinds can be checked this way. By setting the base on the outfeed table of a jointer, the height of each knife can be gauged, and measuring across to the infeed table will tell whether the two tables are parallel. A hand-plane iron could be set in the same way. The indicator is invaluable in setting the bedrolls, outfeed roll and pressure bar of a thickness planer. On a table saw, the indicator will measure tooth height as well as set. Of course, the machinery must be electrically disconnected and revolved by hand. Never attempt to gauge cutting edges at operating speeds.

By setting up on a flat surface such as a saw or jointer table, the indicator becomes a comparator-type of measuring device. It will check the diameters and roundness of dowel pins, or the thickness of veneers. The magnetic base also has angled surfaces which will lock against a cylindrical shaft, and because of its weight the base will set firmly against a flat wooden surface as well. By laying an accurate metal bar across a large flat surface, the surface can be "scanned" to gauge overall flatness and locate irregularities. The base holder by itself also has many uses around the shop. Locked to the saw table, it makes a convenient end-stop for crosscutting multiple pieces. I often use it to position an air hose or to hold excess electric cord out of the way.

Dial indicators are quite similar among reliable brands, although a variety of backs are available for mounting to different holding devices. A good indicator costs between $40 and $80, and a magnetic base is about $40. ☐

The dial indicator easily measures minute variations—here, it is set up for checking chuck concentricity on a drill press. With the dial's spindle bearing against the quill, it will measure bearing runout. Setting it against the shank of a bit will tell whether the bit is centered or bent.

The dial indicator can also gauge surface flatness—here, it checks the height of a jointer knife. Revolving the cutterhead by hand will tell whether all the knives are cutting the same circle. Moving the indicator across a knife will show whether it is parallel from end to end. The spindle can also be extended to the infeed table to check if infeed table and outfeed table are parallel.

Photos: Bruce Hoadley

Making Your Own Machines
Learn what you need to know, then experiment

by Giles Gilson

From the author's sketchbook: a drawing-board sander.

If you need a machine you can't afford or are frustrated by back ordering, poor design or malfunction caused by poor quality control, you should consider building the machine yourself. It will test your creativity, ingenuity and ability to scrounge. It will require time and possibly study, but the result can be a machine custom-built to meet your needs.

Don't be discouraged by someone else's reservations. A good way to start is first to find out what you need to know, second, to get that information and third, to practice applying it. Machines are generally simple. They have a basic function and accessories that support that function. Most woodworking machines simply rotate a cutting tool into the work. Different structures control the speed or orientation of the cutter; hold, move or guide the work; protect the operator; and generally hold the whole thing together. By studying its separate parts, you can uncover a machine's principles.

I have built a number of machines and modified several more; these illustrate what experimentation and makeshift applications can yield. Combining performance, accuracy, safety and convenience is a creative task. If your materials are properly chosen and your construction is sound, your home-built machine can be better than a store-bought one.

In design work, decisions are most easily made through drawings. Some people prefer a detailed technical drawing in which most of the problems can be worked out; others draw only enough to establish reference points or to determine shapes. It is not necessary to use conventional symbols or elaborate instruments. If you plan to show your drawing to designers or suppliers, however, you must be sure they understand your terminology. The basic tool is the standard foot ruler, with which several scale sizes can be read directly; at ¼ size, for example, 3 in. = 1 ft., and ¹⁄₁₆ in. = ¼ in. You'll also need a compass, a 30°-60° triangle, and a protractor. The edges of precut paper are usually square and can be used as references from which to measure.

It may help to make a model in conjunction with the drawing. This is educational and entertaining, and when you get frustrated, you can smash it. Models help you visualize. They point out problems that may not show on the drawing, so there are fewer bugs to be worked out of the final product.

Average auto-maintenance tools will do in most cases. In addition, you should have a set of taps and dies, calipers, some metal snips, spare hacksaw blades, a dial indicator and a surface gauge. For operations that you are not equipped to handle, you can either get the tools as you need them, rent them or farm out that part of the work.

One advantage the woodworker has is that some of his machines need not be as rigid as those used for metal; therefore machine bodies and stands can be made of non-ferrous materials. Wood, including plywood and composition board, is convenient; aluminum and fiberglass might work in some applications. A new material, used in conjunction with fiber-

glass and under development by General Electric Co., has almost the strength of steel, but can be worked with carbide cutters. It is a single-component epoxy called Arnox, which can be bought in sheets, tubes or rods. I have bandsawn and lathe-turned sample pieces, and it has possibilities for many machine parts, including shafts, gears, plates and pulleys. If you work with this material, cut it at slow to moderate speed and feed rates, and use a good dust collector. (For more information contact G.E.'s Plastics Division, Arnox-resin Operation, 1 Plastics Ave., Pittsfield, Mass. 01201.)

One of my favorite materials for models and light-duty machinery structures is MD-44. It is produced by Masonite Corp. and comes in the same sizes as plywood, but is cheaper. It has about the same strength as fir ply, has a smooth finish and holds a clean edge when machined. It can be sculpted, but because the surfaces are tempered, it may chip a little near the faces. If you paint MD-44 or laminate it with plastic or sheet metal, you must do both faces to prevent warping.

Don't get locked into buying only new parts and materials. Wood and composition boards are often in the shop as leftovers from jobs. Metal can be obtained in small quantities and odd shapes from scrapyards. Machine parts can be found in scrapyards and repair shops, or adapted from other applications. An inventory of hardware should be kept in categories: nuts and bolts, handwheels, pulleys and belts. These can be collected over a period of time the same way you collect wood. You do not have to seal and sticker hardware; it is usually dry.

Some design considerations are evident right away, and some may not be. Often convenience to the operator is overlooked. Avoid putting adjustment controls underneath or behind the machine where they are awkward and dangerous to reach for. On some machines, there is no choice, but if there is an alternative, use the most convenient location. This also applies to accessory storage. How often have you had to use a machine whose table was too low or too high? In general, tables, lathe spindles (not ways) and the like should be the same height as your elbows. Make tables large enough for the work you plan to do, or provide for extensions.

Versatility is important as long as it does not require too much time to change from one mode to another and does not compromise performance. Adjustments should be fast and easy. Movable parts should be clamped with devices that are quickly released without additional tools.

When designing a machine, be aware of industry standards. Find out what sizes and methods are most commonly used for attachments. If you are building a disc sander and want to buy the backing disc instead of making it, what size is its centerhole? How is it fastened? These things determine shaft size. If you are building a lathe, what is the most com-

Giles Gilson, a designer/sculptor, lives in Schenectady, N.Y.

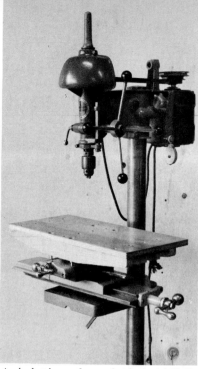

Band-saw accessories, left, include plywood cover latched with Volkswagen convertible-roof holddown and blade guide from roller bearings, angle iron, nuts and bolts. Right, cross-slide and compound-angle jig cannibalized from metal lathe are mounted on drill press.

mon spindle thread for faceplates? Machinery catalogs usually mention spindle diameters, thread pitches, belt sizes, etc.

The choice of bearings is important. Think about how the workloads will be distributed from the shaft through the bearings to the structure of the machine. Which way will the work push against the spindle? What pressure is the drive belt putting on the shaft? What is the maximum speed? Consider the environment of the machine. What kind of foreign material will be present? Normal sawing produces fine chips as well as dust, turning produces curls and dust, and sanding produces abrasive grit and dust. What will these substances do to machinery?

Oil-impregnated bronze (oilite) inserts are made as a single piece and called sleeves, or as two halves usually called clamshells. They are good for many applications, and also inexpensive and quiet. However, they should be used only on precision-ground shafts and often must be align-bored or reamed to size after installation. This can be done by a machine shop if you do not have the facilities.

Anti-friction bearings are generally noisier than sliding types. They are more efficient, however, and sometimes require much less power to run. The most common type of anti-friction bearing is a ball bearing. These withstand sideloading well. Needle or roller bearings are simply a series of cylindrical rollers that replace the balls in a bearing. They sometimes use the shaft as an inner race, and often have no retainer, which means the rollers must be individually placed between the shaft and the outer race. This type of bearing is used where thickness is a problem. A variation on the ball and needle bearing is the thrust bearing, used to handle pressure along the centerline of a shaft. An example is the guide wheel behind the blade on most bandsaws. Thrust bearings use balls, tapered rollers arranged radially, or are simply a Babbitt bearing or bronze shoulder.

Tapered roller bearings handle both axial thrust and side loads. They are quiet, but require preloading. This means they must have a specified amount of pressure holding them in place. A shoulder or snap ring supports one race while the

adjustable support for the other is set to apply the preload and locked in place. The most common method of installing bearings designed for a press fit is to freeze the shaft and heat the bearing in oil to about 200°—do not heat the bearing directly. Refer to "Basic Machine Maintenance," *(FWW # 13, Nov. '78)*, which shows what the bearings look like and how to handle them, and how to align pulleys and shafts.

For mounting bearings, a pillow block is convenient. A self-aligning pillow block with a sealed ball bearing is shown in the center photo on the facing page. The grease fitting in the housing allows lubrication without having to take things apart. The advantage of a self-aligning pillow block is that if the block can't be mounted exactly perpendicular to the shaft, the bearing will line up properly anyway. The outside of the bearing fits inside a spherical casing, allowing the bearing to be oriented to the shaft even if the block is not. Pillow blocks are made with almost any kind of bearing. You must specify rigid or self-aligning, and bearing type. Bearing distributors and their catalogs are helpful. Check the Yellow Pages under "Bearings."

The best operating speed for most cutting tools has been established and can be found in owner's manuals, from manufacturers, repair shops or in reference books. There are cases, though, where experimentation will show that higher or lower speeds are more effective. Variable speed may be important. A pair of step pulleys can allow three or four speeds and, if necessary, a jack shaft can be added to increase the speed choices.

To find the pulley or gear sizes needed to attain a desired spindle RPM, you must know the motor speed. This is most often either 1725 or 3450 RPM. Divide the higher speed by the lower—this gives the ratio. Then use a pair of pulleys whose diameters establish this ratio. For example, if the motor speed is 1725 RPM and the desired spindle speed is 431 RPM, $1725 \div 431 = 4.0023$, or for practical purposes, 4. The ratio is 4:1. One pulley diameter must be four times the other. Since the spindle is to turn more slowly than the motor, the smaller pulley goes on the motor. Usually the speeds need not be exact. If you want 1200 RPM and it's easy to get 1050 RPM, 1050 RPM will probably do. Many gadgets and accessories have maximum speed ratings. Don't exceed them.

Bear in mind that *V*-belts will not bend around very small pulleys. If your calculations call for a small pulley, either find a belt that will make the bend, or enlarge both pulleys.

You will have to decide how to fasten the parts of your contraption. Welding is strong and can save space, if you are equipped to do it or can have it done, but it is difficult to disassemble welded parts. Be sure to allow for changes you may want to make later. Rivets do the same thing as nuts and bolts, but also require special equipment and are difficult to remove. They do not vibrate loose though, and look better. Pop rivets are good for some applications because they are easy to use and readily available.

Threaded fasteners are the most common choice for assembly of parts. They are sturdy and they allow disassembly. They could be inconvenient, however, if used to hold often-moved accessories. Loosening nuts and bolts to remove a guard or change a sanding belt takes time. If a threaded fastener is needed, some convenience can be added by using handwheels, knobs or thumbscrews. Handwheels may be purchased, but they are easily made by burying a nut between two or three layers of plywood, then turning, using the nut (or a bolt threaded into it) as the center. A handwheel should be large enough for leverage and feel comfortable to hold. If the finish is too slick...well, you'll see.

Nonthreaded quick-release fasteners are excellent for holding accessories, but be sure they are strong enough for the application. Latches, buckles, lever and cam devices and Dzus fasteners are listed in industrial hardware catalogs, usually with their measurements and sometimes a technical drawing of their parts. An ideal application for these is guards for band saws and belt sanders, where quick removal can facilitate blade and belt changes. Lever-and-cam clamps are good for holding fences, trunnions, belt tensioners and stops. Dzus fasteners, a form of bayonet plug used primarily in the aircraft industry, hold sheet metal in place. A dime or quarter fits into the slotted, round head to release them. If you use them, keep your pockets full of change. Spring-loaded clamps serve well as depth gauges, such as the ones found on drill presses, and movable stops along fences. Refined adjustments could be built into stops with an added miniature fence and thumbscrew arrangement.

Don't neglect safety. Keep in mind that the structure of the machine must be able to withstand heavy impact, vibration and misuse. Think about what could happen if the cutter or blade suddenly flew off and hit someone. This becomes more important as the speeds get higher. Consult machine designers or mechanical engineers who are familiar with the type of machine you are building, especially if you are not certain the material will hold up.

Remember such things as inherent movement in materials. Wood shrinks and swells; bolts through wood may come loose. Check all materials for faults. Round sharp edges and corners—brackets sticking out or sheet-metal edges can easily cut you. Moving parts like to be covered whenever possible.

No vibration should be transmitted to the machine operator. If there is vibration caused by a malfunctioning part, it should be repaired or replaced. Vibration inherent in the machine can be damped with rubber mounting devices, or where applicable by counterbalancing. Noise should also be kept to a minimum. One way is to construct with wood, which will dampen sound, unless it is a thin panel walling a hollow. Cover resonating panels with sound-deadening material, or fix them with stiffeners.

Most of the time, you can use standard electrical parts. National and local codes show procedures and required precautions. Be certain to use wiring and parts that are rated for the current that the motor calls for. The open-frame motor shown below at right was used for experimental purposes only and has since been changed to a totally enclosed fan-cooled motor in accordance with national electrical codes.

Switches and connections should be mounted in containers, usually metal conduit boxes designed for this purpose. These should be enclosed to keep out dust and chips. Wood is an insulator, so extra shockproofing is an added feature of a wooden machine.

A drawing-board sander — Now let's look at an example of a homebuilt machine. I call this sander "drawing board" because with its table tilted, that's what it looks like. I designed it for light to medium duty, but made allowances for changes to heavier components. I had two functions in mind: light spindle-sanding and foamback-disc and drum finish-sanding. (For more on foamback sanding, see "Turning Spalted Wood," *FWW* #11, Summer '78.) In the spindle-sanding mode, the motorhead and table can be tilted separately for beveling, or as a unit for comfort. The machine has two speeds, 2000 RPM for spindle-sanding and 550 RPM for finishing. I used both modes to make the sculpted boxes shown at the top of the next page, first the spindle to shape and sand the inside walls, then the disc to finish the outside contours to 320 grit.

I did the rough design in my spare time by sketching ideas and forming a basic concept of the major parts. I made re-

The drawing-board sander in spindle mode, left. The table, of aluminum-laminated MD-44, measures 24 in. by 24 in., and is 48 in. high when not tilted. The base consists of 2x6s covered with plywood, and the trunnions, fixed in position by tightening the four-pronged handwheel, are birch ply. Center, the table is removed, the large birch-ply handwheel loosened and the spindle positioned horizontally to receive foam-backed discs or drums. Self-aligning pillow blocks bear the shaft. Right, the ⅓-HP motor fitted with pulleys yields 2000 RPM and 550 RPM at the spindle.

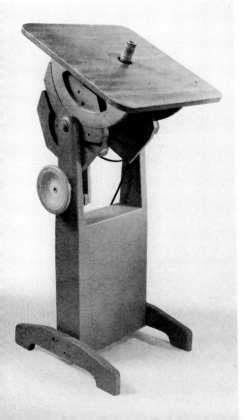

Left to right, boxes finished on the drawing-board sander: 'Geyser of Light,' 13½ in. by 9 in. by 5 in., birch ply, lauan, curly maple, East Indian rosewood; 'Antigravity Box #1: Dumping Karo Syrup on the Enemy,' 14½ in. by 13 in. by 7½ in., padauk, walnut, maple, lucite; and two views of 'Big Brother and Little Joe,' 20 in. by 13 in. by 4½ in., walnut, figured maple, rosewood.

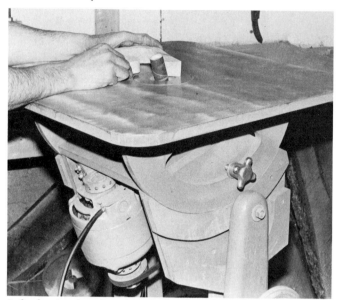 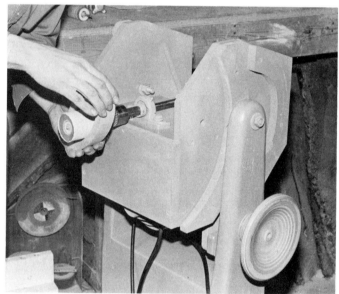

Left, drawing-board sander spindle tilts independently of table. Right, foam-backed drum finishes the inside of a piece.

finements during construction. Because it was necessary to find certain reference points, I made a more technical drawing at the workbench. Lines that didn't provide measurements I sketched freehand to save time. I built the motorhead and table without a preliminary model, although I made a mockup of the base. This proved valuable because it demonstrated where the machine would be unstable, showed some clearance problems and indicated just how comfortable the machine would be at the planned height.

The base is made of 2x6s with plywood covers rabbeted into the fame. The motorhead and table are made from MD-44 with gussets for rigidity. The trunnions are solid birch ply because it will wear well where the parts slide. The table top is aluminum laminated to the MD-44 and finished with a low-speed sanding disc, 320 grit. The large handwheel for the motorhead clamp is made from birch plywood scraps that were on their way to the woodstove. I used self-aligning, ball-bearing pillow blocks simply because they were easiest.

A homebuilt machine is often a prototype, especially if it incorporates new ideas, and therefore will have to be "field tested" to find out what the necessary improvements are. The drawing-board sander is in this stage now. I'm compiling notes evaluating the tool for durability and actual usefulness. Already there is a need for a taller spindle. This will require heavier mountings, which can be installed because of the allowances I made earlier. The machine serves its original pur-

pose well, but it can be changed to do more.

A valuable test is to have people experienced with similar machinery use and evaluate it. (Be sure they know it is experimental and that you know it is safe to use.) Others will spot things you might overlook. You may not want to bother making a change because you've already done a lot of work, and have become used to the tool the way it is—"it does the job," and "that can be done later." But will it? If you're taking the trouble to build a machine, why not build the best? □

Further Reading

Fundamentals of Tool Design, American Society of Tool and Manufacturing Engineers, Prentice-Hall, Englewood, N.J., 1962, $21.95. Principles and techniques of tool design: cutters, dies, jigs and fixtures. I recommend it because the better you understand what the cutter is doing, the better you can design the machine to power it.

Mechanical Design of Machines, Siegel, Maleev and Hartman, Int'l. Textbook Co., Scranton, Pa., 1965 (out of print). Highly technical. Has charts on shaft loading and describes forces on machine members.

Mechanical Engineering Design, Joseph E. Shigley, McGraw-Hill, New York, 1963, $25.50. Starts with fundamentals, and though it becomes very technical, is easy to follow. Includes drawings of welded joints and a fine section on bearings.

Pictorial Handbook of Technical Devices, Otto B. Schwarz and Paul Grafstein, Chemical Publishing Co., New York, 1971, $12.50. Valuable technical drawings of mechanical devices used in machinery; also includes structures, industrial processes and electrical parts.

Shaper Cutters and Fences
For accuracy and flexibility, make your own

by Earl J. Beck

My machine woodworking efforts started in 1934 with making a shaper from two old auto brake drums, using a plan from *Popular Science*. I have for 19 years been using variations of my own design of a single-cutter shaper collar, using mostly freehand-ground cutters, with great success, speed and safety. I got to grinding the cutters in a curious way. I was fortunate in finding a number of old cabinet planes, some of which were molding planes. I wanted to use the nice shape in one of these, but did not want to limit myself to a straight or slightly convex edge, so I ground my first cutter to match the plane iron. When I returned to the plane for the straight cuts, the grain proved difficult and the plane badly tore out the wood. As the shaper cutter didn't, I finished the job with it. I like my collection of beautiful old hand tools, but I love that shaper.

The shaper has many advantages over other tools to do the same work. Now if you enjoy pushing a carving chisel through a complex, knotty, ornery piece of wood for hours on end, fine. I like to do that myself once in a while. But more important to me is the rapid, precise contouring of wood to produce parts that fit together without a lot of hand-finishing, allowing me all the time I want for hand-detailing and removing all traces of machine work. I use a band saw, jointer and shaper, and of these only the shaper is indispensable.

Shaper and router cutters — While the shaper is my tool of choice, there are applications for the portable high-speed router for which I have been unable to adapt a shaper. So I will precede my discussion of shaper cutters with a discussion of router cutters—many of the principles are the same.

A router may be the best choice where the workpiece is large and awkward. It may also be the only machine alternative for the shaping of compound-curved stock—the contouring, for instance, of fancy chair frames that would otherwise be handcarved. To reduce handwork in making a double-wide copy of a French Provincial chair, I made a cutter for the router like the one in figure 1. I could have ground a standard cutter to shape, but I chose to braze a tungsten-carbide metal-cutting chip to a ¼-in. aircraft-quality bolt, rounding the hex head in a lathe (you could also do this by hand-grinding) and slotting it to receive the chip. The important thing with a single-edged cutter (the only type most of us want to fool with, in the absence of sophisticated precision grinders) is to have the dummy side—used only for balance—short enough that it doesn't tear up what the sharp cutter side does. So place the chip slightly off-center and sharpen the slightly longer side. Once when I did not have a large enough chip, I placed a smaller chip more than a little off-center, with no obvious disadvantage or vibration.

Being able to fashion your own cutter gives you the option of producing the same contour in different ways. A conventional ogee cutter looks like the one at *A* in figure 2. The same shape can be produced by *B*, with the advantage that the tool marks are in line with the grain and consequently easier to remove.

While there is no great point in using carbide steel rather than high-speed metal-cutting steel unless you plan to use your cutters continually on abrasive wood or you desire a permanent cutting edge, the carbide can be brazed and heated with impunity (MAPP torches are satisfactory), as overheating does not anneal them. Carbides are inherently hard and unlike tool steels do not depend on quench-hardening. Also, carbide tool bits come in shapes and sizes about right for the job, and don't require extensive sawing or grinding. If you decide to silver-solder tool steels (brazing will probably be too hot), you'll find either *T* or *M*-series high-speed steels will be harder than necessary for wood cutting. If available, the higher numbers in the *M*-series—*M15* or *M33*—will be least susceptible to annealing during silver-soldering.

If you choose carbide, you'll need a silicon-carbide grind-

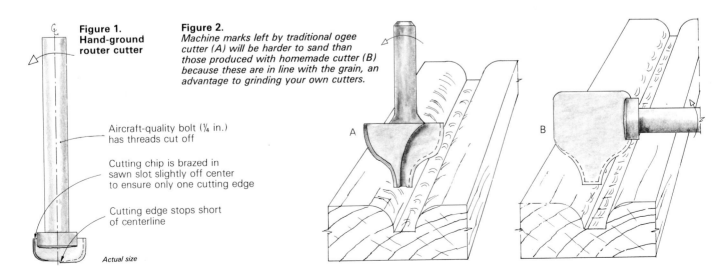

**Figure 1.
Hand-ground
router cutter**

Figure 2.
Machine marks left by traditional ogee cutter (A) will be harder to sand than those produced with homemade cutter (B) because these are in line with the grain, an advantage to grinding your own cutters.

Aircraft-quality bolt (¼ in.) has threads cut off

Cutting chip is brazed in sawn slot slightly off center to ensure only one cutting edge

Cutting edge stops short of centerline

Actual size

A

B

ing wheel; aluminum-oxide grinding wheels are too soft. You can use the soft, green silicon-carbide recommended for this purpose, but I prefer a harder, vitrified wheel made for lapidary. The vitrified wheel is more likely to overheat and while that won't harm a brazed chip, it might melt the silver solder. It is my impression in freehand grinding, where the cutter is not rigidly held, that the vitrified wheel produces a slightly sharper edge.

Tool geometry and sharpening — I have two single-cutter shaper collar systems (figure 3)—to attempt to grind multiple cutters is impractical as it's difficult (if not impossible) to grind two or more cutters to exactly the same shape. The system A cutter consists of two collars separated by a post, which balances the cutter sandwiched opposite it. System B consists of a small cutter held in a slot in a solid-steel disc with an allen screw. For cutters up to about ⅝ in. wide at the cutting edge, system B is my method of choice. The small cutters are heat-treated easily with a small torch, and easily annealed for reshaping. The disc may be any useful size—for small cuts I have had success with a disc 1½ in. to 2 in. in diameter. An advantage of system B is that the holding disc usually doesn't interfere with the wood guide (discussed later), which may then fit closely and all but totally shield the cutter.

Through grinding cutters I attempt to achieve a wood surface that may be sanded easily, has no trace of casehardening (burnishing of the surface), and minimum or no tear-out. This combination is probably impossible, which is why production woodworking involves so much sanding. If you examine all but the finest of new furniture, you'll see that sanding frequently has been substituted for high-speed machining, giving the finished piece a buttery, rounded appearance with excessive radii on corners. Woodworkers who try to speed things up with an abrasive flap wheel know the effect.

For every wood, moisture content, machine and speed there is an optimum combination of rake (cutting) and relief

**Figure 3.
Two single-cutter
shaper systems**

Specialized cutters
for system B

Small dovetail
cutter

Small radius
cutter

Allen screw

System A

System B

(clearance) angles, as shown in figure 4. The desirability of, and in production work the need for, a definite rake angle is a persuasive argument for the shaper instead of the router. The rake angles of the router cutters I have seen to vary all over the place—as do their cutting capabilities. All seem to depend on the machine's high speed to compensate for a lack of attention to detail.

Over the cutting length of a shaper knife from top to bottom, the radius (r_1 and r_2 in figure 4) varies significantly, and thus so do the cutting and relief angles. On straight blades such as used in jointers and planers, you can grind a small second bevel on the face of the knives for a smaller cutting angle. This back-beveling gives more of a scraping than a lifting action, and virtually eliminates tear-out (see *Fine Woodworking*, Nov. '79, p. 34). This tactic is not viable for shaper

Figure 4.
Cutting angle (α) is measured between the face of the blade and the radius of the cutting circle (r). As r_1 changes to r_2 along the contour of the blade, so does α change. The only way the cutting angle can be equalized is by grinding a back bevel on the face of the blade, not practical for contoured blades. Relief angle (β) is measured between the tangent to the cutting circle and the ground bevel. This angle also changes as the radius changes, but it can be equalized by honing a land or burnishing the edge on the bevel at and near r_2.

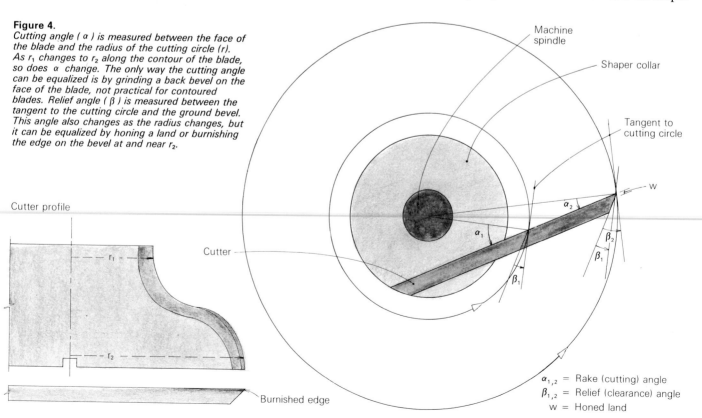

Cutter profile

r_1

r_2

Burnished edge

Machine spindle

Shaper collar

Tangent to cutting circle

w

Cutter

α_2

α_1

β_2

β_1

β_1

$\alpha_{1,2}$ = Rake (cutting) angle
$\beta_{1,2}$ = Relief (clearance) angle
w = Honed land

blades, which are contoured, and so for optimum results you must make an adjustment of another sort: Relieve the extreme edge at and near r_2. Grind initially to the correct angle at r_1 in one pass, then grind a small land, w, at the outer edge of r_2, at the same angle. As an alternative, you could burnish the leading edge of the cutter at the largest radius (as when finishing the edges of hand scrapers), but only if the cutter is not too hard. For a fully hardened cutter, hone the end to produce a land of width w.

The small land on the cutter (which can form through wear as well as by grinding) suppresses tear-out by forcing down the wood fibers just behind the sharp cutting edge. The trade-off, however, is zones that are casehardened. These zones may not be visible, but they are all too apparent during finishing, when they cause the stain to blotch. How casehardening occurs is exaggerated for illustration in figure 5, where both the width of the land, and the travel of the workpiece while the cutter is in the cut are much too large for the real world. However, the depth of cut, another variable that influences the finished surface, is pictured in the detail typically. To achieve the best cut with minimal tear-out and casehardening, try a combination of shallow cuts, slow feed and a slight land on the cutter.

The criteria by which a skilled amateur or small-shop professional judges cutter performance are probably quite different from the criteria used in a high-speed mill producing planed, structural lumber. For one thing, softwood lumber is usually planed wet, and it is the after-dry appearance that the customer observes. Casehardening is irrelevant in structural lumber since the wood will not be stained, and may even be preferred for the smooth, slick finish it imparts. On the other hand, the small-shop woodworker generally seeks two types of surfaces—one to be glued and the other to be finished. If you're gluing, precision is all-important in obtaining the best possible fit. Despite some reports to the contrary, I believe roughing up the surface first with sandpaper gives a better glue bond. Now suppose you have a jointer with an optimum cutting edge. The trailing edge of the cutting bevel causes casehardening. Because the wood is kneaded, however slightly, sanding is difficult and in some woods almost impossible. For gluing, it's usually better to accept a little tear-out, which will disappear under clamping pressure.

The more important type of machined surface for most of us is the one that is shaped, sanded and finished. My idea of a good surface is one from which I am able to remove the cutter marks with a pass or two of medium-grit (say, 100) sandpaper. Again, in this case, a bit of tear-out would be preferable to a bit of casehardening. If the shaped surface is to be painted rather than finished with a clear stain, however, I would opt for a bit of casehardening.

To avoid excessive hand-finishing, I keep cutting edges sharp, with a slight burr and no excessive fine honing. This is a good reason for using high-speed steel cutters instead of tungsten carbide—my tests show that even with the greatest care, grinding tungsten carbide leaves little if any burr.

The shaper and its basic tooling — Just why does the shaper work better than the router, where it can be used? First, the shaper has a larger radius of cut, important in a surface to be sanded. The router partly compensates for this with its high speed, but unless its cutter is very sharp, not enough. Second, the shaper cutter can be honed with a rough stone or ground on a medium-grade aluminum-oxide wheel to produce a slightly torn finish, which is optimum. Third, except for certain unfortunate types of cuts—usually a result of poor cutter design—the shaper is safe. Figure 6 (next page) shows what I believe to be an important feature of shaper use—you can submerge the cuts, and the workpiece being machined protects you from flying debris. That the work, if it leaves the table, moves away, rather than toward the cutter, and thus is less easily ruined, is a bonus.

I use a spindle shaper with a ½-in. diameter shaft. These

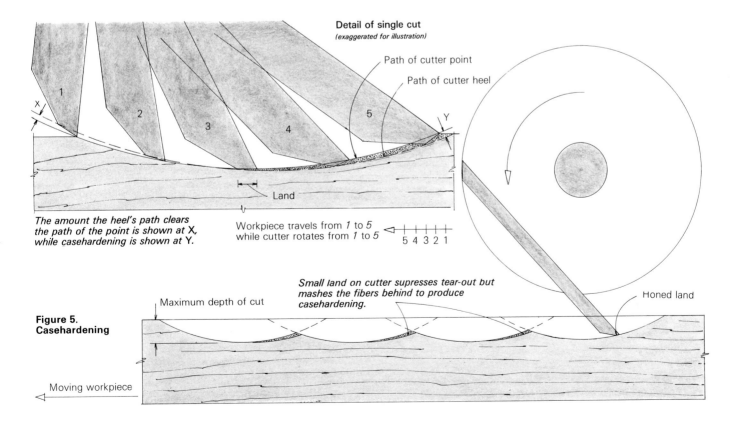

Detail of single cut
(exaggerated for illustration)

Path of cutter point

Path of cutter heel

1 2 3 4 5

X Y

Land

The amount the heel's path clears the path of the point is shown at X, while casehardening is shown at Y.

Workpiece travels from *1* to *5* while cutter rotates from *1* to *5*   5 4 3 2 1

Honed land

Small land on cutter supresses tear-out but mashes the fibers behind to produce casehardening.

Maximum depth of cut

**Figure 5.
Casehardening**

Moving workpiece

**Figure 6.
Submerged cut**

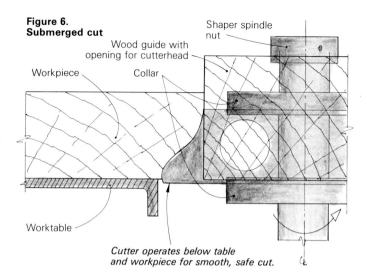

Shaper spindle nut

Wood guide with opening for cutterhead

Workpiece

Collar

Worktable

*Cutter operates below table
and workpiece for smooth, safe cut.*

machines are usually belt-driven by a motor mounted below the table. Some models have direct-drive motors, but these lack flexibility and I don't recommend them. They're also unduly noisy because of the high speed they must achieve. A good shaper should have a fairly heavy table (I prefer ground cast iron) at a comfortable height, with hold-down-bolt holes, an adjustable bearing carrier to elevate and lower the cutter, and well-made auxiliary components (such as spanner nuts and spacers).

I built my ½-in. spindle shaper, and anyone could duplicate it for about $1,500, using local foundries and machine shops. A logical adaptation might be made with low-cost conversion parts for a ½-in. drill press. Don't do it: The only thing I know of that is more dangerous is the myriad of cutoff items that accumulate on shop floors. If you want a good, nice-looking shaper and don't want to make one, buy Sears' model 2392N (97 lb.) at $209.95. Buy a few cutters, but mostly grind your own. They'll be sharper and work better.

If you're planning to buy a shaper, try to buy it without the fence, at lesser cost—I have a nice factory-built adjustable

fence that I simply never use, preferring instead the wooden work guide shown in figure 7. The guide is fashioned from a piece of scrap wood about ¾ in. thick, with an opening for the cutter. When I want to renew the working edge and know so a day or two in advance, I glue a strip of hardwood to the old edge, leaving a space above the surface of the table for chip clearance.

I also like to use another technique for submerged cuts—especially simple with system *B*, but usually practical in any case with a little trimming of the hardwood strip. I clamp the guide down lightly, with the cutter inside, and then move the guide in while running the machine, to allow the cutter to cut its own opening, a little oversize. I relieve the second edge with a skew chisel to provide good entry without hang-up. For vertical clearance, I place two scraps of thin cardboard under the guide after the cut is made, and run the guide into the cutter again. If I can't use a submerged cut because of cutter design or the nature of the cut, and am going to make a lot of cuts, then I build a guard that completely covers the cutter. In this case it is important to shape the guard so chips can be carried away from the work. Chips that circulate around the cutterhead can cause small but noticeable depressions in the finished surface. Even in the open-topped fence, a chip ramp is a good idea.

I regulate the depth of the cut with a cam adjuster attached to the work guide; it requires minimum (for me) tooling and is ideal. As discussed earlier in this article, tear-out and casehardening can be minimized by making a series of light cuts rather than one heavy cut. The cam adjuster facilitates this by allowing incrementally fine cuts without having to stop the machine or reposition the workpiece. In use, you place the fence over the hold-down bolts through the appropriate holes (there is a choice, allowing gross adjustment) and roughly set the depth of cut, shifting the fence in the hold-down-bolt slot. Set the hold-down knobs loosely and move the cam lever to fine-tune the depth of cut. This care is justified only for finished surfaces; for glue joints only accu-

Figure 7. Adjustable wooden work guide

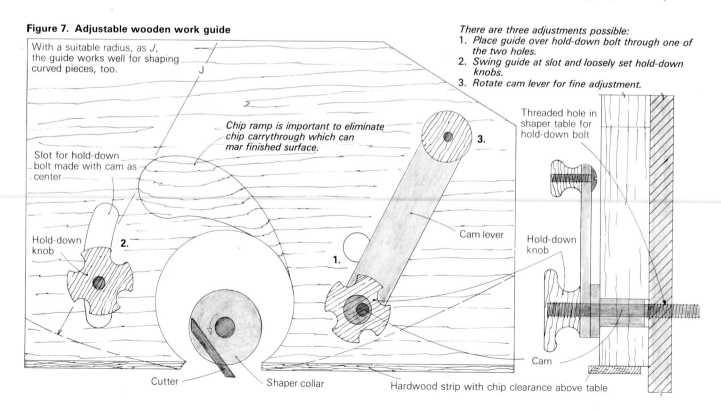

With a suitable radius, as *J*, the guide works well for shaping curved pieces, too.

J

Chip ramp is important to eliminate chip carrythrough which can mar finished surface.

Slot for hold-down bolt made with cam as center

Hold-down knob

2.

1.

Cutter

Shaper collar

There are three adjustments possible:
1. *Place guide over hold-down bolt through one of the two holes.*
2. *Swing guide at slot and loosely set hold-down knobs.*
3. *Rotate cam lever for fine adjustment.*

Threaded hole in shaper table for hold-down bolt

3.

Cam lever

Hold-down knob

Cam

Hardwood strip with chip clearance above table

Figure 8.
Metal guide for concave cuts can be mounted below the cutter, as shown here, or on spacer blocks above the cutter.

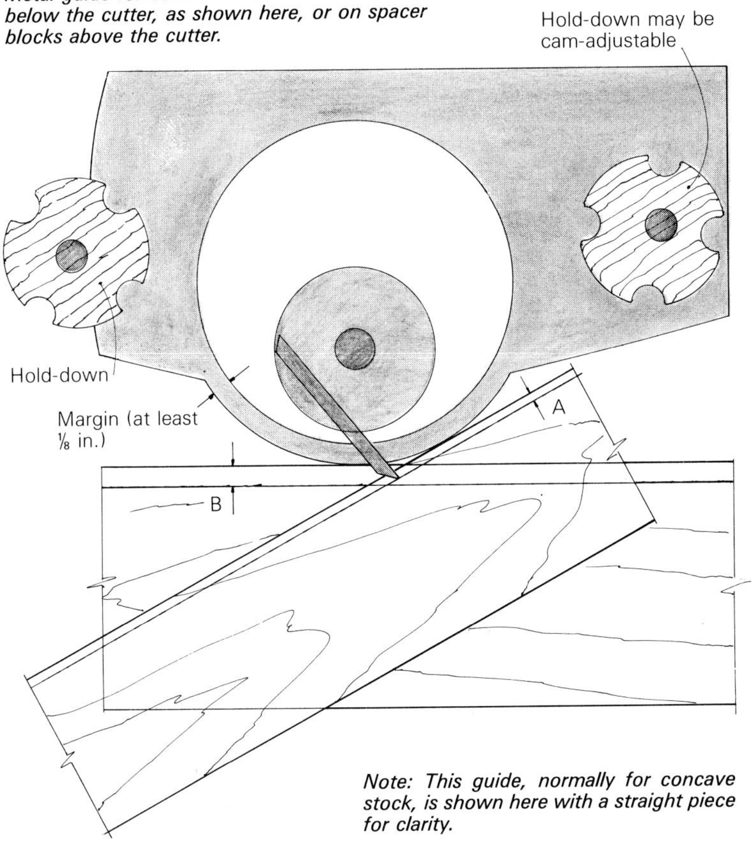

Hold-down may be cam-adjustable

Hold-down

Margin (at least ⅛ in.)

A

B

Note: This guide, normally for concave stock, is shown here with a straight piece for clarity.

Figure 9.
Contour guide

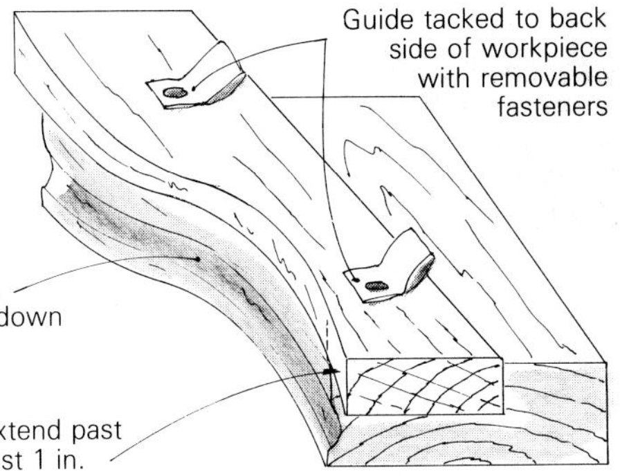

Guide tacked to back side of workpiece with removable fasteners

Workpiece, finish side down

Guide to extend past work at least 1 in.

Figure 10.
Three-sided guide-carriage

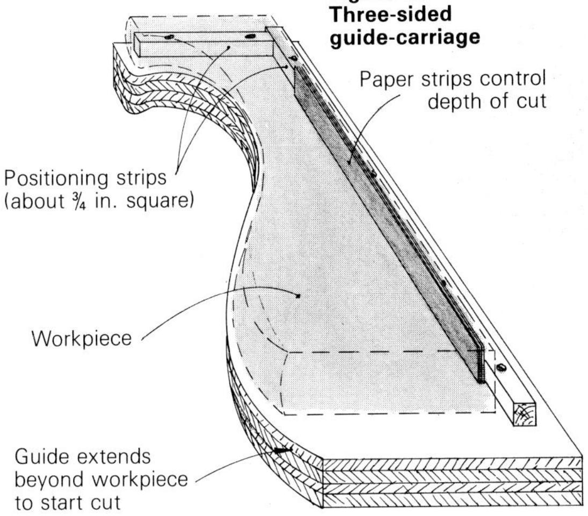

Paper strips control depth of cut

Positioning strips (about ¾ in. square)

Workpiece

Guide extends beyond workpiece to start cut

---

racy is necessary, and in other cases, say, for tongue-and-groove joints, heavy cuts are usually adequate.

More shaper guides — The straight guide is the safest, most accurate and simplest way to ensure a near-perfect cut in a shaper. Unfortunately, it is useful only for straight or convex work. Where molding of concave stock is desired, it is standard practice to run the work past the cutter, holding it either against a ball-bearing rubbing collar attached to the cutter or a steel rubbing collar inset in a well in the table opening (see "Furniture from Photographs," *Fine Woodworking*, July '79). In either case, the cut is started by holding the work against a hold-down stud to avoid having the cutter toss the work back at you—a tricky and dangerous maneuver. There is no rapid, simple way to adjust depth of cut in either of these two methods, and the inset collar tends to interfere with the positioning of the cutter.

The guide shown in figure 8 can be positioned either above the cutter using spacer blocks or bolted to the table and adjusted with the hold-down, cam, or both. It is a useful alternative to the guides discussed above: It provides friction without the rubbing post, a nuisance on certain pieces with small radii, and you can control the depth of cut—change it without turning off the shaper or adjusting the guide—by changing the angle at which the workpiece approaches the cutter. The first shallow cuts, as at *A* in figure 8, are made with the work tangent to the guide at a point to the right or left of center. Final cuts, as at *B*, are made with the work tangent to the center point.

All three types of guides do share certain problems, however. Unless the work is held in a shaped guide that has a surface elevator built in, as in figure 10, you may need a plywood surface elevator. Also, if a template is attached to the workpiece in order to get a precise shape, it's usually necessary to make the pattern slightly different from the shape of the finished piece because the cutting radius and ball-bearing or insert radius are not the same, as anyone with experience in router control using rubbing collars knows.

You can make the concave-cut guide in figure 8 on a metal or wood lathe of aluminum (⅛ in. to ¼ in. thick) or on a metal lathe of steel (⅛ in. thick)—the size of the opening is irrelevant. You could also cut the guide on a drill press using a fly cutter. In any case, for durability it is best to leave a margin around the hole at least ⅛ in. wide.

Where only one side of a workpiece is to be shaped, you can tack a guide to the back side of the workpiece, as in figure 9. Make sure you carefully cut and sand the guide, as imperfections there will be transferred to the work. The guide should be at least 1 in. longer than the workpiece, in order to enter and leave the cut under full control, with the workpiece held at the correct distance. The workpiece should be sawn about 1/16 in. oversize on the edge to be shaped. Make the guide of any material, depending on the number of times it is to be used—pine for short runs, metal for long runs. I find it useful to keep on hand a supply of pine and hardwood planed to about 5/16 in. I never throw a guide away, although occasionally I get in a hurry and rework one.

Figure 10 shows an alternative to tacking the guide piece to the work. In this case the part to be formed had both faces finished, so I made a three-sided carrier to hold the workpiece. Because I had not developed the cam adjuster at the time, I used paper strips to adjust the depth of cut. □

Earl Beck, of Ventura, Calif., is a semi-retired research engineer and lifelong woodworker who generally builds rather than buys his tools.

101

Building a Walking-Beam Saw
Poor man's band saw has almost unlimited capacity

by Mark White

A walking-beam saw uses two parallel arms or beams, and a thin sawblade tensioned between them. The arms can be made of either wood or metal, and they pivot on pins or bearings. A twisted piece of line or a turnbuckle is used to tension the blade, which moves up and down, powered by either a treadle or a motor via a flywheel and crank.

The saw works like a band saw with two notable exceptions. First, since the cutting action is reciprocal, it is neither as smooth nor as continuous as that of a band saw. Second, since the walking-beam saw has only a single section of blade to worry about, it can be used to crosscut stock of almost infinite length. A band saw's width of cut is limited by the diameter of its wheels, but its length of cut is virtually unlimited. The length of cut a walking-beam saw can make is limited primarily by the length of its arms and by the configuration of its supporting members. While a circular saw is generally better for ripping long boards, the walking-beam saw can be used for ripping long stock by mounting the blade at a 90° angle to the arms and adopting a fairly short stroke.

The major advantage of the walking-beam saw is the fact that it can be easily and inexpensively constructed by the average home craftsman. However, it will do some things that the band saw cannot. It can cut an inside hole in a large piece of material, such as through mortises in the legs of a heavy trestle table. It can cut substances such as meat, bone, asbestos board, and metal—things that usually require extensive cleanup or which gum up the works or strip teeth from a band saw. Blades for the walking-beam saw are cheap and easily replaced with little or no adjustment necessary for different widths. The saw can be constructed in various sizes. While a band saw with wheels much bigger than 14 in. is usually quite expensive, a walking-beam saw with 8-ft. or 10-ft. arms will cost only slightly more than one with 3-ft. arms.

The prospective use of the saw will dictate its relative size and the rigidity of its frame. The saw (figures 1 and 2) was designed for trim work and for the precision cutting of boat frames and small parts. It has arms that measure about 3 ft. from the central pivot bearing to the sawblade bearing. When the width of the supporting frame is taken into account, useful throat depth is about 33 in.—enough for most

Fig. 1: *Using his walking-beam saw, White cuts through an 8-in. hardwood block. The saw is well suited for contour cutting, crosscutting and ripping both thick and thin stock, but long rippings require special attachments for the arms. Drive mechanism with ⅙-HP motor produces 144 cutting strokes per minute.*

Bill of materials (all dimensions in inches)
Arms—2 pcs., 2x4x54
Upright supports—2 pcs., 2x8x38
Block between uprights—2x8x6
Table supports—2 pcs., 2x6x48
Legs—4 pcs., 2x3x40
Side rails—2 pcs., 2x3x56
Cross rails—2 pcs., 2x3x32
Main bearing support (near crank)—1 pc., 3x4x41
Table—1 pc. of plywood, approx. 1¼ thick by 23 sq.
Main drive pulley—2 pcs., ½x24x24 ACX or CDX plywood; 1 pc., ⅜x24x24 ACX or CDX plywood
Pivot pins—2 pcs. 1-in. rod, approx. 7½ long, cold-rolled steel
Crank—1 pc., 1-in. cold-rolled steel rod from 18 to 20 in. long
Counterbalance—1 pc., ¼x2x6 steel flatbar
Blades—any dimension and style desired, suggest pruning-saw blades, 20 in. between pins to start
Turnbuckle—⅜ in., min. opening 6 in., max. opening 10 in.
Blade brackets and tensioner supports—approx. 50 in. of ¼ or ⅛x1 steel
1—⅜-in. steel clevis or shackle
Bracket and tensioner bearings—approx. 10 in. of ⅛ or ¼ brass pipe
Leg bolts—16 ea. ⁵⁄₁₆x3½ carriage bolts with washers and nuts
Crank and drive bearings—3 or 4 1-in. pillow-block bearings with zirc fittings
Drive motor—⅓ to 2-HP motor with 2-in. or 3-in. pulley
Misc. nuts, bolts, washers, screws and nails to hold motor, brackets and pieces in place—best determined at construction, rather than from a prescribed list.

Photos: Mark White; Illustrations: Ric Lopez

work. As a general rule, the arms should be about 6 in. longer than the anticipated maximum length of cut.

The arms—Once the arm length has been determined, lay out and construct a set of arms. Straight-grained ash, cherry, and basswood are good choices; they're tough, hard, stable and fairly light for their strength. The top arm is essentially an idler, which tensions and aligns the top of the blade. The bottom, driving arm has a heavier forward section to take the strain of the up-and-down motion imparted by the eccentric drive. A hole, bored a few inches back from the blade, receives the bearing for the drive crank (figure 3).

As with most reciprocating saws, the part of the stroke that does the most work is that part that draws the workpiece toward the table as it cuts. But there is a considerable difference between a cheap saw with a blade that moves merely up and down, and one on which the blade moves into the cut and backs off on the return stroke. The difference can amount to as much as a threefold increase in cutting efficiency and tooth life. One of the features that gives the walking-beam saw its efficiency is the fact that this automatic blade advancement can be easily built into the machine during construction simply by making the forward part of the top arm a little longer than the bottom arm. The parallel arms will then move the blade away from the cut on the up stroke and into the cut on the down stroke (figure 4).

On a saw with a blade length of 20 in., I would make the top arm about ¾ in. longer than the bottom arm. Thus, the distance between the arm pivot and blade bearing hole is 34 in. on the bottom arm and 34¾ in. on the top arm. A small saw with a 6-in. blade should probably have the top arm a scant ³⁄₁₆ in. to ¼ in. longer than the bottom arm. As a result of the relatively short stroke of the blade and the elasticity of the parts, the actual forward/backward motion of the blade is probably less than half of the difference built into the arms. Nevertheless, this difference will add considerably to the saw's cutting efficiency.

Wood/metal bearings—While all of the bearings in the walking-beam saw could have been commercial roller bearings, I went with wood/metal on seven out of ten of them to save time and money. The main pivot bearings for the arms were fashioned from pieces of 1-in. steel rod about 7½ in. long. I bored test holes in a scrap of koa, the wood I used for the arms, with a number of different bits to make sure the hole would be snug. The blade bearing, tensioner bearings and one arm-drive bearing were fashioned from 2-in. lengths of ⅛-in. brass pipe. The blade holders and tensioner brackets I made from ¼-in. by 1-in. mild steel flatbar, as shown in figure 5 on the next page.

Assembly of the arms and frames—The metal bearings that were to run in wood were cleaned up with a file and polished with fine sandpaper. The tensioner supports and blade holders were assembled permanently on the arms. A bit of grease in each hole ensured initial lubrication. Oil holes (¼ in.) drilled before assembly make lubrication easy.

I fitted the arms with a blade and set them in a trial position on a piece of 2x8 stock in order to get an idea of placement for the pivot pins. I tried to get the arms parallel to each

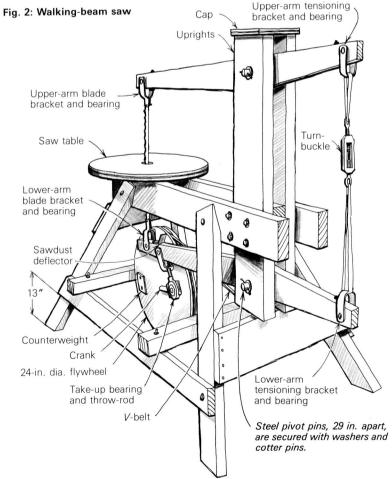

Fig. 2: Walking-beam saw

Cap
Uprights
Upper-arm tensioning bracket and bearing
Upper-arm blade bracket and bearing
Saw table
Turn-buckle
Lower-arm blade bracket and bearing
Sawdust deflector
13"
Counterweight
Crank
24-in. dia. flywheel
Take-up bearing and throw-rod
V-belt
Lower-arm tensioning bracket and bearing

Steel pivot pins, 29 in. apart, are secured with washers and cotter pins.

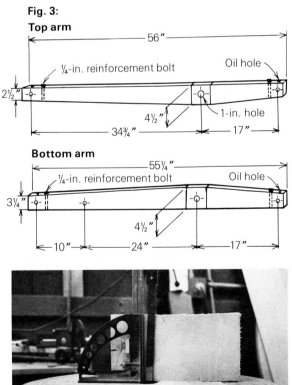

Fig. 3:

Top arm

56"
¼-in. reinforcement bolt
Oil hole
2½"
4½"
1-in. hole
34¾"
17"

Bottom arm

55¼"
¼-in. reinforcement bolt
Oil hole
3¼"
4½"
10"
24"
17"

Fig. 4: Since top arm is longer than bottom arm by ¾ in., blade angles into cut on downstroke and away from cut on upstroke, increasing cutting efficiency and blade life.

Fig. 5:
Top blade bracket

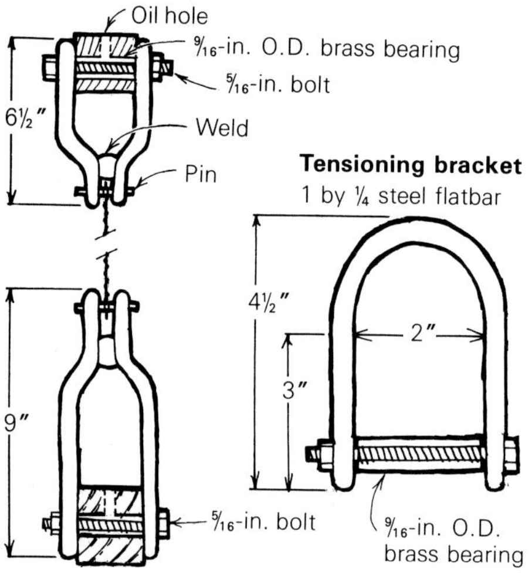

Oil hole
⁹⁄₁₆-in. O.D. brass bearing
⁵⁄₁₆-in. bolt
6½″
Weld
Pin
Tensioning bracket
1 by ¼ steel flatbar
4½″
2″
3″
9″
⁵⁄₁₆-in. bolt
⁹⁄₁₆-in. O.D. brass bearing

Bottom blade bracket

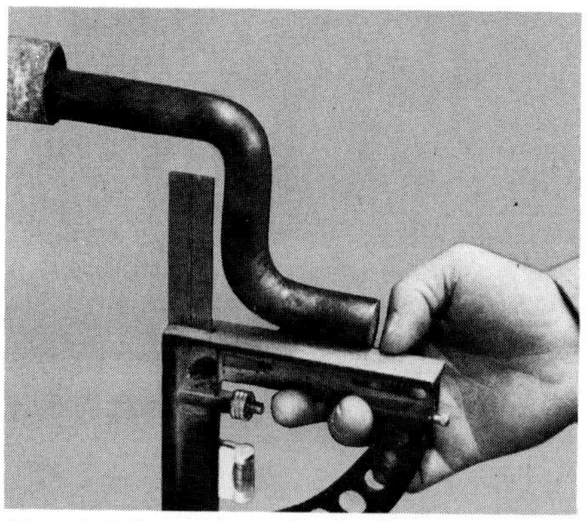

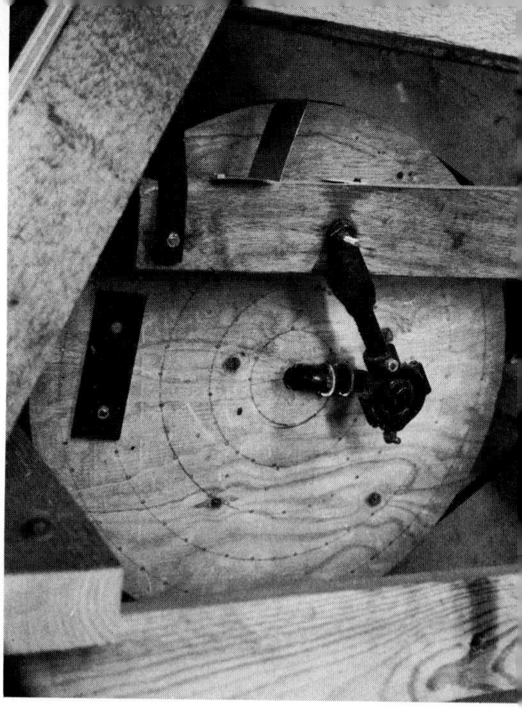

Fig. 6 (above): Crank rod is checked for squareness after being heated cherry red and bent into shape. Fig. 7 (right): Crank, takeup bearing, throw-rod and U-shaped coupling connect flywheel to lower arm of saw. Metal plate bolted to flywheel opposite crank acts as counterbalance.

other—and then spread the turnbuckle ends an extra ½ in. to allow for bearing wear and blade stretch. I noted the vertical distance between pivot pins and cut two pieces of 2x8 plank to serve as upright supports for the arms. These I cut about 12 in. longer than the pin-to-pin distance. They were clamped together and bored for the pivot pins on a drill press to ensure proper alignment. I cut a small block ⅛ in. thicker than the arm, and glued and nailed it in place between the uprights where they would be bolted to the two table-support members, which I cut from 2x6 stock. They were glued and lightly nailed in place on the upright. Then the whole assembly was bolted together with four ⅜-in. threaded rods. The pivot pins were lightly greased and inserted into the assembly, securing the arms (rocking beams) in position.

The assembly was held upright while four 2-in. by 3-in. legs were attached to the table support members. The joining cheeks of the legs were beveled at 15°, splayed to the front and rear and attached with nails, bolts and glue. After leveling the unit, I attached braces and stretchers to stabilize the legs and to support the motor and drive system.

The drive crank—I took my 20-in. piece of 1-in. steel rod over to the local auto shop to use their cutting torch. The section of rod was heated cherry red about 7 in. from one end and inserted into two sections of pipe to bend it to a perfect 90° angle. A friend applied more heat as the metal was being stretched to prevent cracking. After cooling, a section about 4 in. past the first bend was heated cherry red and bent away from the first to complete the crank (figure 6).

The wooden flywheel—The next task was to make a belt-driven flywheel to turn the crank. My power source was an ancient electric washing-machine motor of ⅙ HP. I assumed that it turned at a standard 1,725 RPM. As large a flywheel as practical would give the poor little drive motor a hefty mechanical advantage. I formed the wheel from three plywood discs, the two outer ones of ½-in. plywood scribed to a 24-in. circle and the inner one of ⅜-in. plywood scribed to a 23⅝-in. circle. Then I bored a 1-in. hole in the center of each disc, spread glue over the mating surfaces of the discs and used the 1-in shaft to align them while I nailed them together, evenly spacing the nails on concentric lines for balance.

The crank was fastened to the completed flywheel with two *U*-bolts fashioned from ¼-in. threaded rod. It took about 40 minutes of wedging, bolt tightening and loosening, and fiddling to get the wheel to run true. Once it did, I smeared a lot of epoxy into the cracks and crevices. This seemed to help hold it in alignment, as it continues to run true.

The two pillow-block bearings were installed on the shaft, and support members were added to carry the shaft and motor. The flywheel was mounted so that the throw from the crank was properly aligned beneath the lower arm. I fastened a 1-in. takeup bearing to a short section of ½-in. steel pipe and pinned it in place with a small ⁵⁄₁₆-in. bolt (figure 7).

Adjusting the stroke—With the blade tightened and the arms braced at the upper limit of their stroke, I raised the crank to its upper limit also. On the lower arm I temporarily bolted into place a *U*-shaped piece of ¼-in. by 1-in. flatbar and set the takeup bearing (crank bearing) and pipe throw-rod in place. The pipe was then cut to a length that bridged the gap between the bearing and the *U*-shaped bracket. Then I welded the throw-rod into position at both ends.

Installing the motor—The completed throw-rod was mounted on the crank and bolted into the lower arm. I turned the flywheel by hand and moved the arms up and down to continue the motion. I bolted a piece of ¼-in. by 2-in. steel flatbar about 4 in. long to the wheel to counterbalance the rotating weight of the crank. A 2-in. pulley was mounted on the motor, which was bolted to a ¾-in. plywood base. Part of the bracket and the crank-rod bearing had to be dismantled to install the *V*-belt. This done, the motor was drawn tight against the belt, and I temporarily nailed the base down. With the motor running and the large pulley spinning, I used a small turning gouge to put a mild bevel on the insides of the flywheel pulley groove. Then I repositioned the motor in order to draw the belt up tight.

I let the saw run for a couple of hours while the pieces wore together. A periodic shot of heavy gear oil on the rubbing surfaces and in the oil holes helped considerably. I tacked small flaps of leather over the holes to keep out dirt and grit.

The table—I made the table from a piece of 1¼-in. plywood flooring, screwing it in place on the frame, square with the sides of the blade. I fastened two butt hinges to one side of the frame and to the table. If I need to cut stock at an angle, I remove the mounting screws and pivot the table until the desired angle is achieved. Wedges and a small turnbuckle can be used to hold the table in place. A larger table can be fastened to the existing table for cutting large stock.

Tuning—I had to make sure that the blade ran true on its up-and-down course (viewed from the front). Turning the flywheel slowly by hand revealed that the blade had some side-to-side movement which was caused, I found, by the upper blade bracket being a little crooked. I cured the problem by turning the bracket around and moving the blade over a bit on reassembly.

With a 2-in. drive pulley on the motor and a 24-in. flywheel, the saw produces 144 strokes per minute. While this is a little slow for efficiency's sake, that's about all the little ⅙-HP motor can handle without tripping its breaker. A ½-HP motor with a 3-in. or 4-in. pulley (or a smaller flywheel) would give a better turn of speed. But I have no trouble zipping through a heavy chunk of 8-in. by 12-in. timber. A piece of wood 8 in. thick is about the upper limit simply because the 11-in. stroke on a 20-in. blade leaves only about 8 in. for the wood being cut on the table. A longer blade or a shorter stroke would provide for a greater depth of cut.

Blades—When I designed this particular saw, I decided to use a standard 20-in. pruning-saw blade, available at almost any hardware store. The one difficulty with pruning-saw blades is that they are fairly wide and are designed to cut in both directions. This is fine for cutting firewood, but not very good for precision cutting where greater control is needed. Short sections of a band-saw blade would cut more precise-

ly. Woodcraft Supply (313 Montvale Ave., Woburn, Mass. 01888) supplies blades of any length. I would choose a blade from ½ in. to ¾ in. wide with three or four teeth per inch.

Because band-saw blades are thinner and cut in only one direction they don't catch and hold on the upstroke. Those needing very narrow blades should think about shaving the arms down a bit near the ends and using lightweight blade brackets and a lightweight tensioner. This will reduce the oscillating mass and thus reduce the strain on thinner blades.

Ripping and resawing—A walking-beam saw designed for ripping usually has a moderate throat, and the blade is set at 90° to the arms. The arms must be club-shaped at the ends with a radius sawn around those ends so that the blade stays vertical and in the same plane as it moves up and down. Pins driven into the ends of arms hold the blade 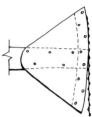 instead of blade brackets and the blade flexes around the ends of the arms, just as it would on the wheels of a band saw.

The walking-beam saw is cheap to make and operate, very quiet to run, and fairly efficient. As with any cutting tool, safety precautions are advised. The greatest danger seems to lie in having the workpiece wrested from your grasp and then attempting to grab it back instead of turning the machine off. Practice, a moderate speed, a sharp, thin blade and some common sense will go a long way toward making your experience with this saw a pleasant and rewarding one. □

Mark White, 40, teaches arctic house construction and boatbuilding at Kodiak (Alaska) Community College.

Treadle Band Saw

With a kit and plans for a 12-in. band saw supplied by Gilliom Mfg. Co. (1109 N. 2nd St., St. Charles, Mo. 63301) and a number of scavenged parts, Andrew Maier of East Orange, N.J., built a treadle-powered band saw that has now been in use in a high-school shop for over a year. Intrigued by Richard Starr's foot-powered lathe (*FWW* #15, March '79, pp. 65-66) that uses a five-speed gear cluster to achieve different operating speeds, Maier decided that the same drive mechanism could be adapted for use with a band saw. Friends discouraged the idea, saying that he'd never be able to develop and sustain enough muscle power to cut stock of usable dimensions. But Maier carried through his scheme, getting parts for the drive system from a used bicycle shop and an auto junkyard, where he bought a Volkswagen flywheel and front-wheel bearings for the drive shaft. The finished machine, he says, will cut rapidly and smoothly through stock 2 in. thick and smaller, but it's slow going through pieces 4 in. thick or more. Maier is very happy with how the machine has performed in its first year of service and with how well it's stood up under use by his students. □

Maier's band saw, right, has frame, housing, column and table made entirely of wood. So this saw can be foot driven, a threaded-rod drive shaft fits into tapered roller bearings (above), which are mortised into cross members in frame. Drive pulley, flywheel and five-speed sprocket cluster were all purchased as used parts. It can, of course, be equipped with an electric motor.

Photos: Gina Scalzulli

Carbide-Tipped Circular Saws

Alloy's hardness is its weakness

by Simon Watts

Most woodworkers now own a carbide-tipped sawblade or have at least considered getting one. The advantages are many. The teeth are accurately aligned so they make a cleaner and more precise cut, producing a good gluing surface directly from the saw; the tooth form stays practically the same after each sharpening; carbide-tipped blades can cut teak and other abrasive materials, and they last about 40 times as long between sharpenings as steel-toothed blades.

The main disadvantage of carbide-tipped blades is the cost. Not only is the initial cost substantial—$75 to $125 for a 10-in. blade—but also since you cannot file them yourself you have to send them out for sharpening, which now averages 25ᶜ a tooth, about $15 for a 60-tooth blade. A good sawblade can be ground more than 30 times before it has to be retipped, so you can expect to spend $450 on sharpening over the life of the blade—three or four times your original investment. Because saw manufacturing is a highly competitive business, a substantially lower price inevitably means inferior materials and poorer workmanship. The cheaper blade will need more frequent sharpenings, which soon will swallow up the original savings.

Woodworkers use their saws for cutting a wide variety of materials and for a number of different operations. Few of us can afford a different saw for each use and so we usually buy combination blades, which may do everything claimed for them, or may not. Carbide-tipped saws come in a bewildering variety of tooth shapes and configurations. How does one choose the right blade for ripping and crosscutting? For hardwood and softwood? Is price the only indication of quality? Is a retipped blade as good as new? What about cutting veneers, plywood, particle board and plastic laminates? Can the same blade be used on a radial arm saw and a table saw? What are the differences between a high-quality blade and an inferior one, and how can one tell?

Before getting into these and related questions, let's take a look at carbide itself and at how a modern carbide-tipped circular saw is manufactured. The alloy tungsten carbide, to give it its full name, can be made only by a process known as sintering, in which powdered tungsten and carbon are mixed together and heated under tremendous pressure. The carbon atoms penetrate the crystal lattices of the metal, creating one of the hardest synthetic materials known. This new alloy retains the granular structure of the original metal powder but the individual grains now have a hardness that is second only to diamond.

It is important to remember that tungsten carbide, although immensely hard, is also extremely brittle. It can be chipped easily by vibration or rough handling and can be used for cutting only when backed by another metal having the tensile strength it lacks. It cannot be drawn to thin edges with very acute angles, cannot be ground thin, and must not be left overhanging and unsupported. It must not be vibrated against a grinding wheel because the particles of carbide will be torn out.

The body of the saw (shown below in figure 1) is made from heat-treated alloy steel, which can be harder and tougher than an ordinary all-steel saw because the teeth don't require filing or setting. Slots are cut in the plate to allow its rim to expand without buckling. To reduce the danger of cracking, the slots end in round holes, which sometimes cause an annoying whistle. This whistling can usually be stopped by plugging the holes with a soft metal such as copper. Pockets are cut into the teeth of the saw, and the little grey blocks of carbide are brazed into them. The carbide tips are then

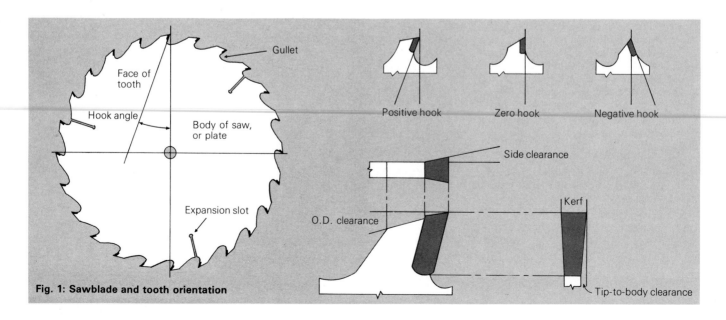

Fig. 1: Sawblade and tooth orientation

Gullet · Face of tooth · Hook angle · Body of saw, or plate · Expansion slot · Positive hook · Zero hook · Negative hook · Side clearance · O.D. clearance · Kerf · Tip-to-body clearance

ground on a diamond abrasive wheel to the required shape and bevel.

All circular saws are subject to centrifugal forces, which tend to make the blade fly apart. These destructive forces are directly proportional to the radius but increase as the square of the speed in rotation. These rotational loads cause the saw to expand unevenly across its diameter, giving it a tendency to buckle. If uncorrected, these forces can prevent the saw from running true, cause noise and vibration, and can even crack the saw body.

To minimize these effects, all good-quality circular saws more than 6 in. or 8 in. in diameter are put through a manufacturing process known as tensioning. This consists of hammering the bodies to an extent determined by their thickness, diameter and operating speed. The work, done with curved hammers on a crowned anvil, puts the middle in compression to compensate for tension of the rim at high speed. Machining done on finished saws (enlarging bores, drilling mounting holes, etc.) will upset the tension and should not be attempted by anyone unfamiliar with this technique. Warped saws can be made flat by hammering, but it is highly skilled work and likewise should be left to the experts.

The thinner the saw body, the more crucial tensioning becomes. Very thick saws have little or no tension added by hammering. Large saws, 20 in. or more, are usually tensioned three times at different stages in their manufacture. Three common types of saw bodies are shown in figure 2. The straight body is the cheapest and most widely used. The other two styles have one or both sides ground away to reduce the width of the saw kerf and are used mainly for cutting thin, non-ferrous tubing and plastics.

The most common tooth form is the flat top (figure 3) also called plain tooth, rip tooth or chisel tooth. The advantages of this tooth form are that since each tooth cuts the full width of the kerf, it has twice as many effective teeth as a staggered-tooth saw. Also, the cutting forces are balanced on the body, the tooth form is easier to maintain, square bottom cuts are ensured and each tooth carries an equally distributed load. The disadvantages are that the chip drags the sides of the cut, reducing the freedom of the chip flow. Chisel teeth can be damaged more easily by side thrust or twisting of the work than can staggered teeth, and the square corners are dulled when cutting abrasive materials. Tooth drag can increase power consumption significantly. Chisel-tooth blades are good for ripping, but when used for crosscutting, they leave a ragged end-grain surface.

All other basic tooth forms (except scoring saws) need more than one tooth to complete the cut. The alternate top bevel (figure 4), known also as a crosscut tooth or simply A.T.B., has the tops of adjacent teeth ground at alternating angles. It makes a very smooth crosscut, particularly across stringy fibers. Its disadvantage is that the leading-point edge is fragile and wears relatively quickly. Also it cannot make a square bottom cut. Crosscut-tooth blades can be used for ripping but easily become overloaded if the work is fed too fast.

To prolong the life of the blade between sharpenings by reducing wear, a rougher tooth, or lead tooth, is introduced. Its function is simply to open a path for the following raker teeth, which take only a finishing cut on the sides of the kerf. Rougher teeth have one or both corners ground at 45°. The raker teeth are usually square, as in figure 5, but they may have the alternate top bevel as in figure 6. Note that the

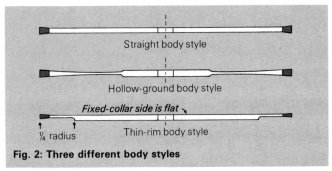

Fig. 2: Three different body styles

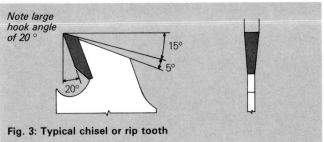

Fig. 3: Typical chisel or rip tooth

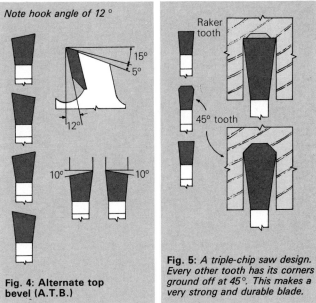

Fig. 4: Alternate top bevel (A.T.B.)

Fig. 5: *A triple-chip saw design. Every other tooth has its corners ground off at 45°. This makes a very strong and durable blade.*

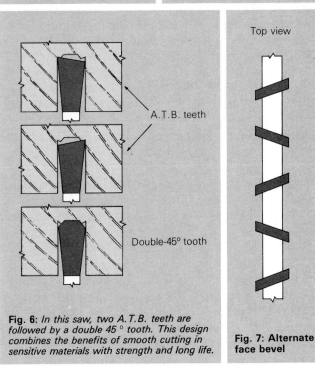

Fig. 6: *In this saw, two A.T.B. teeth are followed by a double 45° tooth. This design combines the benefits of smooth cutting in sensitive materials with strength and long life.*

Fig. 7: Alternate face bevel

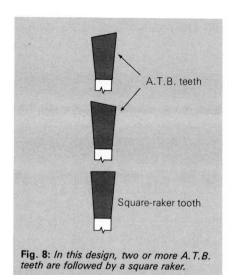

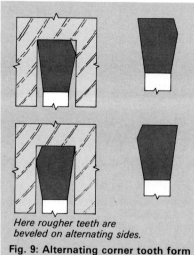

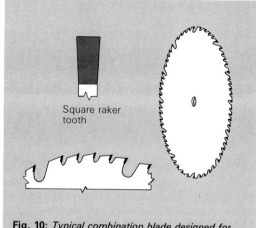

Fig. 8: *In this design, two or more A.T.B. teeth are followed by a square raker.*

Here rougher teeth are beveled on alternating sides.
Fig. 9: **Alternating corner tooth form**

Fig. 10: *Typical combination blade designed for both ripping and crosscutting. Four A.T.B. teeth are followed by square raker.*

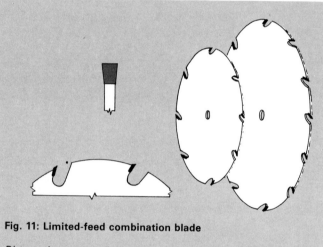

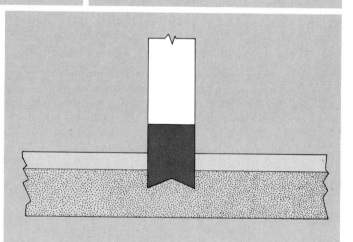

Fig. 11: **Limited-feed combination blade**

Distance between teeth determines maximum rate of feed.

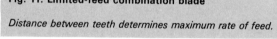

Fig. 12: *A scoring saw is used for cutting thin veneers. Usually its depth of cut is very shallow.*

rougher tooth makes a slightly deeper cut, in order to protect the tips of the rakers.

For abrasive, brittle materials like particle board, the faces of the teeth are slanted alternately right and left (figure 7, previous page), a configuration that reduces chipping out. This arrangement is achieved by placing the teeth in the plate at the required angle or by grinding them.

There are many other possible tooth configurations. For example, every second or third tooth in an A.T.B. can be followed by a square raker (figure 8), or the rougher tooth itself can be beveled first on one side and then the other, as in figure 9.

Figure 10 shows a typical combination blade. It has four alternating beveled teeth followed by a square raker and is designed for both ripping and crosscutting.

Another general-purpose saw is shown in figure 11. It is designed to limit the feed to a predetermined chip load and can be used in portable electric saws, table saws and radial arm saws when smoothness of cut is unimportant.

Most carbide blades can be used on both radial arm saws and table saws. However, as the hook angle increases (see figure 1, p. 106) so does the danger of a radial arm saw grabbing the work (self-feeding). Positive hook angles of 13° to 15° are usual, although some blades designed for swing-and-pivot saws may have a negative hook. Heavy-duty ripsaws go to the other extreme with a 25° positive hook.

Figure 12 shows a scoring saw, which is designed to cut cleanly through fragile veneers. It usually cuts only about $\frac{1}{16}$ in. deep.

Chip loads — For a particular tooth configuration, there are four factors that govern the performance of a circular saw: speed of rotation, number of teeth, rate of feed, and chip load. Chip load is nothing more than the thickness of the chip removed by a sawtooth. There is a simple relationship between these four variables which can be expressed by the following equation:

$$\text{Chip load (in./tooth)} = \frac{\text{feed rate (in./min.)}}{\text{RPM} \times \text{no. of teeth}}.$$

As one would expect, halving the rate of feed or doubling the number of teeth reduces the chip load by half, and it is easy to see that a smooth cut requires a low chip load—either a slow rate of feed, lots of teeth, or both. What is not so obvious is that increasing the chip load increases the life of the blade. This is because the greatest wear on the tooth occurs when the cutting edge strikes the work at high velocity. Therefore, the larger the chip load per tooth, the fewer times each tooth has to separate a chip from the material, and the fewer impacts the tooth withstands in cutting a given length of material. Maximum attainable chip loads are affected by the condition of the machine, the thickness of the blade relative to its diameter and the nature and thickness of the material that is being cut. Accurate alignment of the sawblade with the path of feed makes a considerable difference in the performance of the blade.

Choosing a blade — Once you have decided on the tooth configuration you want, how do you select a good blade? Much of the work that goes into making a high-quality carbide blade is invisible (tensioning, for example), and it is difficult to make an intelligent choice between competing brands. In general, the price, the terms of the warranty and the manufacturer's reputation are the best indicators, but here are some other things to look for: A good blade should be flat. When placed on a true arbor, the total indicator runout of the blade body should not exceed 0.005 in. for a 10-in. blade, and outside-diameter runout should not exceed 0.002 in. With a hand lens, check the quality of grind on the sawteeth. If the carbide looks smooth and shiny, it's good, but if it has deep and irregular grind lines, the teeth will dull rapidly. The teeth should be notched in and neatly brazed to the body of the saw (figure 13). There should be at least ⅛ in. of carbide on each tooth of a 50-tooth saw.

Sharpening — Carbide blades are sharpened on special machines using diamond grinding wheels, and only about 0.005 in. of carbide should be removed each time. This requires skill, and blade life can be considerably shortened by careless or improper grinding. Saws sometimes come back from being sharpened with the tips missing carbide particles on one side because the tip was not properly supported and the pressure between the wheel and the sawtooth produced vibration. Another common way of losing carbide particles is to use coarse-grit wheels for finish-grinding. It may cost less, but the results are expensive. The peaks and valleys left by these wheels leave unsupported particles that can easily be knocked off during the cut, rapidly dulling the saw.

Broken and damaged teeth can be replaced and ground to the exact size and shape of the others. If properly cared for, a good blade can be sharpened 30 to 40 times before it needs to be retipped.

Retipping — When there is not enough carbide left to grind, the remains of the teeth are removed with a torch. The notches are ground out, new teeth are brazed on and then ground to the same shape as the original ones. Next, the body of the saw is checked for flatness and, if necessary, straightened by hammering. The result should be a blade equal in quality to the original one. There will not be a great savings in money, but you will have the satisfaction of making a small stand against our throw-away economy.

Care of blades — Ruining a carbide blade is much easier than you think, and I have been guilty of most, if not all, of the following abuses. Saws are most frequently (and most seriously) damaged by overheating. This is usually caused by continuing to use a blade that is dull but can also happen by trying to feed stock too fast. Saws warped by overheating have to be straightened by hammering and sometimes retensioned as well. When the teeth are very dull they have to have more carbide ground off to make them sharp, and this shortens the life of the blade. Like steel saws, carbide blades gum up when cutting resinous woods. The best way to clean them is by soaking them overnight in kerosene or paint remover.

Faulty alignment is another major source of trouble. To get

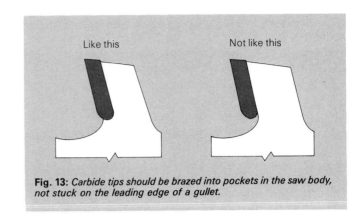

Fig. 13: *Carbide tips should be brazed into pockets in the saw body, not stuck on the leading edge of a gullet.*

a clean, accurate cut, the sawblade must not only run true (no wobble) but also be parallel to the direction of feed, which means parallel to the miter-gauge slots in the saw table. Getting proper alignment (if you don't have it already) usually requires loosening the trunnions and moving the arbor assembly slightly.

Once the sawblade is trued up with the line of feed, you should align the rip fence with the blade, and on this there are two schools of thought. One argues that the blade and fence should be exactly parallel. The other maintains that the fence should be canted slightly away from the line of feed (about 1/32 in. or less) on the outfeed side of the table. This ensures that only those teeth on their downward cutting arc contact the workpiece. Too much of a cant will result in a "heel-and-toe" condition, make feeding difficult and possibly cause the blade to overheat and distort.

To see whether the saw is running true, clamp a machinist's dial indicator to the saw table. Mark a spot near the perimeter of the blade and rotate it slowly through 360°. If you cannot get a dial indicator, clamp a piece of smooth steel almost up to the blade and check the distance between it and the blade with feeler gauges as you rotate the blade. If the indicated runout exceeds 0.005 in., find out the reason. First take the saw off the arbor and make sure the saw collars are clean and not worn. Try the blade on another machine. If the trouble is in the blade and it is not flat, do not take a ball-peen hammer to it, but send it out for correction. Never try to put shims between the saw collars and the blade. This can distort the blade and damage it permanently.

Other factors that will affect a saw's performance, if not its health, are throat plates (table inserts) that are not close enough to the saw or not level with the table, vibration from loose arbors or bearings, tables not flat, and mismatched or loose *V*-belts. Never try to slow down a saw by pressing something against its side. This can generate enough heat to distort the body. Don't drill holes in a blade or enlarge existing holes. This will upset the tension. Keep it on a wooden peg or rack all by itself when not in use. When shipping make sure, if there is a bolt through the arbor hole, that it is not putting pressure on the body. Finally, never lay a carbide saw (or any other edge tool) down on a hard surface like a cast-iron saw table. Remember, the teeth are made of grains of tungsten carbide bonded together—super hard but vulnerable to mistreatment.   □

Contributing editor Simon Watts prepared this article with the help of Steven A. Segal of North American Products in Atlanta, Ga.

An Inflatable Drum Sander
Rubber sleeve conforms to work

by Robert L. Pavey

*Walnut bird,
11 in. high by 8 in. wide,
sanded on homebuilt
pneumatic drum sander.*

An inflatable sanding drum is an invaluable tool for shaping and smoothing wood and other materials—both convex and all but the tightest concave surfaces can be executed with style. The sanding surface conforms to irregularly shaped work and, unlike a hard-backed sanding drum, does not leave deep sanding marks. You can inflate it hard for fast cutting, then release some pressure to make it soft for smooth finishing. It is also easy to change sanding sleeves: Simply release the air pressure, slip off one sleeve, slip on another, reinflate and on with your work. Whether you have compressed air in your shop or a bicycle pump, it takes only seconds.

Making a pneumatic sanding drum is easy. It can be run on a lathe or be driven as mine is by a ⅝-in. shaft supported by pillow-block bearings and powered by a 1725 RPM, ⅓-HP motor. I get variable speeds from half to twice that RPM with a double-flange, spring-loaded pulley system that effectively changes the diameter of the drive pulley by levering the pulleys away from or toward one another. The materials for the drum itself should be available locally:

—1 12-in. length of ½-in. water pipe

—1 tire valve stem

—1 tube silicone rubber sealant

—1 shaft adapter to fit your drive

—1 rubber stopper, ½ in. dia.

—1 10-in. length of 3-in. diameter rubber tubing (Goodyear Spiroflex 2001 water discharge hose works well)

—4 ¾-in. shaft bushings

—2 ¼-in. to ⅜-in. thick by 3½-in. dia. discs: wood, polyethylene, nylon or other material

—wire or strong, thin cord

—1 piece of canvas 12 in. by 12 in.

—2 pieces of ⅛-in. cord, 12 in. long

—Sandpaper and glue to make the sanding sleeves

EDITOR'S NOTE: For those who do not want to make their own, pneumatic sanding drums, their separate parts (with or without drive) and various-sized sanding sleeves are available from Sand-Rite Mfg. Co., 1611 N. Sheffield Ave., Chicago, Ill. 60614.

First cut the ½-in. pipe to length using a pipe cutter. The burr this leaves serves as a flange inside the pipe that will prevent the tire stem from slipping out. The other end of the pipe should be reamed to remove the burr. The tire stem must be turned down to fit snugly into the pipe. Chuck the cap end in a drill or lathe and file while it turns. Then slip the stem through the pipe and before pulling it tight against the flange, place some silicone rubber sealant under the flange to form a seal. Pull tight and let dry.

The next step is to mount the shaft adapter to the opposite end of the pipe. First drill and tap a set-key hole in the pipe approximately ¼ in. from the end to keep the pipe from slipping on the shaft adapter. It's a good idea to use a threaded shaft adapter and to tap a thread in the pipe to fit it.

Before attaching the adapter, insert in the pipe a tight-fitting rubber stopper liberally coated with silicone rubber sealant to form an airtight seal ahead of the shaft adapter. A ⅛-in. hole drilled through the pipe between the stopper and the valve end permits air to enter the drum chamber.

Next construct the ends of the drum. First ream the four ¾-in. bushings to fit over the pipe, which will be approximately ²⁷/₃₂ in. Also drill and ream the center holes of the discs. Place the bushings and the discs on the pipe as shown in the drawing. Before tightening be sure to apply liberal amounts of silicone rubber sealant on each side of the discs next to the bushings; position and tighten the bushings to hold the discs in place 9 in. apart outside to outside.

After the silicone rubber sealant is dry, place the assembly on your drive and turn down the two discs to a 3³/₁₆-in. diameter. This corrects for any wobble in your shaft or off-centering of the hole drilled in the discs. Next turn a groove in the center of each disc for gluing the diaphragm. This groove should be deep enough to permit the wire or cord windings to be pulled below the surface of the completed drum. This will

Sheets of cloth-backed sandpaper with a strip of sand removed and glued over on the back form sleeves for the sander.

The drum, showing tire valve stem (sealed with silicone), wire wrap, canvas sleeve with drawstring, and pillow blocks bearing the belted shaft.

110

Photos: Milton Fanta; Illustration: Christopher Clapp

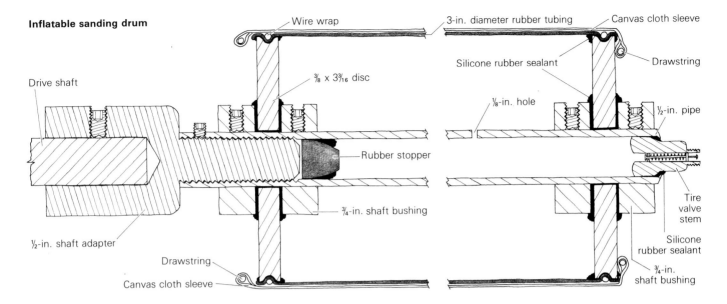

Inflatable sanding drum

Wire wrap

3-in. diameter rubber tubing

Canvas cloth sleeve

Silicone rubber sealant

Drawstring

Drive shaft

⅜ × 3³⁄₁₆ disc

⅛-in. hole

½-in. pipe

Rubber stopper

½-in. shaft adapter

Drawstring

¾-in. shaft bushing

Tire valve stem

Silicone rubber sealant

¾-in. shaft bushing

Canvas cloth sleeve

protect the windings and the protective cover from damage.

Now comes perhaps the most difficult step, that of attaching the diaphragm and obtaining an air-tight seal. The 3-in. diameter rubber tubing should be longer than the drum in order to be able to hold it in place while wrapping and gluing the binding wire or cord. Silicone rubber sealant applied liberally on the inside of each disc will aid in forming an airtight seal. Pull the wire or cord tight so that it bites into the rubber, pressing it tight against the discs. Let the sealant dry thoroughly before testing. If you detect minor air leaks, these may be sealed using bicycle-tire sealing materials. The diaphragm is then covered with a canvas cloth stitched and tied with a drawstring down over the ends.

The last step is to prepare the sanding sleeves to be placed over the drum. First wrap the 9-in. by 11-in. sheet around the drum and mark the sheet at the point of overlap. Scrape a strip of abrasive off one end of the paper, apply glue and then clamp until set. Once the glue is dry, place the sleeve over the deflated drum, inflate and use. For dust collection, I have mounted a 3-in. by 6-in. vacuum nozzle (not shown in the photos) behind the drum. A Sears Shop-vac takes care of most of the dust. My drum rotates counter-clockwise, and I hold work sometimes above, sometimes below it. Try using different pressures and see how it affects your work; you will be amazed at the fine, smooth finish you can achieve on ir-

regularly shaped pieces of wood without leaving flat spots, ridges and sanding marks.

Hand-held adaptations — I am sure that by extending the length of the water pipe to accommodate two handles slipped over the ends, with bearings between the inside diameter of the handles and the outside diameter of the pipe, you would have the beginnings of a rolling-pin sander. The handles could be turned-and-bored wood or plastic or metal pipe. The tire-valve stem would remain protruding from one end of the spindle pipe. To power the unit, a shaft adapter or a plug fixed to the other end of the pipe could be turned to fit a flexible-drive-shaft or portable-drill chuck.

The hand-held adaptations I have actually made are single-handle designs made from nylon bar stock. Efficient use of standard 9x11 sheet sandpaper determined the various drum sizes, all smaller than the original design and ideal for sanding holes and tight curves. To use a 5½-in. by 9-in. half-sheet, the drum must measure 9 in. by 1⁵⁄₁₆ in. in diameter. Taking into consideration ¹⁄₁₆ in. for the inflatable sleeve and ¹⁄₁₆ in. for the canvas covering, the disc has to be turned to 1³⁄₁₆ in. To use a 5½-in. by 4½-in. quarter-sheet, the drum measures 5½ in. by 1³⁄₁₆ in. in diameter and the discs must be turned to 1¹⁄₁₆ in. And to use a 4½-in. by 2¾ in. eighth-sheet, the drum measures 4½ in. by ¾ in. in diameter and the discs must be turned to ⅝ in. These drums were constructed similarly to the large one, however the spindle and discs are one unit turned from 2-in., 1½-in. and 1-in. nylon bar stock, respectively. For a drive shaft I drilled and tapped a hole in the end of the bar stock and screwed in a ⅜-in. bolt, then cut the head off. This shaft can be mounted on any ⅜-in. chuck drive (flex-shaft or portable drill). To attach the tire-valve stem to the opposite end of the shaft, first remove the rubber from the metal portion of the valve stem. Then drill a hole in the end of the spindle, into which the valve stem can be driven for a tight fit. This hole should be deep enough to go past the disc portion of the spindle in order that the ⅛-in. hole that permits air to flow into the chamber can be drilled across the spindle to meet it. The diaphragms for these smaller drums were made from thin-wall latex rubber tubing, attached, sealed and covered as on the larger drum. □

Drum sander smooths irregular contours of a bandsawn bird.

Bob Pavey, a research scientist, lives in Western Springs, Ill.

A Low-Tech Thickness Sander

Homebuilt machine is accurate and cheap

by T.R. Warbey

I make dulcimers, so I need thin pieces of wood sanded to fine tolerances after resawing. Last summer I made an abrasive thicknesser that handles stock down to 0.040 in. The machine cost me less than $20.

My thicknesser uses a drum made of plywood discs glued together and mounted on a steel shaft. The two end discs have ¼-in. grooves routed in them, and the steel shaft is drilled through with two ¼-in. holes to coincide with these grooves. Insert 3-in. lengths of steel rod into the holes when all the discs but the end ones are glued and in position on the shaft. Apply glue to the end discs and position them over the two rods.

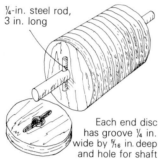

¼-in. steel rod, 3 in. long

Each end disc has groove ¼ in. wide by ⁵⁄₁₆ in. deep and hole for shaft

Clamping the assembly locks the drum onto the shaft. When it's dry, I take it to the local machinist to be turned true.

Next mount the drum/shaft in pillow blocks on wooden spacers on a heavy plywood base. On my machine, the base is the top of a stand to support the machine and to house the motor. For the work-support table under the drum I used 1-in. maple only about 15 in. long, to minimize flexing. The table is hinged at one end (a full-length piano hinge is best) and sits on a wedge at the other.

I glue sanding-belt material to the drum using contact cement, but I use white glue for the joint at the belt ends. Dip the ends in boiling water to remove the abrasive, and dry prior to gluing. Lap the ends at an angle to the axis, a standard belt-gluing procedure.

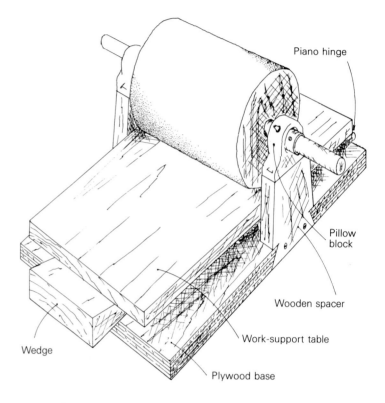

Piano hinge

Pillow block

Wooden spacer

Work-support table

Wedge

Plywood base

I sand both softwoods and hardwoods using 50-grit closed-coat aluminum-oxide belting. My machine is driven by a ¾-HP motor; the 6-in. diameter drum turns bottom toward me at 1600 RPM. I stand at the wedged end, place the work on the table and gently push it in under the drum, which sands and thicknesses at the same time. When one side is done, turn the work over, shift the wedge in a little and sand the other side until your stock is the desired thickness.

The machine is light enough to carry outside; this way I don't have a dust problem. Even so, I wear a mask. My next problem is how to change grits and keep it simple. □

EDITOR'S NOTE: We've come across a number of machines similar to Warbey's thickness sander. One made by Bob Meadow (a lutemaker and resident woodworker at Peters Valley Craftsmen, Layton, N.J.) is shown at right. It has a screw adjustment instead of a wedge to raise and lower the table. Two threaded rods are pinned to two timing pulleys and synchronized by a toothed rubber (timing) belt, which ensures even support. To true his drum, Meadow slid coarse sandpaper under the rotating, roughcut drum. (It is even possible to turn round an octagonal blank, already in the pillow blocks, from a tool rest mounted on the frame.) This both trues the drum and corrects any slight misalignment to the table.

According to R.E. Brune, of Evanston, Ill., another maker, the drum-type thickness sander has been around for several centuries as a luthier's *filertier*. Other variations can be found in the data sheets compiled by the Guild of American Luthiers (8222 S. Park Ave., Tacoma, Wash. 98408). Among the refinements is an answer to Warbey's problem of changing grits simply. *GAL Quarterly* editor Tim Olsen recommends using a steel drum (see data sheet 48). Not only is this more stable than a wooden one, but the sanding strip can be applied with a light, spray-on rubber cement (Olsen uses Weldwood Spray 'n' Glue), which bonds weakly with the steel and is easily removed. Wrapping the strip helically and securing the ends with masking tape provide an adequate hold.

Thickness sander by Bob Meadow uses a pair of synchronized machine screws to raise and lower the table. The machine is powered by a 1½-HP motor that turns the cylinder 1150 RPM.

A Sanding-Disc Jointer

Tapered disc on tilted arbor allows fine adjustment

by H.B. Montgomery

There are various methods for obtaining perfect edges on workpieces from thin veneers to ¾-in. thick hardwoods. With a simple guide jig and a tapered sanding disc mounted on a tilting-arbor table saw, I am getting perfect edges, ready for gluing in a matter of minutes.

A tapered sanding disc can be machined from a piece of ⅜-in. thick aluminum. I prefer a 10-in. disc with 2° to 3° of taper. Use a heavy backing plate while cutting the taper, or the edge will curve away under the pressure of the cutting tool and the surface will not be true. Three degrees is the maximum taper you can expect the sandpaper disc to adhere to. I use Sears pressure-sensitive sanding-disc cement and cut a 3-in. hole in the center of the sandpaper. Use paper-backed sanding discs; cloth or fiber-backed discs will not stay on.

The advantage of a tapered disc is that when mounted on the saw arbor and tilted to compensate for the taper, only a small portion of the disc is at 90° to the saw table, and that portion is moving practically parallel to the grain of the work being fed past. Also, because the arbor is tilted, the crank that raises and lowers the arbor can be used for fine adjustment of the lateral depth of cut of the disc.

The guide jig, which runs between the rip fence and the sanding disc, consists of a top and bottom plate (¾-in. hardwood plywood), a hardwood clamping reinforcement strip, two carriage bolts with wing nuts and two registration dowels. The jig should be slightly longer and wider than the stock you will be jointing. Crown the reinforcing strip about 1/16 in. to even out clamping pressure, and fasten it to the top plate from the bottom, about 1 in. back from the edge, with two countersunk wood screws located about 3 in. on either side of the center. Placing the screws farther apart might bend the

plywood to the slight arc of the reinforcing strip. Now clamp the two plates together and drill through at the ends of the reinforcing strip for the two carriage bolts. Install the bolts, tighten down the wing nuts and drill two holes in the edges of the far side of the jig to receive two ½-in. by 1¼-in. registration dowels. Loosen the wing nuts, install the dowels and retighten the jig.

With the sanding disc on the saw, raise the arbor to its full height and, checking with a try square, tilt the arbor until the disc face is exactly 90° to the table, measured directly over the arbor. This is the only critical adjustment for the jointing operation. Lower the disc to 1¾ in. above the table and set the rip fence so the jig just fits between the two. Turn on the power and run the jig through several times on each edge, raising the arbor slightly between passes, until its edges are true and parallel.

To use the jig for jointing two veneers, lay the pieces side by side as they will be joined, face up, and fold them together with the good faces inside. Clamp this "book" in the jig with only 1/16 in. or so protruding, set the rip fence for the lightest cut and pass the work-loaded jig through the rotating disc. Raise the arbor between passes for a deeper cut until the veneers are flush with the jig edge; depending on the grit size on the disc, from .005 in. to .025 in. can be removed with one pass. I recommend 120 grit for finished edges.

The horizontal locating dowels work best for thin stock. The jig can handle up to ¾-in. thick stock (1½ in. thick total) with a 10-in. disc, but with thick stock vertical registers should be used.   □

H.B. Montgomery, a retired mechanic, lives in Seminole, Fla.

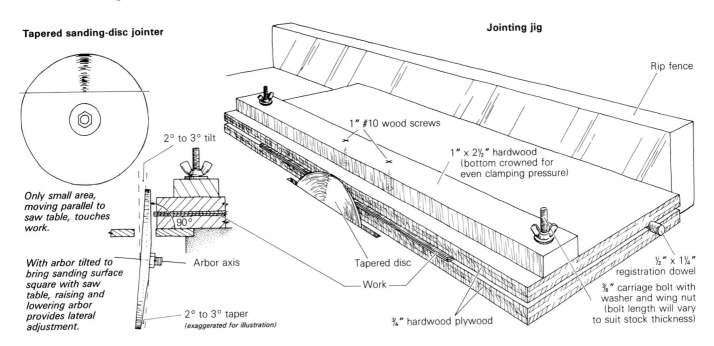

Tapered sanding-disc jointer

2° to 3° tilt

Only small area, moving parallel to saw table, touches work.

With arbor tilted to bring sanding surface square with saw table, raising and lowering arbor provides lateral adjustment.

Arbor axis

90°

2° to 3° taper
(exaggerated for illustration)

Jointing jig

Rip fence

1" #10 wood screws

1" x 2½" hardwood
(bottom crowned for even clamping pressure)

Tapered disc

Work

¾" hardwood plywood

½" x 1¼" registration dowel

⅜" carriage bolt with washer and wing nut (bolt length will vary to suit stock thickness)

Illustration: Christopher Clapp

Tuning Up Your Lathe
Mass and rigidity make clean cutting easier

by Del Stubbs

Most lathes I've seen, in both amateur and professional shops, do not function as they could. Yet improving them is simply a matter of understanding and putting into effect the basic principles of lathe operation. The idea is to have no play anywhere, not in the mounting of the stock on the faceplate or between centers, not in the bearings or the shaft, not in the tool-rest base or the tool rest. Then the lathe needs to be mounted on a base so solid that the vibration of an out-of-balance piece or the jarring of an improperly used tool is immediately damped.

A common misconception is that the less serious you are about turning, the less of a lathe you require. The reverse is true. The beginner has enough problems, without a poorly built lathe adding to the burden. A skilled turner can cope with a sloppy lathe and get by, though there's no question vibration slows down the rate at which he can work and makes clean cutting more difficult. Vibration in a beginner's lathe can drive him to quitting. It should be pointed out, though, that in small-diameter turnings the stock has so little mass and leverage against the tool that a very solid lathe is not so necessary. Faceplate turning and large spindle work are the real test of a lathe.

Though the base is perhaps the most neglected part, it is the first priority in tuning up your lathe. For a test, grip the headstock and see if you can move it. It shouldn't budge. If yours is a sheet-metal base, so common on smaller, less expensive lathes, it will probably have to be braced or replaced. Price, though, is no sure determinant of a lathe's quality; I've seen $2,000 lathes whose mass was not proportioned effectively. One quick, inexpensive and removable way to keep the lathe fixed to the floor and to damp vibration is to use sand. Contain it in boxes or gunny sacks as close to the headstock as possible. Take care that grit doesn't get loose and into the bearings of the motor or lathe; wrap the sand first in a plastic trash bag.

For my lathe I bolted together some old 6x12s into a base that is so massive (it weighs about 500 lb., which I consider a minimum) it must be disassembled to be moved. Timbers damp vibration (without sending it back, as steel may). But putting timbers together rigidly, as they must be, involves a disadvantage: If the base is not sure-footed (if one corner is slightly higher), the whole lathe can rock, causing vibration. The solution here is to wedge and shim carefully until each corner carries the same weight. I also use felt pads to separate the wood from the concrete floor—these stop the lathe's tendency to walk around the shop while an unbalanced piece is turning.

What about bolting the lathe to the floor? If the floor is wood, the whole building may shake as well as the lathe. If the floor is concrete, well, as an old millwright told me, "If you bolt a rigid lathe to a solid floor and turn a heavily unbalanced piece, it could tear up your lathe—something's got to

give." The alternative is not a lathe that walks around, but a base that absorbs vibration and deadens it. That's what's ideal about sand: Bang a steel bar and it resonates, punch a bag of sand and it's dead. Wood and cast iron have similar advantages. An old cast-iron lathe has so much mass that it will not resonate like a light steel one. If you build out of wood, triangulating the structure will help achieve rigidity. Set the legs out at an angle and cross-brace them.

One addition that's rare on lathes is a foot-operated clutch; I consider one important. A clutch allows you to start the motor under no load, which saves the motor and electricity, and makes for quicker starts and stops. A clutch is also a safety feature. Out-of-balance pieces can be started slowly—if a corner hits the tool rest, it just stops, and you have the chance to see if the lathe will shake. A clutch also is a foot release, if ever your hands can't get to the switch.

The most important advantage for me in having a clutch is that by slipping it I can modulate speed readily while cutting—mostly to slow down to help stop chatter in difficult or delicate cuts. I often use speeds about 200 RPM to 300 RPM in getting that final clean-up cut in some faceplate and spindle work, the foot on the clutch constantly adjusting the speed as the cut changes. I also experiment with slower speeds, especially if I'm having trouble with a particular cut. If the tool isn't cutting right when the stock is turning slowly, it won't cut any better at high speed. Adding a handwheel to the outboard end of the lathe and turning the stock by hand so the tool cuts at about the speed of a pocketknife through a piece of whittling wood is one way to see if you're getting the shear cut you want. With a clutch you can move the stock almost this slowly, and still have both hands on the cutting tool.

Probably the simplest clutch is to have some way of lifting the motor and thus lessening the tension on the belt. This method uses only the weight of the motor on a hinged motor mount to provide belt tension. A pulleyed cord, moved by a hinged foot pedal, raises the motor mount and releases tension. There should be enough travel for the belt to slip, but not so much for the belt to come out of the pulley grooves. I include a small turnbuckle in the cord that raises the motor to allow fine adjustment of the clutch. With one foot under the plywood pedal and the other pressing it down, I adjust the clutch to release just as the pedal touches my foot.

Belt quality is important. An unevenly manufactured or worn belt creates vibration. For smooth, positive power I've found a notched *V*-belt best. In some cases, though, these will grab even when tension is relaxed; a solid, stiffer belt should then be used. Old-style flat belts slip best and an adjustable idler pulley can be used as a clutch with these, or with any belt if the motor is too heavy or inconvenient to lift. If in heavy-duty cutting you find a belt slipping, use a cam to lock the motor down or add weight to the motor mount. If

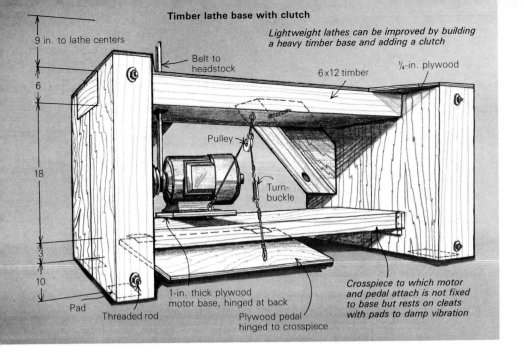

Timber lathe base with clutch

Lightweight lathes can be improved by building a heavy timber base and adding a clutch

9 in. to lathe centers

6

18

3

10

Belt to headstock

6x12 timber

¼-in. plywood

Pulley

Turn-buckle

Pad

Threaded rod

1-in. thick plywood motor base, hinged at back

Plywood pedal hinged to crosspiece

Crosspiece to which motor and pedal attach is not fixed to base but rests on cleats with pads to damp vibration

rebuilding it for a bigger shaft or bearings, as the lathe would still be no more rigid than the rest of it you hadn't souped up. The "weakest link" principle should also be kept in mind in fabricating a lathe.

The mounting of the stock on the lathe is another area that should be checked for play. If it's faceplate turning you're doing, first make sure the faceplate sits securely on the spindle—check for bright spots on the mating surfaces that will indicate only point contact. Next make sure the mating surfaces between faceplate and wood blank are perfectly flat and free of particles. Chamfer the holes in the stock into which the screw or screws will be driven, so the screws raise no splinters that will keep the faceplate and blank from meeting flush. Looseness can also be caused by voids sometimes found in plywood glue blocks. After the blank is mounted, grip it and test-pull it in several directions, checking for movement between the work and the faceplate. Solid mounting is critical for smooth cutting.

In spindle work check the spur center to see that all four spurs are sharp and the same length and that the point extends no more than ⅛ in. beyond the spurs—if it's too long, it will prevent the spurs from making solid contact. I use a small Dremel grinder to true up the spurs while the lathe is turning. Wear safety glasses and grind no farther than the shortest spur. Then take the center to the bench grinder and get the spurs sharp. Thin spindles will be remarkably less flexible if all four spurs are in solid contact. If you have a ball-bearing center, check it with a spindle in place and replace the center if there's play.

The weakest part of most lathes is the tool rest and tool-rest base. To test yours hold one end of the tool rest and press down firmly. If it gives, it will give also under a heavy cut, causing dig-in or chatter. If possible, get a heavier model tool rest and base than is standard for your lathe. For years I had to use a lathe whose tool rest wasn't rigid. I adapted by staying away from using the end of the rest and by applying considerable pressure down on it when cutting. It also taught me to take a lighter, more careful cut, an advantage after all.

Nicks in a tool rest make smooth travel across the workpiece impossible. They are caused by chatter and other impacts, but also by sharp edges on a skew chisel cutting a groove as it is pushed into the work. Check all turning tools for sharp edges and round them over with a stone. Also file the tool rest smooth, then wax it. Be sure the bearing surfaces between the tool rest, its base and the lathe bed are smooth and that they can be tightened together securely. Use a longer wrench for more leverage, if necessary.

If you understand the principles, you can make most lightweight lathes a good deal better than they come straight from the manufacturer. I still use a small Rockwell (with the timber base) for most of my small spindle and faceplate work. If you decide to stick with a sheet-metal base, do a lot of bracing to stop flexing and add weight, at least 100 lb. □

possible mount the motor separately from the lathe, to reduce transferred vibration. If not, include a damping pad between the motor and the lathe.

Testing for play in your shaft and bearings can be a lesson in sensitivity. Have the shop completely quiet. Take the belt off the pulley, and grip the shaft. Try to rock it from side to side and in and out. Listen and feel very carefully for any knocking. End play is as much a problem as side play in faceplate work. All end play and some side play are eliminated in spindle work by the pressure of the tailstock. You felt a knock—now what? If it's end play, the problem might be solved by tightening an allen screw, moving a collar, adding a shim or tightening an outboard faceplate. Side play probably means shot ball bearings, worn sleeves or Babbitt bearings, or a loose fit between shaft and bearing or between bearing and headstock. If it's a ball-bearing lathe, turn the shaft (belt disconnected) and feel for any catch or roughness. Also give it a spin and, with your ear pressed to the headstock, listen for rumble. If you sense either of these, plan on getting new bearings. In lathes with external grease fittings, play can be temporarily reduced by filling the gaps with a shot of grease; don't overdo it.

If you have to replace the bearings, try first to get an assembly drawing of your headstock from a tool supplier or from the manufacturer. Also take care not to apply pressure or impact to any part of a bearing except the inner sleeve (see "Basic Machine Maintenance," *FWW* #13, Nov. '78). I pound on my bearings with a piece of hardwood drilled out to just fit over the shaft and turned down at one end to just the thickness of the sleeve. I replace the bearings every 1,000 to 1,500 hours of lathe time, and this has become a routine operation.

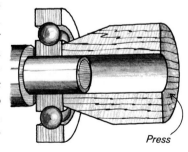

Press

Shaft size is important in selecting or in building a lathe. Flex in a small, ¾-in. shaft is significant, especially in faceplate work. I would recommend 1½ in. as a minimum for serious bowl turning. Not that fine bowls can't be turned on a smaller shaft; I'm talking here about ease of cutting quickly and cleanly. I'd not recommend taking a small lathe and

Del Stubbs is a professional turner in Chico, Calif.

Ferrules from end caps

Over the years I have seen all kinds of homemade tool handles ranging from an old corncob jammed on the tang of a rasp (a surprisingly comfortable improvisation) to ornate, French-polished creations. For most of us whose efforts fall between these extremes, locating a suitable ferrule is a larger problem than turning the handle. Plumbing stores stock an attractive, inexpensive solution—copper-tubing end caps. The end caps, available in several sizes, are tough enough to

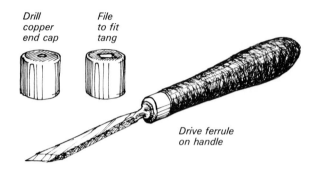

Drill copper end cap

File to fit tang

Drive ferrule on handle

hold up to mallet blows. To make a ferrule, drill a hole for the tool's tang through the soft metal. Shape the hole, if necessary, with a needle file. Drive the ferrule onto the wood handle, which has been sized to give a tight friction-fit. Rubbing the copper with fine steel wool produces a beautiful satin finish and reddish-gold color that complements all woods. An occasional coat of paste wax will protect the copper from tarnish. —*George Mustoe, Bellingham, Wash.*

Lathe sanding drum

This inexpensive but effective drum sander is made and used on the lathe. Center an 18-in. long 4x4 on the lathe and turn a cylinder of 3½-in. diameter. Carefully reduce the diameter of the cylinder until a standard sheet of emery paper wraps around the drum without gap or overlap. Glue the emery cloth (I used 100 grit) to the drum with hide glue. Wrap the entire surface with a sash cord and let dry overnight. Turn

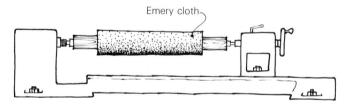

Emery cloth

down the ends of the drum to about 1½ in. to give free working space. The size of the drum can be scaled up or down for different applications. A smaller open-end drum could easily be made using a screw center.

—*Harland Smith, Waterloo, Iowa*

Purfling router guide

In stringed-instrument construction the router is commonly used to cut a small shoulder around the perimeter of the instrument. The dado holds an ornamental inlay (purfling) used to cover the glue seam between top and side. The chore requires a precise cut with a router guide capable of following sharp curves. Though I've tinkered with various adjustable guides, I keep coming back to simple, wooden, preset guides.

The guide consists of a wooden finger glued to a crescent-shaped piece of plywood, which ensures proper positioning. A

single bolt and wing nut provide fast but secure fastening.

For inlay work I have three guides, each made to cut a rabbet width corresponding to one, two or three layers of veneer. Thus, for any given thickness of inlay I just bolt on the right guide. No time is lost making practice cuts.

—*George Mustoe, Bellingham, Wash.*

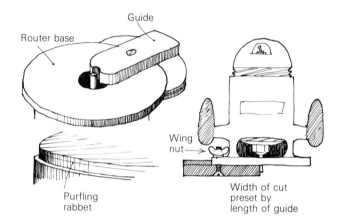

Guide

Router base

Purfling rabbet

Wing nut

Width of cut preset by length of guide

Auxiliary vise

When I acquired a large European workbench, I decided to make an auxiliary vise similar to the one made by Ulmia. Held in the right-hand end vise, the auxiliary vise clamps thin

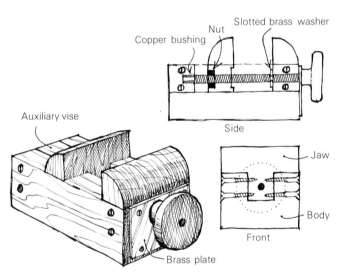

Copper bushing

Nut

Slotted brass washer

Auxiliary vise

Side

Jaw

Body

Front

Brass plate

boards or molding for planing. My version uses maple, a piece of ⅛-in. thick brass, a small handwheel and a length of ordinary ⅜-in. threaded rod.

Make the body of the vise by cutting a 1-in. channel in a maple 2x3. Or glue up two or three pieces of maple into a U. Attach the fixed front jaw and the end block with bolts or screws driven in from the sides. Screw the brass plate to the front of the vise to prevent wear by the knob and threaded rod. Drill a hole through the vise and install the threaded rod and movable jaw as shown in the sketch. I reduced the diameter of the end of the rod and bushed the end block with copper tubing. Recess a nut into the back side of the movable jaw and pin the nut in place with a couple of fine screws, or epoxy it. To keep the threaded rod from slipping out of the vise, file a notch around the rod just inside the front jaw and force a slotted brass washer around the notch as a retainer. Recess the front of the movable jaw to accommodate the washer. —*Ralph Luman, Virginia Beach, Va.*

An Abrasive Planer

Automatic feed and rigid bed offer exceptional accuracy

by Michael Horwitz and Michael Rancourt

Stringed-instrument makers, marquetarians and boxmakers all deal with thin stock that must be thicknessed accurately. Luthiers in particular need to thickness tops, backs and sides often as thin as 0.080 in., and to make bindings and rosette components that commonly measure 0.010 in. or less. Knived planers can rarely handle stock less than ⅛ in. thick, and they produce a scalloped surface. An abrasive planer increases the possibilities for both production and design in thin stock. Simple drum-type, hand-fed sanders (pp. 110, 112, 116) give modest results and do provide an alternative to tedious hand-planing or to purchasing thicknessed wood. However, to the woodworker involved in light production and/or requiring great accuracy, an automatic-feed, continuous-belt abrasive planer can prove valuable. In the seven machines we have built, a rigid bed provides advantages over the conveyor bed of other abrasive planers currently available. The machine detailed here can handle with greater accuracy the most delicate pieces of wood, and its cost and size make it feasible for the small shop. With the construction drawings on the next page, some mechanical know-how and basic machining, a superior abrasive planer can be home-built.

Construction — We make our planers, a 12-in. and an 18-in. size, on a movable base. It consists of eight pieces of angle iron and a half-lapped 2x6 maple frame. The angle iron forms a table whose legs are bolted to the frame, which rides on casters. The top surface of the angle-iron table is 31½ in. high; from it hang the motors (the machine has two motors) and on it is mounted the machine's superstructure. This consists of another 2x6 maple frame into which we mortise 2x4 uprights, attached from beneath with lag bolts. Two cross braces keep the uprights parallel, and two diagonal braces hold them perpendicular to the base.

The machine has two belt rolls: a lower sanding roll, which drives the belt, and an upper belt-tensioning idler. These we make of hardwood plywood discs, stacked and glued together on cold-rolled steel shafts, then turned and sanded with 50 grit. Leaving the bottom roll rough gives necessary belt grab. To prevent warping, the rolls are sealed with sanding sealer and polyurethane. The upper roll is then covered with ³⁄₁₆-in. cork (applied with contact cement) to help belt tracking. A locking pin system keeps each roll from turning on its shaft.

The bearings for the belt rolls are sealed roller-type with double-width races, and must be press-fit onto their respective shafts. The sanding-roll bearings are pressed into housings held in place with setscrews in two steel mounts. The mounts are 1-in. thick

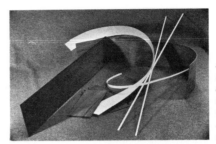

Left, stock thicknessed on abrasive planer, the thinnest pieces to 0.005 in. Below, Michael Horwitz at the 12-in. model.

milled forks, welded to ½-in. steel plates bolted to the machine base. The idler is supported by two belt-tensioning arms that pivot from the uprights on ¾-in. steel rod pinned to the arms. Cutouts drilled with a circle cutter on the insides of the arms receive the bearings for the idler. A snug fit here ensures consistent belt tracking. Slots in the ends of the swing arms receive threaded rods. These pivot from steel angle brackets bolted to the top of the uprights. Each of the two adjustment handles, which control both belt tension and tracking, is a homemade rod-coupler pressed and pinned into a piece of maple shaped like a giant wing nut.

The bed is a piece of ⅝-in. hot-rolled steel covered with Formica. Attached to the underside of the bed by five machine screws is a ¾-in. cold-rolled steel rod, which serves as a pivot mounted in oilite bearings at either end. One end of the pivot is in a fixed maple block; the other adjusts to true the bed parallel to the sanding roll. A piece of threaded rod with a handwheel attached raises and lowers the bed to adjust depth of cut. The rod passes at a 6° angle through a tapped block, welded to a steel cross member. The end of the threaded rod is turned to a soft point to achieve a smaller and more positive contact. A dead stop (two jam nuts on the threaded rod) keeps the bed from contacting the sanding roll.

The accuracy of this machine is achieved in good part by driving the stock past the sanding surface at a steady rate. The three rubber drive rolls are chain driven by a ¼-HP, 18-RPM gear motor. It produces a feed rate of 9 SFM. We made the drive rolls by cutting to length 2-in. medium-hard rubber cylinders and slipping them onto the cold-rolled shafts. We then ribbed the rubber on the table saw and fixed it to the shaft with ¼-in. roll pins. The feed-roll shafts rotate in oilite bearings pressed into collars welded on the end of steel swing arms that pivot on the frame. Tension springs attached between the

arms and the frame provide downward pressure on the stock. Adjustable arm length compensates for chain slackening.

The abrasive belt for the 18-in. machine is driven by a 3-HP, 1725-RPM, totally enclosed, fan-cooled motor, the 12-in. machine by a 2-HP motor. The motor's speed is reduced slightly by a 3½-in. pulley on the motor and a 4¾-in. pulley on the roll. These produce a belt speed of 1,700 SFM. The motor is equipped with an overload button, and all electrical components are matched according to motor amperage.

A vacuum hood mounted directly over the space between the sanding roll and the front drive roll collects dust immediately as it leaves the board. The entire evacuation unit, including the ¼-in. Plexiglas guard, is hinged so it can be swung away during belt changes. For safety, Plexiglas also encloses the drive system and the idler.

For passing many boards through the machine in succession, we designed a stacking attachment to receive stock at the outfeed end. It is a collapsible birch-plywood shelf,

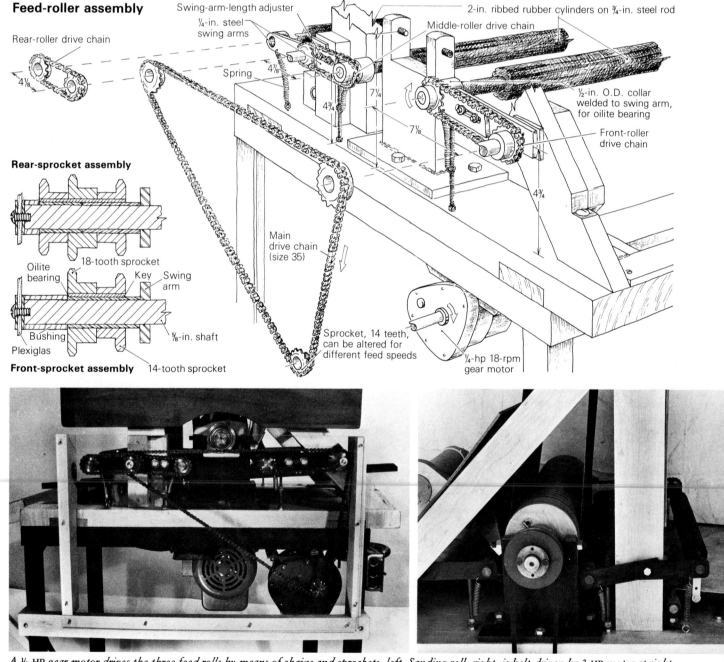

A ¼-HP gear motor drives the three feed rolls by means of chains and sprockets, left. Sanding roll, right, is belt-driven by 3-HP motor at right-hand side of machine. Bed-truing adjuster can be seen attached to back of 2x4 upright.

18-in. abrasive planer

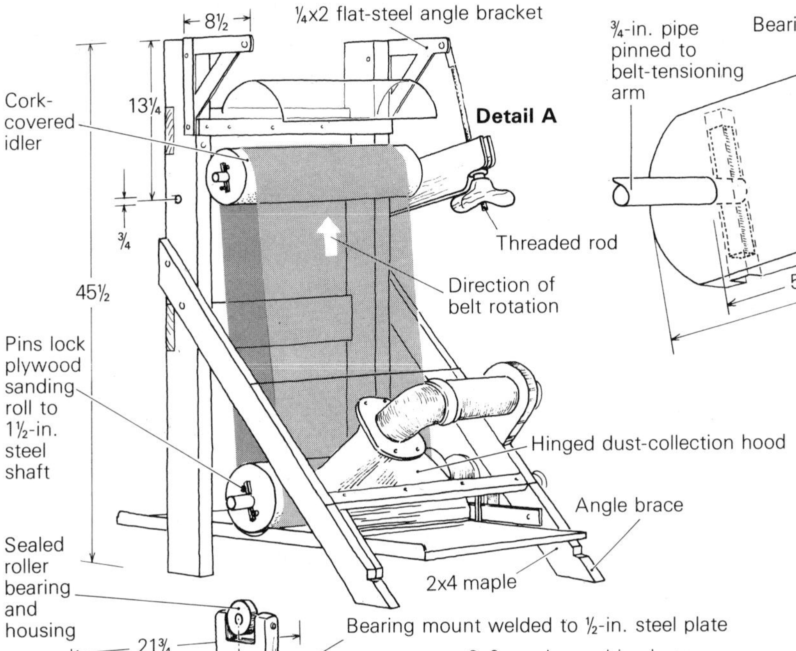
8½
¼x2 flat-steel angle bracket
13¼
Cork-covered idler
Detail A
Threaded rod
¾
45½
Direction of belt rotation
Pins lock plywood sanding roll to 1½-in. steel shaft
Hinged dust-collection hood
Angle brace
Sealed roller bearing and housing
2x4 maple

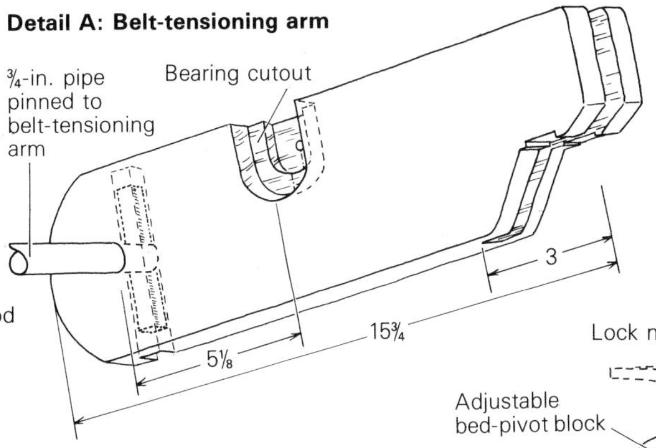
Detail A: Belt-tensioning arm
¾-in. pipe pinned to belt-tensioning arm
Bearing cutout
3
15¾
5⅛

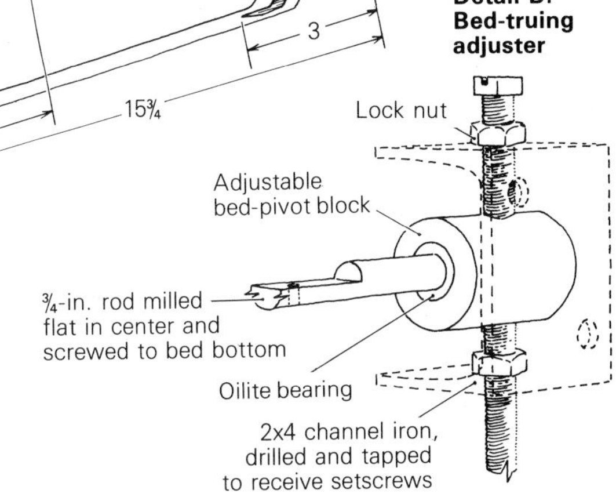
Detail B: Bed-truing adjuster
Lock nut
Adjustable bed-pivot block
¾-in. rod milled flat in center and screwed to bed bottom
Oilite bearing
2x4 channel iron, drilled and tapped to receive setscrews

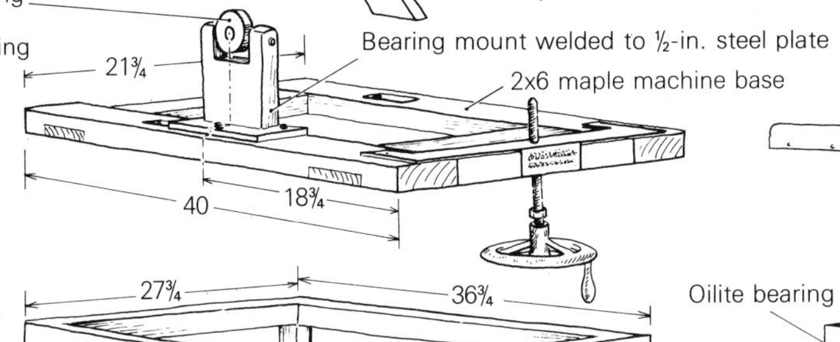
21¾
Bearing mount welded to ½-in. steel plate
2x6 maple machine base
40
18¾

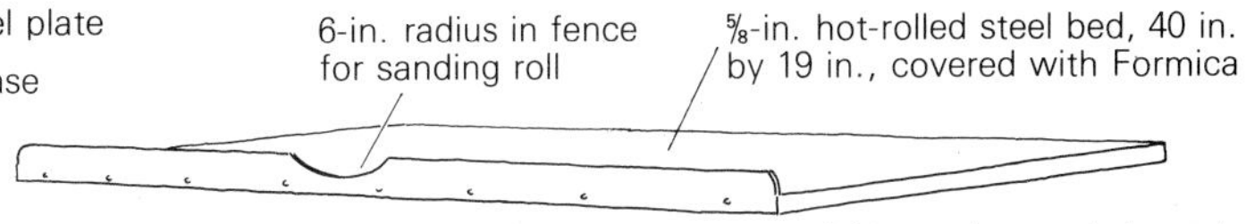
6-in. radius in fence for sanding roll
⅝-in. hot-rolled steel bed, 40 in. by 19 in., covered with Formica

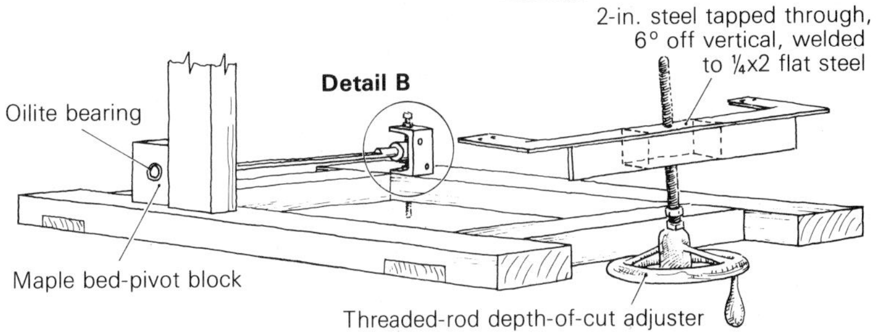
2-in. steel tapped through, 6° off vertical, welded to ¼x2 flat steel
Detail B
Oilite bearing
Maple bed-pivot block
Threaded-rod depth-of-cut adjuster

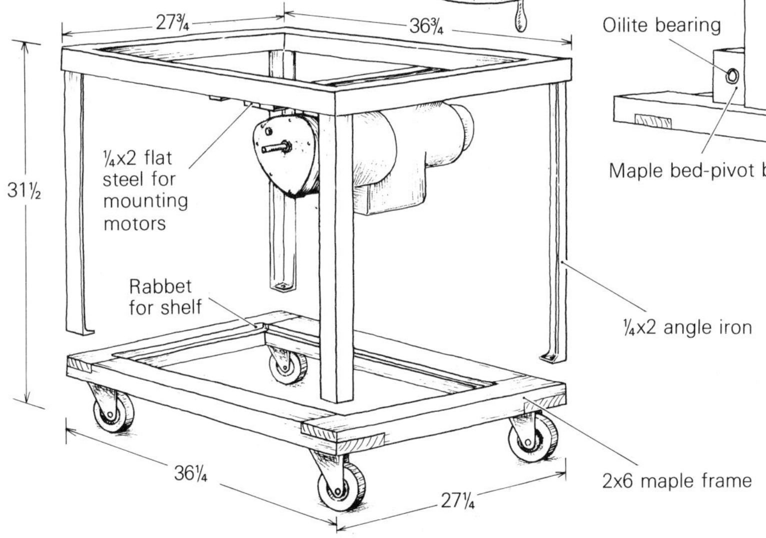
27¾
36¾
31½
¼x2 flat steel for mounting motors
Rabbet for shelf
¼x2 angle iron
36¼
27¼
2x6 maple frame

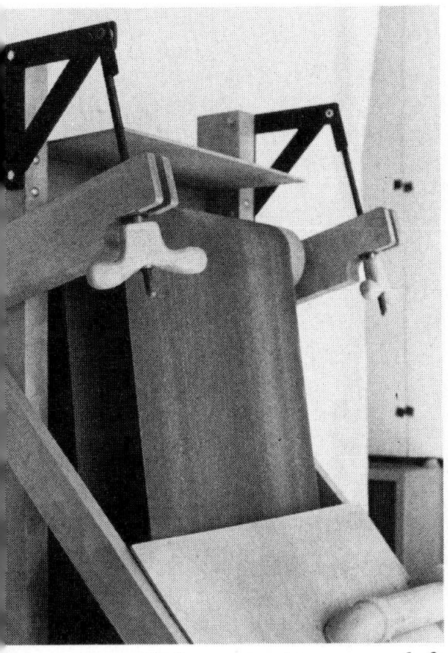

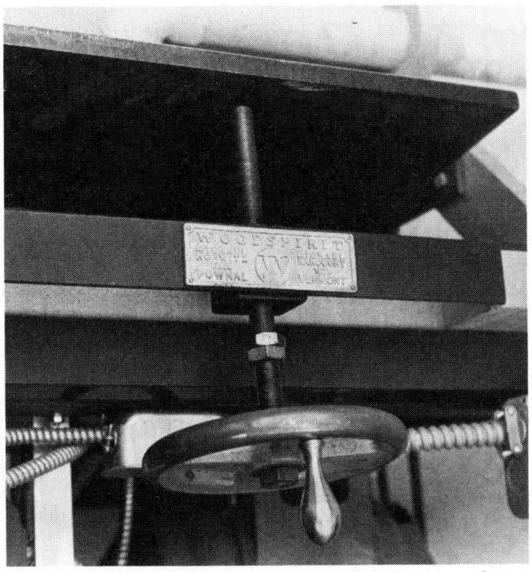

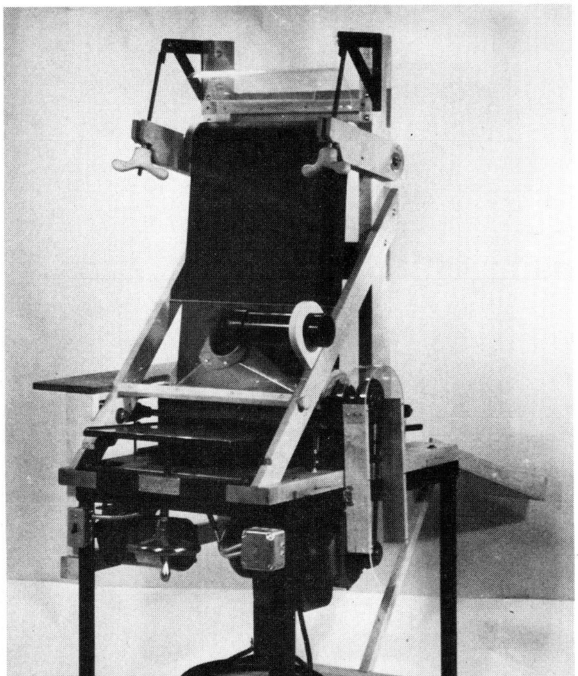

Belt-tensioning arms, left, depth-of-cut adjuster, center, and full view of 18-in machine, right. It measures 76 in. by 44 in. by 34 in. and weighs 800 lb.

Photos: Raymond P. Bub; Illustrations: Christopher Clapp.

hinged from the rear of the base. The rear feed roll eases each piece down onto the stacking shelf.

Operation — To install the belt, loosen the setscrews that retain the sanding roll. Tilt the roller assembly, remove the drive belt and then the roll itself. At the tensioning arms the idler can be removed, passed through the abrasive belt and replaced. Then pass the lower roll through the belt and replace it in the steel mounts. To tension and track the belt, tighten the two wooden wing nuts so that each side is firm but not forcibly stretched. For an initial tracking check, bump the motor on and off. Final tracking is achieved with the motor running. Keep a close eye on the belt for a while, as even a 5° turn of the wing nuts takes minutes to show up as belt movement. Don't get the belt too tight. Tracking can be achieved by loosening as well as tightening the wing nuts.

To get accurate results, the bed must be absolutely parallel to the sanding roll. After turning on the two motors and the vacuum, run narrow test boards through the machine at the sides of the roll, compare their thickness and true the bed using the bed adjuster at the right-hand side of the machine (detail B in the drawing). To begin sanding, lower the bed, using the handwheel at the front, beyond the thickness of the board and pass the board under the feed roll. As the board goes under the sanding roll, raise the bed slowly until light contact is made. Now that the bed is adjusted to the board's thickness, the depth of cut depends on grit, wood density and width of the board. For example, 0.050 in. can be removed from a 10-in. Sitka spruce board with 36 grit, 0.025 in. with 60 grit. In wood as dense as Brazilian rosewood, the maximum cut might be 0.015 in. with 60 grit on an 8-in. board.

Saddle jig with two cam clamps.

Special jigs can hold even the shortest pieces of wood, which to guitar builders can mean the accurate thicknessing of nuts, saddles and bridge blanks. By taping strips of stock to support boards, one can make custom bindings and rosette components. In the repair of a rare Torres guitar, we matched the original binding with maple purfling strips measuring 0.005 in., a size thinner than those available commercially.

We're working on several options to improve the machine. They include a variable-speed feed motor to accelerate taking light cuts and a more powerful sanding motor to make heavier cuts. Another idea is a thickness-calibration system using two dial indicators that would eliminate manual measuring of stock thickness.

The only maintenance necessary on this machine is an occasional oiling of the drive chain, and keeping the machine clean. The vacuum system, which is hooked up to a shop vac, picks up 99% of the dust produced; to achieve accuracy of ± 0.003 in. across the whole width of the planing surface, a relatively dust-free situation is necessary. □

AUTHORS' NOTE: All machine components and complete machines, both the 12-in. and the 18-in. models, are available through us at Woodspirit, Hidden Valley Rd., Pownal, Vt. 05261.

And a Disc Sander

by Donald C. Bjorkman

As the price of tools becomes astronomical, I rely more and more on equipment I build in my own shop. Having been given a ¾-HP., 1,750-RPM motor retired from pumping well water, I felt I was on my way to the sander of my dreams. As with many such projects, procuring parts was most demanding. The materials list at right tells where I got my supplies and what I paid for them last spring.

As I planned to have my sander last me a long time, and because it would cost about one-eighth as much as a comparable commercial machine, I felt I should go first-class on components. I also wanted a sander that would satisfy as many sanding needs as possible. With this in mind I designed a dual 16-in. variable-speed sander with two adjustable tables. As I use both sides of the discs, I have four disc surfaces, each with a different sanding grit: two outboard with tilting tables and two inboard with a stationary table.

Besides the motor, the basic components include ball-bearing, self-aligning pillow blocks to guide the ¾-in. shaft, a hardwood frame joined with mortise and tenon and ⅜-in. Finnish birch plywood for the cabinet stress panels and the sander table. The 30-in. by 44-in. table consists of three layers of plywood laminated together to give a strong 21-ply top, 1⅛ in. thick. (For a simple vacuum press to laminate this top together, see *FWW* #16, May '79.)

Putting the motor down low in the cabinet keeps it out of the dust, allows access to both sides of the discs and makes for a more stable machine. The shaft is fitted with step pulleys. This is helpful when going from rough sanding to medium and then to fine. With 16-in. discs I have found that speeds over 2,000 RPM burn the wood and that speeds less than 1,000 RPM are too slow for good cutting, so I use a 3/3½/4-in. step pulley on the motor and a 4/4½/5-in. step pulley on the shaft. For smaller discs, faster speed could be used.

My only complaint with the machine was the lack of a dust-collection system, which I have recently remedied. As shown in the drawing, the discs run in slots that prevent dust from entering the cabinet. I cut two half-circles of tempered hardboard and glued plywood spacers around the edges. I sanded flat the mouths of two Sears corner nozzles and epoxied them over openings in the hardboard. The covers are attached with wing bolts and T-nuts, and the nozzles connected to a vacuum, which removes most of the dust. □

Don Bjorkman is a professor of fine woodworking and furniture design, industrial design and interior design.

Bjorkman's 16-in. disc sander incorporates tilting tables and uses all four surfaces of the discs. Pulley guard removed for photo.

16-in disc sander

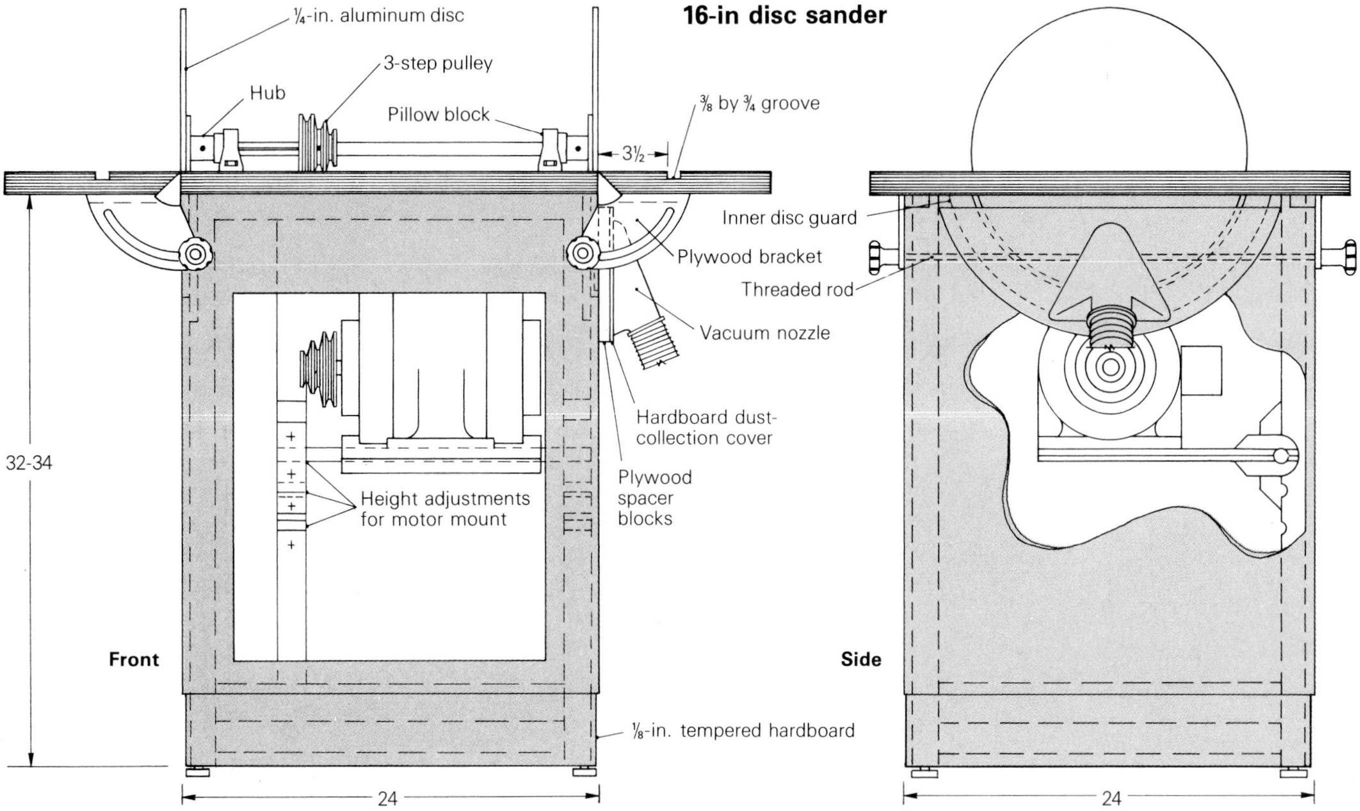

¼-in. aluminum disc
3-step pulley
Hub
Pillow block
⅜ by ¾ groove
3½
Inner disc guard
Plywood bracket
Threaded rod
Vacuum nozzle
Hardboard dust-collection cover
Plywood spacer blocks
Height adjustments for motor mount
32-34
Front
Side
⅛-in. tempered hardboard
24
24

Materials list		
Quantity	Purchased parts	Approx. cost (Spring, 1979)
	Local lumberyard:	
2	⅜x60x60 birch ply	$33.00
5	2x2x34 maple	10.00
8	1½x1½x24 maple	
4	⅛x4x24 hardboard	
2	⅛x8x18 hardboard	1.00
	Machinery supplier:	
1	Manual switch	9.00
24 in.	¾-in. shaft w/keyway	20.00
2	¾-in. ball-bearing pillow block	26.00
2	¾-in. bore step pulley	15.00
4	Adjustable glides	4.00
1	*V*-belt	3.00
	Metals company	
1	¼x16x32 aluminum plate	21.00
	Hardware store:	
6 ft.	Electrical cord	2.50
1	Electrical plug	1.50
2	Cord connectors	.50
1	Tension spring	2.00
24 in.	1¹⁄₁₆-in. continous hinge	3.00
24 in.	2-in. continuous hinge	3.00
4	½x20 *T*-nuts	1.00
4	½x20x1½ wing bolts	1.00
	Bolts, washers, screws	4.00
	Gilliom Mfg., 1109 2nd St., St. Charles, Mo. 63301:	
4	Lock knobs	5.00
2	3 flange hubs	6.00
	Brookstone Co., 127 Vose Farm Rd., Petersborough, N.H. 03458	
4	Thread inserts ⅜-16	1.50
	Sears Roebuck	
2	Corner nozzles (#14277)	3.00
		$176.00

Layout for parts from two sheets of Finnish plywood

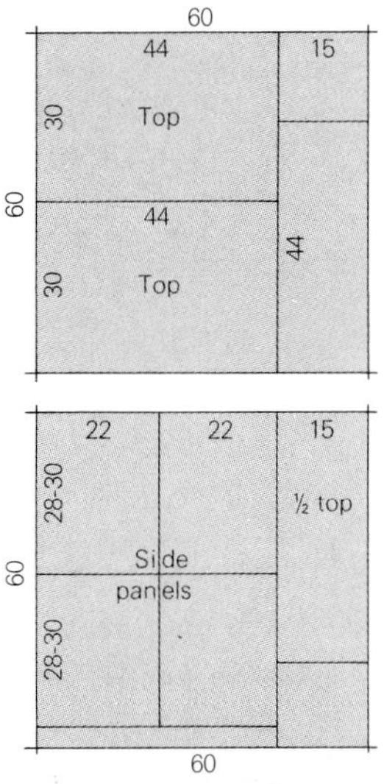

60
44
15
30
Top
60
44
30
Top
44
22
22
15
28-30
½ top
60
Side panels
28-30
60

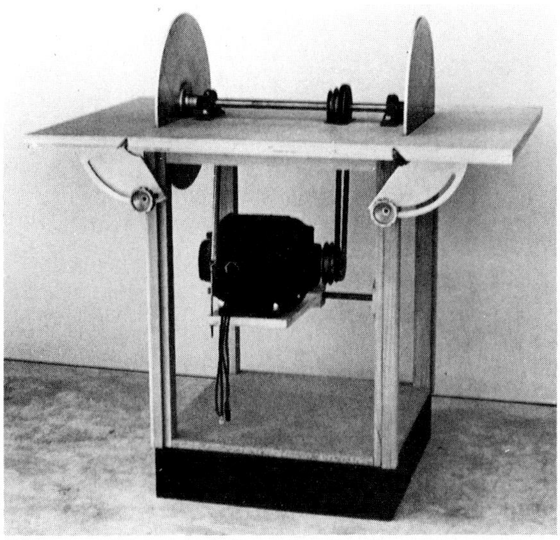

The motor is counterbalanced on its pivot with a spring.

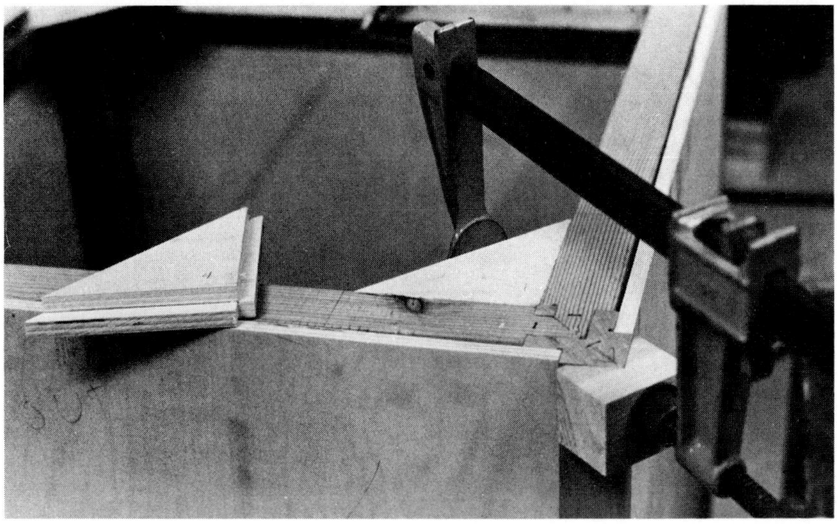

Upper corner bracing is set into groove in frame.

Photos and Illustration: Don Bjorkman

JOINERY

The Butterfly Joint
Double dovetails for strength and beauty

by Frank Klausz

Though the butterfly joint, sometimes called a double dovetail, is ancient, it was hardly ever used in traditional furniture making. Lately, however, it has enjoyed wider use since people have begun to make furniture from solid slabs of wood, from whole flitches or from root sections. George Nakashima's tabletops (*FWW* #14, Jan. '79, p. 43) show how the butterfly can be used for strength and decoration. Across the grain, this joint provides mechanical reinforcement and is especially useful for controlling checks in slabs and for repairing cracks in tabletops and chair seats. The joint can also be used to join separate boards into a single panel or to join up sections that are butted together lengthwise to form a long tabletop or bar top. Recently I put butterflies into a horseshoe-shaped kitchen countertop made from six separate pieces of butcher-block material. These were joined end-to-end with butterflies, three of them for each joint.

I try to make all my butterfly keys the same size, unless the job demands otherwise. So most of the time I cut them 3¾ in. long, 1½ in. wide and ⅝ in. thick. Instead of cutting them one at a time, I like to make a dozen at once. I first cut several strips of wood to a width of 1¾ in. and a thickness of ⅝ in. Then using my radial arm saw and a stop gauge, I cut the strips into pieces exactly 3¾ in. long. I glue 12 of these pieces together, face to face, with just a spot of glue in their centers. I wrap masking tape around the end grain, then I clamp them firmly together. I tilt the arbor on my table saw to a 10° angle and set the fence precisely 1½ in. from the blade where it intersects the plane of the table. The blade should be set 1¹³⁄₁₆ in. high (or slightly less) so the two waste pieces will stay attached to the stock after all four cuts. Make sure you leave an unsawn strip at least ³⁄₁₆ in. wide in the cen-

ter of the wood. With the clamp positioned so it can't contact the blade, I make the cut with one hand, using the bar of the clamp as a handle while pressing down on the stock. It is a hair-raising operation for one who hasn't had much experience using a table saw, but with care it can be done safely.

After making the four necessary cuts, you end up with a stack of perfectly dimensioned butterflies, except for the two waste pieces still attached to the center on both sides. Break these pieces out and clean up the valley by passing a sharp chisel left and right. Now knock the individual butterflies apart. The whole job from gluing to knocking apart shouldn't take longer than a half-hour, or the glue will set hard and you'll have a solid block of wood. Then you'll have to saw the pieces apart.

Instead of gluing 12 or more pieces together, you can cut them all from a single, solid block, if the grain runs in the right direction. This method is economical because you can cut off pieces of whatever thickness you need and save the rest. It also allows you to use short trimmings from wide, thick planks, pieces that ordinarily would be thrown away. Cutting all the keys from one piece is safest because you don't have to clamp the workpiece while sawing and you don't have to worry about them separating during the cut.

If you need only one or two keys, it's best to make a pattern, trace it onto your wood and bandsaw close to the line. Then clean up and straighten the edges with a sharp chisel.

Once you've made the butterflies, you have to set them into the wood. The simplest way is to place a key on the surface (centered across the check or joint and perpendicular to it) and trace around the butterfly with a sharp pencil. With a chisel cut the mortise, being careful to get no closer to the

Butterfly keys are an attractive way to control checks. They can also be used to join single boards into panels.

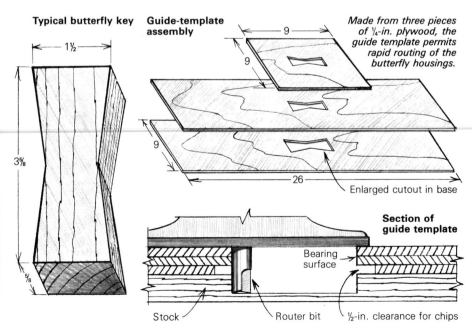

Typical butterfly key

1½

3⅝

⅝

Guide-template assembly

Made from three pieces of ¼-in. plywood, the guide template permits rapid routing of the butterfly housings.

9

9

9

26

Enlarged cutout in base

Section of guide template

Bearing surface

Stock   Router bit   ½-in. clearance for chips

Photos: Frank Klausz and Edward Ludlow; drawings: Ric Lopez

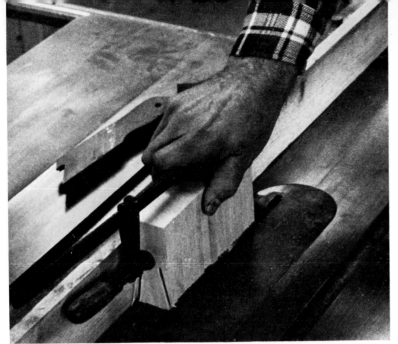

Cutting a dozen keys at one time on his table saw, Klausz uses a bar clamp to help grip the stock. This is a dangerous cut. Do it safely by making sure that the blade clears the clamp jaws and that the thumb is placed high on the workpiece.

To clean up the unsawn center portion of the stock, Klausz holds the chisel askew and slices at the waste, moving from left to right.

lines than ¹⁄₁₆ in. The floor of the cavity can be leveled and smoothed with a router plane and then the walls pared to the line with a chisel.

Because I make a lot of them, I prefer to cut these mortises with my electric router, using a guide template that makes the job quick and easy. So I can make the cutout in the template exactly the same size as the butterfly, I use a two-flute, ¼-in. router bit, which lets the shank bear directly on the template guide. The best bit for this has cutting edges only ½ in. long and is made by Velpec (#4-4-AI) available from Force Machinery Co., Rt. 22, Union, N.J. 07083. You can use other ¼-in. bits, as long as their cutting edges are flush with the shank, but since most of these bits (Rockwell and Sears) have cutting edges longer than ½ in., you'll have to increase the depth of your template so the shank will ride smoothly on the cutout edge with no danger of the bit cutting into the template itself. Remember, the farther the cutting edge is from the router chuck, the more chatter produced and the rougher the cut.

To make the guide template you will need three pieces of good-quality ¼-in. plywood, two of them 9 in. by 26 in. and one 9 in. square. Glue the small square piece in the center of one of the longer pieces. Then lay one of your butterflies on the center of the square piece and draw around it with a sharp pencil. Drill a pilot hole inside one of the corners and saw out the waste with a saber saw, or you can chisel it out. Make sure you are doing very good work here, for all your butterflies will fit like this one. Leave your pencil line on the wood so you can do the final fitting with a file for a perfectly snug fit.

Now take your third piece of plywood, put it beneath the guide template just made and align the outer edges. Trace the cutout onto the bottom piece, remove the guide template and enlarge the tracing by ½ in. all around. Cut out this area with a saber saw. This bottom piece elevates the template the right amount; the enlarged cutout makes room for chips and dust that would otherwise interfere with the bit as its shank bears against the sides of the template. It's a good idea to glue a couple of sandpaper strips to the bottom of the base to help keep it from slipping. Put a little oil on the pattern where the router bit or guide bushing will rub.

Remember that you want the mortise to be about ⅛ in.

shallower than the thickness of the butterfly so you can plane the key flush to the surface. For a butterfly that's ⅝ in. thick, I cut the mortise ½ in. deep.

If you want to use an ordinary straight-face router bit and a guide bushing, then you'll have to make the cutout in your template larger than the butterfly. The exact amount of this enlargement depends on the distance from the cutting arc of your bit to the outer edge of your guide bushing (see "Routing for Inlays," *FWW* #17, July '79).

To rout out the waste, hold the router at an angle so part of the base contacts the surface of the template and center the bit over the cutout. Switch on the power and let the router down flat. Work the tool in a clockwise direction, going from the center to the outside edges, and when you've removed the waste from the center, make a final pass around the edges so that the shank of the bit (or guide bushing) rubs the edge of the template. All that's left to do is to chisel out the four corners, where they've been left rounded by the router bit.

Because the butterfly is usually housed across the grain and the greatest amount of shrinkage and expansion occurs in this direction, a slight undercut on the ends of the mortise is sometimes desirable. This will help prevent the wood from checking if it shrinks against the ends of the key. Butterflies used for repair purposes and visible only from underneath should be cut slightly shorter than their housings, leaving a small gap at either end in case the wood moves.

The butterfly should be glued into its housing, clamped if possible and allowed to dry before you plane it flush with the surface. Avoid using a belt sander to work it down because you can never get the cross-grain scratches out. I use a sharp smoothing plane, followed by a cabinet scraper. Then I sand with 220-grit paper.

Because this joint needs very little material, I try to use dark woods—ebony, rosewood, padauk, purpleheart and black walnut—for contrast with the lighter wood of the tabletop or counter. If, on the other hand, the table is made from a dark wood, I use a light wood for the butterflies, such as lemonwood, satinwood, curly maple or white ash. □

Frank Klausz makes reproduction furniture and restores antiques in Bedminster, N.J.

The Dowel Joint
Why round tenons fall out of round holes, and the elastomer compromise

by R. Bruce Hoadley

Dowel joints must surely be among the oldest methods of joining wood. What could be more basic than a cylindrical tenon fitting a drilled-round mortise, locked forever with good glue? The image of perfection.

But not quite. For our experience suggests that if anything is as old as dowel joints, it is loose dowel joints. We have become resigned to loose and wobbly chairs, and to our mothers warning us not to tilt back at table. Accepting this has always seemed unreasonable to me, so some years ago I set out to study the traditional dowel joint, to find out why they fail and especially to discover the recipe for a joint that would not fail. After many experiments I arrived at the troubling conclusion that no matter how well the joint is made, the conflicting dimensional behavior of the mortise and the tenon in response to humidity variations in our everyday environment can cause self-induced loosening. The very nature of wood ensures that it eventually can come loose. However, some recent research encourages me to believe that soon we will have a dowel joint that is successful, virtually indestructible. In this article I will explore the self-destructive effect of moisture variation on the traditional dowel joint, and I will suggest some remedies and some lines for further exploration.

A plain round tenon in its simplest form, such as an un-shouldered rung inserted into a chair leg, responds to external loading differently from a shouldered tenon, a dowel in a rail/stile frame joint, or a grooved, serrated or precompressed tenon. This article makes no attempt to address such special cases, but focuses on the individual dowel or tenon insertion.

Obviously, the species of wood and the dimensions of a successful joint will accommodate the loads it must sustain. In a typical chair (figure 1), analysis can determine the dimensions and proportions of the joint so that axial stresses along the mating surfaces are safely within the strength properties of the wood. Adding glue provides shear resistance to whatever minor withdrawal load might be imposed. And the commonly used dimensions, which have evolved by experience and tradition, are more than adequate to resist loads imposed by use—or even moderate abuse. Chair rungs are rarely so small in diameter that they fail simply because of excess bending stress and break off at the joint. When they do break here, it is usually because the other end has fallen out of its socket, and someone then steps on the rung. Likewise, as long as the joint remains tight, its bearing areas are usually large enough to distribute the racking loads.

But two common shortcomings lead to problems. First, the mortise may be too shallow in proportion to its diameter. In a Windsor chair, for example, the thickness of the seat limits the mortise to a shallow hole compared with the rather large tenon diameter at the top of the leg. Second, the mating surfaces may be of poor quality. Poor turning or shaping of tenons is not nearly as common as badly bored holes. If the spurs of the auger aren't in top condition, the surface of the

hole is liable to be lined with damaged cells, which can neither support the bearing loads nor develop a successful glue bond. Proper fit is also critical. With water-based emulsion glues (white or yellow), highest withdrawal resistance develops when the dowel diameter is several thousandths of an inch less than the mortise diameter. If the tenon is oversized, the joint will be scraped dry upon assembly; if undersized, the glue line will be excessively thick.

Moisture variation is to blame — If a joint is properly designed and well made, it will carry any reasonable load at the time of assembly. The mystery is why an apparently successful joint loosens due to nothing more than humidity change. The humidity variation in typical indoor situations is wide. In Northern states, humidity in the 80% to 90% range may prevail through August and September, only to plummet to 15% to 20% relative humidity in the subzero days of January and February. This may cause the average equilibrium moisture content of wood to cycle from as low as 4% in winter to as high as 15% in the summer. Even greater extremes occur in such areas as basement rooms, with condensation dampness in summer and a nearby furnace causing excess dryness in winter. Furniture assembled in Scottsdale, Arizona, later moved to New Orleans, and ultimately back to Scottsdale, would go through a similarly drastic moisture cycle. An unfinished wooden ladder, stored flat on the ground and covered with a tarp in summer, then returned to a heated shop for winter storage, would suffer likewise. As a result of moisture cycling, the dimension of wood perpendicular to its

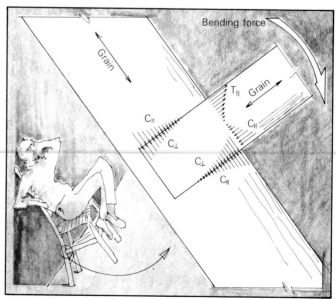

Fig. 1: Tilting back in a chair racks the joints. The rung tends to bend, causing axial stresses (tension, $T_{||}$ and compression, $C_{||}$). In turn the rung tenon bears against the mortise walls, compressing the rung perpendicular to the grain ($C_\perp$) and the mortise parallel to the grain ($C_{||}$).

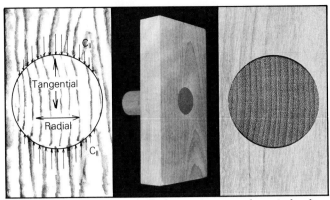

Fig. 2: Paired discs of American beech, left, dramatize the effect of cyclic moisture variation. The top two are as originally turned at 7% moisture content—the wood tightly fits its steel sleeve. The central pair has been moistened to the fiber saturation point (about 30% MC). The lower two were moistened to fiber saturation, then dried to their initial 7% MC. Compression set makes the restrained disc smaller than it started out, whereas the unrestrained disc has returned to about its original size. Right, the handle was tight when this hammer head was sectioned by hacksaw. Then it was stored in a damp place and later redried—the hickory shows severe compression shrinkage, and moisture variation, not the pounding of use, is to blame. This is why soaking a tool in water to tighten a loose handle is a temporary solution at best.

Fig. 3: Increased moisture swells the mortise across the grain by about the same amount as the tenon swells radially. But the mortise doesn't change in height (parallel to the grain). Thus, like the steel sleeve, the end-grain surfaces of the mortise restrain the tangential swelling of the tenon (diagram, left). When the unglued birch joint shown in the photographs was cycled from dry to wet to dry, compression set made the redried tenon smaller tangentially than it originally was, yet still a snug fit radially. Since most woods move more tangentially (in the plane of the annual rings) than radially (perpendicular to the rings), the orientation shown here is not optimum. Turning the tenon 90° in the mortise would be better.

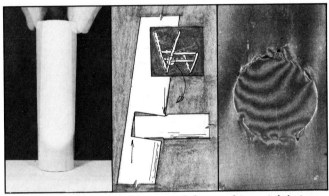

Fig. 4: This white ash ladder rung, left, was driven tightly into a western hemlock rail, then put through a severe moisture cycle. The double exposure shows how loose the joint has become. The diagram shows that once looseness develops in a joint, racking results in concentrated load that may further crush the wood: The worse it is, the worse it gets. Right, a birch dowel in ponderosa pine was coated with moire strain-analysis material and photographed through a grill of undistorted lines. The light-dark patterns show that compression damage extends well into the end grain of the mortise.

grain direction can change by up to 4% of its original dimension. This amounts to a change of 1/32 in. across a 1-in. diameter tenon.

First, consider a wooden dowel confined in a metal socket, such as a hammer handle tightly fitting into its steel head. For our experiments, we simplified this to a dowel of wood fit snugly into a stainless-steel sleeve, then cycled from low to high and back to low moisture content. An unconfined dowel would simply swell and reshrink to approximately its original diameter. However, the restrained dowel crushes itself, and upon redrying to its original moisture content, assumes a smaller-than-original size. Confining a piece of wood to prevent it from swelling by 4% is essentially the same as allowing the piece of wood to swell and then squeezing it back to its original dimension. The trouble is that in confining wood perpendicular to the grain, the limit of elastic behavior (that is, its ability to spring back) is less than 1%. Any additional squeeze will cause permanent deformation, or "set," as in figure 2. In addition, the wood surfaces, already somewhat damaged by machining, do not behave elastically, and seem simply to crush. The result is a concentrated surface layer of crushed and mangled cells.

The wood-to-wood mortise-and-tenon joint is a special situation in that the restraint is unidirectional. The diameter of the mortise does not change parallel to the grain, but its diameter perpendicular to the grain varies right along with the diameter of the tenon. It becomes ovoid during moisture cycling (figure 3). After a dry-wet-dry cycle, compression set is greatest against the end-grain surface of the mortise, while the tenon remains snug at the side-grain surfaces of the mortise. The tenon will therefore be looser in a plane parallel to the grain direction of the mortise.

Such looseness in the side rungs of a post-and-rung chair will allow the chair to rock forward and back. As soon as this

looseness begins, the joint-surface load is no longer distributed evenly, but is concentrated at specific points. The concentrated loads may now exceed the strength of the wood at these points, further crushing the surfaces. So the joint gets looser—the worse it is, the worse it gets (figure 4). With woods of equal density, most of the damage will turn up as crushed tenon because of the lower strength of wood in compression perpendicular to the grain. However, where the mortise is in a lower-density wood than the tenon, such as a hard maple leg tenoned into a white-pine seat, the crushing may be worse on the end-grain walls of the mortise. This bad situation is compounded if the end grain was damaged when the mortise was bored, especially in fragile woods like pine.

Now consider glue. If a good glue bond develops between the tenon and the end grain of the mortise, the shrinking of the compression-set tenon during the drying cycle can be significantly retarded. This is apparent when we make matched samples with and without glue. The unglued joint will open with even the slightest cycle. Glued joints resist moderate moisture variation without failure. With exposure to more

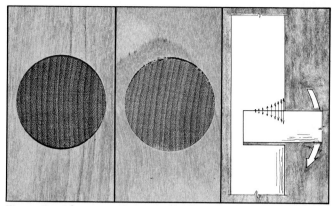

Fig. 5: Dowel joints without glue (left) and with glue, after severe moisture cycling. Once one side of the joint has opened, the other glue line is no match for racking stresses and usually fails in tension. If the mortise was badly drilled, a layer of wood may pull away with the glue.

severe cycles, the joint eventually fails, at first along only one of the end-grain surfaces. The remaining glue bond is now no match for even moderate racking, for the critical stress has become the tensile loading of the glue line (figure 5). When a joint loosens, we assume that "the glue has let go." Close examination may show, however, that a layer of wood tissue has been pulled from the inside of the mortise. This is common where a high-density tenon is glued into a lower-density mortise—the maple leg in the pine seat.

One more point bears elaboration: the behavior of wood in tension perpendicular to the grain. As we have seen, if wood is compressed perpendicular to the grain to well beyond its elastic limit (that is, by several percent of its original dimension), the cell structure is permanently crushed but it remains intact. However, in tension perpendicular to the grain, the strain limit is 1% or 2% of the original dimension, whereupon the wood pulls apart. Therefore if the moisture cycle develops between 1% and 2% compression shrinkage, a glued tenon may be pulled apart during the drying cycle, no matter how perfectly the joint was machined and glued. The tenon actually splits near the glue line. So one way or another, the joint will fail if the moisture cycle is severe.

What to do? — I really didn't appreciate how destructive moisture cycling could be until I ran some experiments. I had arrived at a standard test assembly consisting of a 4-in. by 1-in. dowel inserted into a 1-in.-dia. hole, 1⅛ in. deep, in a 3-in. by 5-in. by 1¼-in. block. In one series, I made 20 similar maple-tenon-in-pine-block joints, using wood that had been conditioned to 6% moisture content. I used a PVA adhesive (white glue). Ten of the joints were stored in sealed plastic bags; the other ten were conditioned up to 18% moisture

content and down to original weight, over a period of several months. The cycled joints weren't wobbly, although visible fracture of the squeezed-out glue along one side of the joints suggested that compression set had developed. Then, by racking the joints with hand pressure, there was an audible snap and the joints became wobbly. When pulled apart in a testing machine, the average withdrawal load of the uncycled specimens was 1,550 lb., while the cycled specimens averaged only 42 lb. This was a terrible predicament, for under commonly encountered moisture variations, even well-made joints were destroying themselves. I didn't want to believe it, but further experiments confirmed this cold, hard truth. To minimize the problem, I arrived at a list of five checkpoints for making joints with the best chance of survival:

1. Proportions. Avoid shallow mortises. I try to make the mortise 1½ times as deep as it is wide. However, if the mortise depth approaches twice its diameter, a new set of problems make the situation worse again.

2. Original moisture content. The wood (especially the tenon) should be slightly drier, not wetter, than its eventual average equilibrium moisture content. Better a little compression than tension at the joint interface.

3. Mortise surface quality. Carefully bore the mortise. Sharpen the bit, especially the spurs, with extreme care to produce the cleanest possible surfaces. Using a drill press or boring guide will improve the hole.

4. Grain/growth-ring orientation. If possible, bore the mortise radially into the female member; orient the tenon with its growth rings perpendicular to the grain direction in the mortise (figure 6). This minimizes the stress by putting radial, rather than tangential, dimensional change in opposition to long-grain structure.

5. Finish the product. Completed work should be given a coat of finish selected to provide maximum protection against short-term, but potentially disastrous, extremes of humidity. Lacquer, varnish or paint is best. And remember to finish all over, especially end-grain surfaces.

All of the above conditions cannot always be optimum, and there will be situations where severe moisture variation cannot be avoided. What other solutions might be possible? For unidirectional stress problems (the chair leg and rung in figure 3), I tried providing stress relief by making a saw-kerf slot in the tenon, thinking that compression would be relieved during the swelling cycle. This helped, but it had the disadvantage of shearing the glue line adjacent to the kerf as each half swelled. Finally I split the tenon—a plane of failure that would relieve stress during the drying phase of the cycle. As compression shrinkage took place, the split could open rather than the glue line failing. In our initial tests with circu-

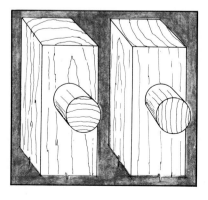

Fig. 6: The optimum condition (left): tangential movement coincides in both mortise and tenon, while the lesser radial dimensional change in the tenon opposes the stable long grain of the mortise. At right, tangential movement varies the depth of the mortise and may 'walk' the tenon out, while compression will cause the greater change in tenon height.

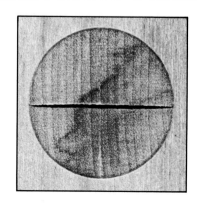

Fig. 7: Birch tenon was split both radially and tangentially before assembly. After moderate moisture cycling, compression shrinkage has developed entirely in one direction, opening the radial split, while the tangential split remains tight. The entire glue line remains intact. This may be what actually happens when tenons are wedged.

lar plugs in flat boards, the presplit tenon opened as predicted, and the glue line remained intact. In matched specimens without splits, the glue line failed. Analysis confirmed that in the compression-shrinkage phase the wood could actually distort itself by enough to relieve the strain. When I made regular, full-depth joints, splitting the tenon to the full depth of insertion, the joint stayed together under moderate moisture cycling (figure 7). I suspect that this mechanism is the real reason why wedged tenons work. Although the wedge is intended to supply lateral pressure to the glue surfaces and perhaps also to splay the tenon for a dovetail-style mechanical lock, it may actually do no more than provide a stress-release slot and thereby help the glue line survive.

Under moisture extremes, a new problem emerges: The mortise depth changes, and the glue line shears. After repeated cycling the tenon remains glued around the bottom of the hole, but shear and compression set develop near the outside junction, and racking eventually completes the break (figure 8). An especially tight fit, good gluing and finishing, and close control of moisture content at assembly can help prevent the mortise from changing depth relative to the tenon. The price is liable to be an unsightly bulge or a check on the back side of the chair leg. So the simple split has promise, but it is not the best solution.

Silicone adhesives — It has always intrigued me to see a heavy motor set into a base with rubber-sleeve motor mounts. Why not set tenons into some kind of rubber sleeves inside the mortise? The rubber might yield enough during the swelling and shrinking phase of the cycle for the glue joint to survive. First, I bonded rubber tubing ⅟₁₆ in. thick around a 1-in.-diameter dowel and glued it into the mortise. A tedious procedure, but I was encouraged when the joint survived severe moisture cycles without failure. Next I experimented with General Electric's RTV (room temperature vulcanizing) silicone elastomers. A translucent formulation, RTV-108 (in hardware stores the product name is Clear Glue and Seal) worked well. To keep the tenon centered and parallel to the mortise while the silicone cured, I glued thin splines onto it at 90° positions (figure 9). Later we figured out how to machine a four-spline tenon with its base diameter undersized by the thickness of the glue line. Hand-carving a dowel to leave four or six thin ribs also works. If the modified portion of the tenon is slightly shorter than the depth of the mortise, the elastomer sleeve can be fully hidden in the joint. Before gluing, slide the tenon into the mortise to be sure the ribs fit snugly. Then wipe a dab of silicone adhesive into all mating surfaces. Next, quickly squeeze a dab into the bottom of the mortise and firmly push the tenon home, allowing the silicone adhesive to flow back up along it. Within an hour it will skin over firmly and you'll soon discover the point at which the squeeze-out solidifies enough to be neatly peeled off. The joint cures within 24 hours but does not reach full strength for a week or more.

I have experimented with various dowel sizes, adhesive layer thicknesses and wood species, and compared the results with conventional assembly glues. Predictably, with fairly thick elastomer layers (0.060-in. layer in 1-in.-diameter mortise) the joints are able to withstand severe moisture cycles (6%-24%-6% MC) without losing withdrawal strength. The same cycle destroys a standard PVA (white glue) joint. For example, in oak joints with white glue, it took an average of

1,100 lb. to pull apart uncycled joints. But after a 6%-24%-6% moisture cycle the average withdrawal resistance was only 41 lb. (most joints were loose enough to be wiggled apart by hand). With RTV-108 (silicone), the original joint strength averages 264 lb.; after cycling, 262 lb. Even though the white-glued joint was stronger in withdrawal to begin with, the silicone-glued joint is strongest after cycling. The silicone joints that withstand the severest moisture cycling are not nearly as rigid as conventional glues and unmodified tenons, and the silicone-glue approach cannot be considered a direct substitute for traditionally made joints. In defense, I point out that after severe cycling, the white-glued joints were often far worse than the silicone joints. However, the rigidity of silicone joints can be improved by increasing the relative depth of the mortise and by making the adhesive layer thinner. It is best to keep the depth of the mortise at

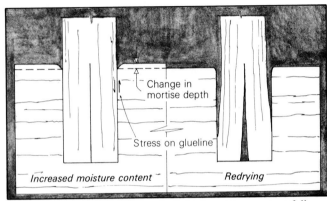

Fig. 8: *In moisture extremes, typically high moisture content followed by redrying, the changing depth of the mortise and compression set near its mouth shear the glue line. The split tenon accommodates stress at the bottom of the hole, but racking will soon break it loose.*

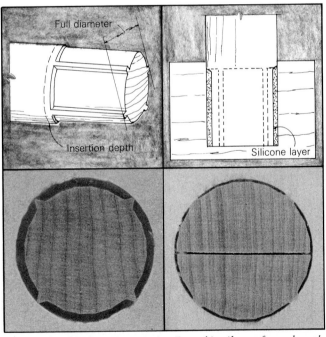

Fig. 9: *The elastomer compromise. Four thin ribs are formed on the tenon, by machining, whittling or by gluing splines onto the tenon. The ribs should be 90° apart, and oriented at 45° to the grain of the mortise. The ribs keep the tenon centered and contribute to rigidity. Their depth determines the thickness of the silicone layer; their length can be short of full mortise depth, thereby concealing the modified portion of the tenon. A split in the tenon contributes to strain relief and allows the silicone layer to be quite thin. The silicone compounds with better adhesion to wood now being developed may solve the problem of wobbly chairs.*

least 1½ times its diameter. With 1-in. tenons, as the glue layer is reduced to about 0.020 in., the joint stays rigid, will have reasonable withdrawal strength and will withstand fairly drastic moisture variation. Effecting this can be a problem in leg-to-seat joints for Windsor chairs, where the seat thickness limits the mortise depth. If the glue layer is too thin, compression will develop. A good point of departure for experiments with 1-in. dowels would be a silicone layer of about ½₂ in. or slightly less. This should give a good compromise between durability under moisture variation, and rigidity.

I have also tried assembling several different types of woods with silicone adhesives. One style of captain's chair, having a pine seat and arms and maple turnings, was assembled using nominal 0.020 in. silicone layers. After six years, all joints are still secure. While seated in the chair, by intentionally racking the frame, you can feel slight springiness due to its non-rigid joints. But nobody who hadn't been told about the special system of joinery has ever commented on the slight wobble. In a set of twelve thumb-back chairs, half the joints were assembled with silicone, half with white glue. The chairs were left in a library lounge for six months of student use. The only failure was in one white-glued joint.

In other items silicone joints seem to be the perfect solution—attaching the smokestack to toy tugboats for the bathtub, where alternate hot-soak and drying of unpainted wood is a most severe exposure. Bathtub toys assembled with conventional glues compression-set and fall apart easily, but silicone joints can take it. Another application is attaching laminated beech sculptor's mallets to their maple handles. Silicone not only solves the loosening problems, but the layer of elastomer seems to contribute to shock absorbancy. I have also used it to reassemble a few pieces of furniture whose

tenons were woefully undersized and loose because of compression shrinkage as well as fist-pounding reassembly many times. Success was predictable according to joint proportions: Shallow mortises didn't work out, but where the tenons were long and the mortises deep, the silicone did a perfect job of filling the gaps and solving the looseness problem, perhaps forever.

Note that all of these remarks apply to rectangular structures, which rely on joinery for rigidity. A triangulated structure, on the other hand, is inherently stable, and silicone glues might be exactly right. I hope some craftsmen may be encouraged to experiment along these lines.

Combining silicone with a stress-relief split in the tenon also looks promising. I found that the glue layer can be held to a minimum (0.010 in. to 0.015 in.), since part of the problem is handled by the opening of the split tenon. Some typical values for direct withdrawal of a maple tenon from a pine mortise, before and after moisture cycling, are: with white glue, 1,553 lb. and a mere 42 lb.; with a layer of silicone 0.010 in. thick, 830 lb. and 290 lb.; and with silicone plus a slit in the tenon, 753 lb. and a surprising 580 lb. The limiting feature of silicone adhesives has been adhesion to the wood surface. Average tensile strengths perpendicular to the surface are only about 200 PSI. Recently, however, we have tested some formulations (not yet on the retail market) which have more than double this strength. I am confident that we will hear a lot more about silicone elastomers, and see them specifically incorporated into joinery work. □

Bruce Hoadley teaches wood science at the University of Massachusetts, in Amherst. For more on repairing wobbly chairs, see p. 157.

One Chairmaker's Answer

(EDITOR'S NOTE: The following is excerpted from *Make a Chair from a Tree: An Introduction to Working Green Wood*, by John D. Alexander, Jr., published by The Taunton Press, 1978.)

The goal is to employ the compressability of green wood without exceeding the elastic limit of the fibers in the tenon. When the moisture balance is right, we can drive in an oversized tenon and create a tight bond between the surface of the mortise and its tenon.... At the time of mortising and assembly, the post should contain about 15% to 20% moisture (air-dried outdoors) and the rung about 5% (dried indoors near the stove).

...I flatten the sides of all the tenons in my chair—slightly more so

on the tenons of the rungs near the top of the front posts. Flats not only prevent posts from splitting during drying, but after drying they act as a lock that prevents the tenon from rotating in the mortise.... Taper the flats a mite so they are broader and deeper toward the shoulders. This makes them slightly dovetailed when viewed from above. If all goes well, the shrinking post locks the dovetailed tenon into its mortise. Last, notch the tops and bottoms of the tenons so that when the compressed end grain of the mortise dries and straightens, a ridge of post wood will be forced into this notch....

When the chair is assembled, the wood rays in the tenon should be oriented vertically, in the same direction as the long axis of the post. This orientation aligns the direction of maximum rung movement (the tangential plane) with the direction of maximum pressure from post shrinkage....Looking from the top of the post, bore the mortises so that the plane of the wood rays bisects the angle between the front and side rungs. This allows each tenon to be compressed equally as the wet wood shrinks....Bore the bottoms of the side mortises about ³⁄₃₂ in. lower than the tangent lines laid out earlier from the tops of the front and rear rung mortises. This locks the rungs together inside the post...I use glue. I use every technique I can that might help the chair hold together.   —J.D.A.

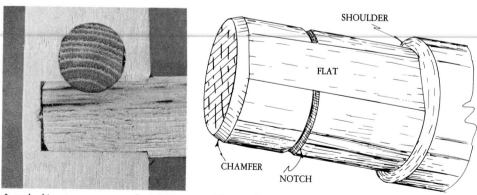

Interlocking tenons secure the joint; tapered flats and notches also help.

SHOULDER

FLAT

CHAMFER

NOTCH

The Frame and Panel
Ancient system still offers infinite possibilities

by Ian J. Kirby

Fig. 1: Section through frame and panel

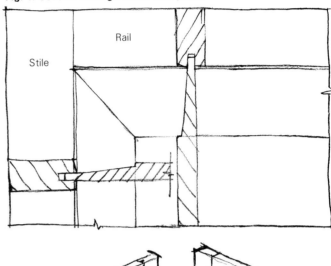

Scarcely another system in the whole range of woodworking has more variation and broader application than the frame and panel. In the frame-and-panel system, pieces of solid wood are joined together into a structure whose overall dimensions do not change. The frame is usually rectangular, mortised and tenoned together, with a groove cut into its inside edge. The panel fits into this groove: tightly on its ends since wood does not move much in length, but with room to spare on the sides because wood moves most in width (figure 1). Wood is not uniform and as it moves in response to changing moisture conditions, it cups, twists, springs and bows. Trapping the panel in the groove inhibits this misbehavior.

Historically, the basic technique that made possible the frame and panel is the mortise-and-tenon joint, on which I have already written extensively. The frame and panel is a basic unit of structure. It can be used singly (a cabinet door) or in combination (to make walls, entry doors, cabinets). The several elements of a single frame and panel may be varied almost without limit, and its aesthetic possibilities are infinite. The little choices made during its manufacture are aesthetic choices, and we can begin to see the interdependence of design and technique. Neither the frame-and-panel system nor its joinery can be thought of as an end in itself. Neither has any importance except in application, toward the end of making a whole thing out of wood.

To overcome the panel's tendency to distort, we make it as thin as the job will allow, while we make the frame relatively thick. By doing this we haven't significantly altered the amount by which the panel will shrink and expand, but we have rendered it weaker so that the frame has a better chance of holding it flat. Panels can be made as thin as ³⁄₁₆ in. but such panels were uncommon before the 19th century because woodworking tools were not readily capable of such refinement. The thickness of the panel was dealt with in a number of ways, the most usual being to raise and field it.

Generally raising and fielding are thought to be the same thing—the process of cutting a shoulder and a bevel on the edges of the panel and thereby elevating the field—that is, the central surface of the panel. I'd like to distinguish between these two terms. Fielding refers to any method of delineating the field of the panel from the frame; raising means cutting a vertical shoulder around the field, which may or may not be accompanied by a bevel.

Given this system for maintaining panel size and shape against the hygroscopic movement of wood, woodworkers in the past found that the system's elements could be varied to produce different aesthetic results in terms of form, color, texture, pattern value, proportion of parts, highlight and shadow (figure 2). By carving the panel, we imprint upon it richness and grandeur. By inlaying it, we make it into a vehicle for the decorative use of other materials, and by using moldings of different profiles, we change the various propor-

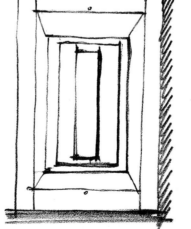

Fig. 2: Proportion and pattern

The pattern possibilities are infinite. The peg holding the panel on center can be an interesting detail for the observer to discover—don't let it become a cliche. It needn't be taken through to the front of the rails.

Illustrations: Ian J. Kirby

tions within the whole. We can alter the mood of a piece by changing the panel's attachment to its frame.

Within the predetermined dimensions of the frame, the relative proportions of the rails and the stiles can vary considerably, though it is common to find the top rails in a door to be about two-thirds the width of the bottom rail, and the stiles to be about three-fourths the width of the top rail. This isn't necessary to produce an acceptable appearance, but many woodworkers build doors as though these proportions were divinely decreed. Altering them within the limits of structural necessity can produce a wholesome diversity of appearances. The proportions of the panel—the dimensions of its field, the depth of its shoulder, the width and slope of its bevel—are all subject to considered alteration.

For showing off highly figured wood, the frame and panel is excellent. The usual way of doing this has been to resaw the figured piece and to edge-join the halves into a bookmatched panel. Edward Barnsley's desk *(FWW #16, May '79)* exhibits how figured wood can be enhanced by a frame. This desk, by the way, incorporates two different types of frame-and-panel construction and shows the discriminating and sensitive use of a frame and panel typical of Barnsley and others, such as Gimson and Vals, who were part of the Arts-and-Crafts movement. Generally, the plainer form of paneling—overlaying it onto the frame—shows a highly figured piece of wood to its greatest advantage. Raising and fielding can look fussy when the wood is highly figured.

The face of the panel can be treated in countless other ways. You can inlay it with mother-of-pearl, ivory, brass or other materials, or the field can serve as a ground for marquetry or wood inlay. Carving on panels has taken many forms. English "joyners" of the 13th to 15th centuries imitated almost slavishly the tracery and linenfold patterns common in stonemasonry. It was also common in this period for panels to be painted with vibrant colors in a variety of abstract geometric designs. In our own century, Mousey Thompson adzed the surface of quartersawn oak panels for a mild rippled texture, subtle to touch and sight.

I wish contemporary panels conveyed such vitality and served the imagination as well. I'm not saying that we have to paint panels or inlay them or dress them up in other ways. I am saying that we ought to realize that the panel is an unexploited vehicle for expression, for there is in fact no woodworking system with as great a potential for individualization within its essential structural features. This invites the woodworker to explore some of the system's possibilities. The easiest way to play with all of these possibilities is to make a

full-size drawing, or several of them, to help you visualize the critical relationships between the parts. A further survey of traditional treatments and manufacture of the solid-wood frame and panel may help contemporary woodworkers to a livelier use of the system.

The frame — Designing a frame and panel begins with a sectional view of the two parts and a decision about the joint to be used in bringing the frame together. The groove is generally placed in the center of the frame stock. If you use a square haunched mortise and tenon to join the frame, then the grooves can be plowed right through the joint without interruption (figure 3). This is no happy accident. The joint was designed for the groove to be continuous, because a plow plane can't cut a stopped groove. When making the haunched mortise and tenon by hand, the question arises about what to do first, plow the grooves or cut the joint. I recommend cutting the mortises and tenons first. If you plow the groove first, you obliterate the gauge lines on the mortise and on the inner edge of the tenon. And nothing is more agonizing than trying to cut an accurate mortise without reference to gauge lines. Also, it's easy to be tricked into thinking that you are cutting the mouth of the mortise at the same time you plow the groove. You can in fact. But if your mortising chisel is not exactly the same width as the groove, you'll find it almost impossible to cut the rest of the mortise in an accurate way. Using a chisel that is too large or too small, even by a minute amount, makes cutting the mortise walls an exercise in guesswork and error.

If you wish to use a mortise and tenon of the sloping haunch type so that the joint shows an uninterrupted straight line, then some means of stopping the groove must be employed. This is quite easily done on a router, shaper or circular saw by the use of end stops.

Another aspect of the frame that deserves attention is the profile of its inner edges. Since standard shaper knives are frequently used to make molding and scribe cuts in rails and stiles, I'd like to describe the less common practice of chamfering the inner edges. It creates a boundary that is decisive and bold, not busy or blurry like poorly conceived moldings. There are three conventional ways to chamfer the inner edges of the frame, two of which require redesigning the joints.

The simplest way is to assemble the frame dry and cut a 45° chamfer with a router, using a bit with a ball-bearing pilot. The cut will be rounded in the corners (figure 4) but can be squared up if desired with a sharp chisel to form what is called a mason's miter (figure 5). But if you want the line of the joint and the outer edges of the chamfer to form one continuous line, then more refined joinery is called for. The first method involves cutting the tenons on the rails as if you were making a long-and-short-shouldered joint (figures 6 and 7). Cut the mortise in the conventional fashion, and then chamfer the inner edge of the stile. To accommodate the chamfer, the long shoulder of the tenon is beveled inward from the shoulder line. A variation of this method also leaves the line of the joint and the outer edge of the chamfer uninterrupted. But instead of beveling the underside of the long shoulder on the rail, you remove a section from the face of the stile to accommodate the long shoulder. Then the chamfers on both rail and stile must be mitered to fit (figure 8). Making this joint requires careful measuring and marking with a mortise gauge and cutting gauge. Chiseling should be done across the

Fig. 3: *Haunched mortise and tenon is designed for an unstopped groove.*

Stile

Rail

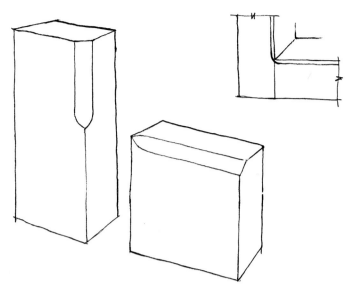

Fig. 4: *To bring the chamfer around the corner in a 90° arc, cut most of the bevel before assembly. The corner round should be completed after gluing up because of the fragile short grain on the rail.*

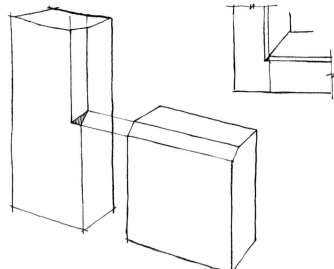

Fig. 5: *Mason's miter brings vertical and horizontal chamfers together. The disadvantages are that the chamfer does not line up with the shoulder of the joint, and a little triangle of end grain spotlights the mitered corner.*

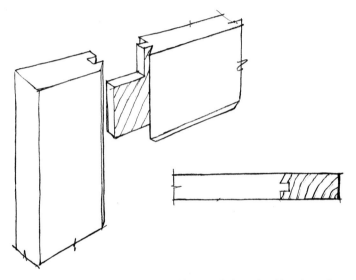

Fig. 6: *Beveled or scribed version of long-and-short-shouldered mortise and tenon permits precise alignment of joint and chamfer lines.*

Scribing line

Original shoulder line

Fig. 7: *Plan of stile/rail joint showing original line of shoulder before undercutting.*

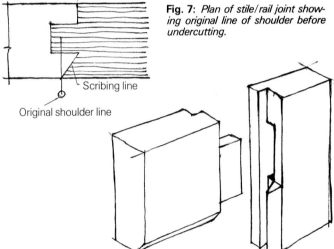

Fig. 8: *Another variation of long-and-short-shouldered mortise and tenon demands care in marking out to get the joint to close properly and the miters to meet on a line.*

grain, and the mouth of the mortise plugged with a softwood block to prevent the tissue from splintering out.

Don't sand the chamfer if you wish to retain its crisp edges and the fine texture of its tooled land. Sandpaper rounds and softens these critical light-reflecting angles and faces. You may try sanding, and even get an apparently satisfactory look until the finish is applied, but then you will find the crispness lost and the clarity of the land muddied.

Yet another variation in the design of the frame is not to use grooves at all, but to lay the panel in a rabbet cut into the edges of rails and stiles. The panel is retained with an applied molding on the show side of the work. Some might think this method to be a good example of bad workmanship, but it is well suited for some types of work, including those using modern materials. It's worth noting that much of the traditional frame-and-panel joinery was done this way.

The panel — When thinking about the design of a panel three possibilities are available: a fielded panel, raised or not, an unfielded panel and an overlapped panel. According to the type of design you choose, you must consider variables such as the size of the field relative to the frame dimensions, the width and slope of the bevel, the depth of the shoulder, and the treatment of the field (carving, inlay, figured wood)—all of which combine to determine the finished look.

You can field a panel without raising it by cutting the bevel right through to the field and eliminating the shoulder. But it's difficult to get good results when you define the field with the bevel alone because invariably that critical line where the two converge will be untrue. It can be straightened out with a hand plane, but it's not easy. Also, panels without shoulders look indecisive, even if the field edge is straight.

It's common practice when raising a panel to cut the shoulder lines first (figure 9). This fields and raises the panel and gives you an idea of its proportions. You can accomplish this by setting the fence on your bench saw to the width of the bevel and the blade to the depth of the shoulder, producing four shallow cuts equidistant from the panel's edges. Saw the bevel by tilting the sawblade to the required angle and setting it to the required depth. When cutting the bevel, a wedge should fall off the waste side of the cut; this means that pressures on the blade are equal right and left. But raised

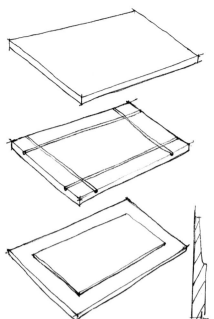

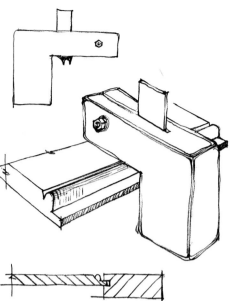

Fig. 9: *The field is defined by saw or router cuts. You can use a nosed cutter in your router to give the shoulder a softer profile. The bevel is angled at the time of sawing or it can be cut with a bench rabbet plane.*

Fig. 10: *A panel edge need not be beveled. Here it is rabbeted and a bead mold run down its edge. The scratch-stock must be held firmly and pushed away from the body. It should settle gently into the cut and not be forced.*

Fig. 11: *The edges of the overlapped panel may be treated in a variety of ways—rounded, beveled or left square. At this stage you introduce details that affect the highlights and shadows of the panel.*

panels are usually more delicate than this will allow. So to minimize blade vibration and consequent scoring of the bevel, use a sharp, stiff tungsten-carbide-tipped saw and feed the work gently into the blade.

However carefully you cut the bevel, its sawn face will need some cleaning up. It can be sanded, but you'll have greater control and get better results using a rabbet plane that's wide enough to clean the whole width of the bevel in a pass. You could also make a jig for your router and make the cuts with a properly profiled bit, or you can obtain the fastest results with a spindle shaper. The latter should be used with great caution, and you should make three or four passes, removing only a little stock with each.

Because the whole system is designed to accommodate the hygroscopic movement of wood, it's not unusual for a panel to travel about in its grooves, sometimes being noticeably off center. This is easily rectified by driving two nails or wooden pegs into holes on the inner edge of the frame, top and bottom, so that they capture the panel on center (figure 2, p. 131). The pegs make interesting little details if left slightly proud and rounded off. You can get the same result by applying a dab of glue in the center of the grooves top and bottom, taking care during assembly to position the panel properly. It is normal for the panel to rattle when tapped. The rattle can be eliminated, but need not be.

The panel doesn't have to be raised and fielded to be held in the frame. One of the sweetest systems brings the groove forward of center to create a flush panel from very thin stock. This system demands accuracy in cutting the top and bottom shoulders so they just touch the rails. The panel edges, which move slightly over the frame, can be molded by using a scratch-stock that you can make yourself (figure 10).

The third possibility exchanges the angular, vigorous look of the usual raised panel for the softer, more subdued look of the overlapped panel. Panels of this sort are rarely seen because most woodworkers hesitate to depart from the more accepted method, yet they are no more difficult to make. The

panel is held in the frame by a set of tongues and grooves, which should not be cut too deep as a long tongue is likely to curl back (figure 11).

Given the possibilities of the frame and panel, it is surprising to find them so little realized by contemporary cabinetmakers working in solid wood. Industry, however, has not ignored their appeal. In one method of quantity production, frame-and-panel doors are molded from a mulch of the sort used to make particle board. After a few seconds of heat and pressure, out pops a frame and panel, raised, fielded and detailed to your requirements, ready for printing with a photocopy of wood grain. Before the offended reach for their pens, consider that if industry will apply its technical and economic resources to such an extent, there must be a strong demand for the frame and panel. Given this market, there is a noticeable lack of frame and panel being used in a refined and exciting way by makers of hand-built, solid-wood furniture. This seems a pity since I've always felt that the cabinetmaker's shop could be the birthplace of technical and aesthetic models for industrial production.

The sad fact of the matter is that there exists an emotional antagonism between the designer/craftsman and the designer/executive, and little productive communication is shared between them. The craftsman suffers the most as a result, because he closes the door on salespeople, designers, decorators and others who work either with or for the larger furniture manufacturers. It does the craftsman little good to have a vast technical knowledge, a keen aesthetic sense and a shop full of tools if he denies himself contact with people who can market his furniture and who can benefit from his fidelity to quality and his innovative thinking. I hope this examination of the frame and panel will promote improved communication between the craftsman in his shop and the larger world of woodworking. □

Ian Kirby, a regular contributor to this magazine, teaches woodworking and makes furniture in Bennington, Vt.

On Dovetailing Carcases
Which to cut first, pins or tails?

by Ian J. Kirby

The through dovetail has become synonymous with quality woodworking, a hallmark of distinction. This is understandable because the joint must be handmade—we don't have a machine that can produce variations in the dimensions and angles of its tails and pins. I do wonder, however, why so many woodworkers see the joint as a standard of craftsmanship. In terms of skill it is considerably easier to make than the mortise and tenon or the secret mitered dovetail. Cutting the through dovetail is little more than sawing to a line. I make this point not to demean the work, but to encourage anyone who might feel inhibited about attempting dovetail joints. The through dovetail is not difficult, and it should not be thought of as the ultimate in woodworking skill.

The through joint was routinely used by 17th and 18th-century cabinetmakers to put a carcase together very quickly. It doesn't take much experience before you can lay out and cut the joint with the minimum of marking out. If you make the end of the board square and knife the depth-line around, the spacing of pins and tails is easy to eyeball *(FWW #17, July '79)*. Lines may be penciled square across the end grain as an assist, but with practice even this is not necessary. It doesn't matter if the angle on the tails varies, since the pins will be marked and sawn from the tails; the interface will still be tight. It was usual 200 years ago to cover the through joint with an applied molding. The outlook and attitude of the times was to conceal structure behind some embellishment. Note the direct contrast with 20th-century attitudes—our urge is to expose structure as part of the dynamic of the object, and to read structural detail as the mark of quality. Figure 1 illustrates some layout possibilities.

The details of laying out and cutting the joint have been written about by other authors *(FWW #2, Spring '76, and #8, Fall '77)*. What I have to say concerns the associated and attendant techniques. There is, however, one point about making the joint itself: whether you should cut the tails first and mark the pins from them, or whether you should start with the pins and mark the tails from them. Woodworkers disagree, and either way will achieve the result. If you understand both, then the answer to which is correct has to be, whichever method you are most comfortable with, and whichever gives the better result. The decision is often determined by which board in a carcase—the vertical or the horizontal—is to have the tails, and which board is the longer. For example, take the proportions of a carcase as shown in figure 2 and assume we want the tails on the longer piece. They will therefore show from the top. If the tails are made first it is simple to put the pins board upright in the vise, position the tails board on it, and mark the pins through the tails. If the pins were made first, then to mark the tails you would have to balance the pins board vertically on the tails board. This is usually done by clamping the pieces in place on the edge of the bench. If the pins board is in any way cupped or twisted,

the problem is compounded by having to clamp straightening battens across it. When the tails are made first, a cupped or warped piece can be straightened by blocks or by clamps put across the bench. Having come this far, I should say that for through or lapped dovetails I make the tails first. It seems to give better control over the marking out and cutting, and better control of the boards themselves. On the other hand, when cutting a secret mitered dovetail, you must make the pins first and mark the tails from them—it can't be done the other way around.

The sawing of the joint also takes on different flavors depending on whether you cut the tails or the pins first. If you make the tails first, then the first thing is to get the sawblade at right angles to the face of the board, and the kerf is made just 1/32 in. or so deep right across the end grain, as shown in figure 3. Make this initial kerf by keeping the saw vertical and don't yet be concerned about the tail angle. The small amount of vertical cut will not affect the extreme tip of the tail. Right-angularity having been achieved, set the saw at the angle to which you wish to cut the tail.

Once started, the angle must not be adjusted or the result will be a bent line. This bent line cannot be "mirrored" on the pin—and anyway, if the angle varies a little from one tail to another, does it matter? The important thing is to have all the sawcuts at right angles to the face of the board. If you make the pins first, cutting them follows this same procedure. But once the tails have been marked from the pins, there is no room for any variation in sawing the angle. The kerf is made across the wood to about 1/32 in. deep, and the

Fig. 1: Dovetail layout

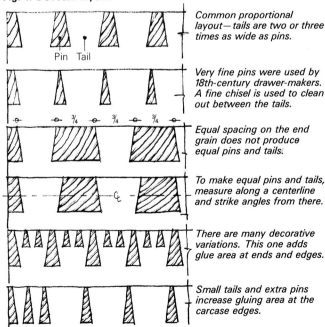

Common proportional layout—tails are two or three times as wide as pins.

Very fine pins were used by 18th-century drawer-makers. A fine chisel is used to clean out between the tails.

Equal spacing on the end grain does not produce equal pins and tails.

To make equal pins and tails, measure along a centerline and strike angles from there.

There are many decorative variations. This one adds glue area at ends and edges.

Small tails and extra pins increase gluing area at the carcase edges.

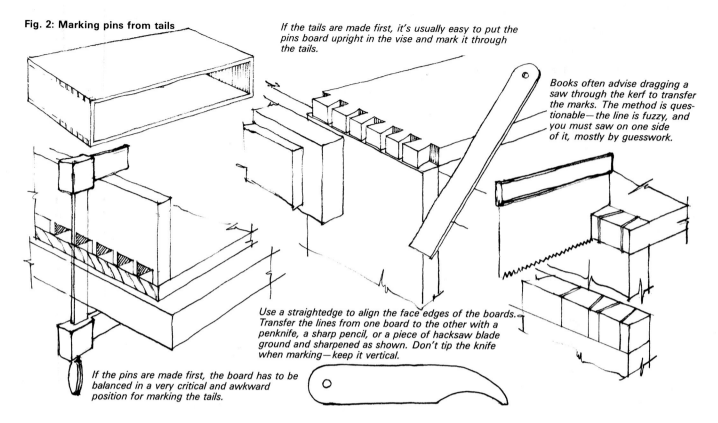

Fig. 2: Marking pins from tails

If the tails are made first, it's usually easy to put the pins board upright in the vise and mark it through the tails.

Books often advise dragging a saw through the kerf to transfer the marks. The method is questionable—the line is fuzzy, and you must saw on one side of it, mostly by guesswork.

Use a straightedge to align the face edges of the boards. Transfer the lines from one board to the other with a penknife, a sharp pencil, or a piece of hacksaw blade ground and sharpened as shown. Don't tip the knife when marking—keep it vertical.

If the pins are made first, the board has to be balanced in a very critical and awkward position for marking the tails.

saw is sighted and set exactly at the angle which must be achieved to give a good interface.

Whatever the method, getting the saw into the correct angle is probably best achieved by beginning the cut on the far side of the wood—not, as one might expect, from the near side. Use light strokes to start, almost lifting the weight of the saw off the wood. Once the shallow cut is made and the saw will remain in the kerf, then saw across the line toward the near side—don't cut any further down the back side of the workpiece. You must concentrate on achieving the angle, not on reaching depth of cut, at this stage. Starting from the far side seems to give better vision into the workpiece—the saw does not hide the line, and the dust is easily blown away. All you have to accomplish is the shallowest kerf across the end grain, to give the saw teeth a register in which to work. If you lift the saw out, the kerf should be well defined across the board but too shallow to have direction downward. Now you can set the saw to the required direction—at an angle for a tail, or vertical for a pin. All of this assumes that you have placed the board vertically in the vise for sawing. If you want to become skilled with the saw, there is no virtue in tilting the wood in the vise. Keep the workpiece square to the bench and learn to saw at the required angle.

To gain skill, the amateur craftsman should look for and take every opportunity to practice. This often leads to experiments in softwood, for utility work around the home and shop, but it can be a disappointment. Generally, softwood tissue is alternately hard and soft, and the soft part readily crumbles if forced into too tight a joint. When cleaning out the bottoms of either pins or tails, that is, when paring across the grain, the wood will crumble badly unless the chisel is absolutely sharp. It helps to ease the under-edges of the tails when working in softwood (figure 3) or when you have made one or more pins a little too tight. With the sharpening bevel of a wide chisel toward the wood, remove a sliver of material from the corner of the tail which is going to come first into

contact with the edge of the pin. Don't cut away any tissue that will be visible, and remove an absolute minimum only. It may seem wasteful to practice with good wood such as a mild-working mahogany, but the feedback of information through your tools and hands, plus success achieved at a critical learning time, makes it worth the expense.

From the outset you should work toward making a through dovetail straight from the saw. The cross-grain surfaces must be chiseled flat, of course, but if the beginner thinks that long-grained surfaces should be sawn fat and chiseled back to the line, adequate results will be a long time coming. You can get the result you want directly from the saw, and to a very high standard, after only a few practice tries.

Having become skilled at making the joint, you may wish to try a mild variation: a very slight off-square cut when making the tails (figure 3). Mark out the joint as usual, with the face side of the board toward the inside of the finished piece. But instead of sawing the line of the tail square to the face, very slightly angle the saw so that the normally parallel gap on the end grain of the tails is wider toward the face side of the board. The gradient of the tail isn't altered, but the tails have a larger pin gap on the face side of the board than on the outside of the carcase. When the pin is subsequently marked from the larger profile, it will tighten as it is driven home and the top interface will be mildly crushed. Be cautious: Overdoing this can ruin an otherwise good joint. The angling of the saw is more an opinion than a visible amount off-square. At worst the outside edges of the pins will be crushed at the top and won't present a parallel line—you went too far.

Use a steel hammer to drive the tails into the pins. A mallet can't be directed at a single tail, if it hits the workpiece on the twist it very easily marks the wood, and its tone upon impact gives no clue as to the tightness of the joint. The hammer should be slightly domed on its face—most hammers are anyway—so that each tail can be struck individually. The hammer will do little damage to the tissue if each blow is

Fig. 3: Sawing dovetails

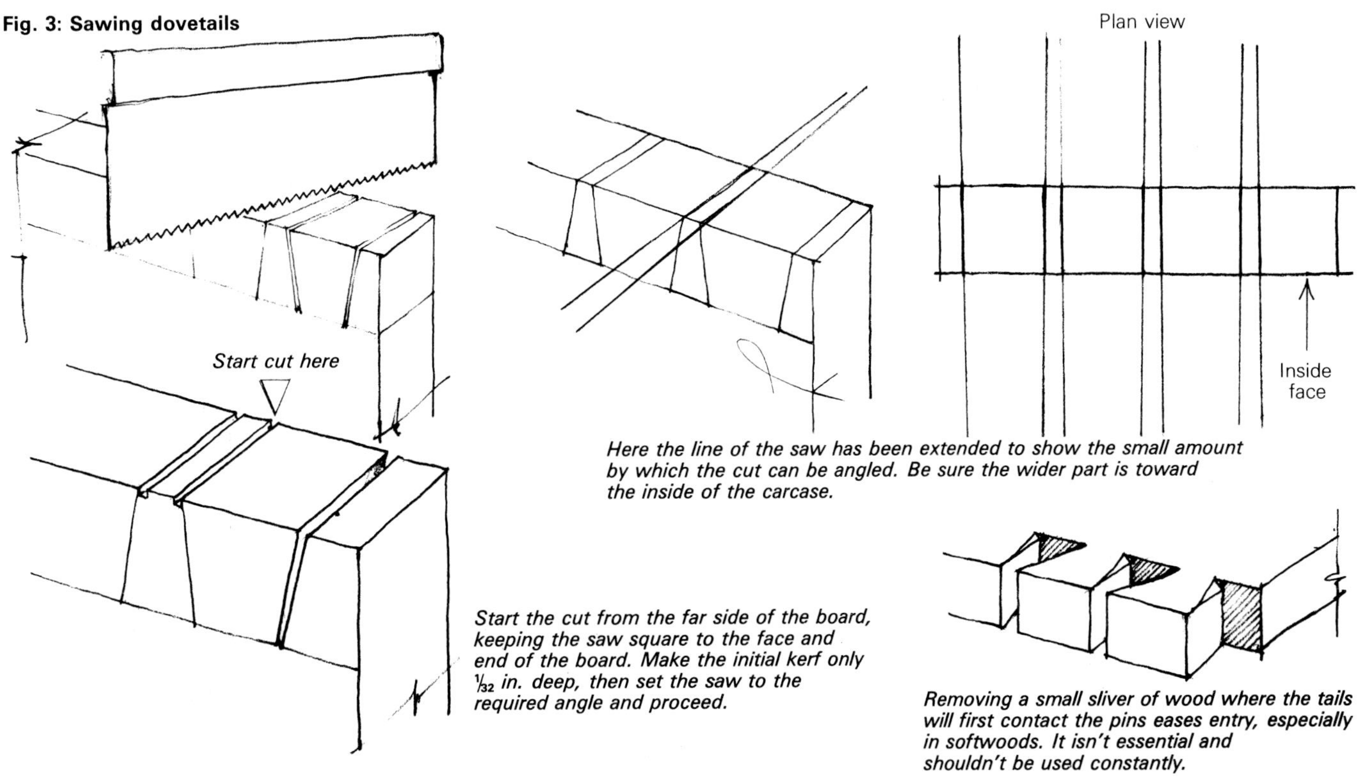

Start cut here

Start the cut from the far side of the board, keeping the saw square to the face and end of the board. Make the initial kerf only 1/32 in. deep, then set the saw to the required angle and proceed.

Here the line of the saw has been extended to show the small amount by which the cut can be angled. Be sure the wider part is toward the inside of the carcase.

Plan view

Inside face

Removing a small sliver of wood where the tails will first contact the pins eases entry, especially in softwoods. It isn't essential and shouldn't be used constantly.

delivered squarely. Each tail can be driven independently, and you will hear a distinct change in tone if a tail is binding and getting too tight. As well as the change in tone, the hammer will now bounce, as though hitting solid end grain. If this makes you queasy, protect the work with a small block of wood. The alternative to a hammer is a bar clamp. It has its greatest effect at the very end of assembling the joint, when the tail should be sitting down tight on the end grain at the base of the pins. When driven with a hammer the tail will travel the last few thousandths of an inch and may then bounce back or simply absorb the shock. Either way you can be fooled into thinking the tail won't sit down tight. Try a clamp and it goes the final fraction without problem, giving a clean, gap-free interface.

One sometimes sees a woodworker making up a set of castellated clamping blocks for each dovetailed carcase—the idea being to put pressure only on the pins or tails on each side of each corner. To me, this practice reflects fundamental misunderstanding of sound cabinetmaking technique.

In a through dovetail, when determining the length of the tail and the pin, we have three options (assuming that the pieces of wood to be joined are all of the same thickness). We can make the tails and pins longer than, equal to or shorter than the thickness of the wood. The method that seems to be most common is to make the tails and pins longer than the thickness of the wood. When the joint is put together the ends of the tails and pins protrude, later to be planed or sanded flush with the carcase sides (see p. 141). Unless you feature this protrusion by carving in some way, there is no virtue here. This approach means you must saw to a greater depth than necessary, only to plane away the effort when cleaning up. In the process, you destroy a vital registered edge. Furthermore, clamping turns into a juggling act with all those little blocks, which tend to crush the tissue mercilessly, or you waste time making a set of special blocks.

Instead, I make the tails and pins fractionally shorter than

the thickness of the stock. Considering this point takes us back to the initial selection of which faces are to go on the inside or the outside of the carcase. Assuming that the more handsome side is to face out, then the less handsome side or inside should be prepared as the face side, having all the normal properties of a face side—it should be flat in length, flat in width, and out of winding or twist (FWW #13, Nov. '78). It is likely that the boards will have been passed through a thickness planer after receiving their face side and face edge, but this is not necessary to the manufacture of the carcase. For the sake of argument, the outside of the boards could be left rough from the mill. But the ends of the boards must be cut to length and squared. The end grain should be clean and free of any tear-out. Do this by knifing round the ends fairly deeply (figure 4), then plane down to the knife line with one of the bench planes—the wider the boards, the larger the plane. A shooting board can be a big help here, since it allows you to lay a heavy plane on its side, gives good vision into the work, and with practice the plane can be made to cut almost like a bacon slicer.

Probably the most useful assist I have found when teaching this and other aspects of woodworking is a magnifying glass about 4 in. in diameter and of 4× or 10× magnification. The enlarged view of the work and the tools brings understanding not only of how and where one is cutting, but also of the quality and sharpness of what one is cutting with.

I am always surprised by how often I meet a woodworker who believes a block plane is the correct tool for end grain. This plane is a small thing, not easy to grasp firmly and push through end grain, where you need the heft and two-hand grip of a larger tool. The fact that the block-plane iron is set at a low angle is of little consequence. Since it is also mounted on the frog with its bevel uppermost, the cutting angle is the same as on a larger plane.

Having got the ends square they need to be knifed round. It is at this point that one has to settle the length of the tails

137

Fig. 4: Planing end grain

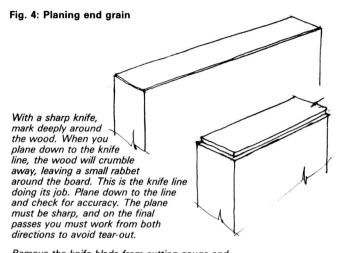

With a sharp knife, mark deeply around the wood. When you plane down to the knife line, the wood will crumble away, leaving a small rabbet around the board. This is the knife line doing its job. Plane down to the line and check for accuracy. The plane must be sharp, and on the final passes you must work from both directions to avoid tear-out.

Remove the knife blade from cutting gauge and sharpen as shown. The flat side faces away from the gauge fence.

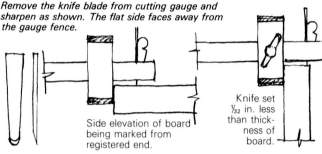

Side elevation of board being marked from registered end.

Knife set 1/32 in. less than thickness of board.

Fig. 5: Making drawers fit well

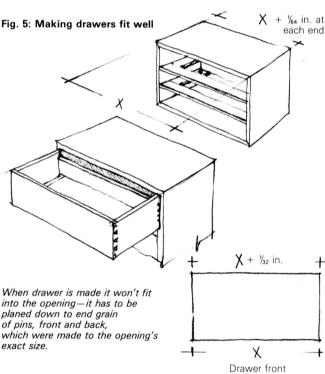

X + 1/64 in. at each end

X

When drawer is made it won't fit into the opening—it has to be planed down to end grain of pins, front and back, which were made to the opening's exact size.

X + 1/32 in.

Drawer front

Fig. 6: Mitering end pins

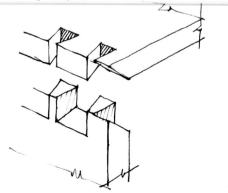

and pins. Set a cutting gauge a bare 1/32 in. less than the thinnest part on the boards. Knife a line round the ends of the boards, using the accurate end of the board as the face from which to gauge. The gauge knife should be sharpened to the profile shown in figure 4, flat side away from the gauge fence. This puts the beveled surface of the knife into the wood on the waste side of the line. Because the pins and tails are marginally short of the outside face of the carcase, during assembly there is no need for special clamping blocks. The clamp heads can be place directly on the tails to press them home, or a straight, simple clamping batten is all it takes. When cleaning up the carcase on the outside, one simply has to plane off the whole surface and come down just to the end grain on the tails and pins—the original end grain prepared by saw or plane. When we reach it and take the finest feather off, then the outside of the carcase is accurate to thickness and parallel to the inside, or face side. This method is not used for the sole purpose of achieving accuracy of carcase thickness—this is only a consequence. Another consequence is that the gauge line from marking out will be removed when cleaning up. Most importantly, carcase squareness was achieved long before the joints were made.

This procedure also permits a delightful refinement in fitting drawers (figure 5). Assume we are making a drawer or set of drawers as shown, and that the carcase is 18 in. deep (front to back). The ends of the top and bottom pieces are made deliberately not square. They are made with 1/64 in. extra on the back edge at each end. Thus the top and bottom pieces are 1/32 in. longer on their back edges than on their front edges. The end-grain edges are prepared as previously explained; the difference being that when one gauges from these edges the assembled carcase will be longer at the back than at the front. When the drawer is made, the boards for its front and back are cut and planed to fit exactly the carcase opening. Then the sides are joined to them with lap dovetails at the front and through dovetails at the back. The drawer sides are also made proud of the end grain of the front and back pieces, then planed down just to the end grain, front and back. Such a drawer will fit exactly into its opening, and will enter the carcase with a mild friction-fit left and right. Because the carcase gets fractionally wider toward the back, this friction does not increase significantly as the drawer goes farther into it. When the drawer is pulled out, the resistance increases as it approaches maximum opening—the action is very sweet. Making a traditional drawer in a traditional carcase relies on this technique of leaving long grain proud on the carcase sides and on the drawer sides. It cannot be done by having end-grain surfaces of tails and pins protrude.

In conclusion, there are two small points to consider when making a carcase with through dovetails. At the outer edges it is generally good to have two or three quite small dovetails, to increase the number of gluing surfaces. This helps if someone should be tempted to lift the piece by grasping the outer edges of the board, and it also increases resistance to cupping. The second consideration is to miter the outside joints, giving a more vital flow to the front edge of the carcase. Making this miter is not difficult—the common mistake is to saw down the line of the first pin, and you don't need to. Figure 6 should make this clear. □

Ian Kirby, a regular contributor to this magazine, teaches woodworking and makes furniture in Bennington, Vt.

Knockdown Tabletops
Dovetails, not hardware, pin top to base

by Kenneth Rower

For storage or shipment it is often advantageous for a tabletop to be quickly removable, while in daily service the top should be fastened securely enough for one person to be able to shift the table within a room. Here are two construction systems that require no hardware—one for tables with apron frames together with a variation for pedestal frames, and the other for trestle frames.

Apron frame — This method uses dovetail pins cut at the tops of the legs and dovetail housings with escapements chopped across the grain of the underside of the top. To assemble, drop the top over the pins and push it across the frame to lock the pins in their housings. To disassemble, push the top from the opposite side until the pins register in their escapements, and lift the top away. Properly dimensioned, the system is invisible when locked up (figure 1).

When sawing the legs, leave extra length at the top end equal to about half the thickness of the tabletop, and when laying out the rail mortises do not omit the customary allowance above the top of the mortise—about ¾ in. for a 4½-in. rail. Square up the top of each leg and take all measurements from there. Build the frame and assemble dry, leaving the rails strong to be trimmed later. Sketch plans and elevations of the leg tops, bearing in mind that all four pins must be offset in the same direction, and that if the system is to be concealed the pin length must be a bit less than half the leg thickness, an allowance being made for seasonal change in the width of the top. Later in the construction, when the frame has been fitted to housings, the escapements will be lengthened as well to accommodate this variation. For frames of ordinary size, about 30 in. across, divide the leg top into two pin lengths plus ⅛ in. at each end (figure 2), then lay out the pins using a mortise gauge for the side and end lines, and

a small adjustable bevel, set to a beveled guide block (about 78°), for the slopes. Gauge the shoulder lines from the end. Make the four cuts outlining the pins, then saw the shoulders. Trim with a sharp chisel, testing the work with the guide block. Finish all work on the frame except polishing.

Build the top and trim it sufficiently to center the frame. Scribe the outline of the pins on the underside of the top to mark their position when locked up (figure 3), but note that the outline is of the crown of the pin rather than its root, which is actually wanted in this space. Mark near each outline the direction the frame will travel when unlocking. Pencil in a benchmark on one leg and nearby on the underside of the top to register the location, and remove the frame.

Lay out the escapements by extending the scribed sidelines in the proper direction a distance equal to the pin length, and connect the new lines with an end line. Find the centerline along the length of this double box. Measure the width at the root of each dovetail pin and transfer it to the layout of the housing, employing the centerline. If the measurements vary from pin to pin, transfer one at a time. Cut the escapements, first boring out with a Forstner or other short-pointed bit, then chopping square. There is no advantage and some danger in going any more than a trifle deeper than the height of the pin. Test the frame in the escapements to be sure that the shoulders of the legs lie flush with the underside of the top. Level as necessary. Now remove the frame and lay out the slopes of the housings, using the adjustable bevel set to the guide block. Bore out, then with a dovetail saw rough out the slope, keeping a little strong of the line. Chop out the waste, again keeping away from the line. Clamp the guide block at the line and trim with a narrow paring chisel, the final cuts to be taken with the chisel right against the block (figure 3).

Lay the frame in the escapements and see that the pins are

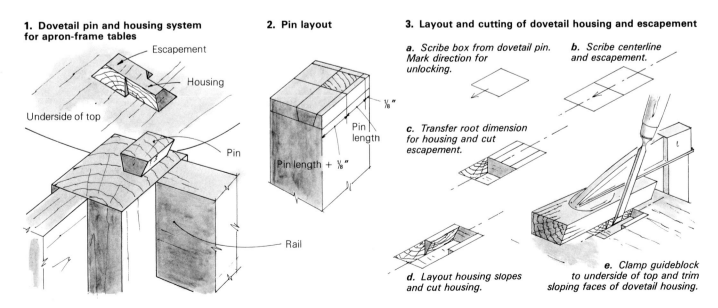

1. Dovetail pin and housing system for apron-frame tables

Escapement

Housing

Underside of top

Pin

Rail

2. Pin layout

⅛"

Pin length

Pin length + ⅛"

Rail

3. Layout and cutting of dovetail housing and escapement

a. Scribe box from dovetail pin. Mark direction for unlocking.

b. Scribe centerline and escapement.

c. Transfer root dimension for housing and cut escapement.

d. Layout housing slopes and cut housing.

e. Clamp guideblock to underside of top and trim sloping faces of dovetail housing.

likely to enter the housings. Then remove the frame and chamfer the leading corners of the pins. Replace and push (or pull). Considerable force may be necessary the first few times—waxing the pins is helpful. However, a driving fit means too much interference. Usually one joint will cause the trouble, or two that are not in parallel across the frame. There will be enough flex in the frame so that tapping at each joint will tell which one is binding. If you trim away too much during adjustments, a piece of veneer or cedar cigar wrapper (.009 in. thick) can be glued into the housing. When all is well, remove the frame and stamp a benchmark into the top of one pin and inside the corresponding escapement. At this point consider the probable shrinkage and expansion of the tabletop, and lengthen the escapements accordingly. Round off all the points and corners of the pins and the entry corners of the housings, as in service the top drops down over the pins, somewhat by feel. Then the near pair of legs can be gripped and the top pushed home with chest or waist.

Pedestal frame — As the arms of a pedestal frame do not offer the appropriate grain for cutting pins, separate pins must be fashioned and joined to the arms. Make up pin blanks of rectangular section, but with one sloping face in the length, then mortise in with a shim to drive the blank against a correspondingly undercut end of the mortise. Saw the slopes once the blank is glued and trimmed.

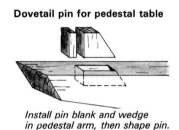

Dovetail pin for pedestal table

Install pin blank and wedge in pedestal arm, then shape pin.

A blank could be fitted up through the underside of the arm and then wedged below, but shrinkage in the depth of the arm would leave the pin standing proud and the joint loose. The best orientation is for one set of arms to be perpendicular to the grain of the top, the other parallel, with room left in the housings perpendicular to the grain for tabletop expansion and contraction. If you orient the arms at 45° to the grain of the top, the system works but the housings won't be as strong.

Trestle frame — In a knockdown trestle frame consisting of two trestles, a stretcher, and two draw-wedges, the action of the wedges in drawing the trestles tight against the stretcher

shoulders can be exploited to clamp the tabletop to the frame. The system consists of a barefaced dovetail cleat formed by extending the post tenon up through each trestle arm, and corresponding housings cut into the underside of the top where it bears on the arms (figure 4).

When cutting the posts, allow for bringing the tenon through the arm, plus an amount equal to about one-half of the thickness of the tabletop, and square the end of the post. Cut the mortise-and-tenon joint, assemble dry, and mark the tenon where the top edge of the arm crosses the cheeks. Remove the post and using a dovetail plane or a wide paring chisel, cut the slope on the inner face (with respect to the middle of the table) of the tenon. The shoulder should be a little behind the line to allow for shrinkage in the depth of the arm (figure 5). Build the rest of the frame.

Make the top and trim to size. Make up a beveled guide block as before though long enough to be clamped from the tabletop edges, and if the underside of the tabletop is not already flat, plane flats where it will bear on the trestle arms. The flats must be parallel, in plane (check with winding sticks) and wide enough to register the guide block.

Invert the assembled frame and center it on the underside of the top. Scribe the outlines of the cleats and remove the frame, benchmarking one end of the system. The outlines mark the location of the cleat crowns, not their roots. With a steel tape, measure the inside distance from root to root of the cleats, add 1/32 in. (more for a very long table) to provide compression to the system, and transfer to the layout of the housings. Draw another line outside the housings to allow the cleats to enter the housings before locking up (figure 6).

Bore and chop out the housings, keeping clear of the sloped faces. Then clamp the guide block in place and chisel back the sloped faces. Leave a little clearance at the bottom of the housings. Round off the entry corners of the housings and the points and corners of the cleats. To assemble, fit the trestles loosely to the stretcher, spacing them out from the shoulders an amount about equal to the swell in the cleat. The top should now drop easily over the cleats. Drive home the wedges to lock up the trestles and the top. Should the system loosen, tighten it by trimming the shoulders at one end of the stretcher, or by installing a shim in one housing.   □

Kenneth Rower, 37, makes furniture in Newbury, Vt.

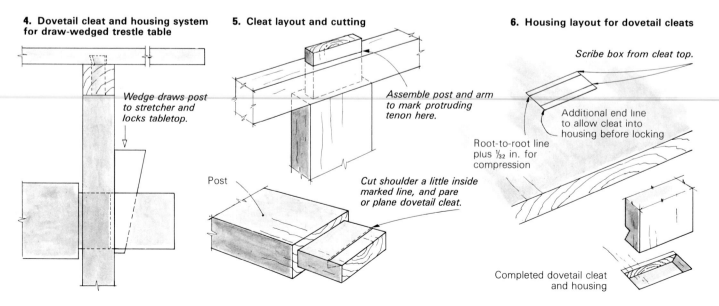

4. Dovetail cleat and housing system for draw-wedged trestle table

Wedge draws post to stretcher and locks tabletop.

5. Cleat layout and cutting

Assemble post and arm to mark protruding tenon here.

Post

Cut shoulder a little inside marked line, and pare or plane dovetail cleat.

6. Housing layout for dovetail cleats

Scribe box from cleat top.

Additional end line to allow cleat into housing before locking

Root-to-root line plus 1/32 in. for compression

Completed dovetail cleat and housing

Making dowels

Here's how to make dowels on your lathe with a router. First build a guide box with sides a little higher than the turning stock. Allow about an inch of clearance between the stock and the box walls. Chuck a ¼-in. straight bit in your router and adjust the depth of cut so that when the bit is over the dowel

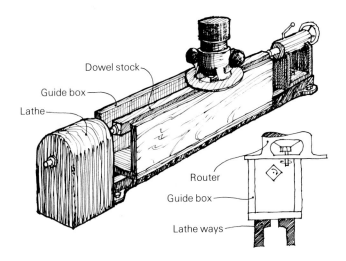

Dowel stock

Guide box

Lathe

Router

Guide box

Lathe ways

stock it will cut the dowel about ¹⁄₁₆ in. oversize. Position the router on the downward side of the stock rotation as shown in the sketch. Turn on the lathe, turn on the router and cut away. Take several light cuts to reduce the possibility of the bit grabbing and breaking the dowel. Lower the bit to the final depth and make one final pass with the router centered over the dowel. *—Lee R. Watkins, Littleton, Colo.*

Although I often need oak or walnut dowels, they're not readily available where I live. Not owning a lathe, I resurrected an ancient but effective dowel-making method that uses a simple jig and hand plane. Dowels made this way are, in my opinion, superior to those made by driving blanks through a steel sizing plate.

Construct the dowel-holding jig by ripping several *V*-grooves in a 2x6. A variety of groove depths will allow a wide range of dowel sizes. Screw a stop on one end of the 2x6. Place a square dowel blank in a groove and plane the top corner. Turn and plane repeatedly until the blank is octagonal.

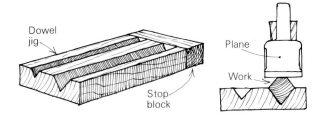

Dowel jig

Plane

Work

Stop block

Successive turn/plane cycles will result in a nearly round dowel, which can then be finished with sandpaper. One small drawback—the blanks must be flipped end for end as the grain direction changes.
 —Frederick C. Wilbur, Shipman, Va.

No-mess doweling

To reduce the glue-all-over-the-hands, sticky mess that goes with dowel work, cut the spout off the glue bottle until the dowel pin just fits inside. Slip a dowel pin into the spout, then invert and squeeze the bottle to cover the dowel with

glue. Turn the bottle right-side-up and twist the dowel out. No mess, no fuss. *—E. Khalsa, Espanola, N. Mex.*

Dovetail marking setup

This setup for scribing pin sockets in hand-dovetail construction eliminates hand-held slipping and repositioning problems. Put a spacer block under a handscrew on the workbench. Align the two workpieces, tighten the handscrew, then lock the whole in position with a *C*-clamp.
 —Richard Kendrot, Windsor, N.Y.

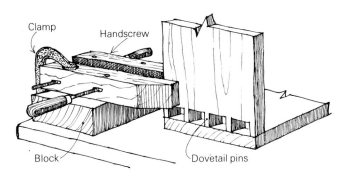

Clamp

Handscrew

Block

Dovetail pins

Trimming dovetails

With through dovetails it's accepted procedure to cut the joints a bit long and trim the ends flush after gluing. The fastest method I've found for trimming the slight overhang is to use a router equipped with a carbide-tipped, ball-bearing flush-trim bit. Start the cut at the very corner to

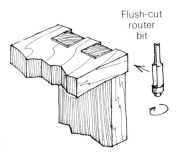

Flush-cut router bit

prevent the bit from grabbing at the beginning. Always feed against the direction of the cutter rotation. After routing, a light planing or sanding will complete the job.
 —Don Herman, Brecksville, Ohio

Drawer joint

This rarely seen drawer joint is my favorite for fine furniture. Properly fitted, it is strong and attractive. The initial cuts, made on the table saw, are similar to those used for the familiar drawer joint. Then cut the tenons with a backsaw, chopping out the waste with a chisel. Tap the tenons into the side

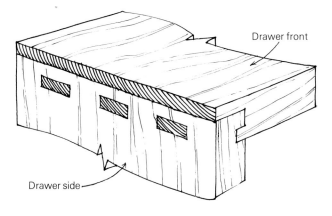

Drawer front

Drawer side

groove and mark the mortise locations. Complete the mortises with a small drill, coping saw and file.
 —John W. Wood, Tyler, Tex.

On Precision in Joinery

How close is close enough?

by Allan J. Boardman

An exemplar of precise joinery, author's full-blind finger-joined music box is 4½ in. on a side. Carcase is flame-figured butternut, dovetailed drawers are English beech with rosewood pulls.

Comparing a machine tool such as a lathe for shaping metal with its counterpart for working wood suggests that entirely different methods and standards are normally applied when operating on these two dissimilar materials. The differences are obvious—finely graduated scales and dials festoon the metal lathe, while the wood lathe probably has no measuring scales at all. What may not be obvious is the fact that woodworkers nonetheless do approach tolerances that might seem appropriate only to metal. The flexibility and compressibility of wood, the acceptability of fillers, moldings and bulk-strength adhesives, the dynamic movement of the material and the omnipresence of shoddy commercial products all contribute to the belief that "precision" is not a word in the woodworker's vocabulary. However, a close look at a truly fine piece of cabinetry will reveal some surprising facts about the dimensional tolerances inherent in its joinery.

Consider the miter joint connecting two adjacent members of a frame made from 3-in. wide stock (figure 1). If the miter were tight at one end and open, say, ⅟₆₄ in. (0.016 in.) at the other, the joint would be quite unacceptable. The frame would be weak, since most adhesives work best in films far thinner than ⅟₆₄ in. Even an untrained eye could easily detect the mismatch, and filler could not disguise it.

Most shops have lots of clamps, and all too often they are used in abundance to bend or press a joint closed while the glue dries. The result may well be a tight joint, but the structure is liable to be distorted—warped, bowed or out-of-square. This distortion may cause extra work in fitting for doors or drawers, perhaps some unanticipated cosmetic repairs, or it may even be uncorrectable and quite obvious in the finished product. And regardless of how well one compensates, the assembly will retain residual stress after the clamps are released. Built-in stress will work against the adhesive for a long time, causing the joints to creep and the dimensions to change. Stress can burst open an otherwise strong joint months or even years later. Improperly seasoned wood and changing humidity, although usually contributory, are sometimes blamed for joint failure when the real problem is faulty joinery initially hidden by clamping pressure. In first-class work, there is no substitute for joints that fit properly.

In figure 1, note that the angle of the tapered space in the miter joint is less than a fifth of a degree. The tolerance in a good miter might be ⅟₁₀ of that, or barely 1 minute of arc. With such a fit, the open end of the tapered gap would be less than 0.002 in., or about half the thickness of a piece of paper. This, in most cases, would be acceptable from the standpoint of strength and appearance. But measurement and tolerances in thousandths of an inch and minutes of arc sound like the language of machinists, not woodworkers. After all, many of

Allan Boardman, 46, of Los Angeles, is an aerospace systems engineer and lifelong amateur woodworker.

our measuring devices are themselves made of this changeable stuff, wood. The protractor scale on a woodworking machine goes no finer than one degree—minutes of arc, never. Parallax caused by the distance between pointer arrow and protractor ensures significant error, depending on where you hold your head. Does no one expect a woodworker to hold to a small fraction of a degree, except perhaps at 90° and 45°, where some machines have detents?

So it is with lineal dimensions too. For the seasoned worker, tricks, techniques, experience and feel (not mutually exclusive terms) compensate for the limitations of the equipment. But to the beginner, the not-quite-square square, the coarse graduations of scales and protractors, the machine's structural flexibility where rigidity is desired, all subtly suggest that only this crude level of accuracy is to be expected. Worse, because of careless use of words like "precision," "accurate," "professional" and "heavy duty" in advertising, the novice comes to believe that plus or minus a thirty-second is precise or that the machine by itself guarantees precision. Consequently, beginners may set personal standards for quality far lower than they should and progress far too slowly in the acquisition of those skills and techniques needed to overcome tool limitations.

Tool quality, measuring and marking—The limitations of our tools are not all bad, once recognized and understood. If a manufacturer were to add the weight, rigidity and precision some of us dream about, the cost of tools would rapidly become prohibitive. Also, because of the properties of wood, some of this extra precision would be wasted: The skilled maker would still have to compensate for the peculiarities of each species and piece.

Some tool limitations may require us to take lighter cuts, and they may inhibit some design options or demand greater skill, but by one means or another, we live with the available tools. Nonetheless, the first thing we must do is correct what can be corrected. For example, a framing square can be made quite true simply by peening the metal at the corner (*FWW* #17, July '79, p. 15). Likewise, cabinetmaker's squares having a metal blade and wooden stock can be filed true. Bench planes require all sorts of fine tuning before one can realized their full potential (*FWW* #14, Jan. '79, p. 52).

Leaving aside heavy-duty production machinery, one should not take for granted the implied precision or quality of tools. If you have the time and patience (and the indulgence of the shopkeeper) to examine and compare all of the squares, planes or chisels in stock, you may find one that is better than the others. The common test for a square, for example, is to mark a line on wood or paper taped to the counter, then flop the square over to see if the blade lines up with the line (figure 2). Any discrepancy is double the inaccuracy of the square. But realize that you will have to spend time on most tools to make them right.

So how do you make them right? Against what do you check for square? There is no way around it: Every shop needs a reliable standard for straight, square and flat. A quality machinist's combination square is a good investment because it provides a reliable 12-in. straightedge, an accurate square and a 45° reference. A 3-ft. metal straightedge is useful and is available at some woodworker and most machinist supply houses. One can also buy a strip of flat tool steel and have a machine shop grind it true. The top of a quality table saw should be flat enough to serve as the reference surface, but it is best to check this if possible by removing it, toting it to a machine shop for measurement and, if necessary, having it ground. Other flat references are granite surface plates and slabs of heavy plate glass or marble, which are generally quite flat but must also be checked. The rule of thumb is that these shop standards should be five to ten times better than anything you are likely to check with them. It is also desirable to have at least one fairly large bench surface be rather flat, say within 1/64 in. over a two or three-foot square, for layout work. This can be prepared with a jointer plane and checked with your reference flat, by rubbing one surface against the other through carbon paper. If your reference surface is not easily moved and inverted, use winding sticks instead (figure 3).

An accurate ruler or scale is also important. Simply because a stick or tape is marked in inches and fractions, it does not follow that the marks are where they should be. Some steel tapes are off as much as 1/8 in. in 10 ft. The machinist's combination square will provide a reliable 1-ft. scale against which others in the shop can be calibrated. The graduations are generally fine and deeply engraved for long life.

These points are about absolute accuracy. More important, most of the time, is relative accuracy. Once the dimensions of a given piece are quite close, the requirement for fit outranks the requirement for hitting the exact dimension on the nose. Consider cutting the four moldings for a picture frame. First, the pieces must be near to the desired length. Second, each piece must be the same length as its opposite, and third, after mitering, the corner joints must be tight (figure 4). Because the molding might not be perfectly true or straight, we trim the miter to fit, and as a result the mating surfaces may be a fraction of a degree off the nominal 45°, or one of the sides may be a deliberate but imperceptible fraction shorter than its opposite. A tiny variation in dimension cannot be observed, whereas an open joint will always be visible and weak. At the stage of final fitting, the ruler or gauge becomes a superfluous intermediary, an unwanted source of error.

This notion of dimension giving way to fit is not radical. It is like the intuitive procedure we use when setting a tool or machine whose protractor or scale has only coarse graduations. We guess at a setting someplace between two markings and then, ignoring the actual number of degrees or thousandths, we make small adjustments by trial and error, perhaps with a piece of scrap, until the fit is just right.

Marking can be done with a sharp pencil, but when the position of the mark impacts final fit, a marking knife should be used. Not only will the line be narrower and therefore better define the position, but a knife will lie much closer to the

Figure 1

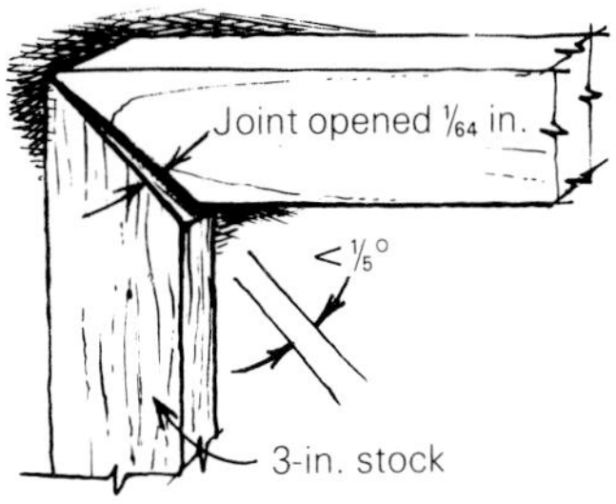

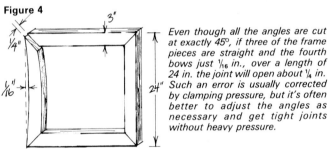

Joint opened 1/64 in.

< 1/5°

3-in. stock

In a frame made of 3-in. stock, a total error of 1/5° in cutting the miters will cause a 1/64-in. gap in the joint. This could result from an error of only 1/10° in setting the saw or in using the miter box, or from warped wood, or even from a tiny chip lodged between the fence and the work. To avoid the error, woodworkers cannot rely on the gross measurement that machine scales provide.

Figure 2

Flopping a 12-in. square to scribe two lines will detect error on the order of 1/20°.

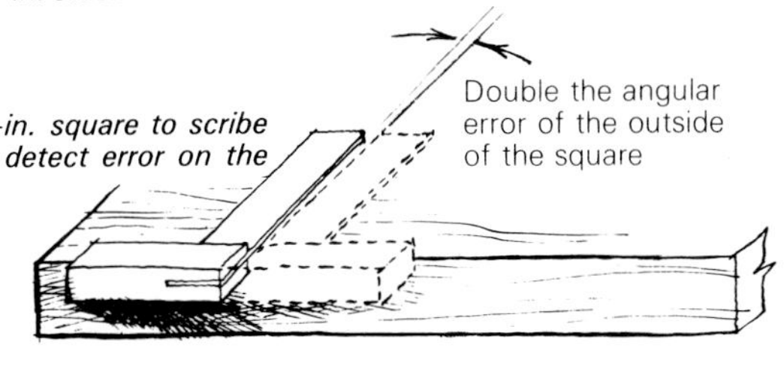

Double the angular error of the outside of the square

Figure 3

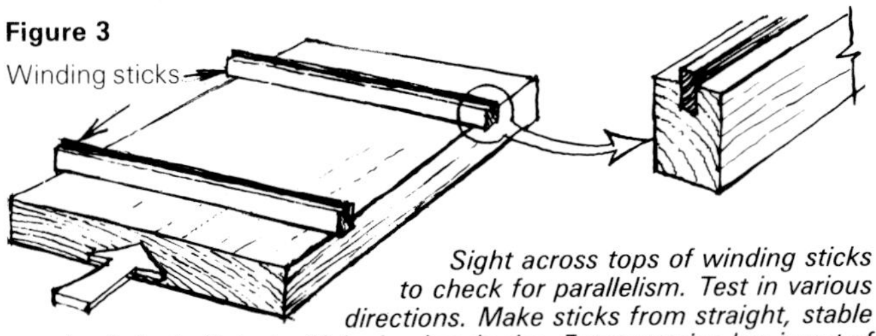

Winding sticks

Sight across tops of winding sticks to check for parallelism. Test in various directions. Make sticks from straight, stable stock — 1/2 in. by 3/4 in. by 18 in. is a handy size. Fancy version has insert of light wood in one stick, dark in the other, for better visibility. Well-made sticks used carefully can find 1/10° of error.

Figure 4

3"
1/4"
1/16"
24"

Even though all the angles are cut at exactly 45°, if three of the frame pieces are straight and the fourth bows just 1/16 in., over a length of 24 in. the joint will open about 1/4 in. Such an error is usually corrected by clamping pressure, but it's often better to adjust the angles as necessary and get tight joints without heavy pressure.

gauge, square or piece used in marking. Furthermore, the mark, being a physical incision in the wood, can often be used to position a chisel for the next operation. A typical example would be marking the shoulder line on a tenon to be cut with hand tools. The knife cut serves simultaneously to locate the shoulder edge, neatly sever the surface grain, and guide a chisel to create a starter groove for the tenon saw.

Cutting to the line—So much for measuring; the marked piece must now be cut. Precision in cutting is the exclusive domain of neither hand nor power tools. I say this despite diehard traditionalists who would argue that truly fine work can be done only by hand, and despite power-tool proponents who believe a plane is what you'd be forced to use if you couldn't afford a machine. There is seldom one best way. A proper table-saw setup would save time if a number of identical tenons were to be cut. The hand-tool method might be best for only one joint, if several different pieces are required or if the shoulder is not perpendicular to the rail.

Often, a combination of hand and power tool methods offers optimum results, taking advantage of the best characteristics of each tool. Suppose tenons are cut at each end of a stile, but for some reason the distance between the tenon shoulders is just a bit fat. (This can usually be avoided by checking with scrap before cutting the work itself.) Moving the table-saw fence a controlled ¹⁄₆₄ in. is tricky. And unless it has just been sharpened, a circular-saw blade is not too effective in trimming off the merest hair. The wood may burn or the blade may deflect, leaving a cocked, charred shoulder.

It is undeniable that power tools save time and physical exertion, but some cuts in precision joinery, such as shaving off that minute error, are clearly better performed with hand edge tools—planes in particular. In practiced hands a shoulder plane can trim that miscut tenon down to size in seconds. End-grain shavings as thin as 0.002 in. can be produced, enabling the scribed line to be approached under the watchful eye of the maker (figure 5). It makes little difference if the waste to be removed is straight or tapered. Because of these factors, it is often advisable when using machines to leave a little margin for hand trimming.

Planes do not cut like most power tools, virtually all of

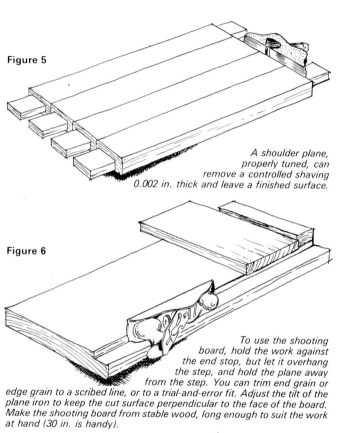

Figure 5

A shoulder plane, properly tuned, can remove a controlled shaving 0.002 in. thick and leave a finished surface.

Figure 6

To use the shooting board, hold the work against the end stop, but let it overhang the step, and hold the plane away from the step. You can trim end grain or edge grain to a scribed line, or to a trial-and-error fit. Adjust the tilt of the plane iron to keep the cut surface perpendicular to the face of the board. Make the shooting board from stable wood, long enough to suit the work at hand (30 in. is handy).

Figure 7

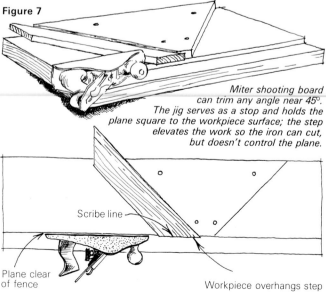

Miter shooting board can trim any angle near 45°. The jig serves as a stop and holds the plane square to the workpiece surface; the step elevates the work so the iron can cut, but doesn't control the plane.

Scribe line

Plane clear of fence

Workpiece overhangs step

which cut intermittently, pounding on the wood fibers and doing inescapable damage on every cut surface (for a close look at the surfaces left by various cutting tools, see p. 212). The unique action of the plane with or across the grain, however, severs the wood fibers cleanly in a continuous, not intermittent, motion. The finished surface in many cases cannot be improved upon. The damaging forces involved in parting the waste from the work are absorbed by the shaving as it breaks or curls. The planed surface, except where the wood grain is particularly cantankerous, shows no evidence of the trauma. Even more important for precision is the fact that the plane can leave a good surface after each pass. The perfect fit can be approached by increments and when achieved, no further clean-up is required. In many routine joinery operations, this objective is far more difficult to reach with sandpaper, files, saws or routers. And as a bonus, all this control comes with no great sacrifice in speed. A plane stroke takes only a couple of seconds.

Paring with chisels and other edge tools offers similar possibilities for working toward precise joints, particularly where the geometry prohibits using a plane. Here the control afforded rather automatically by the plane must be provided by the craftsman. However, the principle is the same—taking off just as much waste as desired, exactly where desired, and leaving a clean surface after each cut.

Jigs—The criteria I apply to virtually all joints are first, in hidden interfaces (the tenon in the mortise) there should be only enough clearance for a thin glueline; and second, visible interfaces (miters, for example) should appear tight with only light clamping. As you approach the final fit a shaving at a time, you quickly discover the need for devices that help keep the hand tools perpendicular, free from wobble, or otherwise aligned. Jigs and fixtures do not guarantee precision, but they can reduce the degrees of freedom the tool has so the craftsman can exercise greater control toward getting the fit.

A jig of continuing use is the shooting board—nothing more than a flat piece of stable wood with a step at the edge and a stop near one end (figure 6). With it, one can simultaneously plane an end or edge of a piece exactly to a scribed line, straight and perpendicular to the surface. Using this same jig and a little blocking or intentional tilt of the plane blade, angles other than 90° can easily be cut for coopered joints or simply to compensate for some special condition.

Other jigs in this same family include several versions of the bench hook, and the miter shooting board—the solution to the problem that began this essay, of how to adjust a miter angle by a fraction of a degree (figure 7). In use, the plane is laid on its side on the ledge while the work is held against the 45° stop. If the plane body is out of square (it usually is), the mitered surface will not be perpendicular to the face of the piece. This can be corrected to some extent by adjusting the tilt of the plane iron, by shimming the work, or maybe 91° is really desired. The 45° angle (or 44° or 46°20′) is not a result of holding the plane firmly against the step in the fixture while pressing the work against the fence. Of course, it could be if the jig were made exactly at the angle desired, but that is too restrictive a use of the shooting board. Rather, one holds the work against the stop but overhung, and the plane sole away from the step. One then planes either to a scribed line or by trial and error to a perfect fit with the mating piece.

In contrast to such "permanent" devices, many simple jigs

can be made for short-term use. The usual reasons such jigs fall into the disposable category are that they get worn or damaged in use or are special in nature or dimensions. Consider cutting dadoes by hand in the two vertical sides of a bookcase (figure 8). A useful multipurpose jig fashioned from two pieces of wood not only simplifies the operation but also facilitates precision. In appearance, the jig is nothing more than a clumsy-looking square, the long leg reaching across the workpiece, the short leg attached accurately at right angles. The width of the members should ensure stiffness and rigidity. The thickness of the short leg should be a trifle less than the workpiece thickness so as not to interfere with clamping. The thickness of the long leg must be sufficient to keep the backsaw perpendicular, but it can also be such that when the saw back hits the jig, the cut is at the desired depth. The jig is clamped to the workpiece and at the one setting serves as a straightedge for scribing, a control for chiseling out a starter groove for the backsaw, a fixture for holding the saw upright, and a depth stop. Two such sequences per dado, followed by cleaning out the waste with chisel or router plane, leave an exceptionally clean joint the width of which can exactly fit the thickness of the shelf. With this method it matters little that the shelves vary in thickness from one to another, or that the dado head on your power saw cuts only in fixed increments that don't match your wood. Notice that in this example since all the scribing and sawing are done on the waste side, both long edges of the jig are used and so must be parallel. Obviously, the same basic technique can be adapted to other and more complicated joints—stopped dadoes, rabbets and dadoes, tapered dovetails and so on.

Precison is relative—In woodworking there is a scale of precision demanded by the nature of each project, from rough to finish carpentry ascending through built-ins to fine cabinetry, furniture-making and ultrafine craft objects like view cameras. Tolerances might range from plus or minus an eighth to one or two thousandths. In addition, we must superimpose a scale of functional tolerances that takes into account the size of the object and the wood's probable movement in response to changes in temperature and humidity. The "precision fit" of a drawer in a fine chest incorporates a neat but wider clearance gap than one would find around the drawer of an equally well-made jewelry box.

Finally, one should not neglect the many different design options that shift the need for one kind of precision to another, or eliminate the need altogether. The results can be quite acceptable and are normally found in abundance on commercial work. Take, for example, the use of a solid nosing around the top of a veneered cabinet (figure 9). To blend the grain of the solid piece with the veneered panel and to join it flush without damaging the thin and delicate veneer would involve considerable skill and risk. This requirement can be virtually eliminated by accentuating the seam instead of hiding it, with a routed or scratched groove used as a design feature. Likewise, moldings can effectively mask imprecise joinery, and overlapping fronts can conceal uneven clearance around cabinet drawers. With design skill, such techniques can permit production shortcuts. Often, they are the best choice in purely design terms, and the fact that less precision is required becomes a bonus.

The characteristics that denote precise woodworking are not limited to joint accuracy and fit. They also include grain

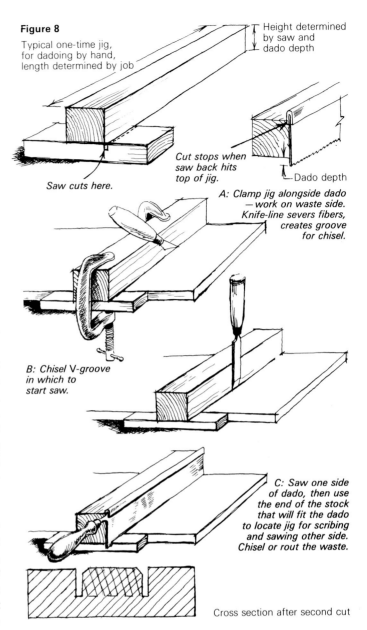

Figure 8
Typical one-time jig, for dadoing by hand, length determined by job

Height determined by saw and dado depth

Saw cuts here.

Cut stops when saw back hits top of jig.

Dado depth

A: Clamp jig alongside dado — work on waste side. Knife-line severs fibers, creates groove for chisel.

B: Chisel V-groove in which to start saw.

C: Saw one side of dado, then use the end of the stock that will fit the dado to locate jig for scribing and sawing other side. Chisel or rout the waste.

Cross section after second cut

Figure 9
Deliberately accenting a joint may be better than trying to hide it.

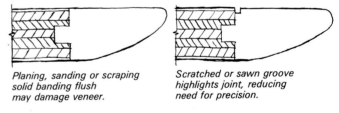

Planing, sanding or scraping solid banding flush may damage veneer.

Scratched or sawn groove highlights joint, reducing need for precision.

and color matching, uniformity of detail and symmetry when intended, clean pre-finish surface preparation, crisp installation of inlays and fittings, minimum use of fillers, and so on.

Precision in joinery is neither for everyone nor for every project. It can be an objective or an attitude that adds pleasure to the craft and quality to the work. It can, on the other hand, become an obsession that goes beyond common sense to the point of inconsistency with the nature of wood itself. But it seems far better for a woodworker to understand the options, recognize that certain skills and techniques can be invented or learned, know what is possible to accomplish, and then exercise free choice, rather than have his or her standards derive from crude scale markings and constant exposure to mediocre work. □

CABINETMAKING

Plans for a Pigeonhole Desk
Design suggests the best woods

by Simon Watts

This folding desk is one of the more complicated pieces, in terms of joinery, made in my shop. The folding front flap is only to make the piece more compact and to give easy access to the drawers. It does not conceal the pigeonholes, as does a conventional roll-top or slant-top desk. I've made nine over the past 14 years, each one a little different from the last. The drawings and photos show the final version, and there are no more changes I want to make to this particular design. It has been made in teak, mahogany, cherry, walnut and padauk but not in any blond woods such as oak or ash.

The matter of choosing an appropriate wood for a particular design is difficult, but not as subjective as it appears to be. Leaving aside questions of cost and availability, there are certain criteria that always apply. Most obviously, the wood chosen has to have the right mechanical properties for its particular function—which may mean using more than one species in the same piece of furniture. Years ago chairs were commonly made out of three different woods: pine for the seat, since it could be easily carved; maple for the legs and rungs, which was ideal for turning; and oak for the back, because of its bending properties. One also needs to think of the suitability of the wood to the tools and construction techniques and the climate to which the finished piece will be exposed. For example, if there is to be a lot of hand-dovetailing, oak is a miserable material because its coarse grain makes it difficult to cut cleanly; if there is a lot of machining and you don't have carbide cutters, you should avoid teak; climates where there are great fluctuations in humidity demand a stable wood such as mahogany.

Stability, ease of working, durability, strength, hardness and resistance to decay—all these have to be considered, but often this still leaves considerable possibilities. Why is it that certain designs look better in one wood than another? Part of the answer lies in the color and texture of the wood. All woods have grain patterns, which range from the almost invisible, as in holly and ebony, to the inescapable, as in red oak. If you use an aggressively grained wood to make a piece like this desk, which is characterized by simplicity and careful proportions, the result is visually confusing. It may be striking and dramatic, but it is not anything a sensible person would want to live with. My general rule is, the smaller the surfaces and the finer the detailing, the more restrained the color and figure should be, but, like any rule, mine can be disregarded by the true genius with triumphant results.

Another point to consider is the hardware that will be used and how it will look. Certain combinations are more pleasing than others: polished brass with walnut or mahogany, wrought iron and oak, stainless steel and rosewood. Similarly, if more than one wood is used, it is important that they enhance each other and that both be subordinated to the overall design. A colleague of mine once made a small oval vanity table, the surface of which was veneered with alternating strips of ash and ebony. Superbly executed, the result was a visual nightmare; but a large table in ash, with a thin edging or inlay of ebony or rosewood, could be both striking and tasteful. If the contrast between the two materials is too subtle, there will be an irritating doubt as to whether, in fact, there is more than one wood and you will get what a teacher of mine called "the monotony of faint variation."

There is also the matter of tradition and historical precedent. A furniture-maker is not bound by these considerations but should be aware of them. This desk has some close relatives in the past at a time when walnut and mahogany were much in vogue, and this may explain why these two woods are my favorites for this particular design.

Some of my customers would want to select a wood not because it was appropriate for the design but because their living room was mostly cherry or oak and they thought that any additional furniture should be in the same wood. My argument is that it is not matching the wood and finish that makes two pieces of furniture good neighbors, but the less easily defined qualities of scale, simplicity and proportion.

Construction — This is a difficult piece of furniture to make, and I urge anyone who is not familiar with a specific technique to try it out first on scrap wood and avoid the frustration of spoiling good material. For example, if you have not made a haunched tenon before, make one, and if necessary, go on making it until you can do it with confidence. It is also prudent, when making a number of identical parts, to make up one or two extras—five legs instead of four, for example. Then, if you make a mistake on one piece, you won't have to repeat each step in its production. The extra piece, if not needed, can be kept as a pattern for future projects.

The time required to construct this piece will vary according to your experience and whether a planer or other machines are available. I would expect to spend about 120 hours in a well-equipped shop. At the end of this article I will discuss how to make up a materials list so that you can estimate the cost and order the right amount of lumber.

Assuming you have a pile of rough lumber, and the plans for this desk, a general cutting procedure would go as follows: Select the best boards for their width, figure, straightness and color. These will be used for the carcase and writing surface. Cut an inch off one end and examine it for checks. If it is clean mark off the length you want and add at least an inch, before cutting. Run the board, concave side down, over a jointer (or hand-plane it) until you have one flat surface.

Putting this flat surface *down*, run it through a thickness planer. Examine it after the first pass and, if it is chipping up, turn it end for end, still keeping the flat surface down. If you're going to glue up, plane to ⅛ in. oversize and, if your planer is wide enough, plane the whole assembly to the final thickness. Otherwise, plane to finished thickness, turning it

Desk of mahogany with rosewood pulls and oak understructure (42½ in. by 28⅞ in. by 42 in.) is a subtle blend of good design, careful choice of woods and hardware and fine joinery. Construction drawings are on the next two pages.

end over end after each pass to avoid moisture imbalance that can cause cupping and to maintain grain direction through the knives.

Next, joint (or plane) the best edge and saw the board to width, allowing ⅛ in. to ¼ in. for cleaning up. With a knife, mark the ends to the exact length and cut off the waste.

The 10½-in. top should be one piece, but unless 18-in. boards are available the side pieces will have to be joined up, then dovetailed into the top, using a half pin at the corners as shown in the drawings on the next two pages. The front and back rails can be either one piece or laminated. They should be lap-dovetailed into the sides as shown. This whole assembly is called the carcase. Now rout the ¼-in. groove for the back panel around the inside of the back of the carcase, taking care to stop the groove in the side pieces so that it does not show from the top. The back panel can then be joined up and planed to its finished thickness of ⅝ in.

The grain of a rectangular panel should parallel the rectangles's long axis, to minimize seasonal change. If your wood is *recently* kiln-dried, you should allow between 5/32 in. and ⅜ in. per foot for expansion, or from ¼ in. to ½ in. for a 16-in. panel. The exact amount depends on the species. Teak and mahogany are at the lower end of the scale, beech and oak at the upper. There is practically no movement along the length of the panel, so it can be fitted quite snugly. With a plane, feather the panel to fit the groove after rough-cutting it to the approximate bevel on the table saw.

To make the understructure, tenon the five drawer supports into the front and back rails, but glue into only the front rail to accommodate seasonal changes in the carcase. Rout or saw a ¾-in. groove ⅜ in. deep in each side to hold the stationary piece of the desk top. Stop these grooves when they meet the back-panel groove, or they will show from the back. After sanding the inside surfaces, glue up the carcase and flush the dovetails off with a sharp plane.

I use Titebond (aliphatic resin) glue and plastic-resin glue such as Weldwood. Titebond sets up quickly (one to two hours) thus freeing up clamps and speeding the work. However, it has a short assembly time (five minutes or less), cannot be easily sanded off and deteriorates in ultraviolet light. It is subject to creep under stress and should not be used for heavy, bent laminations. Plastic resin permits longer assembly time (10 to 20 minutes), but takes at least six hours to set up at 70°F. Unlike Titebond, it is practically waterproof.

In general, I use resin glue for dovetails and any complicated joint requiring long assembly time and for joints exposed to sun and water. I use Titebond for small laminations and for simple joints that will not be heavily stressed.

It is convenient to make up the base now, to have something on which to set the carcase. The legs should be of the straightest stock you can find, for strength and for appearance. Rough-cut the taper on the band saw or table saw (don't use the jointer) and then clean it up with a plane. I like to plane the legs slightly convex, otherwise perspective makes them appear hollow. A haunched tenon attaches the legs to the aprons. The aprons are rounded on the underside and also have a slight curve—an important detail because it helps to keep the desk from looking too severe. After cutting

the groove for the tabletop fasteners or buttons (*Fine Woodworking*, Sept. '79, pp. 63-64) you can glue up the base. Do this in two stages: two pairs of legs first, and then the whole assembly. Check with a tape to make sure the legs are parallel, as shown in the drawing. (They should actually toe out very slightly because perspective makes two verticals, when seen from above, appear to converge.)

Next select the stock for the writing surface, join it up and plane it to fit the ¾-in. groove. The stationary piece can be joined up out of ordinary stock but the front flap, like a table leaf, is not restrained by any structure or frame and should therefore be of vertical-grain stock and preferably one piece. Cut the stationary piece to size and slide it into the carcase until it stops against the sides. It should overhang the front by ½ in. and is kept in place by a single, long wood screw counterbored on each side. But don't fasten it yet; the top must be off to fit the slides and drawers—the next steps.

The slides that support the flap can be of maple or oak, faced with the same wood as the carcase. These facings are offset to act as stops when the slides are pushed all the way in, ½ in. short of the back panel; too close and carcase shrinkage would cause them to project. Attach the facing to the slides with plywood splines as shown in the drawing. Stop the slides in their extended position by putting a peg in the stationary part and a slot in the underside of the slide; the length of this slot determines how far out the slide will travel.

Now set the slides in place and measure the horizontal distance between them, subtracting 2½ in. for the five ½-in. dividers. Divide the remainder by four to get the exact width of each drawer. To avoid the difficulty of making drawers to fit precisely an existing opening, make the drawers first in the usual way (through dovetails at all four corners) and then fit them as follows: Cut some pieces of 3x5 index card. Place the slides, all the drawers and as many of the dividers as will fit. Then slip a piece of card into each gap, at the front and back. Remove, plane and test-fit the dividers until the assembly fits without forcing. Then clamp the dividers and screw them from the underside. (The drawer fronts, which will overhang the drawers, will be stopped against the front edge of the dividers, so not only must they be spaced accurately, but their front edges must be aligned.) When you remove the cards, the drawers will have the right clearance. Now cut out the false fronts and screw them to the drawers from the inside—don't use glue. Make these fronts slightly oversize so they can be trimmed to fit the openings and each other. I like to make the drawer fronts and the slide facings out of the same piece of wood, to give a consistent grain pattern.

The drawer fronts look better set back between 1/16 in. and 1/8 in. from the carcase front. To do this, block them out with one or two pieces of index card, plane or scrape them all off flush with the carcase and remove the card.

Turn the knobs or pulls out of a wood that contrasts with the carcase without being too extreme. For example, a walnut or cherry desk with rosewood pulls looks good, but ebony pulls on a maple desk draw one's attention, detracting from the overall appearance. If no lathe is available, you can carve pulls or substitute small brass knobs.

Cut the front flap as shown in the drawing and attach it to the stationary part using brass hinges, which have to be scribed and set into the writing surface. Rectangular hinges are easier to fit than the ones with semicircular ends. I strongly advise a trial fitting on a piece of scrap before cutting into the desk top.

The final step is to make the pigeonhole unit and fit it into the carcase. Dovetail the outside box together out of ½-in. stock and rout slots for the dividers. Cut a shoulder in the front edges of the dividers to cover the rounded end of the slot left by the router bit. Then slide them in from the back, gluing only the long, vertical ones. The small drawers are best lap-dovetailed but a simple rabbet joint, glued and nailed with panel pins, could be substituted.

Plane the sides of the pigeonhole unit to a slight taper so they fit snugly in the carcase. Then secure the whole assembly with four brass or wood pins as shown. You could make knobs for the small drawers from the same brass rod. All finishing should be done before the unit is fastened in place.

I usually finish with Watco, a synthetic oil that polymerizes on exposure to the air. I apply it at 24-hour intervals until the wood will absorb no more, wet-sanding with the grain, using 600-grit waterproof sandpaper for the final application. If this process is repeated every six months or so, an attractive patina develops. There is no need to oil the understructure because movement within and around it has been allowed in the construction. Wherever wood is sliding on wood I use a good-quality paste wax. This makes for a smooth action and reduces wear. The insides of the drawers are best waxed, too. It makes them easier to keep clean. □

Figuring your materials

When buying lumber wholesale, in quantity, you cannot specify the exact widths and lengths of the boards you want, nor, generally speaking, can you pick them out. Consequently you have to order more than you need—but at a lower price. Buying retail by the board is considerably more expensive, but you have less left over.

If you choose to make this desk in *Afzelia*, or some other exotic wood you don't plan to use again, then buying retail makes sense. If you decide to use a more common wood, such as walnut or cherry, which will be used for other projects, then you should buy wholesale at a better price and have the additional advantage of being able to select boards for their figure and color.

You figure the amount of lumber required by making a complete bill of materials. I follow the format given in the example below:

	Size (in.)	Area (sq. in.)	Area (sq. ft.)	No.	Total (sq. ft.)	Total (bd. ft.)
4/4 stock, walnut						
Aprons	2½ x 40	100	0.69	2	1.39	1.53
Drawer fronts	3¼ x 42	137	0.95	1	0.95	1.05
8/4 stock, walnut						
Legs	26 x 2 x 2	104	0.72	4	2.88	3.17

The last column is arrived at by multiplying the total in square feet by 1.1. You do this because when you buy a board foot, its actual size is 12 in. long by 11 in. to 11¼ in. wide; it shrinks that much across the grain from its cut-green width of 12 in. If you need 141 sq. ft., say, you will have to buy 141 x 12/11 (or approximately 1.1) = 155 bd. ft. A materials table like this one should be made for each different kind of wood and for each thickness. You must also allow for waste. If you buy FAS (first and seconds select), 20% is a commonly accepted figure. A lower grade will mean more waste. In addition to hardwood, you will need ⅛-in. plywood for drawer bottoms. You will also need tabletop fasteners (unless you make your own buttons), three brass hinges and some small pieces of hardwood for the knobs.   *S.W.*

Simon Watts is a contributing editor to this magazine.

Two Easy Pieces
A frame chair and a sofa

by Simon Watts

This chair and sofa are two variations on one simple theme: a wood frame spanned by tensioned canvas that supports loose cushions. The canvas is kept taut by nylon lacing running through brass grommets. Both pieces are light, easy to make and economical.

I designed the chair as a practice project for apprentices in their first six weeks of training. It teaches the mortise and tenon as well as bridle joints, and it can be made from a drawing with minimum supervision. Since little material is involved, a poorly cut joint could be made over again without either the student or myself feeling badly about the waste.

Later I used the same basic design for a small sofa and then for a larger one. The former succeeded but the latter was a failure. Although amply strong to support three adults, it *looked* weak because the end frames were too far apart. The only structural difference between the sofa and the chair is in the thickness of stock—1⅜ in. instead of 1¼ in.—this is as much for the sake of proportion as for strength.

Sofas are bulky and awkward to move so I also made a knockdown version by substituting loose wedges for the glued mortise-and-tenon joints. This detail is shown at *B* in the drawing and can be used for either piece.

This design can be made in any straight-grained hardwood. Before deciding on the wood, consider how it will look against both the canvas and the fabric chosen for the cushion covers. I like a black canvas because it doesn't show dirt, goes with any wood (except walnut) and looks well with brass grommets and white lacing.

Construction — Starting with 6/4 stock, cut out the pieces for the end frames and rails. You will need two pieces 24 in. long, four pieces 22 in., six pieces 32 in., and three pieces for the long rails: 35 in. for the chair and 59 in. for the sofa. If you are making the knockdown version, be sure to add 3 in. extra to two of the long rails to make room for the mortises and wedges. Plane all these pieces down to 1⅜ in. if making the sofa, 1¼ in. for the chair.

The next step is to join up the end frames by bridle joints at each corner. Bridle joints are best cut on the table saw; a carbide blade helps ensure accuracy and smoothness. If I were making this chair by hand, I would use a different joint, a mitered dovetail, because I don't like to do things by hand that are better done by machine and vice-versa. I'll describe how to make the bridle joint first, then the mitered dovetail.

After cutting the pieces to exact length, set a marking gauge to the width of the stock plus 1/16 in. Mark out one of the pairs to be joined on all four surfaces of each piece. If you are using a table saw, there is no need to mark more than one pair because saw and fence settings will take care of the rest. Usual practice is to make the tenon two-fifths of the thickness of the stock—about ½ in. for 5/4 stock.

Holding the stock vertically, saw the tenons first. For this operation I screw a wooden fence 8 in. high to the standard metal one. This gives more support and greater accuracy. The saw should be set a bare ⅛ in. lower than the gauge marks. Then, with a miter gauge accurately set at 90°, saw the shoulders. If you set the blade down so the waste is not quite sawn through, it will not come whistling back in your face. The remaining wood is easily cleaned up with a chisel or a shoulder rabbet plane. If you don't have a good enough blade for finish cuts, mark all the shoulders with a knife, saw 1/16 in. on the waste side and then chisel to the line. The shoulder must be left square, not undercut, because it shows.

Next saw the mortises, vertically, in the same way. They should fit the tenons snugly without any forcing. Remove the waste by drilling a single hole (halfway from each side) or with a coping saw. With a chisel, clean up the end grain to the gauge mark on the inside of the mortise.

The mitered dovetail, the handmade alternative, is a one-pin affair that does the job of a bridle joint, only more elegantly. Begin by marking all four surfaces of each pair to be joined (dotted lines in the drawing at *A*). Mark out the miter lines on each side of both pieces with a knife, but do not saw them yet. Next, mark out the space for the tail on the horizontal piece *(a)* as shown. This can be sawn either on a table saw, with the blade angled, or by hand using a tenon saw. Cut out the waste with a coping saw and chisel to the line *y-y*

Chair in cherry with black canvas sling and woolen cushions.

153

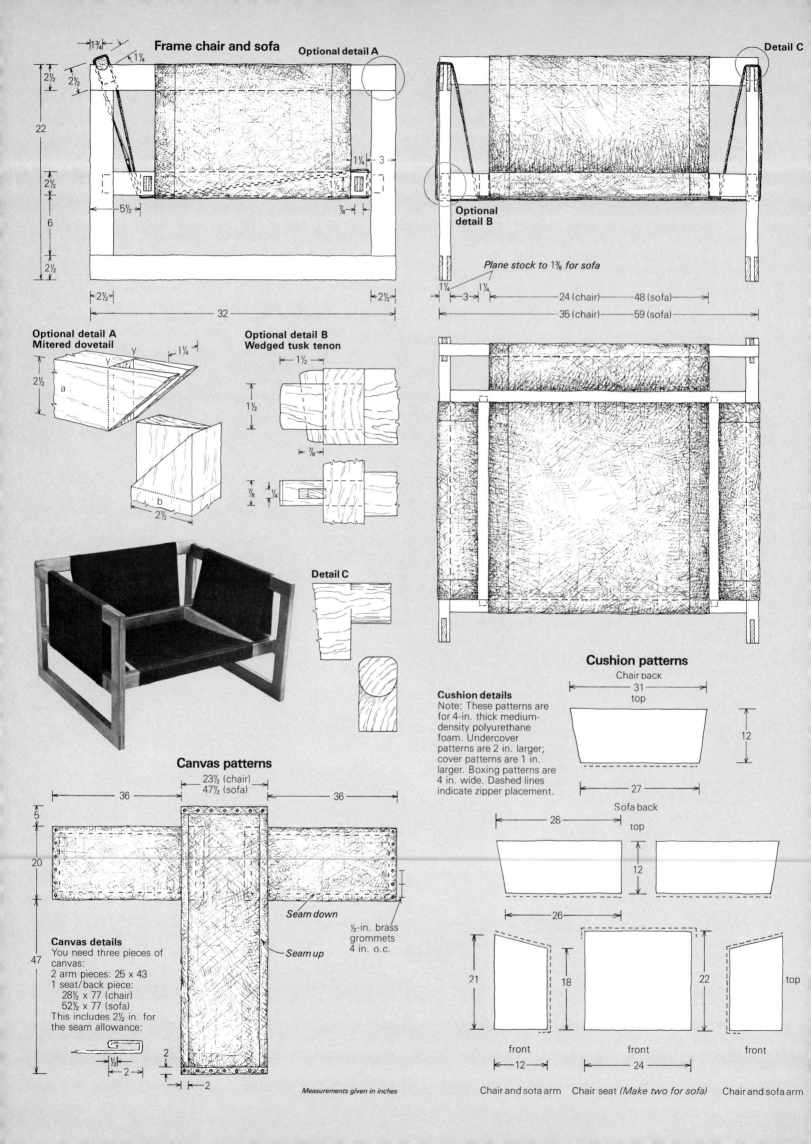

Frame chair and sofa

Optional detail A

Detail C

Optional detail B

Plane stock to 1⅜ for sofa

1¾
1¼
2½
2½
22
2½
6
2½
5½
1¼ 3
1½
⅞
2½
32
2½

1¼ 3 1¼
24 (chair) — 48 (sofa)
35 (chair) — 59 (sofa)

Optional detail A
Mitered dovetail

2½
1¼
y
y
a
b
2½
2½

Optional detail B
Wedged tusk tenon

1½
1½
⅞
⅞
¼
⅞

Detail C

Canvas patterns

23½ (chair)
47½ (sofa)
36
36
5
20
47

Seam down
Seam up
½-in. brass grommets 4 in. o.c.

2
2
½
2
2

Canvas details
You need three pieces of canvas:
2 arm pieces: 25 x 43
1 seat/back piece:
  28½ x 77 (chair)
  52½ x 77 (sofa)
This includes 2½ in. for the seam allowance:

Measurements given in inches

Cushion patterns

Cushion details
Note: These patterns are for 4-in. thick medium-density polyurethane foam. Undercover patterns are 2 in. larger; cover patterns are 1 in. larger. Boxing patterns are 4 in. wide. Dashed lines indicate zipper placement.

Chair back
31
top
12
27

Sofa back
28
top
12
26

21
18
22
top

front
12
front
24
front

Chair and sofa arm
Chair seat (*Make two for sofa*)
Chair and sofa arm

working from both sides. Lay piece *a* firmly on the end of *b* and mark the pin with a scribe or thin-bladed knife. Mark out the other limits of the pin and saw the cheeks. Remember to stop the sawcut when close to the miter line.

The last step is to saw the miters on both pieces and trial-fit the joint. You should saw the miters a little to the waste side of the line, push the joint together and then run a fine saw into the joint, on both sides, until the miter closes.

With the joints in the side members cut, the middle rail is next mortised into the two verticals and then all five frame pieces can be assembled and glued up. When gluing a bridle joint, be sure to put clamping pressure (protecting the work with pads) on the sides of the joint until the glue has set. When gluing a mitered dovetail, put glue on the miters as well as on the pin and tail. Clamp lightly across the cheeks of the tail. Check with a square. After the glue has set (but before it is bone hard) flush off the surfaces with a sharp plane.

Next, cut the through mortises for the two long rails. Mark accurately on both sides with a knife, drill out the waste, then chisel to the knife mark. The semicircular cutouts are best done by clamping the top edges of the two frames together and drilling a single 1¼-in. hole. Remember to use a backing piece to prevent splintering.

The edges of the frames and rails must be rounded over. If they are left sharp, the canvas will eventually wear through on the corners. I use a router with a carbide rounding-over bit fitted with a ball-bearing pilot. It can also be done by hand, with a wood file and sandpaper. All the edges are treated in the same way except where two horizontal rail meet. Here they are left square.

Next, the four pieces of the underframe are cut and joined. The short pieces are stub-tenoned into the long rails because a through mortise would weaken the structure. This assembly is then attached to the end frames using either a glued-and-wedged mortise-and-tenon joint or, for the knockdown alternative, a through mortise and loose wedge. In both cases the wedge is vertical, at right angles to the grain.

When making a tapered mortise *(FWW #16, May '79, p. 46)*, it is best to make the wedges first. Lay a wedge on the outside of the tenon and mark the slope with a pencil. Then, with a mortise gauge and a knife, mark the two mortise openings top and bottom. Most of the waste can be drilled out (working from both ends) and the remainder cleaned out with a chisel. I always leave the wedges 1 in. overlong so when they are tapped home they can be marked, then removed for trimming. The top of the wedge should project slightly more than the bottom. In time they invariably get driven lower.

The top rail, at the back of the chair, is not fastened but is held in place by the tension of the canvas. It is rounded on the upper side and fits loosely into the half-rounds in each frame. Its two ends are best sawn out square and then shaped with a rasp or wood file.

Canvas — The canvas is wrapped around the completed frame and laced across the back and under the seat. You will need 45 ft. of ¼-in. lacing, double for the sofa, which must be of nylon or the equivalent. Don't use clothesline or sash cord. I use

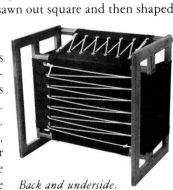

Back and underside.

an 18-oz. treated chair duck, which is a rather heavy material for a domestic sewing machine, and you may want to have the canvas made by a tent and awning manufacturer, a sailmaker or an upholsterer. The 2-in. seams are sewn with the edge turned under ½ in. They must be made exactly as in the drawings so only the smooth side of the seam shows. The brass eyelets, or grommets, are easy to put in yourself. You need about three dozen ½-in. grommets (five dozen for the sofa) and a ½-in. punch-and-die-set.

Cushions — To make the cushions you need a piece of medium-density polyurethane foam 4 in. thick, 1-in. Dacron wrapping, medium-weight unbleached muslin, a 26-in. zipper for each cushion, and fabric for the outside covers.

First make a full-size pattern of each different shape of cushion in heavy, brown wrapping paper. Transfer the patterns to the foam using a soft pencil or blue chalk. If you don't have a band saw, the easiest way to cut polyurethane is with a fine panel saw or hacksaw. An electric carving knife will work, too. Support the foam on the edge of a piece of plywood, saw with light strokes along the lines, and keep the plane of the saw vertical.

The Dacron batting gives the cushions some extra bulk and makes them less hard—both on the seat and on the eye. They are padded a little more on one side than on the other as follows: Using the same patterns, cut out with scissors one piece of batting for each cushion. Lay this on the side of the foam, which, when in place, will be *toward* a person sitting in the chair (away from the canvas). Next wrap each cushion, including the ends, once around with the batting. You may want to keep this in place with a spray glue (foam or fabric adhesive) while making the muslin undercovers. To cover the ends of the foam, either cut the batting over-wide and fold it over the ends, like wrapping a parcel, or cut separate pieces of batting and spray-glue them in place.

Undercovers — Muslin undercovers are essential. Without them it is practically impossible to remove and replace the outer, or slip, covers, for cleaning. Inner and outer covers are made in the same way: two panels joined by a strip (called *boxing)* that runs around the edge of the cushion.

Lay the original patterns on a piece of newspaper and then, with a felt pen, draw a line around them. Draw another line ½ in. outside the patterns and a third one ½ in. outside that. Cut around the outside line. Using these new patterns, cut out two pieces of muslin for each cushion. Next, cut the boxings, strips 4 in. wide and a little longer than the perimeter of the cushion. They don't have to be one piece.

If you are an old hand with a sewing machine, machine-stitch the covers directly, sewing ½ in. in from the edge of the material (the middle line of your pattern). This is best done by putting a piece of tape as a guide on your sewing machine ½ in. from the needle. Sewing the boxing to one panel all the way around and then, starting from one corner, sew the other panel. If you are a novice, pin or hand-stitch (baste) the covers before machining. Leaving one long edge unsewn, turn the covers inside out and insert the wrapped foam. The loose edge is turned under and blind-hemstitched by hand.

Fabric — As in choosing a wood, certain criteria apply when picking fabric for the outer covers. Leaving aside matters of color and pattern, you must choose a fabric that is strong enough. It must not stretch in use—which means a tight weave—or shrink when washed, or wear too quickly. Think of the climate, too. Wool is fine in Vermont, but it would be a poor choice for the heat and humidity of a Washington summer, where linen or heavy cotton would be preferable. Remember that light colors need cleaning more often, blues fade in bright sunlight, and some synthetics not only can melt but are flammable. The chair will require 5 yd. of 30-in. to 36-in. material, the sofa 8 yd. If you use 48-in. or 54-in. material, the chair will require 4 yd. of material, the sofa 6 yd. The undercovers will require roughly the same amount of muslin. Make sure the material is preshrunk. If it is not, you must wash it once to shrink it. Ironing makes the sewing easier.

Outer covers — Taking the same newspaper patterns that were used for the muslin covers, cut ½ in. off the perimeter (to the middle line) all the way around. Then pin the patterns to the fabric and cut out the panels as before, together with enough 4-in. strips for the boxing. The innermost line on the pattern is now the one to sew on.

The alert reader will notice that the muslin-covered cushions are ½ in. bigger than the outer covers. Like putting a sausage in its skin, this helps keep the outer covers tight and free from wrinkles. Wrinkles in the muslin will not show through—the muslin is too thin.

The inner and outer covers are made exactly the same way, the only complication being the zipper. This must be put where it won't show, and the best placement is indicated on the drawing. To install the zipper, take a piece of boxing 1 in. longer than the zipper and fold it in half lengthwise, making a crease. If it won't stay creased, iron it. Lay the zipper down on the crease so that the zipper teeth are just level with the folded edge of the boxing. Pin or tack it in place and then stitch it using the zipper foot of your sewing machine. Now take another piece of 4-in. boxing, crease it lengthwise, and stitch it to the other side of the zipper. You should now have a 4-in. strip of boxing, double thickness, with a zipper running neatly up the middle.

When sewing this piece of boxing to the side panels, remember to face the zipper *in*. Then, when the cover is turned inside out, it will be on the right side. A professional upholsterer covers the two ends of the zipper by overlapping the adjacent boxing. Or you can simply join it with a neat seam.

It is a good policy to sew the seams twice, once along a line ½ in. from the edge and again as near to the edge as you can manage. This prevents the material from unraveling at the seam if it is roughly laundered.

This chair and sofa have never been made in quantity but the design could easily be adapted for production by machine. This is because there is no hand-shaping, boards do not have to be selected for color and grain, and most of the joints can be cut by machine. The design could be further simplified by using only one thickness of stock (1⅜ in.), which would cut the number of separate parts in half. Bridle joints lend themselves to machine production but I would replace the mortise-and-tenon joints with stub mortises using allen-head machine screws and *T*-nuts. The whole piece could then be shipped knocked down and easily reassembled. The canvases could be made in quantity and enclosed with plenty of lacing and suitable instructions in several languages.

Perhaps someone would like to take this up? □

Methods of Work

Masking out squeeze-out
Glue squeeze-out problems can be avoided by covering areas near joints with masking tape. Carefully place the tape during final assembly so that it covers the area but doesn't get caught in the joint. This technique is especially useful on the inside corners of joints (drawers, boxes, etc.) where cleanup is a problem. *—Tim Rodeghier, Highland, Ind.*

Mortising fixture
The sides of a cradle I built recently were made of slats mortised into the frame. The router-based mortising fixture I built for the project helped me cut all those little mortises quickly and easily. The fixture has three simple pieces: a hardwood clamping lip, a birch-plywood router base and a Masonite hold-down. Bolt the 2x3 clamping lip under the workbench flush with the front edge. To permit deeper mor-

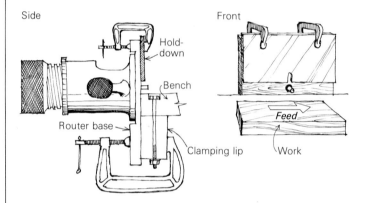

tises, rout a ⅜-in. recess in the plywood base to fit the router. Mount the router in this recess using countersunk screws driven from the face.

To use, clamp the base to the clamping lip, making sure the bit is the right height above the workbench. Then clamp the hold-down in place. Stand behind the router and, sighting from above, pull the workpiece into the router. A router cut or pencil lines on the hold-down are needed to show the left and right boundaries of the cut. Feed the work from right to left. The router produces mortises with rounded ends, which can be squared up with a chisel. But it's easier to round the tenons with a rasp or sandpaper.
—G. R. Livingston, New York, N.Y.

Inexpensive homemade clamp
When you run out of clamps and money at the same time, these simple old-timers can be quickly made from wood scraps and an old leather belt. Make up several sizes of end-blocks to keep the front jaws roughly parallel.
—Larry Humes, Everson, Wash.

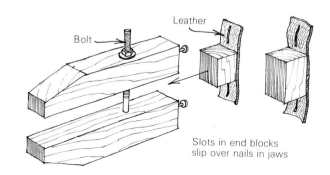

Repairing Wobbly and Broken Chairs
Two shops relate their methods

In the Q&A section of the May '79 issue, David J. Wood inquired as to methods of disassembling a chair that had been repaired with epoxy. George Frank pointed out quite correctly that a "sharp" blow is not really possible with a rubber mallet, and suggested instead the use of a steel hammer. We feel this will result in unacceptable damage to the surface. We have found that the following procedure works well for the five or so chairs a week that we rebuild in our shop.

If the joints are tight, drill the smallest possible hole directly into the bottom of the mortise and inject white vinegar. This will dissolve most glues and loosen others. While vinegar has no effect on epoxy, experience shows that joints repaired with epoxy are rarely cleaned out properly during the repair. The epoxy then is holding the old glue together rather than the wood. Dissolving the old glue effectively loosens the joint.

Knock the chair apart with a Computhane dead-blow hammer. These leave almost no mars and with even less rebound than a steel hammer deliver the better part of the force to the work. Stubborn joints sometimes require fixing one piece, say the rung, in a vise while the leg is knocked off with alternating blows to each side of the joint. This concentrates the energy on breaking the joint rather than moving the piece around the workbench.

If this doesn't do it, leave the joint intact and fix the rest of the chair. We glue with cascamite after a careful cleaning of the joints. Its strength, long open and closed working time, good gap-filling qualities and low pressure requirements for a good set make it unbeatable for most chair repairs. Cascamite glue injected by syringe through a small hole drilled into the joint will strengthen the loose tenon that cannot be removed.

We do not use fox, or blind, wedges to spread tenons because we've seen them split seats and legs rather than be driven down into the tenon during regluing. A more consistent problem is that it is all but impossible to remove a fox-wedged (or, for that matter, a pinned) tenon if it gets loose again, and experience shows that tenons get loose in time whether wedged or not. Seasonal changes in humidity cause the tenon to expand, its confined fibers to be crushed, and the tenon to shrink smaller than it was before expansion. We often see amateur repairs with nails, screws or epoxy—all ineffective and problematic in themselves. The old-timers were right to assume they'd have to disassemble their chairs periodically and reglue them.

—Jane Clarke and George Danziger

When I am called upon to repair a chair leg, stretcher or arm support that has broken in the middle or toward one end, I use Albert Landry's scarf joint (Methods of Work, Jan. '79). However, many times a break will shear exactly at the joint line and perpendicular to the grain direction, especially on a chair stretcher (figure 1). In these cases I use a repair method that is easier than the scarf joint and nearly as

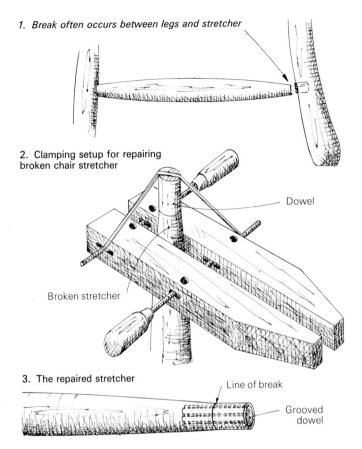

1. *Break often occurs between legs and stretcher*

2. *Clamping setup for repairing broken chair stretcher*

Dowel

Broken stretcher

3. *The repaired stretcher*

Line of break

Grooved dowel

strong. Also, if you are dealing with a chair in original paint or finish, little or no finish touchup is required.

First, file or saw the broken end perfectly square. Find a dowel the same diameter as the broken joint and cut off a piece the same length as the broken end, usually ¾ in. to 1 in. Butt-glue one end of this dowel to the broken member as follows: Take a small handscrew clamp and tighten the section between the threaded rods onto the broken member about an inch down from the top. Glue the end of the dowel to the end of the broken member, securing it by stretching a heavy rubber band between the threaded-rod ends of the clamp and up and over the end of the dowel (figure 2).

When the piece has dried, carefully drill through the dowel and into the old part of the broken piece with a drill ⅛ in. to 3⁄16 in. smaller than the dowel diameter. Glue a new section of smaller dowel into this hole (figure 3). Cut grooves into the sides of this dowel to allow air and excess glue to escape because the broken member's diameter is quite small and easy to split. The second dowel gives the joint all of its strength. Though it is ⅛ in. to 3⁄16 in. less in diameter than the original joint, in my experience it proves to be a sound repair.

—Robert C. Kinghorn

Clarke and Danziger's shop, The House Doctor, is in Leverett, Mass.; Robert Kinghorn repairs furniture in Excelsior, Minn.

Methods of Work

Sliding dovetail bookends

Most furniture designed to hold books doesn't. Shelves must be filled with books end to end or pairs of movable bookends must be used. I make integral, sliding bookends from the same wood as the bookshelf. Cut ½-in. dovetail keys across the bottoms of matched blocks. Then rout a mating dovetail slot in the shelf end to end. The fit of key to slot should be smooth but not loose. Allow for swelling during humid seasons. Slide the bookends into the slot prior to final assembly. Books placed between the bookends supply the necessary leverage to jam the key tight in the slot. Bookends can be easily repositioned if book tension is relaxed.

An alternate approach for open shelves is to stop the slot a few inches from each end. Widen the slot (with a straight router bit) in the middle of the shelf to insert the bookends.
—*Rick Kramer, Beech Creek, Pa.*

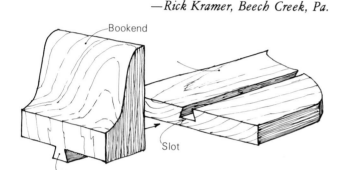

Bookend

Slot

Key

Wooden high-chair mechanism

This high-chair tray adjustment mechanism is simple, won't pinch, rust or jam and is sturdy enough to survive several rowdy babies.

Turn the high-chair arms in a series of rings and flats, then mount them on the chair level and parallel. Install two dowels on the underside of the tray to engage the inside of the arms. This gives the needed in-out adjustment. Two pivoting latch-dowels mounted on ears hold the tray down.
—*J.B. Small, Newville, Pa.*

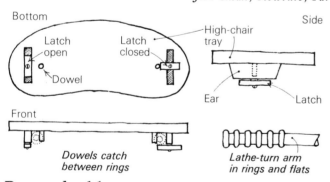

Bottom

Latch open   Latch closed

Dowel

High-chair tray

Side

Ear   Latch

Front

Dowels catch between rings

Lathe-turn arm in rings and flats

Recessed tabletops

Wasting the central area of a top to form a lip on a bedside table or bureau is attractive and functional. Recessing emphasizes the grain, shows that solid wood has been used and prevents pencils and spills from falling to the floor. I cut the recess on the table saw using a dado head with all the chippers to get the widest cut. The circumference of the dado head leaves a pleasant curve at the inner edge of the tabletop.

To cut the recess, first clamp blocks of wood to the saw's rip fence to serve as stops. Then set the dado head to the right depth (¼ in. suits my taste). Holding the wood against the back stop, carefully lower the tabletop into the dado head. Do not cut across to the near edge, as it's liable to split out. Instead, cut halfway across, reverse the tabletop and cut half-

way again from the other edge. Waste the bulk of the material by cutting crossgrain, repeat passes along the grain, then carve out the corners by hand. Finish the surface by scraping and sanding.   —*Pendleton Tompkins, San Mateo, Calif.*

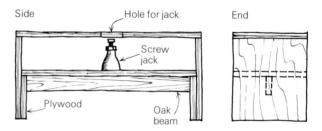

1. Lower work onto dado head

Stop   Stop

2. Cut halfway

Tabletop after cutting

3. Reverse work, cut from other edge

Hand-carve corners

Cabinet-hanging prop

After years of struggling to hang upper cabinets, I built this simple prop. Now I can hang the upper units by myself, regardless of their size. Make the prop from ¾-in. plywood, except for the center support beam, which is oak. Dimensions depend on the height of the jack. For this application, I believe a screw jack works better than a hydraulic jack.

To use, first install the lower units and set the prop on top of one (protecting the countertop with plywood). With the upper cabinet balanced on the prop, screw the jack up until the upper unit contacts the ceiling. Leveling and plumbing can be done after the top band has been anchored to the wall (I use dry-wall screws).   —*James E. Gier, Mesa, Ariz.*

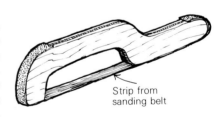

Side   Hole for jack   End

Screw jack

Plywood   Oak beam

Hand sander

Here's an inexpensive, quick-to-make hand sander that's effective for smoothing out gouge marks on curved surfaces or for rounding off a sharp edge. You will need some scrap plywood, a used belt from a belt sander and a little contact cement.

Strip from sanding belt

First, cut the plywood into an 8-in. to 12-in. long hacksaw shape. Tear a strip from an old sanding belt as wide as the plywood you use and a couple of inches longer than the frame you cut. Spread a little contact cement on the backside of the strip and along the bottom surface of the frame and press the abrasive strip along the bottom of the handle to the front.

When completed, the sander has an open section with a little give for sanding curves and a rigid section for sanding flat surfaces. The rounded ends are designed for sanding concave surfaces. By changing the shape of the frame, the applications are virtually endless. When the abrasive is dull, just pull off the old strip and glue another on.

—*Richard Neubauer, Jr., Cincinnati, Ohio*

Working Woven Cane
Spline holds cane firmly on the frame

by G.A. Michaud

Though hand-caning was a staple project in every industrial-arts program around the turn of the century, the time when caning techniques were common knowledge has long since past. The rebirth of interest in restoring antique furniture and the lovely, sometimes startling application of cane in contemporary furniture, however, has created a demand for practical information about this craft. The easiest, most economical way to learn how to insert cane is to install it on a piece of existing furniture. Inserting machine-woven cane into prepared grooves is the quickest method. The photo below shows a chair seat and the materials you'll need: a pattern, a roll of cane, spline and driving and holding wedges.

Open-woven and close-woven cane are the two styles most frequently available to individual craftsmen, though some upholstery-supply houses sell others. Close-woven cane comes in 18-in. widths and costs about $7 a running foot. Open-woven cane comes 12 in. to 24 in. wide, in 2-in. increments, and costs from $5 to $10 a running foot. Spline, the strips used to hold the cane in the grooves, was once available in hickory and reed, but now only reed spline is available. It is classified as light (3/16 in. wide), medium (1/4 in. wide) and heavy (5/16 in. wide).

To begin, remove the old cane and clean the groove of glue, cane and spline. If the seat frame has a series of small holes drilled around the opening, you'll need to hand-weave individual strands of cane—a different process from what is described here. You could rout a groove 1/4 in. back from the holes, but I think it's easier to learn to hand-weave. Check the groove for size. It should measure 3/16 in. across by 1/4 in. deep. Sometimes the groove is 1/4 in. or 5/16 in. wide, usually an indication that the frame has been recaned several times— cleaning the groove of old spline and cane widens it. Buy spline in the size closest to the width of the empty groove.

Draw a pattern of the shape of the opening you wish to cover, allowing at least 1/2 in. beyond the groove. Transfer this pattern shape onto the cane webbing, cut it out and soak it in warm water. I have seen formulas for soaking solution: usually 1½ tablespoons of glycerine per gallon of water. I haven't had great success with this because glycerine absorbs water from the air, and in an area such as the damp, river-valley town where I work, it makes the cane feel sticky. If your area is drier than mine try it, but test a patch first.

Establish the amount of spline needed and soak it along with the cane. Don't be afraid of damaging it—soak it at least an hour, longer if you prefer. The more pliable it is, the easier it is to work. The cane and spline will become not limp, but pliable enough so that when bent over on itself the fibers

will not fracture. While the cane is soaking, seal the frame with sanding sealer so the wood is water-repellent—the cane is wet when you insert it into the groove. Next, make a number of hardwood locking wedges and a driving wedge.

Lay out the soaked cane over the opening with its shiny side up and align the weave parallel to the groove most prominent in design, usually the front groove. Woven cane has two sides—a glossy side and a dull side. The shiny surface is the bark of the rattan cane and is the side you wish to display to wear or view.

Pull out the weavers (horizontal members of the weaving) that run over the groove. You don't have to do this all at once but only where you intend to start. With the driving wedge and a mallet, force the cane with light taps into the groove, and lock it in place with the small wedges. Sponge the cane down from time to time to keep it pliable—sponge the dull side, because the shiny side isn't absorbent. To keep the cane flat and parallel to the groove, begin in the center of the

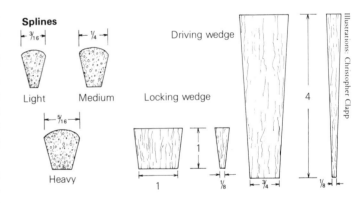

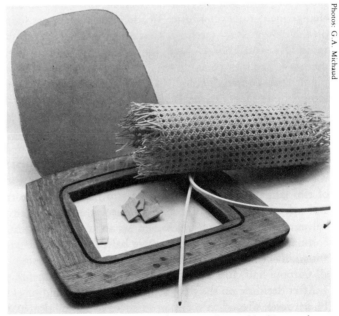

Materials: Pattern, cane, spline, driving wedge and locking wedges.

EDITOR'S NOTE: Three sources of cane and caning supplies are: Cane and Basket Supply Co., 1283 S. Cochran, Los Angeles, Calif. 90019; Inter-Mares Trading Co., 1064 Route 109, Lindenhurst, N.Y. 11757; and H.H. Perkins and Co., P.O. Box AC, Amity Station, Woodbridge, Conn. 06525.

nial Philadelphia and to some extent in other areas. During the Federal period it became common in American production.

The range of construction techniques in 18th-century furniture can also be seen in carcase base-moldings and bracket feet. Scott of Williamsburg followed advanced London practice. He glued base moldings to a series of secondary wood blocks, which were in turn glued to the bottom of the case (photo *F*). The base molding is not attached directly to the carcase, but overlaps it by ⅟₁₆ in. to ⅛ in.—just enough to prevent a visible gap. This arrangement allows the case to expand and contract without great stress developing between the sides and the molding. The gaps between the blocks add some flexibility, and since the blocks are smaller than the sides and bottom and made of a weaker secondary wood (pine or poplar, usually), they give way first.

Scott's base construction is rarely found in other areas of Colonial America. The most common systems are of two types, both of which present shrinkage problems. In one system, the base molding is glued and nailed directly to the sides of the carcase. In the other a wide frame is glued and nailed to the case bottom, the nails often driven through and clenched. These batten frames are sometimes made entirely of primary wood whose edge is molded, but more commonly the primary-wood molding is nailed and glued to a frame of secondary wood. Both of these systems restrict the movement of the crossgrain sides, causing them to crack.

Bracket-foot construction in Scott's shop has two sophisticated features unknown in cabinetwork from other American cities. Both features can be found in production from major London establishments. The ogee bracket feet are formed from two-ply laminated boards, the outer portion of primary wood (walnut or mahogany) and the inner of yellow pine. This two-ply composition provides two grain patterns at the weakest point, where the ogee curve swings inward, therefore

F: *Bottom of the Scott desk-and-bookcase in photo A shows the English method of applying molding to segmented glue blocks instead of directly to the carcase side and front. This system allows the carcase sides and bottom to expand and contract without cracking.*

G: *Typical bracket-foot construction, as in this view of the Massachusetts slant-top desk, (also shown in photo D) employs a corner glue block with the grain running perpendicular to the grain of the bracket members. Cracked bracket feet are common. Note that the base-molding glue blocks run all the way into the corner, unlike the glue-block construction shown in photo F.*

H: *Bracket foot of a Scott bookcase, above, and of a London-made china cabinet, right, both show composite glue-blocking and laminated bracket members: primary wood on the outside and secondary on the inside. These two features, unknown in combination in American shops other than Scott's, have ensured exceptionally good survival of his bracket feet.*

helping to prevent fracturing at this critical location. Additionally, the softer secondary ply provides a resilient core that enables the foot to withstand greater shocks without breaking than if it were constructed entirely of hardwood.

The essential strength of the 18th-century bracket foot is the glue-blocking inside its corner. In the better pieces, the weight of the case is on these glue blocks and not on the brackets. The blocks are directly below the corners of the case, while the brackets are directly below the base molding. In pieces where the weight is taken by the brackets, the base molding is often broken loose, allowing the case corner to slide downward. The typical glue-blocking in bracket feet is made up of a square, vertical piece glued into the corner formed by the two brackets (photo *G*). The grain is perpendicular to the horizontal grain of the brackets. Excessive or sudden changes in relative humidity can cause the brackets to shrink, often breaking the glue joint since the block does not shrink in like amount. In some cases the glue-block joint holds and the brackets split at their weak point where the ogee swings inward. After splitting, each segment shrinks unto itself, leaving a gap at the fracture point.

Another defect of this construction shows up when the case is moved. If slid along the floor, the foot glue block is liable to catch on an uneven area and snap off.

By the mid-18th century, a composite glue-blocking technique that solved these problems had evolved in some London shops. Composite glue-blocking consists of several layers of secondary wood blocks stacked one on the other to build up a vertical foot block. All the grain in the glue blocking runs horizontally, parallel to the grain of the bracket itself. In addition, the blocks are stacked crossgrain, which alternates the grain orientation at the joint between glue-block and bracket-foot member to provide long-grain gluing surfaces to each side of the bracket. The layers are also face-glued together, producing an extremely strong foot (photo *H*). Scott's pieces combine this feature of foot construction with the laminated bracket, and his is the only American shop known to do so. Several other Williamsburg shops used composite-blocked feet, as did some in Norfolk, Va., and Annapolis, Md., but to my knowledge, this construction does not make a single appearance in the furniture of Boston, Newport, New York, Philadelphia or Charleston.

In summary, if it is to 18th-century American furniture that the craftsman and designer look for instruction, it is wise to realize that there were various construction methods as well as levels of sophistication. All American production is an off-shoot of the English techniques that were most highly developed in London. The transition to America involved some loss or distortion of the original systems. Cabinet shops producing furniture closest to London in style and construction centered in Williamsburg. According to the degree of sophistication in typical case constructions, the other centers range, from high-style to provincial, as follows: Charleston, Philadelphia, New York, Newport, and Boston/Salem. Other cities should be in this list, but their production has been too little studied to reach definitive conclusions. □

Wallace Gusler is curator of furniture at Colonial Williamsburg. His book, Furniture of Williamsburg and Eastern Virginia, 1710-1790 *(Virginia Museum of Fine Arts, Box 7260, Richmond, Va. 23221, $24), covers in detail the production of the Scott and other Virgina shops.*

Post-and-Panel Chests
A 19th-century design

by Jim Richey

Experts on antique furniture usually advise, "Buy it and leave it alone." They didn't see the 140-year-old chest of drawers we brought home. Once sturdy and clear-finished, it was wobbly and covered with ugly paint. A previous owner had cured its loosened joints by driving nails through the cheeks of the mortises. Proper restoration had to start with complete disassembly.

While rebuilding, I realized that the post-and-panel construction of this unadorned country antique is really quite sophisticated and deserves to be better known. It is strong and handsome, and not likely to crack apart over the years. Hundreds of these chests survive: They were made throughout the Ohio River Valley states, of local hardwoods by village cabinetmakers who cared more for function than for fashion.

The post-and-panel chest is designed to cope with seasonal humidity changes and long-term panel shrinkage without damage. All the critical dimensions of the chest are determined by long-grain members—posts and rails. Built like a post-and-beam barn, the chest is strong enough to handle the strains of cross-country moving. Yet, there are disadvantages. The joinery is difficult, the material list calls for more and thicker wood than slab-sided construction and the finished chest seems to weigh a ton.

The old chest shown on the next page is 44 in. high, 44½ in. wide and 20½ in. deep. The top, front and sides are solid cherry. The back, drawer sides and drawer bottoms are poplar. The side panels are 16 in. wide, cut from a single board. Nowadays, unless you have access to unusually wide, clear stock, you would have to glue up two boards for the side panels. It is also perfectly acceptable to construct two (or more) panels per side with a stile between that's mortised into the top and bottom rails. Authentic 1830 panels are flat on the outside, beveled on the inside. The bevels can be turned to the outside for an attractive, if not authentic, effect. As with all frame-and-panel construction, the panel is left unglued in its groove, free to move as humidity changes.

If you decide to adapt the post-and-panel design to a chest project, carefully cut and dry-fit all the joints first. The mortise-and-tenon joints where rail meets post are crucial to a strong chest. Single tenons on the ends of the rails will work, but divided tenons mated with divided mortises are stronger and not much harder to make. Drawbore and peg the mortise-and-tenon joints, if desired, to gain extra strength and to reduce the number of clamps needed for assembly. Don't substitute one horizontal tenon for the two vertical tenons shown in the sketch at the ends of the drawer dividers; a horizontal tenon here won't hold, and it will weaken the posts.

Don't try to glue up the carcase all at once. First glue up the more complex side assemblies. The drawer-guide supports (with the drawer guides yet to be screwed on) need not be glued in; the post-and-rail frame will hold them in. With the side assemblies done, you can glue up the back or leave it

Post-and-panel chest construction

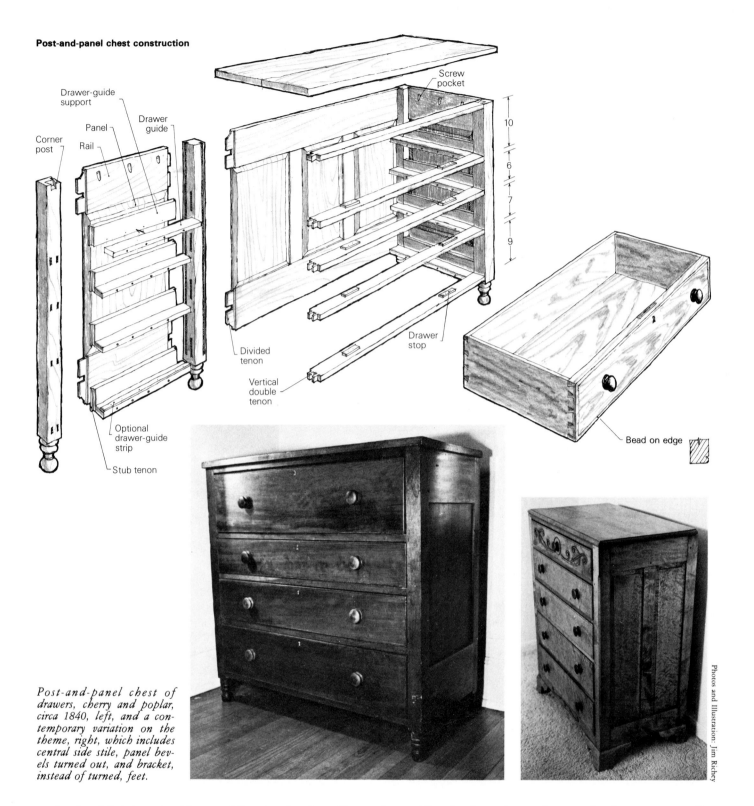

Post-and-panel chest of drawers, cherry and poplar, circa 1840, left, and a contemporary variation on the theme, right, which includes central side stile, panel bevels turned out, and bracket, instead of turned, feet.

unglued and fit it into the side assemblies piece by piece. The best way to assemble the whole carcase is to lay one of the sides on the floor and fit the back rails, panel, and front drawer dividers into the posts. Then fit the other side onto the other end. Turn the carcase upright, clamp it together and glue in the top drawer divider, which is dovetailed into the posts. With the carcase completed, the drawer guides can be screwed in flush with the drawer dividers. The guides will wear in time and so should not be glued, making their replacement easier.

Fasten the top to the frame with screws through screw-pockets cut in the top side rails. The screw holes should be large enough to allow for some movement of the top. If the top is warped, put the concave side down to reduce gapping at the front. After the frame is together, cut the drawer parts to fit the drawer openings. Use traditional drawer construction with dovetailed corners and solid, beveled-panel bottoms.

Most antique chests have a turned foot at the bottom of the legs ending at the floor with a ball. If you prefer molded bracket feet to turned posts, just rabbet out a portion of the face and side at the bottom of the front posts equal to the height of the foot. Fasten the bracket foot below the resulting shoulder with screws from the back. Since part of the post touches the floor and backs up the feet, the arrangement is quite strong. ☐

Jim Richey, of Ponca City, Okla., is Methods of Work editor of Fine Woodworking *magazine.*

Methods of Work

Wooden pull/catch

This cabinet door pull serves a double function—it's also a locking catch. The material cost is negligible but you'll spend about an hour making and installing the pull. The catch is designed for doors hung flush with the framing, so a separate door-stop must be incorporated.

First, square a line from the edge of the cabinet door at the position you want the pull. Bore a ⅝-in. hole through the cabinet door 1 in. from the door's edge and centered on the line. Then cut a 1-in. deep, ¼-in. wide mortise into the door edge. Start the mortise ⅛ in. below the position line and stop the mortise 1 in. above the line. Cut a corresponding ⅜-in. deep mortise in the frame.

After the mortises are completed, lathe-turn the pull handle with a knob on the front and a round tenon on the back. The tenon should slip-fit in the ⅝-in. hole and be as long as the door is thick. Dry-fit the pull in the hole and, while holding the knob at the locked position, reach through

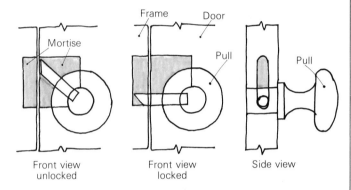

Front view
unlocked

Front view
locked

Side view

the mortise and drill a ¼-in. hole in the tenon to receive the latch/dowel.

To complete the pull/catch, coat the tenon with beeswax, put a drop of glue in the latch-dowel hole and set the pull in place. Insert the latch-dowel through the mortise into the hole. Then, with the handle turned to the unlock position, cut the latch-dowel flush with the door edge.
—*Michael Lynch, San Francisco, Calif.*

Quick-adjust picture-frame clamp-nut

To make this clamp-nut, tap a ¾-in. section of ¾-in. aluminum or steel rod. Then cut through the tapped hole on an angle with an end-mill cutter to clear the threads. Use a ¹⁷⁄₆₄-in. end-mill cutter for a ¼-in. tap and a ²⁵⁄₆₄-in. cutter for a ⅜-in. tap.

To use, tilt the nut on the threaded rod and slide into position for quick adjustment. Then straighten out the nut for fine adjustment and locking. The nut works well not only on picture-frame clamps but also in other locking-knob or quick-adjust situations. —*Walter W. Yaeger, Maple Shade, N.J.*

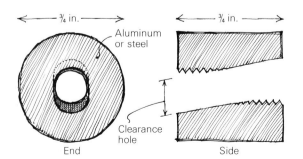

End

Side

Building Blockfronts
Improving traditional constructions

by E. F. Schultz

Blockfront furniture has always been regarded by antiquarians and craftsmen alike as a unique, beautiful and important American decorative-arts creation. Students of furniture and design admire the blockfront for its boldly sculptured form, its fine proportions and its superlative moldings. This article attempts to deal with some of the demanding constructional features particular to Boston and Newport (R.I.) blockfront furniture. The cabinetmaker today can construct period reproductions either exactly like the original in every detail or with modifications, incorporating contemporary improvements in the joinery without visually altering the piece's magnificence. I choose to improve the construction where time has shown the originals to have shortcomings.

Before beginning, it is important to note the complexity of these designs and the meticulous execution they warrant. Be prepared to spend several months in a well-equipped shop to complete a blockfront like the ones discussed here. A time-consuming, but indispensable, first step is to draft full-scale plans. They indicate the relation of all the parts, their joinery and detailing, and thus prove whether or not your planned method of construction will work. In effect, once you have successfully completed a set of plans, you will have mentally assembled the piece of furniture. The plans are then a record of information often not easy to recall in the midst of actual construction. They also can be elaborated upon in designing more sophisticated pieces. I prefer full-scale plans when the size of the piece permits, as you can measure from them directly and use them to make and check templates.

Much of the beauty of blockfront furniture is attributed to

Schultz's reproduction of a Boston blockfront chest of drawers, 40 in. by 35⅜ in. by 22½ in., Honduras mahogany. Full-size blueprints for this piece and for the Newport blockfront slant-top desk on p. 168 can be purchased from Boston Cabinet-Making, Inc., 27 Kingston St., Boston, Mass. 02111.

Fig. 1: Newport case construction

Carcase dovetailed together in usual fashion

Bare-faced mortise and tenon

½″ screw slots

Dust frame and panel, glued to back edge of drawer divider

Spline miter

Base frame is screwed to carcase bottom

Detail of slot screwing

#12 screw

½-in. slot filed in base frame

#16 brass washer with slot filed in it

Countersunk hole

Splined and mitered bracket feet, glued to base frame. Glue blocks are also used.

Newport blockfront slant-top desk in construction. One-piece mahogany side is 20¾ in. wide.

From the back, base frame (left) shows bare-faced mortise and tenon, and half-blind dovetails between back feet and braces. Segmenting the bracket-foot glue blocks (right) minimizes the chance that the bracket pieces, which run crossgrain, will crack.

the wide, one-piece ends and top. A mahogany board of the required width will usually display quite diverse visual grain characteristics: flame figure, dark (almost black) stripes, rich swirls and beautiful iridescent colors. To make a visually accurate blockfront reproduction, the cabinetmaker must first deal with the problem of locating suitable and worthy stock, and then plan his construction to cope with the constant movement of even well-seasoned boards. However they move, they must provide a stable carcase for the sculptured drawers they contain. With both Boston and Newport furniture, these wide boards must also attach to a sculptured base molding and to bracket feet. Because the grain direction of the carcase sides is perpendicular to that of the base molding, the traditional construction techniques—gluing and nailing this molding to the carcase side—is troublesome. Many cases have loose moldings and/or cracks originating from the molding because it constrained the movement of the sides and thus caused them to relieve their internal stresses through checking. Also, the ogee bracket feet were glued across the grain of the wide boards, so this joint too loosens in time.

One possible solution to this problem is to allow the wide boards to move, but to direct their movement. The aim is to have the exterior remain visually perfect, so we construct the piece for the movement of the wide boards to occur from front to back. The visual facade of the piece remains tight while expansion and contraction occur "behind" its exterior surface. This can become somewhat of an engineering job.

The construction that I suggest for the Newport case is shown in figure 1. In simplified terms, a dovetailed carcase is attached to a molded base frame. The front corners of the base frame are mitered and splined, with bare-faced tenons cut on the back rail and mortises on the sides. The front and sides of the base are glued up first, the back rail afterward. Remember when gluing up the miters that only the outermost edge shows; therefore, this edge should be tightly fitted even if the inner edge of the miter is not.

Next, the front two ogee bracket feet are splined and glued together while the back feet are half-blind dovetailed to the back braces (photo, above). All four are then glued directly to the base frame. Glue blocks are used as well. For the bracket feet themselves, cutting several short glue blocks instead of one long one should keep the deleterious effect of wood movement to a minimum.

The entire base has now been assembled as a separate unit. The bottom surface of the case and the top surface of the base frame should now be trued with a plane and straightedge prior to slot-screwing the base into place. I use a Starrett 36-in. straightedge because of its heft and resistance to bending. Slot the screwholes in the center and rear of the base frame only; thus the carcase is fixed to the base frame at the front and allowed to expand and contract at the back.

With Boston blockfronts the suggested construction for attaching the base molding must differ somewhat from the Newport style because of the absence of a drawer divider between the bottom drawer and the molding. This, along with the absence of a drawer divider between the top drawer and the carcase top, gives the Boston chest a more starkly linear appearance. The joinery for constructing and attaching the base on the Boston blockfront is more complicated than with the Newport style, but the principles are the same (figure 2). A major difference here from the Newport construction is that the base, once installed, is not removable. The molded base front, incorporating its giant dovetail, is glued permanently to the case bottom's leading edge. The base sides are then glued to the front of the base with a lap miter joint. Thus the base molding is held secure to the front of the case, allowing the carcase to move in slotted screwholes from front to back. The rear rail of this base "cradle" is fitted and lap-joined to the base molding sides *after* the sides are screwed to the bottom of the case. This sequence is followed to ensure a tight fit between the case sides and the *L*-shaped, molded base sides. The bracket feet are applied to the base in the same manner as in the Newport blockfront, using segmented glue blocks. When completed, and even with the bottom drawer removed, unless one looks underneath the Boston case, it is not possible to differentiate this type of construction from the original.

Because the wide boards, whose movement we have been taking into account in our construction, must also be an integral part of a sturdy carcase for supporting the large, sculptured drawers, the joinery between drawer dividers and carcase sides deserves attention. Newport pieces traditionally have exposed sliding dovetails with cockbeading on both drawer dividers and carcase sides. Boston pieces usually cover the drawer-divider dovetails with thin cockbeaded strips of wood the length of the carcase sides. In both Boston and Newport blockfronts there are no dust panels. The period pieces, for the most part, have drawer runners dadoed and glue-blocked to the carcase sides, a crossgrain construction that can result in cracked sides.

I prefer to incorporate dust panels whose frames provide more than adequate drawer support while allowing the runners to float free of the carcase sides (figure 1). The extra time and stock required for this construction is negligible when compared to the sturdier, more durable and more finished piece that results. Figures 3 and 4 contrast the Newport and Boston-style joints between carcase side and drawer divider. The cockbeading and its mitering in both cases present a special challenge in fine joinery. □

Gene Schultz, 34, builds custom furniture at Boston Cabinet-Making, Inc., in Boston, Mass.

Fig. 2: Boston case construction

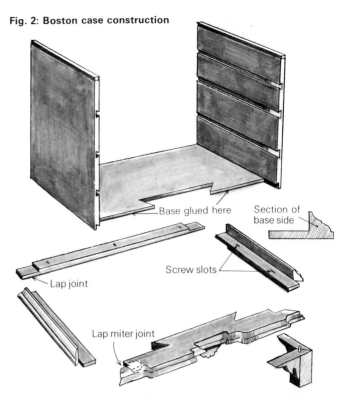

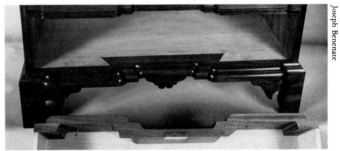

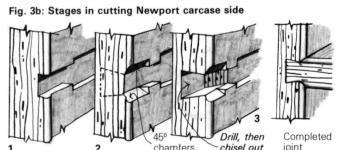

A giant dovetail joins Boston-style base frame to carcase bottom.

Fig. 3a: Stages in cutting Newport drawer divider

Use tenon to locate dovetail when scribing it to carcase edge.

Fig. 3b: Stages in cutting Newport carcase side

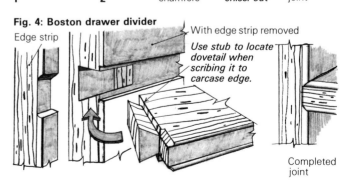

Fig. 4: Boston drawer divider

Edge strip

With edge strip removed

Use stub to locate dovetail when scribing it to carcase edge.

Completed joint

Head blank is tenoned and pegged into partially carved neck. Mortises for forelegs have already been cut in lower chest.

Holzman puts finishing touches on head with carving gouge.

Carving complete, the undercoat is applied. Flaring nostrils, perky ears and tensed neck muscles impart vitality to wooden steed.

doweled into the rump and made to flow into a leg where it can be attached. This prevents it from being easily broken off. The tails of many horses were of real hair, not difficult to obtain when horses could still be seen on city streets. Still others were carved.

Carousel carvers like to emphasize muscles, tendons and bone structure. Common are flaring nostrils, prominent teeth, straining heads and bodies. To reduce the difficulty of the undertaking, it is advisable to carve the legs, neck, head and body independently of each other. Each part should be taken to a near-completed state, leaving a couple of inches undone where each piece will be joined to another. After that the pieces can be faired into each other. There are decided advantages to working this way and not having to manipulate a glued-up horse that may be bigger than you are.

It is best to bandsaw the rump and chest profiles if possible. Use a large, three-sweep fishtail gouge for roughing out the body. Where there are depressions in the flanks, use deeper gouges. Straps, blanket and saddle are drawn in and outlined with a *V*-parting tool and carved with appropriate gouges. Some carvers suggest leaving the head for last to allow time for the wood and tools to be gotten used to, especially since this part of the anatomy is the most difficult to do. Templates can be used to gauge symmetry and contours. More detailed photos of the head will be required than of any other part of the body. Generally, the head was made from two or four pieces of wood glued up face to face. The neck is a separate piece, also a lamination, with the grain running sometimes parallel to the body. This was done because manes would not flow down but would wrap around the neck, and horizontal grain would facilitate carving the hair. The ears should not be carved too soon, as they are delicate and may break off. Once finished, the head and neck can be attached to the body and faired in.

Here is a technique used by Speiser for setting in the kind of glass eyes that can be purchased from a taxidermist. Draw a rough profile of the head on a piece of stiff paper and cut a small triangular hole for the socket. Try inserting the glass eye edgewise through this hole. Keep making the hole larger until the eye falls through. Transfer the outline of this hole to the carving. Gouge out and undercut the hole enough for the eye to be rotated. Remove it and partially fill the cavity with plastic wood. Immediately insert the eye, rotate and press it into the proper position. The displaced plastic wood will ooze out, and the excess can be removed. After the plastic wood has hardened, you carve the details of the eyebrows and eyelids.

Once the horse has been carved and sanded smooth, a heavy-bodied paint sealer should be applied. Sand this coat lightly when it's dry and apply another coat, which this time should be tinted with the colors that will finish the horse. Give each separately painted area its own tinted undercoating. Choice of paints may be individual, but flat oil-base colors flow together better. As a final step, apply a coat of clear varnish.

Additional touches might include gold leafing on the blanket fringes, harnesses and other trappings, and adding flat-back mirrored jewels to the blanket. □

EDITOR'S NOTE: Two publications about the design, construction and lore of carousel animals are Frederick Fried's *A Pictorial History of the Carousel* ($17.50 from A. S. Barnes and Co., Box 421, Cranbury, N.J. 08512) and *Carousel Art*, a quarterly magazine ($10 a year from Box 667, Garden Grove, Calif. 92642).

French Fitting
Making the presentation case presentable

by John Lively

Though the term is most often applied to arms cases, a box, a drawer or a chest can be French-fitted to hold almost anything. Drafting, optical and photographic equipment, large pieces of jewelry, hand tools and musical instruments are but a few of the items that can benefit from being snuggled into a closely fitting, leather-lined recess. The method I will describe deals specifically with cases for handguns.

In the last quarter of the 18th century, a gentleman's purchase of a pair of new pistols was no casual matter. As much objects of art as instruments of defense, the custom-built pistols of Georgian times involved the cooperative efforts of many skilled artisans. Master gunsmiths, acting much like general contractors, retained the services of independent founders, barrelmakers, lockmakers, woodcarvers, goldsmiths, silversmiths and engravers. After designing the parts and farming out the various jobs, the gunsmith's work was done, except for collecting and assembling the finished pieces. Then the pistols were delivered to one more specialist—the casemaker. It is the work of these casemakers that has ensured the survival into our time of so many splendid examples of 18th-century gunsmithing. Thanks to them, it is not unusual for an auctioneer's bulletin to describe the condition of 200-year-old firearms as "excellent" or "original."

Though these cases served well enough for storage and display, they were designed for traveling by coach. They were usually shallow, rectangular boxes in sturdy oak or mahogany, dovetailed together, with their flush-fitting lids secured by hinges at the rear and an inlet, keyed lock at the front. On the outside, these cases were paradigms of unadorned simplicity, relying on the wood's figure and color for decoration.

Yet on the inside, things were not so simple. Muzzle-load-ing arms required a number of accessory tools that had also to be fitted into the case, and all the pieces had to be kept from coming into damaging and possibly dangerous contact with one another. Two distinct methods of casefitting arose to address this necessity—the English and the French. English casemakers found it expedient to divide the case into straight-sided, cloth-lined compartments, each conforming, more or less, to the shape of the piece it contained. The inside of the typical English case appears labyrinthine. The French casemakers chose instead to fashion compartments in the precise shape of the pieces. They created these negative spaces either by cutting the shapes into a solid panel of wood or by making molded impressions. In either event, they usually glued cloth inside the impressions as well as to the ground surface above, so it covered the entire inside of the case. Though elevations vary from case to case, the typical French-fitted box presents its contents in half relief, the metal of the pistols contrasting nicely with the cloth-covered ground.

The fitted pistol case remained an indispensable part of a gentleman's traveling gear until the advent of repeating arms and pocket pistols toward the middle of the 19th century. The wooden carrying case then gave way to the leather holster and the vest pocket. But as a presentation case for custom-made or special-issue arms, the fitted wooden case continued to be made, and even today the major arms manufacturers sell them as accessories. Their cases are inferior, however, and in recent years the interest of collectors in black-powder and reproduction firearms has created a new demand for custom-fitted presentation cases. The woodworker is in a good position to compete. Too, the marketplace is accessible via the well-attended gun shows held several times a year in most

Black walnut main case holds Colt dragoon revolver and powder flask, while cleaning and bullet-making tools fit into lidded inner box at right.

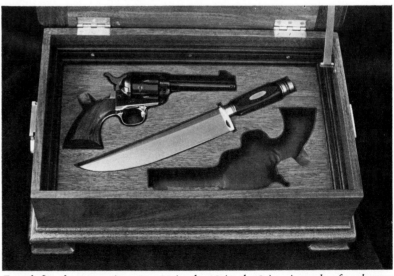

French-fitted presentation case, 21 in. by 18 in. by 5 in., is made of mahogany with padauk molding inside, and red leather lining. An inner lid (not shown) rests atop the molding inside the case.

Photos: John Barretto; Illustration: Ric Lopez

major cities. With samples to show, the casemaker is sure to generate considerable interest.

Before proceeding, I have to point out that my fitting method differs in several significant respects from the traditional treatment. First, I line the case with leather instead of cloth. I've found that fabric wears quickly where it contacts the pieces, and it eventually becomes grimy from gun oil and other residues. Also, it is almost impossible to line the cavities with fabric without unsightly wrinkles. Second, I don't make a molded impression of the pieces, but rather I cut the shapes into a solid panel of wood (called an inset panel), line their inner edges with leather, and secure the panel above a leather-covered cushion that fills the bottom of the case. Using wood rather than cloth as the visible ground not only allows me greater opportunity to create visual effects, but also makes for a more durable interior. And because it is small, the inset panel is the perfect place for using a nicely figured scrap from the stash under my bench.

Making the inset panel — French fitting begins where casework ordinarily leaves off, though it's good to have all the materials on hand before starting the case itself. If you want to use several different species of wood on the interior, you will need to coordinate these with the color of the lining material. Leather comes in lots of colors, but they may not all be available all of the time. At a leathercraft supply store, select upholstery leather that is finished on one side but left unfinished or sueded on the other. Buy enough to cover double the bottom surface area of the case.

Finished upholstery leather is many times more durable than cloth, its finished surface will not soak up oil and dirt, and it can be cleaned with a damp cloth. The leather's unfinished side has just the right texture for gluing to wood with contact adhesive, and its finished side will resist glue penetration. You can wipe off glue smears with your finger.

Once the case is made, cut four cleats ¾ in. square by its inner dimensions. Miter them to length and glue them to the bottom and inner sides of the case. Next, obtain a piece of medium-density upholstery foam exactly 1 in. thick, and cut it to fit snugly between the cleats. As you will see later, the ¼-in. difference between the thickness of the foam and the thickness of the cleats is important. Now cut a piece of leather to the inner dimensions of the case and tack it securely along

its edges to the top of the cleats, one tack every 1½ in. The leather should be taut, but not stretched across the cushion. When the leather is tacked down, there must be no wrinkles or bulges caused by uneven tension.

Start by making templates from the pistols or whatever is to be fitted. This requires tracing around the contours so that the completed outline is larger than the object piece by the thickness of the leather. Leather does not come uniformly off the cow, but if your outline is 1/16 in. larger than the piece you are fitting, your template will be close enough. To make this tracing, clamp the object over a piece of poster board. I use a bench holdfast with a pad of foam and a small scrap of wood. To produce the slightly enlarged outline, use a device similar to the one described by Carlisle Lynch (*FWW* #18, Sept. '79, p. 83). But make yours with a *V*-shaped base (because it must follow tight curves) and a tracer positioned 1/16 in. in advance of the scribing tool.

Once you have completed the template, dimension the stock you have chosen to the inside measurements of your case, and at least half as thick as the object you are fitting—¾ in. does well for pistols. Lay the template on the stock and move it around until you are satisfied; if more than one object must fit, try different arrangements until you find one that is both pleasing and practical. Trace the outline of the templates onto the bottom face of the panel. If you have a jigsaw, drill starter holes and cut out the shapes, being careful not to stray beyond the inside edge of the traced lines. Don't risk ruination by sawing too close to tight corners. These areas will be properly enlarged by filing later.

Rather than jigsawing, I prefer the band saw. But instead of attempting to weld a blade threaded through a pilot hole, I simply rip the panel in two so the saw kerf passes through all the proposed negative spaces at once. Joint the sawn edges, dry-clamp the two pieces together, and reposition the templates on the top surface to make new tracings corresponding to the ones on the bottom. This is necessary because the ripping destroys the original proportions. Then I unclamp, saw out the spaces, and glue the two parts back together. You will probably need to clamp from the inner edges of the sawn-out spaces, using several small handscrews, along with bar clamps at either end of the panel. Different panels will call for different strategies.

Before proceeding any further, saw a slot along each end-grain edge to receive a spline ¼ in. thick by at least ½ in. wide, the full width of the panel. Rip the two splines from solid material. They should seat tightly enough to require a few gentle taps with hammer and block. Do not omit this step or postpone it; without reinforcement, the short-grain portions of the panel won't stand up to subsequent handling, and it will crack the first time you give it a hard look. I usually take the additional precaution of boring through narrow short-grain walls and gluing in bits of ¼-in. dowel.

Now you should begin to clean up the bandsawn inner edges with bastard files—a half-round, a triangular and a small round. Assuming the entire width of your traced outline is still visible, as it should be, you will want to file the sawn-out spaces just to the other edge of the line. Do not obliterate the line, but leave a visible trace of it all around.

The next steps are quick and easy. Make sure the panel fits easily in the case, bearing in mind probable movement across the grain. With a marking gauge, scribe the panel's upper face ⅜ in. in from all four edges. Then mark equidistant

Section through case

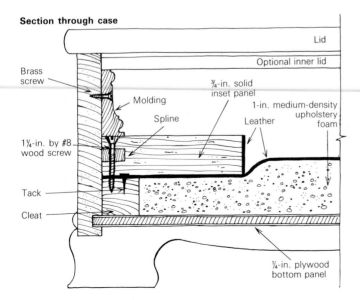

Lid

Optional inner lid

Brass screw

Molding

¾-in. solid inset panel

Spline

Leather

1-in. medium-density upholstery foam

1¼-in. by #8 wood screw

Tack

Cleat

¼-in. plywood bottom panel

Halved panel stock is reassembled after spaces are bandsawn.   *Leather is cemented into place. Note reinforcing spline in panel's edge.*

centers for pilot holes, three of them along the length and two on the width. Bore and counterbore on these centers for 1¼-in. by #8 wood screws. If you anticipate more than negligible movement, slot appropriate holes to allow for it. Transfer the centers to the leather-covered cleats on the bottom of the case, and bore pilot holes in them, too.

Lining the spaces — At last it is time for an initial fitting. Return the panel to the case and screw it down. Since the foam cushion is higher than the cleats, it will be compressed. Tighten the panel as you would tighten a drum-head—not all at once on any one side, but in even stages all around. When it is firmly seated, you will see that the covering has welled up into the cavities, forming a firm, neatly crowned pillow. Now you can nestle the items into their compartments. Cut several patches of leather and slip them between the edges of the cut-out and the object pieces at various places along their contours. Then study the unfilled spaces to determine whether a proper fit will be achieved once the entire inner edge is lined with leather. Remember that you want a smooth fit, but not one that is tight. Whatever you are fitting should settle into its compartment by its own weight. Once settled in, there should be an absolute minimum of slop. If you try to wiggle it around, it should not move more than ⅟32 in. in any direction and preferably it should remain dead still. Shade the tight spots with a pencil, remove the panel from the case and file some more. Then test it again.

When the fit is correct, seal the surfaces of the panel so that they will resist the glue you will apply inside the cavities later. Take care to prevent the finish from dripping over the edges of the cut-outs, as this will interfere with gluing the leather.

When the faces of the panel are sealed, you are ready to line its inner contours with leather, which should be cut (straightedge and sharp knife) into long strips a uniform 1 in. wide. These strips must be long enough to run the entire distance—any attempt to splice will leave ugly gaps. Now lay the strips face down and apply three coats of contact cement to their unfinished sides, waiting for each coat to dry. Do the same to the inner edges of the panel. When the final coats have dried, clamp the panel in a vise and begin sticking the strips of leather to the contoured edges, allowing the strips to overhang about ⅛ in. to each side. Begin and end in the same

corner to make the junction as unobtrusive as possible.

Press the leather firmly into place with your fingers. For those tight little curves and culs-de-sac, use a round screwdriver shaft or the like to put pressure where it belongs. Don't rush this operation, and don't permit the leather to touch the tacky surfaces ahead of the spot you are working on. If it sticks to the wrong place and you try to pull it loose, half of the leather strip will remain stuck to the wood. Should this happen, pull all the leather loose and clean up the mess with lacquer thinner, which will probably also dissolve the finish on the panel's face. Be assured of a nasty tussle if you let the leather stick where it doesn't belong.

When the inner edges are lined, take a pair of manicure scissors and trim the leather flush with the top and bottom surfaces of the panel. Before going further, you need to work in a bead of yellow glue with your fingertip to stiffen the raw edges of the leather so that they will not roll over in use. When the glue has hardened, sand the face of the panel with 220-grit paper. A subsequent sanding with 400-grit paper will leave the panel ready for final finishing, which should be done before it is fastened to the cleats.

The final step is to design and make a molding to trim out the inside corners of the case. The only requirement of the design is that the base of the molding be thick enough to obscure the heads of the screws that fasten the inset panel. You might attach this molding with small brass screws, so you can remove the panel should the need for repair arise.

Having said little about the design of the case itself, I would like to close with a few prejudicial remarks. For a contemporary collector, a presentation case is seldom used as a traveling container. It's an article of household furniture with the specific function of preserving and displaying objects of significance and value. Though it may be carried about from time to time, there is no need to feel restricted by the design requirements of a traveling case. Apart from structural necessities, your design should be aimed at achieving harmony, balance and continuity between the case and its contents, so that the two can be perceived as one thing.   □

John Lively, 35, has joined Fine Woodworking *magazine as assistant editor. He used to make cabinets and billiard tables in Dallas, Tex.*

Tambours in the Weed kitchen allow cabinets (all made of black willow) to remain open without swinging doors on which to bump your head or to obstruct access. Weed says this design requires no more work to make than a set of frame-and-panel doors. Right, tambour curtain disappears behind faceboard and false back, painted white. A stiffener strip neatens the top edge of the false back. Cabinet is deep enough for stacks of 10-in. plates.

Tambour Kitchen Cabinets
The conveniently disappearing door

by Richard Starr

"These doors are incomparable as far as convenience is concerned," says Hazel Weed about the kitchen cabinets built by her husband, Walker. "When I'm in here working, I just open them up and have everything where I can get at it." Weed, a woodworker who directs the student craft shops at Dartmouth College, feels that traditional doors are always in the way, obstructing other cabinets and banging you on the head. When planning the kitchen for their old farmhouse in the hills above Hanover, N.H., the Weeds chose disappearing doors—vertically opening tambours.

Most cabinets are boxes with doors hung on them, but a tambour must be designed into the cabinet structure. Weed routed the curtain track into the inner sides of the carcase (front, top and back) before assembly; the three straightaways were joined by tight curves. To ensure that the left and right tracks were identical, Weed used a template to guide the router. A false back, hung in grooves in the sides and trimmed with a stiffener strip at the top, hides the back of the open door from view. To cover the curve of the door as it arches into the cabinet, Weed installed a faceboard whose inner surface was contoured to match the track. Thus the vis-

ible section of the door is flat, creating the illusion that it is disappearing into the air over the cabinet as it is opened.

For the curtain to run properly the cabinet must be perfectly square; Weed emphasizes the need for accurate joinery. He fixed the cabinets to the wall only at the top so they would not be distorted by any settling of the house. The carcases are joined with half-blind dovetails at the corners. The dividers in the double and triple cabinets are set in dadoes; their front ends are housed dovetails that extend about 1½ in. back into the cabinet.

To make the curtains, Weed cut a board slightly longer than the width of the cabinet and planed it to ½ in. thick, the width of the strips. He rounded the edge of the board with a router, then ripped off this half-round strip, ½ in. thick, on the table saw. The newly sawn edge of the board was shaped again and the process repeated until he had enough strips.

The finished tambour curtain must be long enough to occupy both curves of the track when closed; its width will be slightly narrower than the distance from one groove bottom to the other. After washing and ironing the 14-oz. canvas backing, Weed cut it to a width slightly less than the inside of

Photos: Richard Starr; drawing: Joe Esposito

Tambour kitchen cabinet

Overall dimensions:
30 in. high by 36 in. wide
by 11¼ in. deep

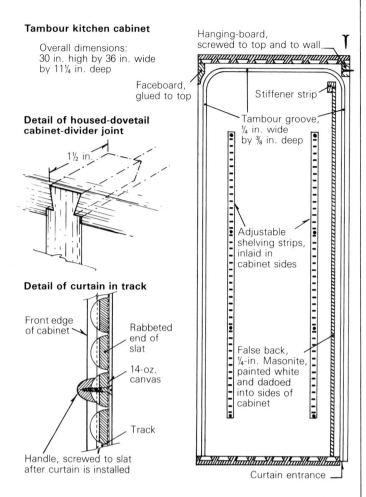

Hanging-board,
screwed to top and to wall

Faceboard,
glued to top

Stiffener strip

Tambour groove,
¼ in. wide
by ⅜ in. deep

Adjustable
shelving strips,
inlaid in
cabinet sides

False back,
¼-in. Masonite,
painted white
and dadoed
into sides of
cabinet

Curtain entrance

Detail of housed-dovetail cabinet-divider joint

1½ in.

Detail of curtain in track

Front edge
of cabinet

Rabbeted
end of
slat

14-oz.
canvas

Track

Handle, screwed to slat
after curtain is installed

---

the cabinet, not counting the track. He left the canvas longer than the finished curtain, and trimmed it after gluing. Each strip was fixed to the cloth with a thin line of Titebond glue down its back, its length centered on the width of the fabric. The wood strips were butted closely together and weighted under plywood to dry. Weed suggests running the curtain over the edge of a table to break the hardened oozed glue, then folding it back on itself to scrape excess dry glue from the edges of the strips. The curtain was trimmed to width, then its edges were rabbeted on the table saw using a batten to hold it down on the saw table. Weed compares this step to fitting a drawer: Both surfaces of the rabbet must fit the groove closely but there must also be sufficient clearance.

After the cabinet is hung, the curtain slides into the track from the back end. Weed suggests waxing the rabbet before installation to ensure smooth running. Some friction is desirable since the tambour is perfectly counterbalanced only when half open; when more or less than half open, it wants to slide up or down. In actuality, the curtain stays put everywhere but a few inches from the ends of its travel. With the curtain in place, a fitted handle was screwed to the predrilled second slat. The handle stops the curtain against the facing at the top of the cabinet.

Weed estimates that a set of tambour kitchen cabinets would take no more time to make than a set with well-crafted frame-and-panel doors. The function of cabinet doors is to hide the clutter and to keep out the dust. Vertical tambours do it efficiently and beautifully. ☐

For a detailed discussion of the design and construction of tambours, see FWW #12, pp. 52-57.

Another kitchen idea: rosemaling

We didn't hope to create a totally different kitchen design. We wanted it to be unique without seeming modernistic, so we kept to the traditional and currently popular raised-panel cabinets. For innovation we decided to employ my wife's talent to hand-paint the panels of the upper cabinet doors with Norwegian rosemaling.

Norway's folk art has a long and colorful history. It goes back to the Vikings and Roman times. The Vikings traveled extensively so their art was developed with ideas taken from the Mediterranean peoples. Rosemaling, the freehand painting of colorful flowers (*rosemaling* means rose painting in Norwegian), became popular during the 18th and 19th centuries, taking the place of more common stenciled decorations. Decorative painting on furniture and cabinets has been popular enough to be mass-produced, the Lambert Hitchcock chairs of the early 1800s being the first notable example. Although ours are the only kitchen cabinets we've seen decorated with rosemaling, the techniques we used can be applied to any kind of decorative painting on wood.

We used clear pine for the raised panels of the upper cabinet doors. To prepare them for rosemaling they were first coated on both sides with an oil-paint primer, followed by a light-colored gloss enamel, to match the appliances. We applied a gloss varnish over this to make corrections in painting easier. On this surface, smoothed with wet 400-grit paper, the pattern outlines were drawn.

All painting was done with oil rather than acrylics. We mixed solid pigment (available through art-supply stores) with a medium made of equal parts of linseed oil, turpentine and varnish. The shades and hues were blended by carrying two colors on the brush simultaneously, which avoided sharp outlines between the two. As a protection for the decorations and to subdue the gloss background, we applied two coats of satin varnish to the completed paintings.

With the panels decorated and sealed, we assembled the cabinets and doors and finished the unpainted parts with two coats of Watco Danish oil, the second coat rubbed down lightly with 400-grit silicon-carbide paper.

—*William A. Julien, Chatham, Mass.*

William A. Julien

Norwegian floral painting (rosemaling) enhances traditional frame-and-panel kitchen cabinetry. Pine panels are primed, enameled and varnished before painting flowers, which are protected with varnish top coat.

Bandsaw Boxes

The quick and easy way to make a complicated container

by John Alcock-White

The versatile band saw can be your primary tool for making small wooden containers. I have been experimenting with the band-saw technique and have found that with it I can produce attractive containers in comparable or even less time than by turning or conventional joinery. Since the container is made from a single (or laminated) block of wood and all the grain remains parallel, movement caused by humidity change is uniform—the bandsaw box is not adversely affected by changing moisture conditions. The method is so direct it has an inherent beauty.

Bandsaw boxes became popular and widely imitated after Arthur (Espenet) Carpenter developed his version in the late 1960s (see *FWW* #25, Nov. '80, p. 66). In addition to boxes, Carpenter made such things as pigeonholes and drawers inside roll-top desks. Carpenter, of Bolinas, Calif., is a quiet person who becomes shy when discussing his own work. Asked about bandsaw boxes, he replies that his technique is so simple it hardly needs explanation. Be that as it may, it has the elegant simplicity common to all important innovation.

I found this technique when I first began to use the band saw. The method is first to saw off the sides of a block of wood, to turn the block on its side and saw out the center, then to glue the sides back on. The procedure can be extended to make drawers (figure 1). After the sides of a block are sawn off, drawer pieces can be sawn out, resawn into smaller containers, and finally replaced in their original positions within the larger block. If the saw is set up correctly—top and bottom guides snug, blade sharp and tensioned as much as possible—the cut pieces can be glued directly back together with little or no smoothing. Because the kerf cut by the saw governs angles and clearances, very little fitting and measuring are required.

Although this technique had struck me as a marvelous way to make containers, I forgot about it for some years until a friend, who markets a line of bathroom accessories, was telling me how profitable it was to manufacture such items as oak toilet seats. However, to increase sales he had to offer a full line of accessories, most of them of good quality, simple design and easy construction. One exception was a box designed to cover a tissue package, constructed with an elaborate finger joint. He was getting $8 for it and it retailed for $15, and he admitted it was a money-loser but still an essential part of his line. Instead of sawing and gluing up the finger joints, I proposed he make the box from a solid or laminated block of wood. He'd then have only four operations: bandsawing, regluing, routing the opening, and sanding (figure 2). The waste wood would be used to make something else, and the $8 price might become more feasible.

This experience got me making bandsaw containers again, and I became convinced it is a viable technique with lots of potential. Mainly the method is fast, perhaps faster than anything else. It is economical if the sawn-out sections are used to make smaller containers or if they can be used in other phases of your operation. Expansion and contraction of the wood is not a serious consideration. Making these containers does not depend on a lot of equipment—apart from the band saw, a few clamps and some smoothing tools are all you need. Lastly, compared to traditional joinery, there is practically no measuring and fitting. You can build freehand and end up with some interesting shapes, without tooling contortions. Although purists may decide bandsawn containers are gimmicky, I find them an enjoyable relief from conventional, more exacting woodwork. They look complicated yet are easy to make, and best of all, people like them. I can sell for a profit what I make. I wish that were always the case. □

John Alcock-White, 31, makes furniture and bandsaw boxes in Nanaimo, on Vancouver Island, B.C.

Fig. 1: Bandsawing a container with drawers

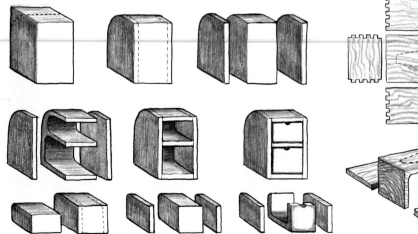

Fig. 2: Bottomless finger-joined box compared to bandsaw box

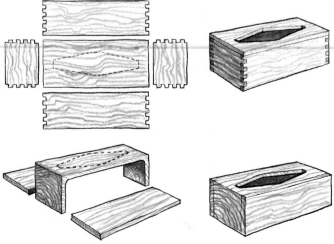

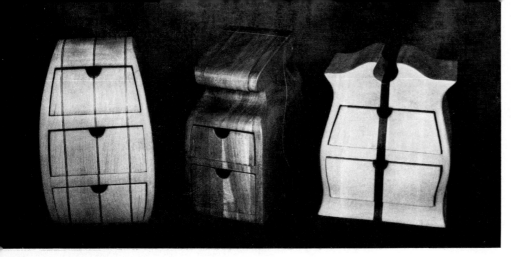

The boxes above, made by the author, have curved fronts and sides made by regluing along a curved kerf. The glueline is generally very clean; the major difficulty of holding the parts while sawing the interior is solved with improvised jigs and clamps.

A. To make a bandsaw box, start with a solid or laminated block of wood; shown are a small piece of myrtle taken from a bent section of the tree and a laminated block of Central American walnut with Honduras mahogany. Saw the block to contours you like, using a four-tooth, ¼-in. blade for heavy cuts and a six-tooth, ¼-in. blade for lighter cuts. Make simple containers with at least two flat sides before trying more complex shapes.

B. Set up a fence on the band saw and remove about 1 cm. (⅜ in.) from each side of the block. These pieces become the sides of the box, **C**, and since end grain does not glue well, saw them with the grain. The saw should leave surfaces smooth enough to reglue later, but for a perfect fit you can joint the cut-off sides and the central block.

D. Draw the interior of the container, and drill for the hinged lid. These boxes are fairly complicated, with a secret ledge above the drawer in the laminated block.

E. Saw along the lines, striving for smooth cuts. Resaw the blocks taken from the drawer openings. Rasp and sand any rough spots now, while they are still accessible.

F. Carefully glue the sides back on. Once the glue has set, insert dowels (or brass rods) through the hinges. Be sure the lid opens smoothly before driving the dowels home.

G. Trim off the dowels, cut a drawer pull, sand the outside of the box, and finish.

A

B

C

D

E

F

G

Methods of Work

Finger-joint jig

Here is a box or finger-joint jig like Tage Frid's (*Fine Wood-working*, Winter '76), except that it uses the table-saw rip fence rather than the miter gauge—a sturdier, easier-to-adjust arrangement. It consists of a guide rail bolted to the saw's rip fence, and a sliding-fence assembly that holds the work. Make the guide rail from particle board or hardwood plywood and cover both sides with plastic laminate to reduce sliding friction. Bolt the rail to the rip fence with four ¼-in. bolts. Countersink the bolt heads on the inboard side.

As with the rail, the sliding-fence assembly is made from particle board or plywood with plastic laminate glued to the bearing surfaces. An essential part of the jig is the hardwood tongue installed in the rail that slides in a groove in the fence assembly. Tack nylon furniture glides to the bottom of the fence asssembly to allow the jig to ride freely along the table.

Set-up time is fast—a good-fitting joint can usually be achieved in two test runs. The first step is to install a dado blade for the desired finger size, say ⅜ in. Raise the dado blade about ⅟₃₂ in. above the thickness of the stock to be cut. Now screw a scrap of ¾-in. material to the front of the sliding fence assembly to serve as a disposable fence. Drill a ⅜-in. hole in the center of the scrap fence about ½ in. from the saw table. Insert a short ⅜-in. dowel in the hole to act as a guide pin. Now adjust the rip fence/rail so that the distance between the guide pin and the dado blade is equal to the size of the dado—⅜ in. in our example.

Using a piece of scrap, start a test pass. While holding the stock vertically against the fence assembly and against the guide pin, pass the stock over the dado blade. After each cut, shift the stock to the right so that the previous cut registers

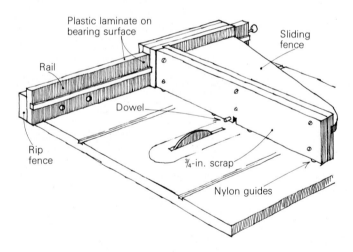

over the guide pin. Start the cut in the second test piece by lining it up with the sawcut in the fence (rather than the guide pin). The joint should be snug but loose enough to allow gluing. If the joint is too tight, move the rip fence to the left. If it's too loose, move the fence to the right.

—*Tom Burwell, St. Paul, Minn.*

Horizontal boring jig

My boring jig, whch uses a ½-in. portable drill, is similar to a conventional horizontal-boring machine except that the table moves rather than the drill. The jig consists of a base, a hinged drill platform and a sliding table.

Make the base and sliding table from ¾-in. hardwood plywood. The drill platform should be extra stiff, so laminate two pieces of ½-in. plywood to give a 1-in. thick platform. Spindle elevation is adjusted by raising or lowering the

hinged drill platform. Install a piano hinge on one edge and two or three bolts with wing nuts for adjustment on the other edge. If adjustment is needed over a wide range (say, 3 in.), some sort of pivoting arrangement would be required for the adjustment bolts.

Most ½-in. drills have a threaded handle socket on the top or side that will accept standard ¾-in. threaded pipe. Secure the drill to the platform with a short piece of threaded pipe and a standard floor flange.

Elevating the platform swings the drill through a short arc, so the fence on the sliding table must be mounted through slotted bolt holes to allow for movement. Hardwood rails on the bottom of the table mated with hardwood guide blocks on the base provide the tracking action for the sliding table.

—*Vanessa Skedzielewski, Sierra Madre, Calif.*

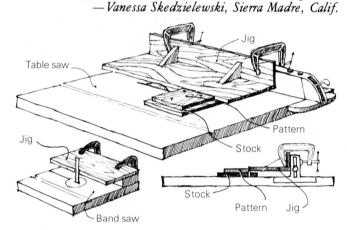

Doweling *T*-jig

A *T*-jig, used in doweling edge joints, ensures alignment of dowel pins and holes. Boards joined with the jig will mate better on the finish side, and sanding or planing misaligned joints is virtually eliminated. The jig's bar and leg are made of steel. High-carbon steel is best (anneal for machining, then harden later), but cold-rolled, mild steel will do. Wood will wear too fast. Drill common-dowel-size holes (¼ in. and ⅜ in.) in the center of the ¾-in. bar on each side of the leg. Two allen-head machine screws secure the leg to the bar.

In use, the *T*-jig serves as both a gauge (all the pin holes are equidistant from the face) and a copier (all the pin holes are mated from one edge to the other). First use the jig to drill all the pin holes in board *A*. Clamp the leg of the jig to the face of the board. No exact measurement of pin locations is needed—the holes in board *B* will be copied from the pins in board *A*. Install an extra-long registration pin in the first hole and regular-length pins in all the other holes.

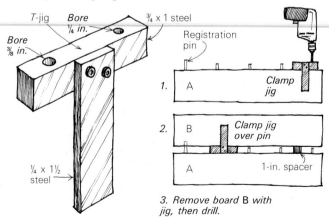

3. Remove board B with jig, then drill.

Horses and wagon

by Robert Ruffner

A simple piece wit[h] charm, this horse-a[nd] made of poplar, waln[ut] ations are easy enoug[h] cedures are given in th[e]

Robert Ruffner lives i[n]

Plan for horses and wagon

Cut s[...] with [...]

³⁄₈ [...]

Contour horse from 5/4 stock.

8 × ³⁄₄ × [...]

Position tongue at proper [...] and drill side for ¼-in. dow[el]. Use dowel centers to loca[te] holes in opposite horse.

A triangular drop-leaf tab[le] with rotating [...]

by Pendleton Tompki[ns]

Now clamp the jig to board *B* (leg to face) and drill the registration pin hole. Place the *T*-jig over one of the regular-length pins on board *A*, leg up, and fit the registration hole over the registration pin. Clamp the jig in place on board *B*, remove the board and drill. Repeat this operation for each pin in turn. Cut and use 1-in. spacer blocks to aid the pin-copying process.

After all the holes are drilled, trim the registration pin to size, spread glue on the joint and press the boards together, keeping the ends even as the boards go together.

—*Wallace Smith, Newport Beach, Calif.*

Duplicating wood parts

You can produce exact duplicates from a master pattern using this overhanging jig on your table saw. To make the jig, glue the pieces of ½-in. plywood in an *L*, reinforcing the joint with braces and screws. Clamp the smaller side of the jig to the saw's rip fence with two *C*-clamps. Allow ⅛-in. clearance between the underside of the jig and the stock to be cut. Now, by moving the rip fence, set the guide edge of the jig directly over the outside of the blade.

Cut a master pattern from ½-in. plywood to the exact size and shape of the part to be duplicated. Fasten the pattern to oversize precut blanks with tacks or double-sided tape. Now

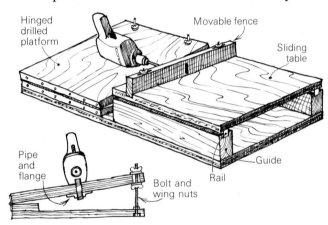

you are ready to cut the duplicate part. Press the master pattern against the guide edge of the jig and push through the blade. For safety's sake remove scraps from under the jig as you cut and stand to one side of the line of cut. Otherwise you'll be dodging projectiles of scrap that pile up under the jig and eventually get fired out by the blade.

The table-saw jig is limited to duplicating straight-edged parts in plywood and thin, solid stock. To reproduce thicker parts, and those with curved edges, set up a similar jig on the band saw. —*Ed Stevenson, Hammonton, N.J.*

Table-saw tenons

This method for cutting tenons on the table saw uses two blades with spacers between. The beauty of this system is that the tenon thickness is "locked in" and does not depend on variables such as stock thickness or pressure against the fence.

I keep a pair of special hollow-ground blades for tenon work. They are jointed as a pair and filed for ripping. Since the hub and tooth thickness are the same, cutting a ⁵⁄₁₆-in. tenon, for example, simply requires mounting the two blades with a ¼-in. and a ¹⁄₁₆-in. spacer between. My set of custom-machined spacers are 2½-in. discs drilled to slip over the saw arbor. Spacer thicknesses range from ¼ in. to 0.005 in. To pass the work through the blades, I use a standard miter gauge tracked in a plywood fence as shown above. This ap-

proach eliminates vertical rocking and thus is safer and more accurate than other methods.

—*Mac Campbell, Harvey Station, N.B., Canada*

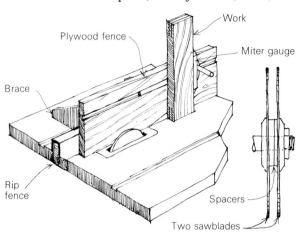

Spacing dadoes

Recently, while building a cabinet for cassette tapes, I experimented with several methods for spacing the numerous dadoes needed. Using an auxiliary miter-gauge fence gave the measure of accuracy and easy use I sought.

Bolt a piece of wood the length of the saw table and about 1 in. wide to the miter gauge. This auxiliary fence becomes an extension of the gauge, stabilizing long pieces of work and preventing twisting on the saw. The auxiliary fence should be the same thickness as the workpiece. After the dado width is set and tested on scrap, make a cut into the auxiliary fence. Mark the right and left edges of the cut on the top of the fence. The workpiece, marked for spacing, is moved along the auxiliary fence. When the lines meet, slide the gauge into the dado blade, making the cut.

—*Paul Saffron, Rockville Centre, N.Y.*

EDITOR'S NOTE: A variation of Saffron's method is common practice in many cabinet shops. Screw a new auxiliary fence to the miter gauge and trim off the excess by pushing the fence through the saw. Since the end of the fence now coincides exactly with the saw kerf, it can be used for accurate cut-off work. Just slide the mark on the workpiece up to the end of the fence and push through the saw.

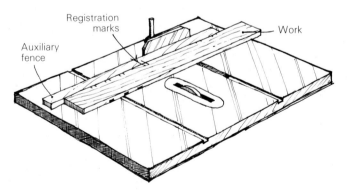

Bandsawing duplicate parts

To bandsaw multiples of intricate wooden-toy parts, I stack several blanks together with double-sided tape between. The tape holds firm during bandsawing, drilling and edge-sanding operations. Double-sided tape eliminates nail holes, replaces awkward clamps and reduces layout time (lines need be drawn only once). Parts are easily separated by inserting a chisel into the tape joint and tapping lightly.

—*Larry D. Sawyer, Ridgecrest, Calif.*

Small I...

EDITOR'S NOTE: Sma...
appeal—they migh...
end. There's alwa...
yourself, who dese...
time, even if there'...
ideas that follow r...
skills. They are from...
contributed, simple...
ects. If you've got o...
in. We'll be makin...
more of these.

Candelabr...
from Chin...
ideograms

by Warren Durbi...

I have always adm...
Chinese calligrapl...
press its elegance...
able object. Last w...
a series of candela...
here draw thei...
Chinese character...
was interested in...

Candelabrum of tea...
the character for u...

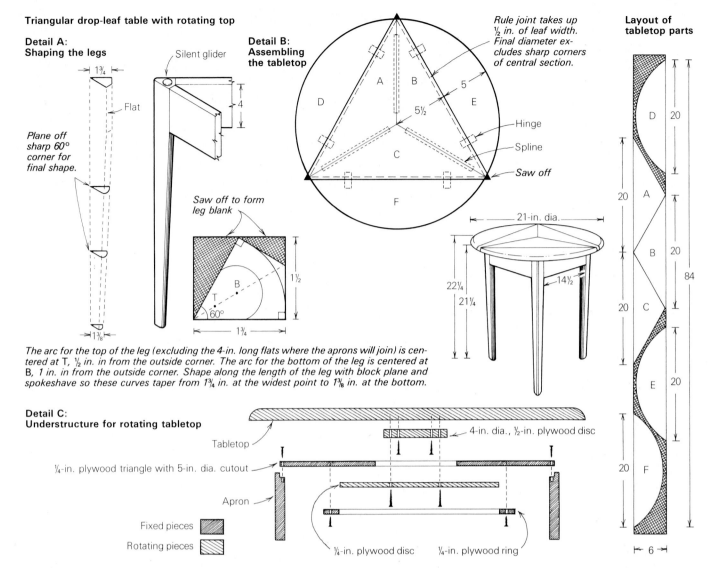

Triangular drop-leaf table with rotating top

Detail A:
Shaping the legs

Silent glider

1¾

Flat

4

Plane off sharp 60° corner for final shape.

Saw off to form leg blank

1½

B

T
60°

1¾

1⅞

The arc for the top of the leg (excluding the 4-in. long flats where the aprons will join) is centered at T, ½ in. from the outside corner. The arc for the bottom of the leg is centered at B, 1 in. in from the outside corner. Shape along the length of the leg with block plane and spokeshave so these curves taper from 1¾ in. at the widest point to 1⅜ in. at the bottom.

Rule joint takes up ½ in. of leaf width. Final diameter excludes sharp corners of central section.

Detail B:
Assembling the tabletop

A B

D 5 E

5½

Hinge

C

Spline

Saw off

F

Layout of tabletop parts

D 20

A 20
20

B 20

84

C 20

E 20

F 20

6

21-in. dia.

22¼
21¼

14½

Detail C:
Understructure for rotating tabletop

Tabletop

4-in. dia., ½-in. plywood disc

¼-in. plywood triangle with 5-in. dia. cutout

Apron

Fixed pieces
Rotating pieces

¼-in. plywood disc

¼-in. plywood ring

spline together the three triangles that form the center of the top and cut the rule joints (*FWW* #18, Sept. '79) between this section and the three drop-leaves. All six pieces can be laid out and sawn from a 7-ft. long 1x6, as shown in detail *B*. With the hinges mounted, first bandsaw the top roughly round, then trim it to a circle with a router mounted on a plywood trammel that pivots on a temporary screw block in the center of the tabletop bottom. Note that the 5½-in. wide leaves have lost ½ in. to the rule joint and that the final diameter of the tabletop (21 in.) excludes the sharp corners of the central section. The edge can be molded to taste.

Now cut a tenon on one end of each of the three aprons and fit two aprons into one leg. Lay the hinged tabletop upside-down on the workbench, turn up two leaves and fit the leg with aprons into the angle between the leaves. Cut the aprons to a length that, with the remaining two legs attached, will exactly fit the tabletop with the leaves folded. Cut tenons and fit the legs and remain-

ing apron together. Before assembling, cut a ¼-in. rabbet on the top inside edge of the aprons to receive a plywood triangle, yet to be made. Gluing up the legs and aprons requires a deft touch; it's best to fit the tenons a bit at a time in sequence and use a strap clamp to bring the joints together.

While the glue is drying, cut a triangle from ¼-in. plywood to fit in the apron rabbets. Then cut a 5-in. diameter hole in the center of the plywood, and screw and glue the plywood into the rabbeted aprons.

Now cut a ¼-in. plywood disc just large enough to fit snugly inside the triangle formed by the legs and aprons. Cut from within this disc another disc of 1-in. shorter radius, producing also a 1-in. wide ring with an entrance kerf that can later adjust the ring's size. Both discs should be near-perfect circles; the inner one must turn smoothly within the outer ring, so make this cut with a jig (*FWW* #16, May '79, p. 16). Sand the saw kerf lightly. Center the outer ring inside the aprons and glue and screw it

to the underside of the plywood triangle in the table. To ease the top's movement over the base, drive ⅝-in. silent gliders into the top of each leg.

Once again with the hinged tabletop upside-down on the bench, set the base inside the triangular center section. From ½-in. plywood cut a 4-in. diameter disc and screw it to the underside of the tabletop approximately in the center, inside the 5-in. diameter hole that you've already cut in the plywood triangle. Take care not to screw into the splined joints of the top. Now place the disc of ¼-in. plywood within the outer ring and screw it to the disc of ½-in. plywood; detail *C* shows the relation of these parts. When the table is lifted by its top, this set of screws will hold the base on, so use screws long enough to enter the top. But before driving more than a couple, rotate the base 120° in each direction to see if the leaves can be folded without interference.

Pendleton Tompkins, a surgeon, lives in San Mateo, Calif.

Flip-open box from one piece of wood

by Daniel Mosheim

I've been making these boxes as gifts for a couple of years, and each one has proved popular and challenging to make. The design can be adapted to many uses with only slight changes. Here I'll cover the most complex one I've done, for business cards. I've fed the woodstove with one or two of these; you can spoil it with the last pass of the plane so work carefully and don't rush.

I've used apple, maple, chestnut, walnut and cherry, but quartersawn zebrawood remains my favorite. In general the darker and more straight-grained the hardwood, the better the overall effect. To start, you will need a piece about $3\frac{1}{4}$ in. by 6 in. by $\frac{3}{4}$ in., with faces and edges straight and parallel. Strike a witness mark across the face, as shown in figure 1. Put a sharp blade in your table saw and check your fence settings on scrap wood before making each cut on your good stock. You have four ripping cuts to make; after planing and scraping the edges smooth and pressing them together to check the fit, you should have two pieces about $\frac{5}{16}$ in.

wide, two pieces $\frac{1}{16}$ in. wide and one piece that is slightly wider than your business card, usually 2 in. Place your card on the face of this piece and mark the center and a little past the ends of the card. Lightly square these marks around the pieces and make a $\frac{1}{4}$-in. slot for half the card all the way through the width of the stock, as shown in figure 2. I use a $\frac{1}{4}$-in. bit in the drill press to rough it out and a sharp chisel to true up the walls. Get this slot smooth now, it's your last chance.

Now glue the two $\frac{1}{16}$-in. pieces to this center one, using your witness marks and all the clamps you have room for. Get good glue lines here. After the glue dries, cut a second slot through the width of the stock for the rest of the length of the card (figure 3). This slot will open into the first slot between the two $\frac{1}{16}$-in. pieces. Don't spend a lot of time here because you can smooth this slot after the next two cuts. Using a beveled scrap block as a guide, cut with a backsaw two 45° angles at the ends of the second slot, *A* and *B* in figure 3. Separate the halves and smooth the insides. The ends of the slot at *C* and *D* can be cut on the table saw with the miter guide and your blade set at the right height. Be careful to keep your fingers where they belong.

Put all the pieces back together, including the two outside $\frac{5}{16}$-in. pieces,

and clamp them temporarily. To locate centers for the dowel hinges, strike a sharp line across the face of the pieces $\frac{1}{4}$ in. from the end of the first slot, at *E* in figure 4. Unclamp the three pieces and continue line *E* down the outside edges of the assembly and down the inside edges of the $\frac{5}{16}$-in. pieces. With a marking gauge set to half the thickness of your stock, mark four points on these lines. Be accurate; the location of the dowel hinge is critical for your box to open and close properly. Using a $\frac{3}{16}$-in. bit, drill into the center assembly to a depth of $\frac{3}{8}$ in. and halfway through the thickness of the $\frac{5}{16}$-in. pieces. Cut and place the dowels and put the whole thing back together again. If everything seems to fit and the box opens and closes, you're ready to glue. Paste-wax the sides of the big half of the center assembly and put a thin coat of glue on the sides of the small half and on the mating surface of each of the $\frac{5}{16}$-in. pieces. Glue neatly so you have a minimum of cleaning up to do inside. And don't forget to put in the dowel hinges. Clamp lightly and open and close the box. If it works, clamp tightly.

When it's dry, cut the box to final length, shape it and finish it as you like. Be careful during the shaping that you don't cut away too much of the bevel or you'll have a gap to the inside and some fuel for the woodstove. □

Fig. 1: Ripping the stock

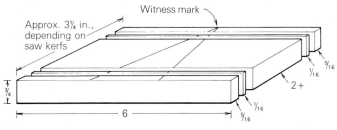

Fig. 2: Cutting the first slot

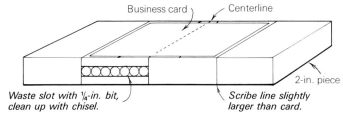

Waste slot with $\frac{1}{4}$-in. bit, clean up with chisel.

Scribe line slightly larger than card.

Fig. 3: Dividing the center assembly

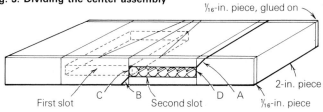

Saw apart at A and B, smooth C and D on table saw.

Precise sawing, boring and gluing yield a box whose design can adapt to other purposes. These are of zebrawood, left, and cherry.

Fig. 4: Locating the dowel hinges

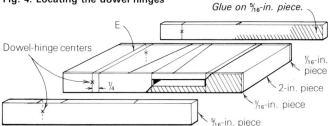

Turning Thin Spindles

Lacemaker's bobbins demand speed and precision

by Mike Darlow

Turning small yet clean, crisp spindles, such as bobbins for lacemaking, requires a special technique. The professional woodturner who's interested in achieving both speed and quality cannot rely on complicated jigs and lathe attachments because they take time to make and set up and because they limit the range and versatility of his work. But with a simple driving device and a practiced method, ordinary tools can produce the desired results.

Lace bobbins are usually made from fine, straight-grained woods—plum, olive, boxwood and walnut were most commonly used in the past. Bone, ivory and hard softwoods such as yew are also ideal. Being small and slender, lace bobbins require a sound turning technique, particularly with the skew chisel. Though there are varying methods of work, the one I'll describe here is straightforward. Begin by preparing the stock for turning, sawing it into square-sectioned strips whose lengths are determined by the finished length of the bobbin plus an allowance for chucking and parting off.

There are four common methods of holding the wood at the headstock. The traditional way employs a small, pronged driving center. One can be made by turning a piece of hardwood to the appropriate taper and pushing it into the swallow of the headstock spindle. Start the lathe, flush off the projecting end and mark its center with the long point of a skew chisel. Next, stop the lathe, drive a brad into the center and pinch it off about 6 mm (¼ in.) from the face of the wood. Then with the lathe running, file the brad to a slim point. Now stop the lathe and hammer in two more brads about 3 mm (⅛ in.) from the center pin and diametrically opposite to one another. Pinch them off about 3 mm (⅛ in.) from the face. With this method there is no need to stop the lathe in order to remove the finished bobbin and to center a new blank. To avoid damage to both the skew and the drive center, part off just to the right of the drive center.

The second way uses a steel driving socket on an arbor of appropriate taper. The socket may have either a cone-shaped cavity, with an internal thread to grip the wood, or a pyramidal one. You can easily make the latter from hardwood.

A third way to drive the stock is by means of a jaw chuck. I prefer the Jacobs type because it is small in diameter and has no dangerous projections. This method allows both ends of the bobbin to be finished in the lathe. And because the left-hand end of the stock is held rigidly along the lathe's axis of rotation, the effective diameter of the turning bobbin is increased and there is less chance of breaking it while cutting the long neck. The fourth and simplest method is to push the blank directly into the swallow of the headstock spindle, providing the opening is small enough. Pressure from the ram will keep the wood from slipping while it's being tooled.

Bobbins are usually turned with their heads at the tailstock

What bobbins do

Bedfordshire bobbins work a lace collar. Threads are plaited around pins stuck through holes in the stiff paper pattern into the pillow below.

There are two main types of lace—needlepoint, made by sewing and oversewing with a needle and thread, using mainly buttonhole stitches; and bobbin lace, which uses the weaving and plaiting of threads. It is this latter method of lacemaking that chiefly concerns the woodturner, for he produces much of the necessary equipment, most notably bobbins. Each separate length of thread used in a piece of lace must be wound on a bobbin at each end. Hence, lacemakers refer to a number of bobbins as so many pairs and many prefer to buy their bobbins in identical pairs. A piece of lace can require several hundred pairs of bobbins, but thirty pairs is about average.

Lace bobbins have three distinct functions. First, they store the thread, sometimes up to seven meters in length, and allow it to be fed out as required. Second, they tension the thread. The lacemaker relies upon the weight of the bobbin (and the attached spangles) to provide this tension, and therefore all the bobbins used for a particular piece of lace need to weigh pretty much the same. Third, they weave and plait the threads without soiling them, because the shank of the bobbin is used as a handle.

There are three main bobbin styles. Continental bobbins follow traditional styles that evolved in particular European lacemaking centers. Honiton bobbins are indigenous to southwestern England. They are used for a fine lace that is usually built up from sprigs—small, complete pieces of lace representing flowers and figures, which are then joined or set into a new ground, using the bobbins as needles. This is why Honiton bobbins have smooth, narrow shanks with pointed ends.

East Midlands Bedfordshire bobbins are slim and basically cylindrical. Most of the bobbin's weight is provided by the spangle. The turner supplies the bobbin drilled, but the spangle is supplied and fixed by the lacemaker. How this unlikely appendage originated is unknown, but spangles—glass beads used as weights—were threaded into 17th and 18th-century laces as decoration. Perhaps a lacemaker wishing to increase the weight of her bobbins tied on some of these spangles, and this evolved into the nine-bead spangle found on East Midlands bobbins from the late 18th century. —*M.D.*

Photos: Henry Strasburger; Illustration: Ric Lopez

end. In the overhand turning method, which is the most common, the left hand either rests on the turning tool or acts as a mobile steady with the left thumb assisting in controlling the tool. The fingers are wrapped over and behind the bobbin to give it support. With this method it's wise to turn the long neck at the tailstock end, as the left hand can more easily support the shank and is clear of the drive center.

I prefer the less common underhand turning method (photo, right) in which the index finger of the left hand goes beneath the tool rest and supports the work, while the thumb and remaining three fingers grip the tool. With this method it's best to turn with the head toward the headstock. This allows the bottom end of the shank to be finished off in the lathe. Finishing off is tricky but can be accomplished by passing the last three fingers of the left hand beneath the bobbin and bracing them against the tool rest, while steadying the right-hand end of the bobbin between the thumb and forefinger. Slacken the tailstock a little to facilitate parting off with the long point of a skew. After withdrawing the tailstock further, you can sand the free end of the bobbin while still supporting it with the thumb and forefinger. Then part off the head. With a little practice you can catch and present the bobbin in your left hand.

Once you've decided on which way to drive the stock, prepare a pin gauge by drawing the bobbin full size on a piece of wood about 13 mm (½ in.) thick. Project main bobbin features onto its edge where you drive in brads that are pinched off to a length of ³⁄₁₆ in. Then sharpen the brads with a file to screwdriver-like points. When centering your stock, take care not to force the tailstock as the wood may split, and once you've centered it, back off slightly on the ram. Excess axial pressure will cause the spindle to spring into a bow when the long neck is cut.

With the lathe running at its fastest speed, rough out the stock using a shallow-nosed gouge about 19 mm (¾ in.) wide and partially ground off on its left-hand side so that you can rough right up to the headstock. A 7-mm (about ⁵⁄₁₆ in.) gouge and a 7-mm skew chisel complete the tool kit. With the lathe still running, lightly press the points of the pin gauge into the rotating wood and then proceed to turn the spindle in the order prescribed in the diagram.

On your first few attempts you may want to caliper the diameters, but it's best to train your eye to gauge them properly. It is preferable to use the skew chisel as much as possible since it's a less risky tool than the gouge. It is possible that the wood will climb up over the nose of the gouge and fracture. When using the gouge, turn it on its side and approach the work obliquely, using it like a skew chisel. The long neck has to be cut with the skew chisel, while either the skew or the gouge may be used to cut the short neck.

I usually sand with 180, then 220-grit aluminum-oxide paper. Traditionally bobbins were not polished, and an attractive patina developed during use. Some turners finish in the lathe, either with beeswax or with a friction polish. I recommend neither, since the wax could soil the thread and the friction polish is slow to apply and too glossy for my taste. After any required hole-drilling, I finish just by dipping in a penetrating oil, which dries completely, brings out the wood colors and leaves an attractive satin sheen. □

Mike Darlow, 36, is a professional turner and cabinetmaker in Sydney, Australia.

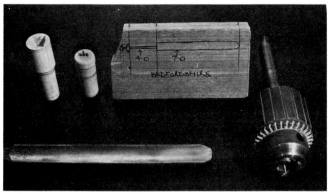

Bobbin turner's tools: wooden driving socket, pronged driving center, pin gauge and Jacobs chuck. Note shape of roughing gouge, ground from a standard spindle gouge.

Turning the long neck using the underhand method. Index finger of left hand reaches below tool rest to support work beneath cutting edge of skew chisel.

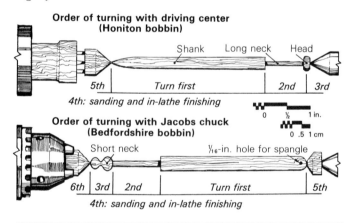

Order of turning with driving center (Honiton bobbin)

Shank   Long neck   Head

5th   Turn first   2nd   3rd

4th: sanding and in-lathe finishing

0   ½   1 in.

0 .5 1 cm

Order of turning with Jacobs chuck (Bedfordshire bobbin)

Short neck   ¹⁄₁₆-in. hole for spangle

6th   3rd   2nd   Turn first   5th

4th: sanding and in-lathe finishing

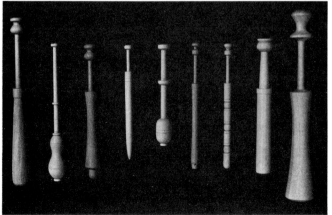

Bobbins, some traditional, some of author's design. The stout ones are for coarse or woolly fibers.

start anew. This was how pianos were finished before the advent of sprays, and the surface that resulted was phenomenally lustrous and durable. However, this was often done over a period of 60 days—certainly not economical today.

To get your layers of polish to lie flat, apply the polish with firm, steady pressure using the three basic motions shown on the previous page: straight pulls, circles and figure eights. If you were to do nothing but straight pulls, ridges would develop and mistakes, such as streaks, would be harder to eliminate. Generally, until this becomes second nature, it is best to do five or six straight pulls to each set of circles and figure eights. Never rub in a circle exceeding 8 in. in diameter, to avoid leaning too hard on the rubber. Both the figure-eight and the circular motions form whips in the polish, and these are difficult to remove when the rubber has been pressed down with too much force. Bearing down too heavily can also cause the polish to pick up previous layers.

Work as drily as you can while getting used to the surface. Too much polish too quickly will look good for a minute, but with subsequent rubbing the rubber will stick and pick up the polish. The way to keep the rubber under control is to charge the fad with polish a little at a time, removing the cotton cloth each time you do so. When the fad is charged, remake the rubber and squeeze out excess polish through the point of the rubber. When you accidentally put too much polish on the surface, let it dry for 10 to 15 minutes and then work straight over the streak, rubbing hard. You might need to add a drop of linseed oil to the rubber for lubrication.

Though oil keeps the rubber from sticking, the novice will find the use of oil difficult to master. Oil can fool you into thinking you have put a beautiful finish down, when in fact there is still plenty of oil to be removed. One way to tell is to blow on the surface—if it clouds there is too much oil. Leaving on excess oil will cause the polish either to crackle or go white. Sometimes this happens in a week, sometimes in a year, but eventually it will happen.

In England the traditional oil is raw linseed, though lemon oil can also be used. If you need it (and often no oil whatsoever is needed), apply about half a drop to the rubber, or flick a bit on the wood with a finger. The total amount of oil I used recently on a dining table was approximately a quarter-teaspoonful. If you put too much on you can either draw a rubber that is charged sparingly with alcohol across the surface with straight strokes, or work the oil out with the polish by rubbing (the dried oil will accumulate on the sides of the rubber). When the surface is free of oil, the rubber will begin to stick slightly, and you'll hear a faint squeak as you draw the rubber along.

French-polish whole surfaces at a time, such as an entire leaf of a dining table or the top of a sideboard, otherwise the surface will have ridges. Large surfaces are the easiest to polish because the "skin" in one area is drying while you're polishing another area. The hardest surfaces to polish are the smallest ones—it's tempting to polish incessantly, but work with deliberation and try not to speed up the routine. You will know when the job is finished when the surface is lustrous and free of streaks, specks and ridges.

As the polisher works, a residue of material will build up on the hands, but cleanup need not be a problem. A generous amount of baking soda dissolved in a container of warm water cleans well and is also reusable. Keep the solution in a pot and simply reheat it when you put down your rubber for the day. □

Clinton Howell is a furniture conservator and publisher of the Antique Furniture Newsletter, *which costs $12 for 6 issues and can be obtained by writing to 445 Bedford Center Rd., Bedford Hills, N.Y. 10507.*

Seedlac Varnish

by Sidney Greenstein

When you combine seedlac, the hardened secretions of the *Laccifer lacca* insect, with alcohol, you get a magnificent spirit varnish that was used for centuries past and is still used today by people in the know. Unfortunately, there are still too few people in the know, and seedlac is often left out of otherwise comprehensive literature about finishes, such as Don Newell's article, "Finishing Materials" *(Fine Woodworking, July '79)*. Seedlac is scraped off the twigs of trees; if it is melted down the result is shellac, but this heating and refining process robs the seedlac of many valuable properties.

Seedlac varnish is pale amber in color and unlike shellac, does not tend toward opacity. Seedlac is also highly scuff and water-resistant and dries fast. You can apply it over any traditional water or alcohol stain, or tint the varnish itself with alcohol-soluble colors.

Seedlac varnish boasts a long, honorable history. The first definite reference in Indian writings to the use of lac resin occurs in 1590 A.D., in the *Ain-e-Akbari*, the official records of Akbar, the Mogul emperor. Details of using lac resin in "lacquering" and polishing wood in public buildings are given. One of the earliest references in the English language is to be found in *A Treatise of Japanning and Varnishing* by Stalker and Parker, printed in London in 1688.

The fine finishes we associate with 18th and 19th-century French and English furniture are seedlac-based. The finishes of the old Italian violinmakers of Cremona are also thought to be seedlac, either wholly or in part. Violinmakers today are divided on the question of whether oil or spirit varnish is best. Those who choose the latter opt for seedlac and would never entertain the idea of shellac on a fine violin.

Tons of seedlac are imported yearly from India for uses in the paint, textile and medical industries. Until recently, modest amounts were available to artisans and small users. These sources are now drying up—the tendency nowadays among conglomerates is to discontinue special (and slow-moving) items. Harpsichord makers William and Nora Smith (1530 Sunset Cliffs Blvd., San Diego, Calif. 92107) import seedlac in 200-lb. lots, and usually have the material on hand to sell in small lots.

To shellac adherents I say: Forgo both ready-mixed products and those you make from buttons and/or flakes, and substitute seedlac. You will obtain a superior material that can be brushed, sprayed or French-polished to produce a coating of much greater transparency, faster drying time and greater water resistance than shellac. □

Sidney Greenstein, 71, lives in San Diego, Calif.

Four ideas for edge-finishing plywood

Here's how to edge-finish plywood and match the color and grain exactly. Buy enough extra plywood so you can saw strips from the edge and ends of the panel slightly wider than the plywood is thick. Now saw off the face veneer from the strips using a thin-rim plywood blade on a table saw. To prevent the

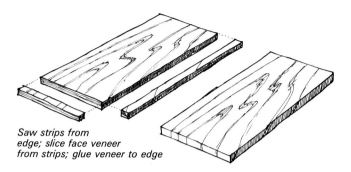

Saw strips from edge; slice face veneer from strips; glue veneer to edge

veneer from falling through the gap between blade and table insert, tape a piece of ¼-in. plywood to the saw-table top and elevate the blade through it. If you are careful in sawing the veneer, you can match the edge strips with the face to create a continuous grain pattern that's quite attractive. Glue the strips in place, then sand off the slight overhang.

—*Floyd L. Lien, Aptos, Calif.*

On a recent platform-bed project I needed to glue ¼-in. oak strips to the edge of a plywood panel. Only two of my bar clamps were long enough for the job. Luckily I hit on a way to combine the two clamps with a double-wedge clamping method I use in guitar construction. I simply clamped a stur-

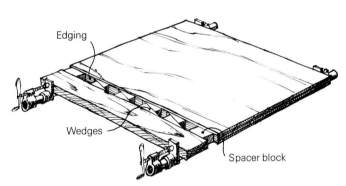

Edging

Wedges

Spacer block

dy oak 1x4 to the edge I wanted to glue, separating the board from the edge with two spacer blocks. The resulting gap left room all along the edge to drive home pairs of wedges. The system worked better than I expected. I was able to control the clamping pressure at many points along the edge without wrestling with a lot of clamps.

—*Willis Overholt, Wichita, Kans.*

In the small custom furniture shop where I worked some time ago, we glued solid oak edging to the unsightly edges of fibercore, oak-veneer panels. Because this required a bar clamp every 8 in. for a tight joint, we soon depleted our supply of clamps, time and patience. My solution is a springboard which applies even pressure to the edging using far fewer clamps. Cut the springboard about 20 in. long from ¾-in. thick, 1½-in. wide hardwood (I used red oak for its resiliency in bending). Place the middle of the front edge to produce a concave shape, about ¼ in. deeper in the center than at the ends. Fasten with screws a couple of sheet-metal fingers to the back edge to hold the springboard in position on the

clamp face while you're adjusting the work to be glued. As you tighten the bar clamp and close the gap, pressure will

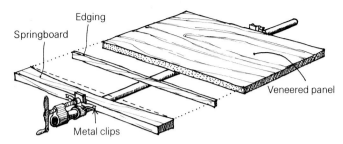

Edging

Springboard

Veneered panel

Metal clips

equalize along the concave face of the springboard.

—*Michael Mikutowski, South St. Paul, Minn.*

I use a hot-water clamp-table to speed up edge-gluing on plywood cabinet parts. When I clamp the plywood and edge strip to the rectangular steel tube (maintained at 160°F by circulating hot water) the plastic resin glue sets in 15 to 20 minutes. I trim the just-glued piece while the next one sets.

The device consists of a hot-water tank, a pump, hoses, fittings, a table and the 48-in. rectangular tube. Two points of caution: Use a pump designed for hot water (check with demolition companies—they salvage these pumps from old buildings) and install a pressure-relief valve. The valve is especially important if your system is closed, as is mine. Cover the work table with plastic laminate and wax so the glue will chip off easily after it has set. Leave a space between the rec-

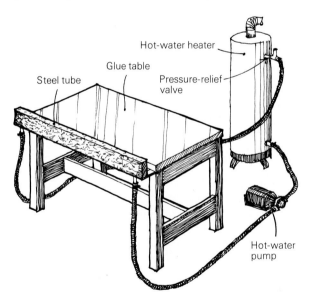

Hot-water heater

Glue table

Steel tube

Pressure-relief valve

Hot-water pump

tangular tube and the table so that you can adjust the edging and leave an overhang on the bottom.

To use, apply glue to both surfaces, position the strip, then bring the edge against the hot tube. Start clamping with the plywood angled up slightly so the bottom glueline is tight but there's a gap on top. Apply pressure until the gap closes.

—*Richard Esteb, Olympia, Wash.*

No-mess epoxy mixing

To mix small amounts of epoxy, simply squeeze equal amounts of resin and hardener into the corner of a plastic sandwich bag. Twist and mix the two until a uniform color appears. Then puncture the bag with a pin and squeeze out the glue as required. No clean-up is required—just throw the bag away.

—*Edgar E. Gardner, Nashua, N.H.*

A Close Look

Micrographs illuminate sanding, scraping and planing

Photos by Stephen Smulski

The photomicrographs on these two pages show the surfaces left on hard maple *(Acer saccharum)* by various woodworking tools, along with the cutting edges of some of the tools themselves. The wood samples are all tangential surfaces from a plainsawn board, and the grain runs from lower left to upper right. The micrographs were made on Polaroid positive-negative film with an ETEC Autoscan scanning electron microscope. All but the last photo were taken at 50× magnification, although the first one, of planed wood, has been

photographically enlarged to about 100×. For comparison we've reproduced at right the *B* from the word LIBERTY on the face of a Lincoln penny, also at 50×. The first and last photos are accompanied by further enlargements of the boxed portions of the *B*, at matching scales. To get the full impact of these photos, find yourself a penny before reading further.

Stephen Smulski, a graduate student in wood science, took these photographs at the University of Massachusetts, Amherst.

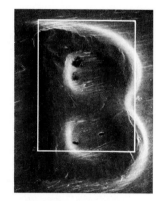

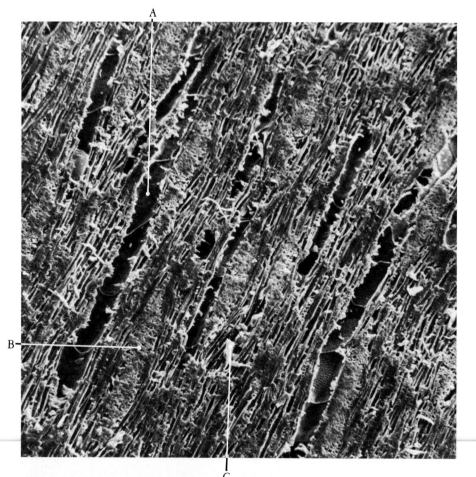

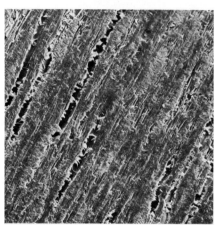

Machine-planed maple still shows open vessel elements, but the smaller features are obscured by torn and pounded fibers. The knife has moved across the surface from lower left to upper right, burnishing the fibers over onto one another. The jointer that did the work is routinely kept in good shape, and nothing special was done to it for this job.

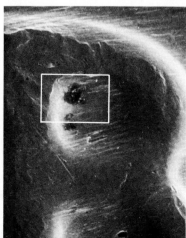

The cleanest surface, as you might expect, comes from a well-tuned smoothing plane. The long openings are vessel elements (cells) of various kinds (A), some of them divided by cross-walls. The lighter, more densely structured areas are ray cells in cross section (B). It's possible to see minute details of the wood's fiber structure, and most of the fibers are cleanly severed. White flecks (C) are small shavings.

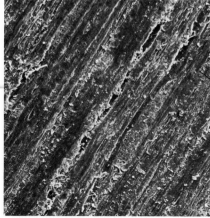

The machined surface has been worked with a cabinet scraper. Most of the wood vessels are filled in by torn and rolled tissue, and the surface is scratched by the minute raggedness of the scraper's edge.

Maple hand-sanded with 220-grit sandpaper (Norton open-coat garnet) is just about as clean as the scraped surface, but there are more scratches. Dust (the white specks), rather than torn fibers, seems to have filled the vessel elements.

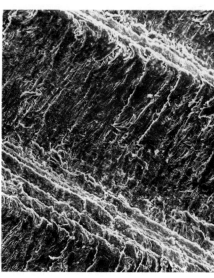

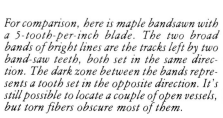

For comparison, here is maple bandsawn with a 5-tooth-per-inch blade. The two broad bands of bright lines are the tracks left by two band-saw teeth, both set in the same direction. The dark zone between the bands represents a tooth set in the opposite direction. It's still possible to locate a couple of open vessels, but torn fibers obscure most of them.

Sandpaper (Norton 220-A Openkote garnet finishing paper), new (far left) and after sanding the maple (left). What makes garnet good for sandpaper is its crystalline structure—the grit fractures into smaller, similarly angular particles. The used paper is littered with broken bits of garnet, maple dust and a few stringy wood fibers.

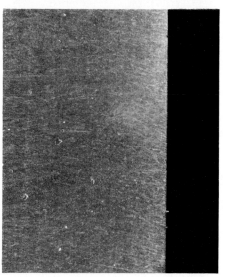

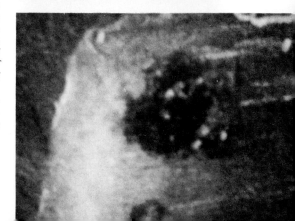

How sharp is a sharp edge? This section of a planer knife (small enough to fit in the vacuum chamber of the electron microscope) was sharpened using the same techniques as for the smoothing-plane iron that cut the wood so cleanly. All three photos are of the beveled side of the iron. Left, the blade has been ground on a Mark II belt-type sharpening machine, using a Norton 100X aluminum-oxide closed-coat belt. Center, contributing editor Bruce Hoadley whetted and honed both sides of the blade, using light machine oil and moving it always in the direction of cut, progressing from a fine India to a Washita stone, then to a white hard Arkansas. He finished by stropping on mimeograph paper, as if he were going to use the blade to clean up a carving. Hoadley swore it was perfectly clean, and at 50 × it does look pretty good, but the microscope reveals two tiny blips projecting from the edge. Right, at 500 × (the bit of B below is at the same scale), they seem to be tiny curls of metal clinging to the now jagged-looking cutting edge, not much bigger than the grain structure of the steel itself.

Some Abrasive Facts

by Lyle Laske

Abrasives fall into two categories: natural mineral and synthetic mineral. Natural minerals include flint, garnet and emery. Since 1900 the synthetic minerals aluminum oxide and silicon carbide have become more and more popular, both in industry and in the home shop. Because of the superior qualities of synthetics and also as a result of the development of power tools, sanding has become a shaping method as well as a finishing method.

Abrasive hardness is routinely measured on two scales. The Mohs scale runs from 1 (talc) to 10 (diamond). Ratings are determined by abrading a soft mineral with a harder one; they do not indicate equal or proportional differences. The Knoop scale, which goes from 1 to 8500, determines hardness with a pressure indenter, and more accurately measures the proportional hardness of minerals. Toughness, which differs from hardness, is determined by a ball-mill test: rotating a given grit in a steel drum with steel balls for a standard period of time and noting how much of the grit survives at the original size.

Each abrasive has advantages and disadvantages, and comparing them will help you choose the right one for the job at hand.

Flint is used in an inexpensive sandpaper. Because its sharp edges break down quickly, it is not used in production work, but is good for sanding resinous and waxy surfaces and for removing paint and sealers, which clog sandpaper quickly.

Garnet abrasive is obtained by crushing semiprecious garnet jewel stock and heat-treating it to increase its natural hardness and toughness. It is used for production woodwork and sanding between coats of paint and sealers. In use, garnet fractures, generating new cutting edges (see p. 213). The furniture industry prefers garnet because it is less expensive than aluminum oxide and because garnet's cutting edges scrape rather than scratch the wood. This promotes finish consistency and resistance to burning on most end-grain sanding operations. Garnet is manufactured in grits from 12 to 320. It is not recommended for metal.

Emery, the second hardest natural mineral after diamond, is the toughest abrasive listed here. However, because it has round, blocky, heat-generating cutting edges, it is usually used with lubricants to polish metal. The dull fracture and lack of chip clearance make it unsuitable for woodworking.

Aluminum oxide is made of heat-treated bauxite and lesser amounts of titania. There are only four minerals harder (three synthetic and diamond). Its heavy, wedge-shaped cutting edge is the reason for its toughness. Aluminum oxide is well suited to high-speed sanding machines working hardwoods and hard metals; its higher cost is offset by its durability. However, when sanding resinous softwoods which clog the cutting edges, thus shortening the work life, and where burning is a problem, garnet is a more economical abrasive.

Silicon carbide is made from heat-treated silica sand and petroleum coke. Only boron carbide and diamond are harder. Of all abrasives, silicon carbide has the longest cutting edges and the best concave sides for chip clearance. Unfortunately it breaks down rapidly on hard metals and reacts chemically with ferrous metals. Because of this it is commonly marketed in finer grits—from 180 to 600, although grits as coarse as 24 are useful on particle board and plywood. The best uses for silicon carbide are in sanding soft materials, hardwoods and low tensile-strength materials such as stone, plastic and glass. Silicon car-

Flint *(quartz)*
Color: buff
Mohs: 6.8 to 7.0
Knoop: 820
Toughness: 20%

Garnet *(almandite)*
Color: reddish-brown
Mohs: 7.5 to 8.5
Knoop: 1360
Toughness: 60%

Emery *(corundum and magnetite)*
Color: grey to black
Mohs: 8.5 to 9.0
Knoop: 1750
Toughness: 80%

Aluminum oxide
Color: tan or white
Mohs: 9.4
Knoop: 2050
Toughness: 75%

Silicon carbide
Color: greenish-black
Mohs: 9.6
Knoop: 2480
Toughness: 55%

bide abrasive is also used for sanding hard lacquers, varnish and baked-enamel finishes.

Abrasives are sold by grit size, a measure of how coarse or fine they are. Three grading systems are commonly used. The *grit symbol*, the oldest, is an arbitrary system. Number 4½ is the coarsest and 10/0 is the finest. The grit symbol is being de-emphasized by manufacturers. The *mesh number* or *grit number* indicates the approximate number of apertures per running inch in the vibrating silk or wire screen that sorts that grade of stock. Thus 120 grit means there are 14,400 (120 × 120) openings per square inch; discounting the size of the silk thread, each opening (and each grit that falls through it) is about 0.0052 in. across. *Simplified labels* used on flint sheet and emery cloth are Extra Fine, Fine, Medium, Coarse, and Extra Coarse. (For a comparison of grit gradings, see "Sanding," *FWW* #12, Sept. '78.)

Abrasives are applied to their backing either by gravity or electrostatically. First the backing is given a *make coat* of glue (either hide or resin, the latter being stronger). In the electrostatic process, the glued backing is conveyed in a strip above a belt conveying the sorted grit through a high-voltage field. This causes the grit to lift off the conveyor and adhere, with maximum evenness and with their sharp points (least mass) outward, to the glued backing. After the make coat has dried, a second, thinner *size coat* (again of either hide or resin glue) is applied over the abrasive surface. Resin-over-resin bonds are used for heavy-duty grinding and in waterproof papers for rubbing out finishes.

The grit can be applied to cover the complete surface *(closed coat)*, or to cover 50% to 70% of the surface *(open coat)*. The spaces in the open coat promote self-cleaning when sanding gummy or resinous materials, and extreme flexibility when bonded to cloth. For fast cutting, use light pressure to avoid heating. A closed coat has more abrading points per square inch, will last longer and produce a smoother surface. It is best for hardwoods and other hard materials that will not clog; it can be put to the work with heavy, constant pressure.

There are four types of abrasive backing: paper, cloth, fiber and combination. Paper backing is manufactured in four weights. A-weight paper, or finishing paper, is used mainly for light hand and vibration sanding. Its flexibility allows the operator to feel defects, and it conforms to small contours and narrow openings without breaking. C-weight and D-weight (cabinet) paper backings are heavier, stronger and less flexible than finishing paper. They are used for hand or vibration sanding with coarse grits and greater pressure. These papers are strong enough not to buckle, yet flexible enough to conform to irregular contours. E-weight paper (roll stock cylinder paper) is strong and durable. It is used on belt, disc and drum sanders. This paper withstands heavy pressures without becoming soft or raggy.

Cloth backings are of two types. J-weight, or "jeans," is lightweight and flexible. It is used in roll form for sanding irregular shapes, especially with pneumatic drums. X-weight, or "drills," is medium-weight, strong cloth backing. It lacks flexibility, hence it is used for mechanical sanders in high-pressure and high-tension operations.

Fiber backing—mainly for disc and drum sanding—is made from vulcanized or hardened rag-stock paper. Combination backing is sturdy and shock-resistant. Laminated paper and cloth is used for high-speed drum sanders. Laminated fiber and cloth is used for discs.

Three abrasives used in surfacing finishes should be mentioned here. Steel wool in pad or roll form is sold in grades from 0000 (very fine) to no. 3 (coarse). Pumice, made from lava, is a white powder that is combined with rubbing oil or water and rubbed with a felt pad. The common grades for woodworking are FF and FFF. Rottenstone, a brown or dark grey substance made from decayed limestone, is finer and softer than pumice and is used in the same way. □

Lyle Laske, a sculptor, of Moorhead, Minn., prepared this article with help from 3M Company and from Norton Company.

Furniture Conservation

Historic objects can outlast us all

by Robert F. McGiffin

Hudson river valley kas, c. 1745.

Probably the greatest threat to furniture is man. Historical furniture is subjected to restoration abuse, misuse, damage and disfigurement by well-meaning individuals who are undoubtedly very proud of their work. Most of my work as a furniture conservator involves correcting theirs. I have seen many pieces of furniture damaged by modifications or inadequate repairs. It is all too easy to pick up a hammer or saw and go to work. I recently treated a Hudson river valley kas (large chest), c. 1745, whose shelves were originally large, single planks. At one point, probably within the last three decades, a section was cut out of one of the shelves to make room for a fire extinguisher, causing irreversible damage.

I feel that with luck, a piece of historical furniture will outlast all of us many times over, and we should do nothing to disturb it. Each of us should develop an attitude that we have no right to remove original material and evidence of an object's history, even if we own the object. This includes the aged finish. Unlike paintings, where darkened varnishes, scratches and later additions are considered disfiguring, historical furniture was designed to be functional, subjected to daily abuse and wear. Scratches, dents, stains and burns that may have occurred during its existence are part of its history.

Many times a beautiful and secure patina is dissolved in a stripping vat or is sanded and scraped away, because the owner, dealer or custodian of the piece is trying to "recapture the beauty of the wood" or to "return the piece to its original appearance." No one knows exactly how the piece appeared when new, although laboratory analysis may indicate what type of finish was used. We may even have some idea of the concentrations, but cannot tell for certain how the stain and/or the finish saturated the newly made object. We probably can't tell the degree of gloss or dullness that the finish originally had. Seasonal changes have made joints and moldings expand and contract, causing them to reach an equilibrium that is slightly different from when new. How about scratches, dents, abrasions and checks? Most can be minimized or camouflaged, but not all. Dents and scratches usually cause a traumatic shock to the wood fibers, obvious

Kas was irreversibly damaged when a section of one of its shelves was cut out to make room for a fire extinguisher.

under a microscope. What would be gained by removing a burn from a tabletop, caused by a trivet or kettle placed there sometime in the 18th century? Wouldn't a part of history be removed if the table's finish, along with the burn, were sanded or stripped away? I am not saying that today's cigarette burn on a piece of antique furniture is adding to its history—a modern burn is disfigurement, because the piece should be preserved from daily wear and tear.

Care of historical furniture — The treatment of the kas (photo, above) involved replacing the separated shelf portion, and a general cleaning. But this treatment won't work on all furniture. When you apply the following procedures to your own furniture, act with caution.

First, the surface of the kas was vacuumed with a soft brush attachment. Had there been cleaving veneer or upholstery, a piece of window screen, with all four edges covered with tape, would have been held between the object and the brush, to keep pieces of veneer or fabric from being pulled into the vacuum. To test the finish, a cotton-tipped applicator was dampened with distilled water and gently rolled over a small obscure area. The applicator picked up surface grime and didn't soften the finish. Whitening, which tells that the finish is reacting badly to water, did not occur after the area dried for a few minutes. Whitening may not be easily reversible—if it is visible, remove it, if possible, using the method described later, and continue cleaning not with water but with solvents.

A bucket was then filled with clean room-temperature distilled water, and the water applied with a clean, dampened (not dripping) sponge, by working in small areas and not rubbing too hard. The areas were dried with soft toweling to absorb any remaining moisture, then the entire process was repeated with clean water. The kas still had grimy area remaining, so we repeated the same steps with one teaspoon of

Robert F. McGiffin, 36, is conservator of the Collections Care Center, Bureau of Historic Sites, Waterford, N.Y. The Center is responsible for 35 state historic sites in New York.

Nails and screws where there were none originally can restrict wood movement, causing checks, or splits and disfiguring holes.

detergent stirred into a gallon of water. Use either a commercial woodwork detergent such as Soilax, or the anionic concentration, Orvus. Rinse away any detergent residue with a sponge dampened in clean water. We waxed the kas with a formula I will describe later. If you still have grime, further cleaning is possible with solvents. However, improper use of solvents can cause irreversible damage, and solvents are not safe for all finishes. The safer solvents are paint thinner (preferably odorless), turpentine and benzine (sometimes called petroleum benzine or VMP naphtha). Benzine is not benzene, which is toxic. Use these solvents in a well-ventilated area with no open flames or electrical sparks.

To test the solvent, dampen a cotton-tipped applicator with it, wring it out and roll it over a small portion of the grimy area. A lot of solvent on the surface can slow down evaporation and may soften the finish below the grime and wax, as well as surface wax, so be sparing. After removing some of the grime and wax from the test area, apply more solvent, making sure it is not softening the finish. Continue working in small areas with the cotton-tipped applicator and immediately dry the area with a soft, clean rag. At this point you have to decide if you are going to continue your grime removal to the point of removing old wax build-up from the entire piece of furniture.

Veneer cleavage — If there is veneer cleavage, you may be able to apply some glue under the veneer with a small brush. If you have a syringe, inject a little distilled water under the cleavage, clamp the area and wait a minute or so to let the original glue soften. Remove the clamp and wipe up any water that runs out on the finish. Dilute some hide glue 50% with distilled water and inject it under the veneer until it runs out. Wipe up the excess, then clamp. I prefer wooden cam-action clamps, such as the ones made by Klemmsia.

If you don't have proper clamps, hold the veneer down for about 24 hours with tape or a weight. Shield the veneer from the clamp surface with a small piece of Plexiglas, to keep the clamp from adhering to the wood and to prevent denting. Waxed paper will also shield the clamps from the glue. After the glue has dried, the Plexiglas may be stuck to the surface, but a gentle push from the side will pop it loose. Use hot hide glue or liquid hide glue, such as Franklin's. They are soluble

in water, easily removed many years later and similar to the glue used when the furniture was made.

Don't be fooled by white polyvinyl acetate emulsion glues. Although they are soluble in water when they come from the bottle, they are less so after aging. On drying, they form a continuous film by fusion of the polymer droplets present in the emulsion. They also penetrate deeply and once in, are almost impossible to remove. If you repair using a white glue and are dissatisfied, or someone wants to reverse it later on, damage could result. If a treatment involves reconstruction and perhaps the replacement of a missing primary support, such as a leg, hot hide glue is strong enough, yet reversible.

Wood fillers, losses and separated elements — If you have losses, or holes, don't plug them with commercial wood fillers. They won't look like wood and may shrink or fall out during the seasonal dimensional changes of the wood. If someone tries to remove them, damage may result to the surrounding areas. Under no circumstances should a separated element be reattached with nails and screws where there were none originally. Not only are they hard to remove, but the restriction of the movement of wood results in checks or splits. They also leave disfiguring holes after they are removed.

For a small area, say a nail hole, I often use a pigmented wax stick that matches the wood. If the loss was caused by a screw head, you can cut your own plug from new wood of similar grain. Dowels or some commercially made tapered plugs won't camouflage the loss unless it is in end grain.

If the loss is more extensive, let in a patch. Obviously, this is time-consuming. I do not remove original material around the area to be filled unless it has jagged edges or splinters. I first find a piece of the same kind of wood with similar figure. Various methods, such as rubbings or measured drawings, are used to transfer the loss configuration to the new wood. The patch is then cut out and shaped.

At this point, I test stains and finishes on the waste portion of the new wood until I can duplicate exactly the original appearance. Sometimes I can finish the patch before pressing and gluing it into place. If the color is wrong, it is safer to find out before the patch is attached. Usually, the patch is fixed in place, the profile is leveled off, and then the new color and finish are applied to match the original surrounding area.

Finishes — After cleaning and repairing, you may want to apply a new finish over the old. Instead of applying varnish, shellac or lacquer over the original, I usually prefer to use wax. Wax protects, and is easy to apply. It can look like a shellac finish, is generally harmless and can be removed at any time. I formulate my own wax recipe and you can do the same. It contains two parts Cosmolloid 80H (a microcrystalline wax) and five parts odorless paint thinner: for example, 20 gm microcrystalline wax and 50 ml paint thinner.

Weigh the Cosmolloid and melt it in a double boiler, bringing the water to a boil on a hot plate, not over an open flame. Keep checking the water to make sure it hasn't all evaporated. Work in a well-ventilated room. The wax may take about 45 minutes to melt. When most has melted, pour the thinner into a glass jar large enough to hold both the wax and the thinner, and place the jar in boiling water to warm for a few minutes. By now all of the wax should be melted. The thinner is heated so that when the molten wax is added it won't gel and form a lumpy mixture. Quickly pour in the wax. Remove the jar from the heat and let it cool. Apply the wax once every year or two, but dust the object once a week. Store the wax jar in a warm area.

You may wish to use another recipe if you don't have a double boiler, or simply don't wish to play around with hot materials. Use two parts by weight of wax plus five parts solvent. Simply place the wax in a jar and add the solvent. Keep tightly covered until a homogeneous mixture has formed. This may take several days with periodic stirring by rotating the jar, and it may be necessary to add a little solvent from time to time to keep the wax soft.

To apply, put a small amount on a soft cloth and rub in. If it seems to go on a little hard (some objects can't take hard rubbing because the joints might be loosened), dip the cloth in a little odorless thinner. Rub in a circular motion, followed by strokes in the direction of the grain. Do not overload the cloth with wax, which can cause the surface to remain sticky. Let the solvent evaporate a few minutes after the wax has been applied to the furniture, then buff in the direction of the grain with a clean, soft, lintless rag. You may want to buff again after 24 hours, after more solvent evaporates.

The wax formula may remain sticky for several days and therefore may not be appropriate for a piece of furniture that has daily handling. A useful product is Renaissance wax, which I recommend both because I know its ingredients and because it doesn't remain sticky. It's hard to buff on large areas, however, and will streak. Dampen the cloth in odorless thinner to overcome this. While polishing, watch for loose pieces of veneer, moldings or hardware that may be pulled loose, bent or broken by the cloth. In general, most conservators try to avoid commercial products because they can contain materials that, on aging, may undergo changes in color or transparency and become inseparable from the object to which they are applied. The Cosmolloid mixture and the Renaissance wax are not panaceas, and if there is wax build-up already on the surface, either may soften it and the surface could remain sticky. Wax build-up should be removed.

I would not use polyurethane varnishes on historical furniture. They are good moisture barriers, but never apply them over an original finish, because they are irreversible.

Avoid recipes for "feeding" the finish, a term from old wives' tales and 19th-century restorers' recipes. Feeding recipes, found in many books, often contain linseed oil, an irreversible drying oil that penetrates the surface, saturating the original finish or pigment particles. In a few years when the object becomes darker and darker, someone will try to remove it and may discover he must either leave it alone or destroy much of the original finish. Linseed oil changes chemically as it dries, forming a tough, hard film.

Some books suggest inpainting losses on painted furniture with oil paints, but never apply anything to painted surfaces. Oil paints discolor and are irreversible except by methods that may harm the original. Painted surfaces can be complex, and only someone with conservation experience should deal with them. Beware of "cure-alls." What may work for one treatment may be the opposite of what works for another. By not fully understanding the chemical and physical properties of a particular paint film, damage may result.

Furniture hardware — I don't use commercial emulsion-type brass polishes for hardware on historical furniture

Sloppy application of brass polish can damage a finish. White material around edges of pull is brass polish residue.

because repeated use can damage the hardware and, if you're not careful, the finish on the wood as well. I also stay away from copper brighteners or dip cleaners, the old home recipe of vinegar and salt, and steel wool or buffing wheels.

I use rubbing, isopropyl or ethyl alcohol to clean brass hardware, cleaning it on the object if the brasses appear original. If I can, I slip a piece of aluminum foil behind the brass to protect the wood, then wipe over the brass with a dampened cotton-tipped applicator to remove greasy fingerprints and allow a protective brown patina to form.

Whitening of finish — Water, condensation from a glass, or a fast-evaporating commercial cleaner can give the finish a milky-white appearance, but this is one area where we can rely on home remedies, moderately used. Try a little cooking oil mixed with cigar or cigarette ash. Rub on the whitish area with your fingertip for a short time, then wipe the area dry with a soft rag. If that doesn't work, try a little of the same oil and a small amount of whiting, pumice or rottenstone, or try wiping the area briefly with a little alcohol on a rag with your fingertip or cotton-tipped applicators. Be careful, because the alcohol may soften the finish, and can actually remove a French polish. If this happens, leave the area alone for a while to give the finish a chance to reharden. Any of these treatments may get rid of the white, but may make the area glossier than its surroundings. If this happens, rub a little 4/0 steel wool in the area. Pull off a small amount of fine steel wool from the pad and wrap it around a round wooden stick from a cotton-tipped applicator or toothpick. This can be followed by an overall waxing of the piece.

These treatments may also work on dark stains or burns, but make sure that the stain or burn is not relevant to the object's history. If the burn is recent, such as from a cigarette, use the same methods described for white rings. It may be a little deeper though and you might have to resort to 4/0 steel wool with a little turpentine or paint thinner. The finish will be destroyed in the area so you can tone with stains, or sometimes you can get by with acrylic emulsion paints or watercolors. Take a fine camel-hair brush and reapply a finish of shellac only in the damaged area. You may need to blend in the new shellac with 4/0 steel wool and wax. □

EDITOR'S NOTE: Orvus detergent, Cosmolloid 80H and Renaissance wax are available at Talas, 104 Fifth Ave., New York, N.Y. 10011. Pigmented wax sticks are available from Mohawk Finishing Products, Amsterdam, N.Y. 12010.

Methods of Work

Two router-table/table-saw extensions

My shop is too small to endure much more big equipment. So when I needed both a router table and additional outfeed support on my table saw, I combined both functions in the extension table shown in the sketch. Since the table is bolted to the saw, alignment between extension and saw table is better and the table is easy to clean under.

I made the ¾-in. flakeboard table 32 in. wide. Added to the saw table, this gives 44 in. of support. Leave a gap be-

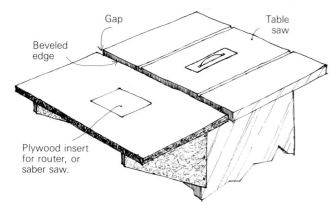

tween the saw table and extension so that a plywood panel can be ripped, then crosscut with a saber saw or circular saw without moving the panel off the table. The blade will travel between saw table and extension. Bevel the front edge of the table so it won't catch work as it leaves the saw table. Cut a 10-in. square hole in the middle of the outfeed table to hold a router or saber saw mounted on 10-in. plywood inserts. Cut another insert blank to fill the hole when not in use.

—*W. Davis Smoot, Duncanville, Tex.*

By mounting a router table to the side of the table saw as shown, you can combine the control of the saw's miter gauge and rip fence with the safe, crisp cuts of the router. You'll find the saw's miter gauge useful in cutting cross-grain dadoes, dovetails and finger joints. Cut mortises, tenons and with-grain grooves using the saw's rip fence. The combination saves shop space and increases the surface area of your table saw. There's no need ever to remove the router table—just lower the bit when not in use.

—*Mark Duginske, Wausau, Wis.*

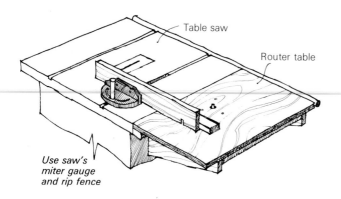

Square cuts

Most table-saw and radial-arm-saw blades that I've worked with have a tendency to climb and squirm when crosscutting. The result is an out-of-square cut. I've found, quite by accident, that if the crosscut is very thin, say one half the kerf, the saw cuts amazingly true. This approach does require that you

make two cuts—one to rough length (leaving a half-kerf extra) and the second to final length. Of course if the machine is out of square to begin with, all bets are off.

—*Pat Warner, Escondido, Calif.*

Cutting circles on the table saw

Round tabletops, lazy-susan shelves and other large circles can be cut on the table saw with a simple jig. Cut a dado in the underside of a ¾-in. high-density particle-board base and glue in a hardwood key, sized for a sliding fit in the saw's left-hand miter slot. Wax the jig bottom and key to reduce friction. Measuring from the blade, accurately locate and paste sheets of ¼-in. graph paper to the jig top to aid in layout.

To use, first cut the circle blank somewhat oversize and locate its center. Next mark the radius of the finished circle on the graph paper and pin the center of the circle blank at this mark. Make sure the blank will rotate freely but is firmly pinned to the jig. Start by lopping off the corners of the blank. Hold the blank and jig firmly while sliding them past the blade. If hand-holding the work appears unsafe, mount a hold-down clamp on the base to lock the blank while cutting. Continue cutting off the corners of the blank until it is almost round. Then, with the work just touching the blade, rotate the blank to trim off all the high spots. The smoothest circles are produced using high-quality, sharp carbide blades.

—*Philip Margraff, Coeur d'Alene, Idaho*

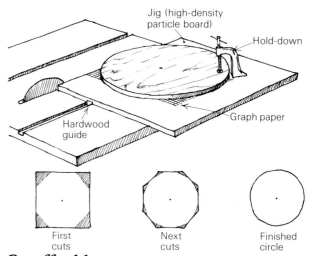

Cutoff table

Back in the days before I had a radial arm saw in my shop, I worked out a cutoff table to use with my portable circular saw. The fixture consists of a 2x12 table, a 2x4 fence and a guide bridge. The rabbets on the two bridge pieces should face each other and be spaced just wide enough to fit the base of your portable circular saw. If desired, a stop block can be C-clamped to the fence for accurate duplicate cutoff work.

—*C.G. Fader, Ketchikan, Alaska*

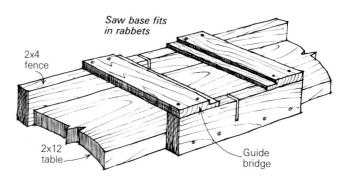

INDEX

INDEX